Written under the auspices of the
Center of International Studies,
Princeton University

STRATEGIC CAPITALISM

PRIVATE BUSINESS AND
PUBLIC PURPOSE IN
JAPANESE INDUSTRIAL FINANCE

Kent E. Calder

PRINCETON UNIVERSITY PRESS   PRINCETON, NEW JERSEY

Copyright © 1993 by Princeton University Press
Published by Princeton University Press, 41 William Street,
Princeton, New Jersey 08540
In the United Kingdom: Princeton University Press, Chichester,
West Sussex
All Rights Reserved

Library of Congress Cataloging-in-Publication Data
Calder, Kent E.
Strategic capitalism : private business and public purpose in
Japanese industrial finance / Kent E. Calder.
p. cm.
Includes bibliographical references and index.
ISBN 0-691-04318-3 (cloth : alk. paper)
1. Japan—Commercial policy.   2. Industry and state—Japan.
3. Industrial organization—Japan.   4. Corporations—Japan—
Finance.   5. Industrial concentration—Japan. 6. Industrial
promotion—Japan.   7. Japan—Foreign economic relations.
I. Title.
HF1601.C35   1993
338.7'0952—dc20   92-39043   CIP

This book has been composed in Adobe Trump

Princeton University Press books are printed
on acid-free paper and meet the guidelines for
permanence and durability of the Committee
on Production Guidelines for Book Longevity
of the Council on Library Resources

Printed in the United States of America

1 3 5 7 9 10 8 6 4 2

It is the highest impertinence and
presumption, therefore, in kings and
ministers to pretend to watch over the
economy of private people, and to
restrain their expense.
—ADAM SMITH

. . . for without vision the people perish.
—ISAIAH

Contents

Figures

Tables

Abbreviations

BIS	Bank for International Settlements
BOJ	Bank of Japan
BPA	Bicycle Promotion Association
DIKB	Dai Ichi Kangyō Bank
DSP	Democratic Socialist party
EPA	Economic Planning Agency
ESB	Economic Stabilization Board
ESS	Economic and Scientific Section
FAIR	Foundation for Advanced Information and Research
FEFTCL	Foreign Exchange and Foreign Trade Control Law
FILP	Fiscal Investment and Loan Program
FTC	Fair Trade Commission
IBF	International Banking Facility
IHI	Ishikawajima Harima Heavy Industries
IMF	International Monetary Fund
ITB	International Trade Bureau
JAPIA	Japan Auto Parts Industrial Association
JCIF	Japan Center for International Finance
JCP	Japan Communist party
JDB	Japan Development Bank
JECC	Japan Electronic Computer Corporation
JETRO	Japan External Trade Organization
JIHAI	Regional Automobile Maintenance and Distribution Corp.
JIPDC	Japan Information Processing Development Center
JNR	Japan National Railways
JSP	Japan Socialist party
LDP	Liberal Democratic party
LMB	Loan Mediation Bureau
MCI	Ministry of Commerce and Industry
MHW	Ministry of Health and Welfare
MITI	Ministry of International Trade and Industry
MOC	Ministry of Construction
MOF	Ministry of Finance
MOT	Ministry of Transportation
MPT	Ministry of Post and Telecommunications
NEDO	New Energy Development Organization
NTT	Nippon Telephone and Telegraph

OECD	Organization for Economic Cooperation and Development
RFB	Reconstruction Finance Bank
SBIC	Small Business Investment Company
SCAP	Supreme Commander Allied Powers
SHI	Sasebo Heavy Industries
SII	Structural Impediments Initiative
VEC	Venture Enterprise Center

A Note on Conventions

JAPANESE personal names throughout the text are presented in Japanese form—that is, with the surname followed by the given name, in reversal of standard Western practice. Exceptions to this convention are made only in the case of Japanese scholars long resident outside Japan, whose names are conventionally presented in Western fashion in the English-language literature. In such cases Western conventions are observed here. Macron marks have been used where relevant in all cases except where the word in question appears so commonly in English discourse without macrons that such usage has become relatively standard. Tōkyō and Kyōto are the two major cases in which macrons would be relevant where this convention is employed. Most figures are given in yen, but when currency translations are undertaken, they are made at contemporaneous exchange rates for the item in question, unless otherwise indicated.

Preface

BRINGING ORDER and purpose to the turbulent world of reality is one of the strongest human impulses. Nowhere has it seemed more clearly and urgently a national imperative than in twentieth-century Japan. Thrust abruptly into the industrialized world near the high noon of Western imperialism, with few natural allies, Japan has long felt itself struggling for economic and strategic survival in an unpredictable broader world. Bringing order and purpose to the economic universe has long seemed a primary imperative to many Japanese.

In the Anglo-Saxon West we take it as truism that order and purpose are not easily achieved, certainly not in the turbulent capitalist world of innately and continually warring self-interests that has dominated our own economic life since the Industrial Revolution. Yet, at a distance, we often tend to see Japan and its capitalism as different—as a world where somehow the tumult of egotism and factiousness so endemic in economic life elsewhere are submerged in the selfless pursuit of broader objectives.

I first got interested in the Japanese political economy during the early 1970s, when I took Edwin O. Reischauer's course in Japanese politics at Harvard in the wake of the 1971 Nixon Shocks. What intrigued me from the very beginning was Japanese economic decision making, which had somehow brought that nation so meteorically to the fore in international affairs, and yet somehow so clearly needed to shift gears as Japan grew larger and other nations more critical of its self-serving ways. Were the Japanese really as consensual and purposive as they appeared? Could they remain so in the face of the epochal pressures then beginning to build in Japan's relations with the broader world? Did they practice a separate version of capitalism?

Studying Japanese capitalism seemed a good way to probe the complexities of Japanese economic life, because the concept was interdisciplinary. Only such an approach, I felt, could capture the prevailing realities of Japan, where economic, political, and social phenomena were so clearly intertwined. My interest in an interdisciplinary understanding of Japanese capitalism was further provoked by intellectual trends in both politics and economics as I began my work. The shifting political parameters of international economic life as the Bretton Woods system dissolved and as an increasingly global economy simultaneously emerged were stimulating a new consciousness, epitomized in the work of Gilpin, Keohane, Nye, Vernon, and Williamson, among others, that economic and political phenomena were deeply interrelated and that serious theorizing could and should take account of this reality.

The conventional wisdom regarding Japan, as I began puzzling my way through the prevailing literature, was the notion of "Japan, Inc."—the rather vague and never very systematic conception that somehow government, business, and the conservative political world all functioned as a consensual unit. Together, these groups pursued Japan's global economic interests in highly strategic, indeed mercantilist fashion, it was argued, although the precise decision-making processes within "Japan, Inc." remained unclear, nearly a decade before Chalmers Johnson's MITI and the Japanese Miracle. But to most accounts that did not matter very much, since the system was so apparently consensual.

These early notions of Japanese capitalism seemed rather facile, and in need of more systematic exploration—a perfectly straightforward task for a graduate student with new momentum from general examinations. In the fall of 1974, I went to Japan, in the shadow of the Oil Shock, for a year of language study and dissertation research before a quick thesis write-up. I stayed for five years.

What I came to see better and better, the longer I remained in Japan, was how profoundly important knowing the trees is to understanding the forest. To understand policy outputs in the Japanese political economy as a whole, I began to realize, one has to grasp both how central institutions of that system function internally and how they are linked—through concrete interpersonal networks, information flows, and incentive structures—to other ministries, political parties, or corporations with which they must interact to generate policy decisions. There is no substitute for a micropolitical, economic, and social perspective, combined with a detailed sense of the interpersonal networks that integrate the nation as a whole.

I also became firmly convinced of the value and the need to understand the Japanese political economy, including its seemingly distinctive capitalism, in comparative terms. Before arriving in Japan, I had spent six of the previous sixteen years outside the United States, including time as a student in Germany. There was much in Japanese institutions at the micro-level, I could clearly see, that was common with patterns elsewhere, particular those in continental Europe. Japanese capitalism was certainly not, despite some distinctive features, an exotic anomaly. The occasional glimpses of commonality with the West, especially with Europe, convinced me that economic competition with Japan was more than simply a confrontation of "Western" and "Eastern" systems.

Since my early encounters with the "Japan, Inc." concept a bit more than twenty years ago, I have spent extended periods in residence at MITI's Research Institute on Trade and Industry, MOF's Institute of Fiscal and Monetary Policy, the Bank of Japan's Institute of Monetary Policy, and the Japan Development Bank's various research centers. I have also paid periodic visits over the years to the Industrial Bank of Japan's Industrial Research Department, the Japan Economic Research Center, Keidanren, the All-Japan Bankers Federation, the Ministry of Posts and Telecommunications, the Fair Trade Commission, and the Economic Planning Agency, as well as innumerable private banks and industrial firms. My dominant impression, from considerable familiarity with all these organizations over a period of years, is the diversity of their viewpoints and internal organizational processes—even though all are institutions centrally concerned with the same rather narrowly specified task of allocating industrial credit in Japan. The easy assumption of common purpose and constant consensus among them, or of the persistent dominance of any one among them over the others, is simply facile.

Industrial finance has, by its very nature, been central both to the interaction of government and business in Japan and to that nation's broader economic achievements. For this reason an in-depth study of industrial finance has long impressed me as an especially appropriate vehicle for exploring the relationship of government and business to Japan's economic success in a way that recognizes the striking pluralism among the elite government offices and the largest private firms of Japan. Such a study of industrial finance also offers a chance to consider concretely the mechanisms that capitalist economies use to direct resources in support of national priorities. These analytical concerns come together in *Strategic Capitalism*, a book that deals primarily with Japanese experience, but tries to raise issues of broader relevance.

Over the sixteen years and more since I first began serious work on the politics of industrial credit in Japan, my debts for assistance and intellectual stimulation are legion. At the top of the list are the literally hundreds of scholars, government officials, politicians, business people, and especially economic journalists—in Tokyo, and throughout Japan—with whom I have puzzled over the details of Japanese public and private credit allocation, in search of a larger picture. It started in the fall of 1976 when Yamato Hiroshi of Representative Kosaka Tokusaburō's office introduced me to the editor-in-chief of the *Nihon Keizai Shimbun*, Kojima Yasunobu, and his assistants, Ōta Hisashi and Sugita Ryōki, themselves both subsequent editors of Japan's principal business daily. They introduced me to the irreverent and knowledgeable economic reporter Higuchi Takeshi, his colleague Kojima Akira, and others. Throughout my work the *Nikkei*, and insightful skeptics elsewhere in the journalistic world, such as Funabashi Yōichi of the *Asahi Shimbun*, have given me valuable perspectives on the informal, subterranean side of Japanese decision-making processes, and advice on dealing with the formal side, for which I am sincerely grateful.

The Japanese bureaucracy can often seem, on first encounter, inscrutably opaque. For early insights into government financial policymaking, I am deeply indebted to an informal circle of young Ministry of Finance bureaucrats in the late 1970s, Research Institute 21 (Kenkyū Shitsu 21), led by Noguchi Yukio and Sakakibara Eisuke, with whom I often met in my graduate-student days. At MITI, Fukukawa Shinji, head of the Industrial Capital Section and ultimately vice-minister, as well as Yamada Katsuhisa were most helpful, as were Imazato Hiroki, Takenaka Heizō, and Hashiyama Reijirō at the Japan Development Bank, together with Nakagawa Yuitsugu at the Bank of Japan. I have also benefited intellectually from my association with Princeton's distinguished corps of alumni in Tokyo, headed by Gyohten Toyoo, currently chairman of the Bank of Tokyo, and formerly vice-minister of finance for international affairs, with whom I had the pleasure of co-teaching a seminar on Japanese economic poliycmaking at Princeton in the fall of 1990 that helped refine the ideas presented here. I am also indebted to Fujikawa Daisuke, Ishii Hiroaki, Sakai Tatsu, Shizume Masato, and Taniguchi Tomohiko, who have helped with needed data for my research.

Private-sector dynamism is a major theme of this work, and private-sector business people have certainly given me numerous specific insights. Some of the most detailed and colorful have been over the dinner table, over many years, from Matsuura Shigenobu, my wife's father, who was witness to many of the events described in these pages. The staff of Keidanren, beginning with managing directors Nukazawa Kazuo and Fusano Natsuaki, have been extraordinarily helpful as this research has progressed over the years, together with the All-Japan Bankers Federation, and especially its longtime executive director, Mizutani Hiroshi. I am also highly indebted to the Industrial Bank of Japan Industrial Research Department, especially its director, Hayashi Nobumichi; his assistant, Tabei Hiroshi; and Ms. Lona Satō of their Washington office. At IBI International, which taught me much about the trees of the Japanese industrial and financial world while I worked there in the late 1970s, Tait Ratcliffe, Yoshizaki Kimio, and Jim Rudy provided important insights and assistance.

Over nearly a decade of research visits to Tokyo, the International House of Japan has been my home away from home. To its director, Nagai Michio, and innumerable members of its staff, I am deeply indebted. In particular, Koide Izumi, chief librarian; Kurita Junko; and other library staff have sought sources at the National Diet Library, made copies, and selflessly aided me, as well as other researchers, in ways that I will never forget.

On this side of the Pacific, I am deeply indebted to a loyal corps of researchers who have worked on this project over the years, never guessing that it might someday actually end: Scott Callon, Ijiri Mayumi, Kojo Yoshiko, Sakurai Rie, Zenda Kuo, Emily Thornton, Xiao-wei Yu, Kyoko Shimizu Hull, David Plimpton, Xiaoyang Liu, and others. Edwin O. Reischauer and Raymond Vernon provided provocative and useful comments on the original dissertation. Richard Missner has been an invaluable supporter in many ways, while the Sumitomo Bank Fund of Princeton's Center of International Studies, the Fulbright Fellowship Program, the Japan Foundation, the Zengin Foundation for Studies on Finance and Economics, and the Social Science Research Council have all generously provided more narrow financial support to this effort, without which it could not have been completed. James Abegglen, Aoki Masahiko, Tristan Beplat, Henry Bienen, Scott Callon, Jenny Corbett, Kenneth Courtis, Albert Craig, Timothy Dickinson, Ronald Dore, Sheldon Garon, Robert Gilpin, Gyohten Toyoo, Roger Haydon, Inoue Munemichi, Marius Jansen, Chalmers Johnson, Peter Katzenstein, Atul Kohli, Michael Loriaux, Miwa Yoshihiko, Nagatomi Yūichirō, Noguchi Yukio, Nukazawa Kazuo, Hugh Patrick, Susan Pharr, Sakakibara Eisuke, Bruce Scott, Ezra Suleiman, Takenaka Heizō, Taniguchi Tomohiko, Ezra Vogel, and Lynn White, as well as participants at research seminars at Princeton, Harvard, Stanford, and Keidanren, have read and commented on portions of the manuscript or offered important suggestions at various stages, while John Goodman, Ed Lincoln, Anthony Marcus, Max Otte, and John Waterbury have read it in its entirety. For all the comments and suggestions I am grateful; for the final product, I alone assume full responsibility.

The production side of this volume could not have proceeded at all without Edna Lloyd. She has been working on this project more than nine years, and I am sure was long convinced it would never end. Without her systematic organizational sense and uncanny ability to read non-word-processed scribbling, this project would clearly never have been finished. At Princeton University Press, Jack Rep-check, the longtime economics editor; his able successor, Peter Dougherty; Beth Gianfagna, who coordinated production; Lois Krie-ger, who handled copyediting; Richard Boscarino, who produced the illustrations; and Diana Witt, who prepared the index, all have my sincere thanks.

Mari Calder, our oldest daughter, was born three months after this project began. She and her younger brother Ryan, both students now at Princeton High School, know their father in no other capacity than as the ongoing author of this book. For their patience, and help with details along the way, I am grateful, as I also am to my mother, Rose E. Calder, for her support throughout, and for typing the first draft many years ago.

Toshiko Calder can remember the staccato sound of a solitary typewriter pecking late into the night in Kamakura, with which this book began, less than two years after we first met. Many years ago she became intolerant of this project. But the advice she gave, before she gave up, had a strong impact on the book at its initial concep-tion. Toshiko has sacrificed a great deal to allow this project to go forward, and it is with the deepest appreciation that I dedicate this book to her.

Princeton
May 1993

STRATEGIC CAPITALISM

Introduction

JAPAN HAS BEEN a nation under siege, at least in its self-perception, since first emerging into the international political and economic system from the shadows of isolation well over a century ago. At times the external threat to Japan was perceived as military, at times economic. On few occasions has a profound separation between national security in these two dimensions been made.

As in other late-developing industrial nations such as France, Germany, and Italy, the state in Japan has traditionally loomed large in economic life, the one force strong enough to galvanize society in the face of mortal challenge from abroad, persistently concerned with reshaping the economy and its role in global affairs. Most analysts see the Japanese state not just as a strong state, but as a successful one.[1] Japan has combined high rates of economic growth, rising industrial production, and successful movement toward a high value-added product mix, with many ascribing this success to government intervention.

Yet as researchers have begun to scrutinize the Japanese political economy in greater detail, its structural complexities and the difficulties in moving the Japanese state to purposeful action have grown increasingly evident.[2] The notion that the Japanese state automatically acts strategically has come into question, even where the success of the Japanese economy as a whole is not doubted. Yet no clear alternative paradigm for understanding the functioning of the Japanese state, or relating it to the operation of the Japanese economy, has decisively emerged.

THE PROBLEM FOR ANALYSIS

This study concerns itself with the inclination and ability of government to engineer economic success, by understanding the variant of capitalism pursued by that conspicuous recent economic success story, Japan, and the role of government in its industrial transformation. It focuses on government's attempts to transform Japanese industrial structure in strategic fashion,[3] because those attempts lie at the heart of important theoretical and policy debates relating to Japan.

If it were true that Japan's bureaucracy has been both inclined to strategically transform industrial structure so as to generate national competitiveness and also successful in its intentions, prospective competitors such as the United States would need either parallel industrial policies or at least a strategic trade policy that reduces the adverse consequences of Japan's state-led efforts to capture comparative advantage.[4] If, on the other hand, the Japanese state's role in national industrial success has been less strategic and salient—or even dysfunctional—then the policy argument for parallel or retaliatory practices may be less compelling. At the theoretical level,[5] such findings of state incapacity would, of course, cast doubt on the persuasiveness of the developmental state arguments, emphasizing the state's role in economic growth,[6] thus opening the way for alternative interpretations of Japanese state-society relations. Casual evidence suggests some empirical support for both interpretations of the state's role in Japanese economic life.

Important instances of incapacity clearly exist where the Japanese state has failed to galvanize society to deal strategically with emerging imperatives. Sometimes the failure has been one of conception, as when many government officials in the early postwar period failed to grasp the potential of emerging sectors such as automobiles and consumer electronics to contribute to long-term economic growth. Similarly, officials of the 1950s and 1960s were often slow to recognize the value of competition in basic sectors such as steel, with many of them obstructing the emergence of efficient new producers such as Kawasaki Steel, Sumitomo Metals, and Sharp Corporation in electronics.

There have also been failures due to co-optation: interest group politics and clientelist government-business networks often prevented government from redeploying resources toward new strategic objectives even when the importance of doing so was broadly recognized. Such resources were often squandered on politically influential industries of the past. Persistent large-scale policy support for ocean shipping and coal mining, long after those sectors had become sunset industries, was a clear case of such irrationality at work.

Even where policy has been coherent, there have also been private-sector alternatives to the state architect of industrial strategy. Indeed, a key defining feature of Japanese capitalism has been precisely the dynamism and farsightedness of its organized private sector. In many of Japan's most successful infant sectors, such as VCRs, audio equipment, and motorcycles, the state's role has been minimal. Even where the state has ultimately intervened, private initiative has typically led the way in industrial development, with government concerning itself with restraining overexpansion. Government has often been more conspicuous and important as a stabilizer than as a proactive strategist.

Japanese economic policymaking as a whole has had multiple, often conflicting, central actors. Many of them have been private firms and groups of firms, including long-term credit banks and *keiretsu*, or industrial groups. Policymaking thus has not generally been a rational, unified, and state-dominated process. Yet sometimes state strategists, centered at the Ministry of International Trade and Industry (MITI), have brilliantly formulated and pursued national objectives in strategic, developmental fashion. In important instances, such as in helping to stimulate the mechatronics revolution, they have triumphed.[7] The verdict is hence not clear regarding how and when state industrial strategists, struggling against varied political, market, and bureaucratic forces, have been able to achieve their designs, and when they have left—or been forced to leave—definition of emerging industrial structure to other influences.

Important issues for analysis thus arise: what social and political forces have determined the parameters and the outcomes of Japan's remarkable recent industrial development? Under what conditions are strategists within the Japanese state central to the palpable economic success of Japanese capitalism? When have private forces—rather than the state itself—been decisive in achieving Japan's economic transition? How have they typically interacted with the state?

Transcending Japan, the more general problem for analysis is understanding the relationship between state efforts at industrial transformation and the actual process of industrial change. It can be expressed, albeit in oversimplified form, in the typology presented in figure I-1. As figure I-1 suggests, nations vary in the degree of state intervention in their economic life—from the heavily mobilized Socialist states such as North Korea to the radical laissez-faire political economies such as Hong Kong. They also vary along another axis, in terms of the degree to which they engage in efforts at strategic resource allocation—that is, in attempts to move scarce resources systematically toward priority sectors through directive means.

Conceptually, this propensity to allocate through command decision is a distinct dimension from that of state intervention. Some nations where state intervention is pervasive (India, Egypt, or many of the sub-Saharan African states, for example) may either not attempt strategic resource allocation or find government efforts to prioritize frustrated by clientelism or other social pressures. Conversely, some nations where state intervention is relatively limited in economic affairs, such as Germany, may have important nonstate

STATE INTERVENTION

	YES	NO
YES	Developmental State (A)	**Corporate-led Strategic Capitalism (B)**
NO	**Clientelized State (C)**	Silicon Valley Capitalism (D)

STRATEGIC RESOURCE ALLOCATION

Figure I-1. The State and Industrial Transformation

mechanisms for prioritizing use of key resources (universal banking in Germany's case) and for directing those resources systematically toward priority objectives.

The analysis implicit in figure I-1 can also be applied at the subnational level. The extent of state intervention and the intensity with which key sociopolitical actors pursue strategic resource allocation vary among the composite industrial sectors of most nations, just as they do at the aggregate level between nations. To be sure, there are some extreme, almost ideal-typical cases—North Korea is an example of uniform state dominance, and Hong Kong is a case of laissez-faire, for example—where intersectoral variation along these dimensions is limited. But the major political economies of the world, such as the United States, Japan, those of the European Community, and most of those in East Asia, have mixed, nuanced patterns of state economic involvement; even the long-Socialist states of Eastern Europe and Asia are moving toward hybrid economic management.

The central concern of this analysis is in understanding the distribution of cases among quadrants A, B, and C of figure I-1—instances of state-dominated strategic resource allocation and related permutations. Proponents of the "developmental state" interpretation of Japanese economic activity take for granted that Japan in the aggregate falls into quadrant A, and that major sectors with high value-added and long-range growth potential, such as steel in the 1950s, computers in the 1960s, and perhaps telematics in the 1990s, belong there as well.[8] But this is an empirical question on which, as will be seen elsewhere in this volume, actual sectoral patterns often differ significantly from the broad generalizations of developmental state theory. Strategy through private initiative ("corporate-led strategic capitalism," represented by quadrant B) or clientelized state intervention (quadrant C) are also conceptually possible; indeed, experience shows that they are common—both in Japan and elsewhere in the industrialized world. The central issue is why cases fall into one quadrant rather than another, and how aggregate patterns in Japan relate both to the developmental state model and to actual patterns of state-society relations elsewhere in the world.

To allow concrete, detached examination of what are highly interactive government-business relationships, the analysis here will be confined to state dealings with private firms in the single highly strategic area of industrial finance. The rationale for this relatively narrow, focused approach is threefold.

First, state efforts at industrial credit allocation provide a critical case testing the notion of Japan as a developmental state.[9] They represent a clear instance, in the words of our earlier typology, in which the state could be expected to be both interventionist and strategic. Chalmers Johnson, John Zysman, and others subscribing to the developmental view of the Japanese political economy argue that credit allocation has been one of the Japanese state's most crucial levers for effecting strategic industrial transformation; Zysman, for example, views the financial system centered on credit relationships as "the eyes and hands of the state's industrial brain."[10]

Credit allocation is also an important area for study due to the insights it yields into intragovernmental relationships. State efforts at industrial transformation in Japan have historically been directed by MITI and its predecessors. But other ministries with very different views on economic management, principally the Ministry of Finance (MOF) and the Bank of Japan (BOJ) have administered financial policy and supervised the major financial institutions through which credit allocation was inevitably carried out. How have these diverse governmental entities related to one another in this area of overlapping jurisdiction, where exclusive control has held crucial institutional significance for all of them?

A third conceptual rationale for the focus on industrial credit allocation is the way it illuminates the private-sector response to public control efforts. Faced with broadly consistent state efforts to allocate credit, individual sectors and even firms have responded in highly divergent fashion. In some cases—especially where industrial groups and long-term credit banks are well developed, as in post–World War II Japan and Germany—the private sector has actually taken allocative decisions into its own hands, in accordance with the "corporate-led strategic capitalism" paradigm outlined above. The prominence of financial-based industrial groups in Japan makes credit-allocation decisions there an especially rich area for examining private-sector alternatives to government-directed allocation. Credit allocation thus provides a useful vehicle for transcending state-centric models and understanding the deeper dynamics of national variants of capitalism, although doing so requires detailed case studies and sectoral analysis of public-private interaction.

In exploring Japanese state intention and capacity through the credit-allocation case, we will engage in extensive historical analysis to determine concretely the kinds of activities government has undertaken, with particular attention to its control over investment decisions.[11] We will look at concrete instruments, institutions, and processes of national goal setting, since we are convinced that a crucial element of understanding national variants of capitalism is grasping how actual public and private organizations operate at the micro level.[12] We will consider the broader patterns of centralization both within the state and among political forces in the political economy as a whole. And we will consider extensive time-series data on the lending decisions of both public and private financial institutions over time. For it is only by situating our analysis in the details of Japanese political-economic evolution over the past five decades and more that we can truly understand the nature of Japanese capitalism and its broader international implications.

GAPS IN EXISTING THEORIES

A broad range of analytical constructs, including functionalist models, cultural analysis, public-choice theory, and group theories, can help to explain state involvement in the process of economic policy formation without a specific emphasis on the state as an independent unit of analysis.[13] In an explicit attempt to understand a state's capacity, however, we must focus more clearly on the specific institutions of which it is composed and their relationship to the broader society in which they are embedded. We are likely to find both state-centered theories and broader institutional approaches to state-society relations useful in this endeavor.[14]

State-centric perspectives held considerable vogue during the 1980s in both comparative and international political analyses, as well as in studies focused more narrowly on Japan. Arguing that policy is not principally a reaction to pressure from social groups, theorists of this school have contended that the state has interests and policy preferences of its own, as well as the ability to impose these preferences in the face of societal resistance.[15] Stephen Krasner, for example, argues that a conception of "national interest" led U.S. policymakers to develop a foreign economic policy independent of domestic pressures,[16] while Eric Nordlinger suggests that "the democratic state is frequently autonomous in translating its own preferences into authoritative actions . . . even when in doing so they diverge from those held by the politically weightiest groups in civil society."[17]

Such analyses have also been influential in the study of the Japanese political economy. Chalmers Johnson, in the most influential piece of such research, developed the notion of Japan as a "developmental state" and its government as the central agent of economic transformation.[18] Like Johnson, John Zysman also sees the state as the key to understanding the Japanese political economy, with an additional emphasis on the relation of government to the Japanese financial system. Zysman draws strong parallels between Japan and France, seeing both as examples of state-led growth flowing from credit-based, price-administered financial systems.[19] Much more categorically than Johnson, Zysman maps out a picture of a strategic Japanese state, directing resources from traditional uses to support the efforts of new expanding sectors.[20] T. J. Pempel, writing in the late 1970s, also emphasized the central importance of the state in the formation of economic policy, stressing among other features the ascendancy of the Bank of Japan in the financial system.[21]

We should distinguish two major variants of state-centric analysis. One treats the state as an undifferentiated unitary actor, or as one with centralized coordinating mechanisms. This view, with a special emphasis on the coordinating role of MITI or the Bank of Japan, was highly influential in Western analyses of the Japanese political economy throughout the 1960s and the 1970s.[22] The other, more subtle variant, while agreeing that elements of the bureaucracy are preeminent in policymaking, suggests that these elements are often disunified and only make policy through a pluralistic bargaining process within the state apparatus.[23] Although less prominent in the scholarly literature on Japan than analyses that stress coordination, this more various model of a state-dominated system has also been influential, particularly through the work of political scientists such as Inoguchi Takashi, Ellis Krauss, and Muramatsu Michio.[24] An extreme version of this pluralist but politics-centered model, arguing that the Japanese policy apparatus is so fragmented and disparate that it should not be considered a coherent state, appears in the popularly oriented but influential work of Karel van Wolferen.[25] Both versions of state-centric analysis present an aspect of Japanese political-economic reality, but typically overgeneralize from narrow empirical bases.

Major gaps in the scholarly literature on Japanese capitalism have made the formulation of clear alternatives to the statist paradigm difficult. In the analysis of the Japanese state itself, one of the most important gaps in the existing literature is the limited number of institutional histories examining just how the central ministries and administrative agencies of the Japanese government function and how they view their institutional priorities. Apart from Johnson's classic study of MITI in English,[26] there are multivolume histories of the various ministries and other administrative agencies published in Japanese by those ministries themselves.[27] But the bureaucratic publications, though highly precise and detailed on legal and institutional changes, are circumspect on other matters; they yield few insights into the informal side of Japanese administration or regarding linkages with either the private sector or the political world. Apart from these works, there are a small number of serious nongovernmental studies of Japanese government administration by Japanese authors—again focusing predominantly on MITI.[28]

The picture we currently have of Japanese administration is thus highly MITI-centric. Yet MITI is but one of twelve ministries. It has a staff of less than thirteen thousand,[29] limited political influence, and little or at best contested jurisdiction over such important sectors of the Japanese economy as finance, taxation, communications, shipping, and shipbuilding. The government financial institutions over which it has administrative authority allocate significantly less than half of all government credit.[30] Yet there is lamentably little detailed evidence on how broadly MITI's "developmental" view of Japan's appropriate economic course has been shared among influencial agencies elsewhere in the Japanese government, or on how conflicting bureaucratic visions of the economic policy process have been coordinated.

Beyond the study of state institutions and their contending visions of Japan's economic future, an important gap exists in the literature on how party and interest-group politics relate to economic policy formation in Japan. Johnson dismisses the influence of political parties in policymaking out of hand and likewise stresses the primacy of MITI over private-interest groups.[31] Okimoto notes distinctions among sectors of the Japanese economy in the salience of political forces in economic policymaking,[32] but considers party and interest-group political intrusiveness to have remarkably little impact on the industrial-policy formation process and does not consider such phenomena in detail.[33]

A few recent works have begun to explicitly consider the linkages of politics and the regulatory framework of the Japanese economy in highly specialized dimensions. Samuels examines how political processes have helped shape configurations of state ownership in the Japanese energy industry.[34] Rosenbluth probes political involvement in legislation and administrative decisions transforming the regulatory structure of the Japanese financial system.[35] But little has been published on Japanese government allocative processes, although these are, as Lasswell and others have pointed out, a quintessential concern of political analysis at its very core.[36]

A third major empirical gap with critical implications for an understanding of Japanese capitalism is the current lack of detailed studies of corporate behavior, exploring how Japanese firms go about dealing with the state. Samuels has suggested the notion of "reciprocal consent" as a means of characterizing government-business interaction.[37] This is a useful corrective in some contexts to previous overgeneralizations about state dominance. But "reciprocal consent" provides little operational guide to what concrete strategies corporations might adopt in relation to the state in specific instances, or to why government responds the way it does to private firms. To illuminate private-sector behavior, corporate histories and case studies of management strategy abound in both Japanese and English. But remarkably little of this material deals with government-business relations in any detail.

Private institutions are important in public-sector Japanese decision making partly because, as in some instances in France, high levels of state regulation encourage the private sector to actively attempt to co-opt public power.[38] But there are still deeper reasons, rooted in national historical experience and social structure, why the analyst of Japanese public policy must pay careful heed to private-sector initiatives. First, Japan, like the Scandinavian nations but unlike much of the rest of the industrialized world, is a highly homogeneous country. It has few distinctive ethnic or class divisions to polarize society and to force the state, as has been common in France, into an active role as arbiter among contending forces.

Japanese banks, in particular, are much more rooted in domestic society and less cosmopolitan in their interests than European analogues; Mitsubishi Bank and the Iwasaki family, which long ran it, can in no sense be considered an analogue to the Rothschilds or the French Huguenot financiers. Domestic steel mills, coal, and shipping rather than Spanish railways, the Suez Canal, or East Asian analogues were consistently the Japanese banks' concern, obviating the need for dirigiste intervention explicitly directing the private banks to support state developmental goals. Furthermore, the Japanese private sector has since the early twentieth century been extraordinarily organized and experienced in self-regulation, the product of incorporation strategies employed by the Meiji modernizers beginning in the late nineteenth century. For various reasons, then, the dialogue between public and private in Japan tends to be an intense, two-way discussion. It is often cooperative, but cannot well be understood by looking exclusively at the state. This dialogue often involves in the end "reciprocal consent," but that notion fails to capture its nuance or provide an operative guide to the specifics of either corporate strategy or government policy.

In the United States and in Japan, a particularly important gap has long existed in the understanding of the Japanese state's role in industrial finance. Johnson's state-oriented analysis carefully documents the aspirations of MITI to transform the industrial structure,[39] and numerous analyses assume some kind of decisive and strategic state direction of industrial finance.[40] These assumptions are conceptually crucial, because such assumed state dominance has been cited as a major piece of evidence to support prevailing notions of Japan as a "strong state." But little detailed empirical work has been done, either in Japan or in the West, to confirm or refute these widely held impressions of state decisiveness and strength, beyond the MITI-centered analyses. Rosenbluth examines how changes are made in the general regulatory parameters of the financial system, but without considering the ability or inclination of the state to direct resources toward particular sectors.[41]

The political world and the private sector have both at times significantly constrained and even supplanted the Japanese administrative state in its struggle for strategy. Yet their role has all too often been given short shrift or treated in terms of nonoperational abstractions. Nowhere do the deficiencies of the conventional wisdom appear more clearly than with respect to industrial finance.

Beyond the details of the Japanese political economy and the scholarly literature examining it, there are also major emerging conceptual issues in comparative political research to which the Japanese experience speaks. Aberbach, Putnam, Rockman, and others have begun to pursue the relationships of politicians and bureaucrats in policymaking processes;[42] these relationships take distinctive and instructive forms in the Japanese case, especially since the early 1970s. But the relevance of Japan's experience is only beginning to be considered systematically in theoretic terms.[43] The process of selective credit allocation in Japan, where political-bureaucratic interaction has become intense and complex in many sectors as the character of state involvement has changed, provides evidence of broader comparative importance in this regard.

The blurring of old institutional boundaries within nations inevitably also spurs comparative research on just how governments go about achieving public purposes. Apart from a recent body of work on public corporations and privatization,[44] private bodies with public functions—"parastatals" in Katzenstein's terminology[45]—are also becoming a major focus of analysis. Japanese credit allocation provides a wealth of theoretically interesting cases in this regard.

As transnational economic relationships intensify and transnational factor mobility across national borders becomes more pronounced, new processes of transnational politics are emerging in the advanced industrial world. Robert Keohane, Joseph Nye, Peter Gourevitch, Stephen Krasner, and others have been dealing with this phenomenon for a decade and more.[46] But the concrete impact on the domestic political decisions of individual nation-states is less well understood. Their policymaking is being shaped by a complex interaction of transnational forces with longstanding domestic structures—an interaction that cannot be understood without reference to their institutional histories. With a domestic financial system even now in the throes of momentous change and influenced profoundly by transnational forces, Japan's experience since the 1970s also provides material for a theoretically interesting analysis of transnational politics and its relationship to the transformation of domestic political and economic systems.

THE ARGUMENT IN BRIEF

Japan's enduring vulnerabilities as a resource-poor nation lacking empire, a continental market, and natural geopolitical allies have given it strong incentives to be strategic; its ethnic homogeneity, periodic shortages of capital and technology, and sophisticated, interventionist government institutions for economic management have given the Japanese state some potential to act strategically as well. Yet centrifugal pressures, especially a well-developed private industrial-group structure based on powerful banks and increasingly powerful transnational economic and political forces, have limited the power of the state alone to manage the economy. Japanese industrial-credit policymaking, like Japanese economic-policy formation more generally, has thus been a struggle for strategy—a political process in which state industrial strategists, based particularly at MITI, have tried to transform the Japanese economy along developmental lines, with mixed success. Both policymaking and policy implementation within the Japanese capitalist system have been pluralistic bargaining processes in which public and private sector have alternated as catalyst for structural change.

The capacity of government industrial strategists to strategically allocate credit has thus been sharply constrained not only by the structure of the state itself, but also crucially by the role of the private sector, the influence of party politicians, and occasionally by foreign actors. In Japan powerful industrial groups, a long-established bankers' federation, and the sporadic intervention of party politicians have confronted a Japanese administrative state less centralized, more understaffed, and less consistently committed to industrial transformation than often supposed. Industrial strategists within the government have lacked wide-ranging ability to shape the financial system to their vision of priorities, although they played an important role in orchestrating the early Japanese postwar recovery and the heavy industrialization of the ensuing decade. The private sector has conversely been unusually dynamic and farsighted by international standards, although not generally antagonistic to government. The result has been an economic order at once market-conforming and sensitive to long-term national competitiveness—in a word, strategic capitalism.

After 1970 broader market forces, including rising liquidity and global economic interdependence, also intruded with increasing persistence, to undermine the position of state industrial strategists still further. With their prerogatives threatened, these officials often responded with creative policy initiatives to maintain influence with the private sector. But preserving influence was always an uphill struggle, and it was difficult for bureaucrats systematically to control increasingly important Japanese multinational corporations, in any case.

State credit allocation clearly helped Japan direct resources toward heavy industrial sectors such as steel and shipbuilding more rapidly and at lower cost to borrowers than the market could have done, while also at critical junctures aiding in the modernization of industries with limited independent access to capital like auto parts. On occasion it directed corporate attention to new cross-sectoral opportunities for synergism, as in the case of mechatronics. But state-directed control allocation was unambiguously successful, one may argue, only when a relatively unusual configuration of state and societal characteristics simultaneously prevailed: (1) when power in the Japanese state was relatively centralized, (2) the private sector in question was disorganized, (3) domestic political intervention and transnational linkages were limited, and (4) the demand for credit was sharply greater than supply at prevailing interest rates. This confluence of circumstances appeared unevenly across sectors of the political economy, as will be seen. It was achieved most clearly across Japan as a whole during 1946–1954, the period of Ichimada Naoto's governorship at the Bank of Japan, although conspicuous breakdowns in the state's ability to allocate occurred even then, as chapters 2, 3, and 6 suggest.

The Japanese state, this research shows, has been persistently plagued in its industrial credit behavior by dual problems at the opposing ends of the product life cycle: hesitancy and clientelism. It has been remarkably cautious—and reactive—in supporting new industries, waiting for dramatic international developments to force its hand. This was true, for example, in the case of computers during the 1960s. Conversely, the Japanese government has poured large amounts of money into declining sectors—without much clear success at rationalization—as in the cases of shipping and coal mining, largely for clientelistic reasons, even when the high cost and the low strategic benefit of such actions were clear to dispassionate observers.

One transcendent problem for the Japanese state in its credit-allocation behavior has been interpersonal networks—particularly the flow of former senior government officials to the private sector. This flow is typically much heavier to established, often declining firms than to entrepreneurial startup ventures. Networks linking bureaucracy with the political world compound this bias toward the past rather than the future.

Within the Japanese state itself, organizational dynamics—especially the powerful hold of routine and risk avoidance on consensus-oriented organizations that practice lifetime employment—compound an approach to allocation decisions already rendered cautious by culture and ideology. Important interministerial differences in organizational goals further reinforce a conservative bias. The Ministry of International Trade and Industry has long supported, at least in theory, a developmental approach to industrial transformation. But within the broader Japanese political economy, MITI's influence is often constrained by more conservative "regulatory" agencies, pre-eminently the Ministry of Finance.

Japanese capitalism has had dramatic success in fostering dynamic industries with formidable international competitiveness. But the origins of that success, this volume contends, have been misspecified. Direction has resided not so much in the developmental state, which proves itself on close inspection to be often hesitant and reactive, or in the abstract functioning of a disembodied "invisible hand" of the market, but most importantly in a formidable and distinctive set of private-sector institutions, including long-term credit banks and industrial groups in combination with the state. Entrepreneurial, persistent private borrowers—insistently manipulating a surprisingly pluralistic financial system for hybrid private and public support in accordance with their own grass-roots calculations—have also themselves in the final analysis provided crucial initiative. This hybrid public-private system, driven preeminently by market-oriented private-sector calculations, but with active public-sector involvement to encourage public spiritedness and long-range vision, can be considered "strategic capitalism."

CONTOURS OF THE RESEARCH EFFORT

This research, as noted earlier, is conceived as a theoretically guided case study that provides a critical case for testing widely pervasive notions of Japanese state strength and state autonomy; it also supplies evidence for developing more nuanced perspectives on how private-sector organization and behavior influence public policy outputs, and thus shape the distinctive Japanese variant of modern capitalism. To gain a broad, balanced view of Japanese governmental credit-allocation attempts and their outcomes, this volume examines both government loans to the private sector and government attempts to influence the lending behavior of private banks. Emphasis is placed on understanding the Fiscal Investment and Loan Program (FILP), which has never before been systematically studied in the English language, together with the lending decisions of the eleven Japanese government banks. Examining the activities of these banks directly provides the most straightforward data possible on such questions as how extensively government has attempted to defuse risk in major projects within priority sectors of the economy, and how oriented its credit-allocation efforts have in fact been to the claims of particular constituents.

We plan to evaluate existing arguments about Japanese capitalism, focusing on the developmental state contentions that have dominated analysis of the Japanese political economy for a decade, by looking first at the situation of state strategists within the Japanese state and the obstacles they have confronted in achieving their objectives. These considerations are presented in chapters 1, 2, 3, and 4. Then the book develops an alternative interpretation of industrial credit policy outcomes, emphasizing the role of the private sector in spurring Japan's remarkable industrial transformation. The private sector's dynamic role is explored first through consideration of Japan's unusual private financial intermediaries and then through a microeconomic and political look via case studies at how entrepreneurial private-sector borrowers manipulate a fragmented and reactive Japanese state.

Historical analysis is clearly crucial to understanding the complex story of Japanese government-business relations with respect to industrial credit. It is especially relevant in understanding institutional origins—both state instruments of control and the unusual strength of Japan's organized private sector in the broader political economy, which stems in part from historical precedence. Some might ask why the book as a whole is not simply presented in chronological fashion, continuing on from the pattern of chapter 1.[47]

Chronological treatment, for all its superficial attractiveness, could not persuasively develop the most central themes of this volume. It would not provide sufficient understanding of structural complexities and decentralization within the Japanese state, which inhibit the state from playing an ambitious proactive role. Similarly, chronology could not systematically probe the organizational ethos of MITI with respect to industrial-credit issues or explain how and why it diverges from the orientation of other ministries. Consideration of such organizational and micropolitical matters is crucial for understanding why the Japanese state has so often ceded initiative to the private sector in the operation of Japanese capitalism.

Most importantly a chronological approach could not present a succinct critique of the developmental-state concept. Such treatment would simply yield the unexceptional conclusion that the Japanese state is slowly losing control capabilities over time. The more fundamental point is not evolutionary patterns—which are increasingly well appreciated in both the academic and popular literature on the Japanese political economy—but rather the surprisingly reactive character of the Japanese state and the contrasting activism of its private sector at any point in time. These dual realities can only be demonstrated through consideration of actual lending patterns, structural analysis of both state and private institutions, and focused case studies of how private borrowers and financial intermediaries, in interaction with state strategists, actually operate.

Evidence presented in this book is drawn from a wide range of public- and private-sector Japanese sources, as well as relevant secondary literature on Western Europe and the United States. Nearly one hundred Japanese and former Allied Occupation officials were also interviewed during 1977–1978 and 1986–1992, to supplement generalizations in the written record concerning actual Japanese financial decision-making processes. Perspective on private-sector contributions to public policymaking was drawn from Japanese-language official histories of relevant corporations and industry associations, supplemented by executive interviews and cross-checks for corroboration with the recollections of government officials.

The year 1946 was chosen as a point of departure for four major reasons. First, it marked the beginning of the postwar political system; the first postwar general elections were held on April 10, 1946. Second, 1946 marks the initiation of major *zaibatsu* dissolution measures, which were critical in stimulating rivalry for credit and market share among Japanese corporations. Third, 1946 marks the advent of serious organizational rivalry among governmental actors in the Japanese credit-allocation system—due to the postwar purge of two hundred thousand wartime government and business leaders, including the controversial finance minister, Ishibashi Tanzan, which began that year.[48] Finally, 1946 marks the clear beginning of the banker-dominated system of Japanese corporate finance, which was strongly reinforced by a series of measures taken by MOF that year that were highly favorable to the practically insolvent commercial banks.[49]

The early 1990s also mark an appropriate conclusion to the analysis in that they represent the transition from a highly segmented, heavily regulated financial system, with manifest possibilities for state suasion in matters of industrial credit, to one where the scope for market forces is considerably greater, and the leverage of the state correspondingly less. In 1991 Bank of Japan window guidance, once a formidable tool for influencing banking behavior, was formally abolished, after having been of reduced importance for several years. In 1992 the Diet passed historic legislation to gradually end the highly segmented character of Japanese industrial finance, which was implemented in 1993. The years 1993–1994 also promised at last the deregulation of savings deposit rates, a fundamental and longstanding obstacle to full financial reform. As Japan approached the mid-1990s, the days of its corporatist Bankers' Kingdom were at last clearly drawing to a close, although the nation's financial authorities and industrial strategists did make the best of the new, less-regulated environment through a revived bureaucratic entrepreneurship of their own—still another tranformation of strategic capitalism.

IMPLICATIONS OF THE ANALYSIS

Although in form a rather specialized empirical study of Japanese efforts to allocate industrial credit since World War II, this volume has a larger concern: the manner in which nations dream, and then seek to transform their dreams of the industrial future into reality, amid the complex counterpressures of an interdependent world with strong tendencies toward entropy. Although not denying the intensity of the dreams entertained by MITI industrial strategists, or the entrepreneurial flair of many who pursued them, this analysis suggests that Japanese bureaucrats had more difficulty attaining their sector-specific objectives than commonly thought, and that the course of Japanese capitalism, outside infrastructure provision, was set primarily by the private sector. The primary obstacles to realizing the dreams of postwar state strategists, it is argued, have been the weak centralization of allocative controls and the vulnerability of such state strategists in their broader domestic economic and political contexts.

To say that Japanese bureaucratic protagonists are constrained in their struggle for strategy is not, it should be stressed, to imply that they are incapable of constructive action. There are important, if clearly delimited, areas in which the unusual technocratic vision of an industrial bureaucracy as gifted as Japan's can greatly contribute to national competitiveness and economic transformation. Their work is a central element of strategic capitalism. With respect to investment decisions, state guidance is most likely to succeed, as has been noted, where the operative allocational responsibilities are centralized in a single ministry and where there is no cohesive, countervailing business or party-political intervention. These conditions are best satisfied in the provision of industrial infrastructure and in intrasectoral assistance to small manufacturing firms in priority sectors that lack extensive independent financial ties, as case studies in chapter 6 demonstrate. Mixed public-private lending enterprises, where limited public equity participation defuses risk without unduly constraining the role of market forces in project selection, may also be effective in fostering certain infant technologies, as chapter 4 suggests.

Three major implications flow from the travails of the Japanese industrial bureaucracy's struggle for strategy. First, *one cannot assume the rationality and effectiveness of industrial policy in developmentally transforming an economy from the statements and actions of industrial bureaucrats alone.* Much more sophisticated cross-societal analysis is necessary to identify the conditions under which successful state-led industrial strategy is possible, as well as those under which alternative outcomes (identified here as "corporate-led strategic capitalism," "Silicon Valley capitalism," and "the clientelized state") are more likely.

Second, as Skowronek, Johnson, and other institutionalists have emphasized, *state structure clearly matters.*[50] In assessing the implications of structure for politics and policymaking, however, one must guard against the perils of overgeneralization from even the in-depth study of just a few government agencies. When a relatively entrepreneurial ministry such as MITI has free rein to order an industrial sector's development and to hone its international competitiveness, as it did in the case of auto parts or computer mainframes during the 1960s, that ministry can clearly achieve strategic results, with little need to struggle in achieving desired outcomes. But the Japanese state's ability to achieve planned sectoral development is affected profoundly by the boundaries of administrative jurisdiction, which are not apparent from studies of individual state institutions. A mixture of detail and broader cross-institutional study of the state is required.

More generally, it is important in the analysis of Japanese public policy to distinguish industrial sectors such as semiconductors, where a single ministry has control and policies can as a result be systematically developed and implemented, from sectors where jurisdiction is shared and where both coherent policy formation and implementation are consequently much more difficult. Telematics, the emerging information industry at the interface of telecommunications and data processing, is a case in point. Interministerial rivalries are unusually salient in Japan due to the strong institutional consciousness that lifetime commitments inevitably bring and due to relatively weak horizontal communication among ministries, much of it occurring formalistically at the vice-ministerial level. The degree of cohesion in the structure of state regulatory authority over a particular sector can thus greatly affect policy coherence and policy outcomes.

Finally, and perhaps most important, an assessment of strategic capitalism as it operates in Japanese industrial-credit allocation suggests that *one must understand the private sector and the incentives that operate upon it.* Only in relatively unusual circumstances have the industrial strategists of MITI displayed enough vision, and been able to centralize enough political influence, to achieve industrial transformation in dirigiste, developmental fashion. All too often the Japanese state has been paralyzed by decentralization of responsibility or been clientelized. Yet remarkable and internationally distinctive economic growth and structural transformation have clearly occurred in postwar Japan. After viewing the organizational pathologies of the Japanese state, the reality of Japanese growth looms as a paradox, only to be unraveled by understanding the sophisticated organization of the Japanese private sector in detail.

This research presents the long-term credit banks and the *keiretsu* industrial structure as key elements in the "corporate-led strategic capitalism" that has been central to the prosperity of Japan's most successful industrial sectors. Michael Porter, in his classic 1990 treatise, *The Competitive Advantage of Nations*, identified transportation equipment and electronics as at the heart of Japan's current underlying global competitiveness.[51] It has been precisely this complex of industries that Japan's organized private sector, particularly its long-term credit banks, has most systematically fostered over the past fifteen years. The Japanese government, as chapter 4 clearly points out, has been preoccupied elsewhere.

The implications for future research are clearly posed: how do the distinctive institutions of the Japanese private sector—long-term credit banks, general trading companies, and industrial groups in particular— influence public policy and promote international competitiveness? Are they—rather than the fragmented, hesitant Japanese state—ultimately the central element in the Japanese economic miracle? How must the very real contribution of government in infrastructure provision, training, and support for technology diffusion be factored in? How has Japanese capitalism developed the flexible, market-sensitive orientation that has allowed it to navigate the volatile economic shoals of the two post–Oil Shock decades on which so many once-successful statist economies—from France to the Soviet Union—have dramatically foundered?

If it is indeed the Japanese private sector that is the principal agent of economic success, with the state largely a reactive, if often vital, accomplice, what does this portend for the future, and for theory in the field of comparative politics and political economy? We begin the exploration of these questions with a detailed examination of just how the entanglement of the state, through industrial credit, in the definition of Japan's economic future came to be, and the institutional heritage that involvement generated for the future of Japan's "strategic capitalism."

CHAPTER 1

The Weight of the Past:
A Complex Heritage
of Control

STATES CHANGE, or fail to do so, through political struggles that are rooted in and mediated by preexisting institutional arrangements.[1] Those arrangements do not just spontaneously arise, nor do they often adapt flexibly to changed circumstances. Indeed, the institutions that so profoundly shape the playing field of political behavior are typically created or transformed in short, sharp periods of turbulence, under strong external pressures. They then persist for long periods in equilibrium, even as the world around them continues to change. As Machiavelli pointed out, there is nothing so difficult, or so improbable of success, as to inaugurate a new order of things.[2]

To fully understand policy, especially in comparative international perspective, one must thus engage first in political archeology—a search for the often buried and forgotten origins of the institutional frameworks that dominate the present, and indeed the immediate future. The very conservatism of institutions—and the salience of institutional frameworks in policymaking—often makes the distant past the best explanation for what we see before us. In the case of modern France, Napoleon, the Liberation of 1944, and even the Vichy Occupation heritage continue to live through the persisting institutions to which they gave birth, much as the New Deal and the cold war heritage dominate American policymaking today even as it confronts a new era. In Japan the heritage of an unusual late developer—emerging into the international economy at the high noon of nineteenth-century imperialism, yet with a richly organized private society as counterpoint to the state—continues to dominate Japan's approach to economic management both at home and abroad. It is that fateful dual heritage of public control and private organization—one that has constrained as well as strengthened the Japanese state and profoundly shaped its distinctive strategic capitalism—that is the central concern of this chapter.

INTERNATIONAL CONSTRAINTS ON
JAPANESE STATE POWER

Japan's early encounters with nineteenth-century imperialism generated a profound sense of internal crisis, but a subtly different institutional response than in other late developers. Japan emerged from more than two hundred years of international isolation in 1854 grievously disadvantaged in terms of techno-military prowess and financial strength, although it had an educated populace, sophisticated social institutions, and more political coherence than most of the new European powers. As a "follower" nation, incapable of competing successfully with the industrialized and increasingly imperialistic West, Japan had strong national economic security incentives for artificially insulating its economy from the outside and encouraging priority sectors through governmental controls and subsidies. Yet there were major complications in doing so—many more than in the major continental and maritime empires of the West, which were much more powerful and potentially self-sufficient in international affairs.

The problem was that the Western imperial powers preferred for Japan—then as now—a more formally open system. And in the 1870s they had the leverage and initially the inclination to impose it. They insisted on a low-tariff treaty-port regime that kept Japanese customs duties at an average of 5 percent throughout the 1870s, even as tariff walls were beginning to rise in the United States, Germany, and elsewhere.[3] Despite persistent Japanese resistance, a low-tariff system enforced by international agreement ordered Japanese trade with the world until 1911. This arrangement constrained the state, encouraged government to acquiesce in the rise of powerful private industrial groups, and stimulated a more market-sensitive approach to international economic competitiveness than prevailed in other great powers insulated by colonies or huge continental scale from these broader market forces. The forces set in motion during this period generated an early adaptive orientation in some ways remarkably parallel to that of twentieth-century Switzerland and Austria,[4] however different the mechanisms of adaptation might prove to be.

As the pressures of import competition and the need to maintain economic sovereignty grew ever more intense for Japan during the 1880s, the Meiji government inaugurated the *shokusan kōgyō* ("develop industry and promote enterprise") policies. This multifaceted attempt at strategic economic development took low tariffs—and uncontrollable foreign markets—as a given. These policies had four major aspects: (1) the promotion of a national banking system; (2) the building of railroad, postal, and telegraph networks; (3) the building of factories ultimately to be sold to private interests; and (4) the leasing and sale of equipment, reinforced by loans, to promising firms.[5]

The *shokusan kōgyō* interlude, although a state initiative, powerfully strengthened the emerging private-sector *zaibatsu*, direct ancestors of today's powerful industrial groups. It did so through the massive sale of government assets, including mines, shipyards, and factories, to these interests throughout the 1880s.[6] Mitsubishi, for example, was awarded extensive real estate fronting on the Imperial Palace in Tokyo for virtually nothing. Today this property is worth tens of billions of dollars. While *shokusan kōgyō* policies strengthened the private-sector *zaibatsu*, they also strongly established the tradition of state involvement in providing business credit and subsidies to private firms. Subsidies for the Japanese shipping industry, to sustain it in the face of foreign competition and to assist the state in military emergencies, date, for example, from 1874–1875.[7]

As Yukisawa points out, however, the initial state support for shipbuilding was relatively small. Between 1868 and 1885, only ¥51 million had been spent on subsidies and loans to the private sector, and ¥151 million on the entire complex of policies.[8] These figures compared to total national fiscal expenditures of around ¥60–100 million annually during the latter part of this period.[9]

After the Sino-Japanese War the scale of *shokusan kōgyō* policies began to expand, mainly in support of private-sector industrialization efforts. By 1896 the government was spurring development of the shipbuilding industry, as well as supporting machinery sectors, through the Shipbuilding Promotion Law and the Navigation Promotion Law and through incentives for the establishment of ocean shipping lines as well as the construction of large iron oceangoing vessels.[10] In addition, a government-operated steelworks was set up at Yawata in Kyūshū, financed from the Chinese indemnity.

All these measures nurtured strategic sectors and helped establish the principle of central government participation in industrial finance. Particularly in shipping, support ultimately became quite large.[11] But it was mainly in support of private-sector objectives; a strong institutional structure of state controls with developmental objectives did not begin to develop vigorously until the onset of the Depression and mobilization for total war, from the late 1920s through the 1930s. Institutionally speaking, the role of the private sector in the Japanese economy was thus prior to that of the state.

While establishing the role of the state in industrial finance, *shokusan kōgyō* policies also helped create many of the private institutions that were to challenge, and ultimately to compromise, the state's ability to control the allocation of credit. Nakamura and Kumon point out that in Japan, as in tsarist Russia, finance, transportation, and communications developed well ahead of manufacturing;[12] this temporal precedence, together with the Meiji leadership's preference for major *zaibatsu* such as Mitsubishi, operated to create powerful private industrial groups centered on financial institutions and holding companies. The prominence of banks and their affiliate industrial groups in Japan paralleled patterns in Germany and Sweden, giving stimulus to corporate-led industrial development, while offering contrasts to France. French developmental policies, in contrast to those of late-Meiji Japan, never encouraged the rise of private-sector economic power centers analogous to Japan's industrial groups; French state power was thus manipulated and countervailed only through the less coherent and efficient private forces of such divided cartels as the Comité de Forges.

THE PROMINENT EARLY ROLE OF PRIVATE BANKS

Paralleling the emergence of the strategic Japanese state from its very beginning has been an unusually prominent role for private banks as financial intermediaries and industrial organizers. Indeed, such private banks have in important respects preceded the financial and industrial policy bureaucracy as a force in Japanese industrial and commercial affairs, compounding the constraints on state control capabilities introduced by neocolonialist extraterritorialism described above. Even during the Edo period (1608–1868) Japan had a vigorous infrastructure of remarkably sophisticated financial institutions, including exchange houses for changing one form of local money into others, money-lending houses, lottery associations (*mujins*), and pawnshops.[13] The Japanese private commercial banking structure was established before many of the government institutions regulating these private financial institutions assumed their modern form. Exchange companies (*kawase kaisha*) in Japan date from 1870, national banks from 1874, the Mitsui Bank from 1876, and the Yokohama Specie Bank (forerunner of the Bank of Tokyo) from 1881; it was only in October 1882 that the Bank of Japan, the national central bank, was founded.

Currently existing government financial institutions are, by and large, a product of the post–World War II period, especially of the forty years since the Dodge Line; a number of other bodies created to mobilize the economy for war were abolished after 1945. Private long-term credit banks, which frequently assumed public-policy functions before 1945, date from the beginning of this century. The private Industrial Bank of Japan (IBJ), for example, which has performed the important quasi-governmental functions described in chapter 4 for nine decades, was established in 1902; the public Japan Development Bank (JDB) was established in 1951. Even the JDB's forerunner as a public dispenser of strategic credit, the Reconstruction Finance Bank (RFB), was not founded until 1947.

The historical precedence of private commercial banks in the Japanese financial system, especially that of industrial-group affiliates such as the Mitsubishi, Sumitomo, Sakura (Mitsui), and Dai Ichi banks, is especially important; it was this privately dominated financial structure that was in place at the time of the formative crisis in the Japanese financial system during the late 1920s. Crises, as suggested above, are typically the periods when the political system of an otherwise bureaucratized developmental industrial state is most malleable and susceptible to major structural transformation; in time of crisis state structure and the linkages of the state with the broader society typically play a decisive role in giving form to subsequent policies and in ordering the evolution of institutions that persist to influence policy outputs for long periods thereafter.[14]

The Panic of 1927 preceded by a decade the mobilization for World War II, which brought the Japanese state pervasively into industrial-credit policy. Thus, one may argue, the Japanese financial system was consolidated in a fashion more congenial with conservative large-scale private banking interests than with any strategic concerns of the state for industrial structure transformation; this consolidation occurred before the state itself had strong incentives to direct restructuring in a fashion consonant with industrial strategy. To be sure, the Japanese state of World War II and shortly thereafter often took successful strategic initiatives. But in asserting its strategic interest, the state always subsequently had to reconcile its concerns with this historical legacy of preexisting private-sector financial power, which frequently had other preoccupations.

Prominent among these private concerns—shared also by the financial authorities—was a concern for stability. The Panic of 1927— caused by the insolvency first of several regional banks and ultimately of the Bank of Taiwan, the Fifteenth Bank (the so-called Peers' Bank, headed by the oldest son of former Prime Minister Matsukata Masayoshi), and the powerful trading company Suzuki Shōten—sent deep tremors through the entire Japanese financial system. At its height, Bank of Japan loans and issuance of bank notes increased by more than ¥1 billion in a single day; the central bank was so overwhelmed by accelerating demand that on April 25, 1927, it printed and issued ¥200 notes entirely blank on one side.[15] After declaring a bank holiday, the Bank of Japan finally announced extensive emergency loans to major institutions, together with emergency legislation permitting ¥200 million in loans to the Bank of Taiwan.[16]

One major consequence of the Panic of 1927 was the accelerated consolidation of the banking system. Even before the Panic the bureaucracy had been pondering seriously the need for concentration. Minister of Finance Takahashi Korekiyo had, for example, recommended the consolidation of the small regional banks in 1921; following the great Kantō earthquake of 1923 the MOF outlined its plans more comprehensively. In the worst days of 1927 new legislation provided the legal basis for reordering, which was given further momentum by MOF administrative measures. The emergency funds supplied by the Bank of Japan during the Panic went to the large banks; at the same time, operating funds available at the smaller banks were drastically reduced, as ordinary deposits fled for safety to the larger institutions and to postal savings.

This desertion of the smaller banks sharply cut back the resources available to small business; through intense lobbying small firms were able to convince the Tanaka Giichi cabinet in May 1929 to prohibit such smaller banks as remained from compounding their liquidity problem by diverting loans to big business.[17] Political pressure from the lesser financial institutions also prevented MOF from consolidating small banks through mandatory capital base requirements as rapidly as it wished. The combination of market forces and the consolidation enforced by a new banking law, promulgated at the height of the financial crisis on March 30, 1927, reduced the number of banks in Japan from 1,417 in 1925 to 680 by 1931.

Radical centralization of the banking system was also systematically pursued by MOF during World War II; the number of private banks in Japan declined further from 505 in 1934 to 295 in 1940, and to only 65 by 1945.[18] There was a particular concentration of banking activities at the top five banks, largely *zaibatsu* affiliates, whose share of all bank loans rose from 18.4 percent in 1925 to 57.1 percent in 1940.[19] Except for a small increase in a number of banks during the U.S. Occupation, there was virtually no change in Japanese domestic banking structure for more than forty years after the end of World War II, apart from an increase in the presence of foreign banks in Japan.[20] The combined total of city, regional, trust, and long-term credit banks at the end of 1990, for example, was almost exactly the same number (86 rather than 87) as in 1955.

Together with the emergency Banking Law of 1927, MOF and the BOJ acquired vague yet clearly expanded supervisory powers. Yet policy changes in the wake of 1927 also strengthened the position of private commercial banks in relation to corporate borrowers, laying the basis for the indirect Bankers' Kingdom regulatory structure, whereby the financial authorities closely supervised banks that supervised industry, and which so influenced later credit allocation.

In contrast to the post–World War II years, Japanese corporations in the 1920s and 1930s had relied heavily on bond finance. Even in 1931 bonds provided 29.9 percent of external corporate funding and bank loans only 13.6 percent. But in 1933, with the support of MOF and the Industrial Bank of Japan, around thirty of the largest private bond underwriting banks established the Kisai Kondan Kai, or Bond Issue Arrangement Committee, in order to restore stability and soundness to the bond market.

At its inception the Kisai Kondan Kai, or Kisai Kai for short, established the principle, persisting inviolate until the Sears Roebuck Tokyo issue of 1979, that corporate bonds would not be issued in Japan without sufficient collateral, usually in the form of real estate or specified government bonds. The banks also succeeded in structuring Kisai Kai regulations so that only "trustee banks" (jutaku ginkō) were allowed to manage relevant collateral until maturity of a bond, in return for a fee. Thus, with MOF concurrence was born an important circle of compensation, private-sector dominated, that played a major credit-allocation role in later years.

At the heart of the Kisai Kai were eight private banks, headed by the Industrial Bank of Japan. Securities companies participated as underwriting members of the Bond Committee, but only banks could earn the collateral fee. Yamaichi Securities tried to take over a trustee bank during the late 1920s to gain collateral-management business, but MOF blocked this move, thus sustaining the claim of the commercial banks on a highly lucrative source of revenue.[21]

Collateral requirements urged by the powerful private banks after the Panic of 1927 thus played a crucial role in destroying the Japanese corporate bond market; by the late 1930s corporations issued virtually no bonds at all.[22] Equity continued, however, to be a major source of corporate finance, constituting over half of corporate funding every year from 1934 through the onset of the Sino-Japanese War in 1937.[23] It was sudden expansion of heavy industrial investment demand under the pressure of war with China, and the onset of patriotic savings drives by the banks to provide funds to meet this demand, coupled with the uncertainties a wartime environment created for capital markets, that led to the decline of equity and to heavy corporate reliance on debt.

In December 1945 MOF's Financial System Research Council (Kinyū Seidō Chōsa Kai) again raised the issue of bond markets, this time setting up a study subcommittee. The banking and securities industries disagreed sharply with each other on whether banks should be allowed to underwrite bonds, and proceedings reached no definitive conclusion before most members were purged.[24] Article 65 of Japan's 1948 Securities Exchange Act precluded banks from underwriting bonds for public placement, but it did uphold the principle of collateral for all corporate bond issues. The Kisai Kai, long-term credit banks, and the extensive legal controls introduced in mobilizing the Japanese financial system for World War II also survived, creating a debt-oriented, bank-dominated financial system with a strong bias toward growth along established lines. Such a structure lay in subtle tension with the more radical transforming impulses of government industrial planners, intensifying the struggle for strategy that these planners confronted.

The early institutional preeminence of private banks, coupled with the trauma of 1927 and the wartime mobilization, had made these banks the principal financial intermediaries before 1945, and market forces in the early postwar period, centering on reconstruction from World War II, reinforced and deepened this bias. The problem was not simply one of rebuilding from catastrophic damage five times the magnitude of that wrought by the Great Kantō earthquake of 1923.[25] Beside the tremendous difficulties created by elementary destruction, there were also problems of structural readjustment, most pressingly the crisis in coal production.[26] Defeat had cost Japan access to the critically strategic coal fields in its conquests Manchuria, Korea, and north China; both large-scale investment and construction steel were desperately needed to repair existing equipment and facilities, and to increase Kyūshū and Hokkaidō coal production enough to compensate for supply losses that followed the fall of the continental empire.

Shortages of coal became a bottleneck choking such other sectors as rail transportation, steel production, and the chemical fertilizer industry (essential to food production). Not just capital alone was necessary, but its strategic, efficient direction toward the complex of crucial industries. The private industrial groups that had played a central prewar role in this process were in a state of economic collapse compounded by occupation-decreed dissolution and could no longer play this function. State direction was thus inevitable. It was also in some ways desirable. The life-and-death economic problems confronting Japan were also issues of synergy among industrial sectors, which centralized, government-led strategic credit allocation was especially well placed to address.

Between the end of World War II and termination of the Allied Occupation in April 1952, Japan concentrated on repairing war damage and replacing at home the industrial facilities lost abroad. The so-called priority-production policy (*keisha seisan hōshiki*) of Yoshida's adviser Arisawa Hiromi concentrated on breaking industrial bottlenecks centering on coal by strategically focusing capital investment in the steel, coal, shipping, and fertilizer industries; this state strategy proved broadly effective, although the impetus to growth after this early reconstruction was given primarily by private-sector competitive rivalry rather than by government incentives.[27] Private firms were ready to invest aggressively, since a chronic shortage of goods throughout the period, coupled with import constraints due to lack of foreign exchange, kept domestic market prices high relative to the variable production costs incurred by industry.[28]

This high marginal productivity of capital was particularly pronounced in the consumer goods sector, hit especially hard by wartime destruction and dislocation. Capital equipment costs were high. Yet firms were still willing to invest, since market prices for finished goods were high, government credit and production subsidies reduced the price of capital goods to would-be industrial consumers, and the prospective productivity gains were substantial. Once recovery was under way, competitive private-sector rivalry fueled investment still further.

The necessity of reducing production costs became the dominant rationale for Japanese capital investment during the 1950s. The government sharply cut back its production-cost subsidies; export subsidies became a problem overseas; great new advances technologically diminished the likely cost of introducing new equipment. In short, there was a sharp increase in the marginal productivity of capital in Japan, creating strong incentives for private investment. The economics of the steel industry, for example, were transformed by the invention of the basic oxygen furnace in Austria during 1953 and the development of high-speed strip mills at roughly the same time.[29]

Upon these developments followed the introduction of continuous casting and mammoth blast furnaces in the 1950s; the economies of scale were great, in turn promising a decisive cost advantage to whoever raised the capital to exploit them. Similar technological advances in petrochemicals, synthetic textiles, nonferrous metal refining, and other industries served as a decisive stimulus to investment. So did the development of entirely new product categories, such as electronic calculators, color television sets, and single-lens reflex cameras. In 1969, for example, 10.5 percent of Japan's entire industrial output was of products not even invented five years before;[30] the facilities to produce such a high proportion of technologically advanced goods could be generated only by an overwhelming desire to invest.

Rising labor costs also provided a significant incentive to large-scale investment, and ultimately to rapid investment-led growth. Such investment and growth in turn promoted higher productivity and lower unit labor costs. Extremely rapid corporate sales growth also increased aggregate demand for labor within larger firms, permitting increased hiring. Since large Japanese firms, operating under the lifetime employment system, hire predominantly young workers at low wage levels, their labor-force expansion significantly reduced average labor costs. Aside from readily calculable cost considerations and technological opportunities, subjective expectations concerning the future growth of the Japanese and world economies sharply enhanced the desire of Japanese corporations to invest, particularly during the pre–Oil Shock period. The effect of these expectations was also frequently compounded by the intense rivalry among Japanese firms for market share.

The industrial policy of MITI, to be sure, increased incentives for capital investment during the high-growth period. Through government-sponsored recession and rationalization cartels, through export-promotion activities, and after 1978 through government subsidies to scrap redundant production facilities, MITI consistently tried to reduce the risks of investment so that business would feel free to invest aggressively with confidence. Thus MITI artificially attempted to create the same "no-risk" investment situation that had prevailed in the early postwar reconstruction.

The expectation that MITI industrial policy would, by supporting demand levels in a given sector or by artificially curtailing levels of supply, assure a profit for prospective investors reduced uncertainty, and thereby sharply increased private incentives to invest. But MITI still had difficulty restraining entry into favored sectors where economic barriers to entry were already low; indeed, its support for particular industries positively encouraged aggressive market entry and capacity expansion. As will be seen later, neither MITI nor MOF could adequately control the "excess competition" stemming directly from Japan's unusual banking-industrial relationships and industrial policies, which removed much of the risk from large-scale investment. This irrepressible market-share rivalry both stimulated the emergence of new industries and complicated the reciprocal administrative necessity of limiting "excess competition" and overexpansion in those emergent sectors. The result was gigantic steel, petrochemical, and shipbuilding industries, far larger than either government or the leaders of private industry desired, which had to be radically downsized after the Oil Shock of 1973.

FOREIGN EXCHANGE AS AN INSTRUMENT OF FINANCIAL CONTROL

In the preceding pages we have seen the deeply rooted institutional power of private banks in the Japanese system of industrial finance. To control them the state for much of the twentieth century has relied heavily on exchange controls.[31] These insulated the Japanese financial system from international market forces that might otherwise have impeded the functioning of economic restrictions at home, although their strategic impact depended profoundly on who was administering the controls and why.

Japanese exchange controls were established under the Capital Flight Prevention Law (Shihon Tōhi Bōshi Hō), enacted in early 1932 to suppress flight capital and foreign-exchange speculation following the Manchurian incident and Japan's December 1931 decision to leave the gold standard.[32] They were expressly administered under the authority of MOF and the Bank of Japan, rather than that of the industrial bureaucracy, with important policy implications detailed in chapters 2 and 3. Until 1936 MOF exercised its new powers with great restraint, employing the law in limited fashion only to restrain capital exports and foreign-exchange speculation. Only in 1937 were exchange controls extended to imports and made a vehicle for systematically managing the balance of payments.[33] Because sectors of the Japanese economy varied in their contribution to Japan's balance-of-payments position, some tendency to discriminate among sectors also emerged, although this was driven by short-run balance-of-payments expedients rather than long-term industrial strategy.

In 1949 the Capital Flight Prevention Law was succeeded almost verbatim by the Foreign Exchange and Foreign Trade Control Law (FEFTCL). This remained the basic legislation governing Japanese foreign-exchange transactions until 1980. Ironically, Article 2 of both the prewar and early postwar laws stipulated that they were only temporary measures, in effect until otherwise suspended.

One key element of the 1949 FEFTCL was its exclusionary character. All financial transactions with foreign countries were prohibited unless explicitly authorized, either by provisions of the statute or through application to the Ministry of Finance. The exclusionary rule generated vast amounts of data for MOF, much of it concerning the internal transactions of banks, by requiring an extraordinarily large number of private-sector applications for public approval; its many discretionary provisions created leverage for the bureaucracy, while its reserve powers afforded the legal basis for much sterner exchange controls should they become politically expedient.

The second distinguishing element of the 1949 act was its "concentration principle," under which foreign exchange (along with precious metals, claims in foreign currency, and foreign securities) could be legally held only by the government foreign-exchange fund special account, the Bank of Japan, the authorized foreign-exchange banks, and such others *as the Ministry of Finance should designate.* For many years corporations and individuals were required to sell foreign exchange to the government within one month of acquiring it. In 1952 MOF began allowing foreign-exchange banks to hold a limited amount of foreign currency, initially restricted to dollars. Then in January 1966 trading companies were allowed to do the same thing, and in February 1970 manufacturers directly engaged in foreign trade.[34] By the end of 1978 any individual in Japan could finally hold foreign currency should he or she desire to do so and could even establish an account denominated in dollars with a Japanese bank. But the formal *structure* of concentration remained until 1980, with designation by MOF (albeit automatically obtained) remaining a prerequisite for legally holding foreign exchange until that time.

Until around 1970 the foreign-exchange laws were rigorously applied, the control structure providing two significant reinforcements of official power. First, it administered foreign-exchange controls and rationed all available foreign exchange under the Foreign Exchange and Foreign Trade Control Law. After the Supreme Commander Allied Powers (SCAP) relinquished direct allocation of foreign exchange in February 1949, these powers passed first to an independent Foreign Exchange Control Board and then in August 1952 to the Budget Section of MITI's International Trade Bureau, becoming one of the ministry's most powerful tools of industrial policy. The foreign-exchange allocation function of MITI, which continued until 1964, was particularly critical in enforcing state industrial policy prescriptions for such sectors as oil refining, where foreign exchange was a constant and pressing necessity. Such controls were especially attractive to MITI because they were one of the few credit tools that it could manipulate in a coherent, strategic fashion.[35] For a bit more than a decade—no more and no less—they were thus a major bulwark of the developmental state.

Overall, exchange controls were more important in their financial than in their industrial policy dimensions, especially since they were generally (the 1952–1964 period partially excepted) administered by MOF rather than by MITI. Controls gave Japan the crucial freedom to determine its interest rates in isolation from the rest of the world, without provoking a flight of the domestic capital needed for development or allowing the inflow of unwanted foreign funds. Needless to say, there were substantial market incentives for private financial institutions to circumvent the controls or to seek their modification, with interest rate differentials with foreign countries frequently running 3–4 percent in a system of fixed exchange rates.[36] Japanese commercial banks attempted a concerted campaign of arbitrage in 1960–1961 by borrowing substantial foreign funds at low interest rates and seeking to convert them into yen. The Ministry of Finance responded in June 1962 with its "foreign exchange reserve deposit system," which largely restrained this threat to exchange controls for most of the ensuing decade.

CONTROLS OVER BANK LENDING

A second state mechanism for limiting the underlying institutional strength of private banks in Japan was controls over their lending. The initial basis for central control of private-bank lending decisions was the Temporary Funds Adjustment Law (Rinji Shikin Chōsei Hō) of September 1937, promulgated just two months after Japan plunged into full-scale war with China.[37] The law required that financial institutions and underwriters obtain permission from the Ministry of Finance when either making long-term loans or subscribing to or underwriting securities in amounts over ¥100,000.[38] This 1937 law also set up the bureaucratic machinery to administer such controls.

The Temporary Funds Adjustment Law categorized loans as "favored," "permitted," or "proscribed"—and established criteria for defining each of these. For instance, capital goods, raw-material processing, and military-related loans were "favored." Most of these categories remained in place until formally abolished in 1963; only "military-related" loans lost authorization after the war. The law set up a Funds Utilization Committee in the Ministry of Finance to formulate general capital-allocation plans for the economy and established a companion Funds Adjustment Bureau (Shikin Chōsei Kyoku) in the Bank of Japan that ruled on specific private-sector applications to extend long-term funds. Both of these institutions also survived the war.

Other survivors of the 1930s also persisted through the turbulent early postwar years. Many of these were administrative measures rather than laws, promulgated under the sweeping National General Mobilization Law (Kokka Sōdōin Hō) of April 1938, itself passed over considerable business opposition at the insistence of radical control elements in the military.[39] This gave the bureaucracy virtual carte blanche to mobilize the economy for war. It also created the legal basis for wide-ranging "administrative guidance," which has been a central feature of Japanese industrial and financial policy ever since.[40] Although the National Mobilization Law itself was repealed under Occupation pressure on December 20, 1945, its broad-ranging powers were reestablished under the Temporary Supply and Demand Law less than a year later (September 30, 1946) and continued in effect throughout the postwar reconstruction.

Among the original law's formidable and enduring offspring were the Companies' Benefits, Dividends, and Accommodations Order (limiting dividend payout) of April 1939; the Ordinance for Control of Corporate Finance and Accounting of October 1940; and the Bank Funds Utilization Order, also of October 1940.[41] These measures, progressively more drastic in character, were implemented to coerce the reluctant commercial banks, particularly the *zaibatsu* banks, into greater cooperation with military plans for a radical redistribution of funds toward war-industry firms. Many of these war-industry firms were financially troubled, poorly managed, and most important, not *zaibatsu*-affiliated. In preference to loaning long-term to the war industries, many banks in 1938–1940 were lending speculatively at high return to short-term civilian ventures.[42] The Ministry of Finance and the military decided to tighten the screws.

The collective effect of these more draconian controls was to make it standard practice for the BOJ and MOF routinely to review the internal financial practices and operating strategies of the banks, as well as their long-term lending decisions. This was a major new penetration of corporate secrecy by the state in a nation where such secrecy had long been one of the crucial preconditions for the private sector's autonomy. Under the Ordinance for Control of Corporate Finance and Accounting, for example, MOF was empowered to prescribe by fiat items of accounts and forms of books, rates of depreciation of fixed assets, and internal disposition of bank funds. It was also given the right to compel purchases of government bonds and to investigate such matters relating to the financial operations of a given bank as pertained to that bank's ability to finance war industry. The Bank Funds Utilization Order imposed controls on the allocation of short-term funds by banks, both by quantity and sector, while also empowering MOF to order banks to lend to specific companies or to subscribe, underwrite, or purchase specific securities.

In sum, these measures of 1939–1940 established the tradition of sweeping state intervention in the internal operations of private banks. This precedent in turn set the stage for wide-ranging "window guidance" and other nonstatutory exercises of administrative discretion in postwar years. But this intervention, it is crucial to note, was to be undertaken by the *financial* bureaucracy, particularly the Bank of Japan; industrial-policy bureaucrats at the Ministry of Commerce and Industry (MCI), with their more developmental orientation, had no direct role in the process. As chapter 3 shows in detail, the objectives of these financial bureaucrats were generally different from those of the industrial strategists at MITI, and their supervision of the private banks was in any event far *less* intrusive than the conventional wisdom suggests.

There was, surprisingly, no legislation explicitly controlling interest rates enacted before 1945. From the days of Meiji, the structure of interest rates had been set, within the constraints established by monetary policy, through cartel-like consultations within the private sector. Beginning in 1932, the Bank of Japan began to exert downward administrative pressure on private-sector interest rates to facilitate absorption of government bonds. Such pressure became increasingly persistent and effective as both the range of controls and the financial needs of government increased under the pressures of war.

Ultimately, interest rates came under almost total de facto government control, despite the dearth of legislation, although the lingering practice of compensating balances left the private sector with some informal autonomy to determine de facto lending rates.[43] After the war government continued to intervene in setting the price of credit, this being formalized in the Temporary Interest Rate Adjustment Law (Rinji Kinri Chōsei Hō) of December 1947. This law empowered the BOJ governor to set interest-rate ceilings for financial institutions and became one of the central legal supports for control-oriented financial policies. It was passed because that October the newly established Fair Trade Commission (FTC) had outlawed the previous collusive determination of interest rates by the private-sector banks. The FTC thus ironically strengthened administrative determination of interest rates, only shifting coordinating authority from the private banks to the bureaucracy, rather than to the market.[44] But once again industrial-policy bureaucrats were given no direct role in the process, complicating their attempts to impose a developmental orientation on credit flows. Ultimately the law was used primarily to keep savings deposit rates below market levels, and aided the private banks much more than it did industry.

New government financial institutions to which MCI did have some relationship had, to be sure, also proliferated under the pressures of wartime mobilization. These new government bodies included the Wartime Finance Bank (Senji Kinyū Ginkō), Industrial Facilities Corporation (Sangyō Setsubi Eidan), Southern Development Treasury (Nanpō Kaihatsu Kōko), the Foreign Capital Treasury, Cooperative Loan Banks (Kyōdō Yūshi Ginkō), and Capital Integration Bank (Shikin Tōgō Ginkō).[45] But none of these organizations survived the war, leaving more room for a resurgence of private initiative than would otherwise have been the case.

The experience of wartime financial controls led to a sharply expanded role for the Bank of Japan, which complicated rather than facilitated MITI's postwar struggle for strategy, as is explained in chapter 3. As Patrick points out, "In the period before World War II, and particularly before 1932, the Bank of Japan did not have a close relationship with the commercial banks and the money market except in times of crisis, when it acted as lender of last resort."[46] Liquidity, when needed, generally flowed into the market via the government-controlled Yokohama Specie Bank (predecessor of the current Bank of Tokyo) rather than through the Bank of Japan. This passive role of the BOJ in relation to the private banking system changed radically as the control period began in earnest, creating some prospect of centralized control in industrial finance under BOJ auspices.

The first significant expansion of the BOJ's role came in 1932 with the advent of exchange controls, which it was called upon to supervise, and with the floating of substantial government debt to finance expanding military expenditures. Its primary concerns were financial rather than developmental. The BOJ stepped in to limit interest charges by the banks on private debt in order to make government bonds more attractive by comparison, thus artificially shifting credit preference toward government securities.

In 1937, under the Temporary Funds Adjustment Law, the BOJ greatly expanded its bill discounting relations with the commercial banks, which consequently forced it more deeply into controlling the disposition of private bank credit. But in doing so it relied primarily on strategic judgments by the Industrial Bank of Japan rather than on the BOJ's own in-house expertise. The BOJ established differential rediscount rates that accorded the most favorable rates to military procurement bills already approved by the IBJ. This differential rediscount rate device was one of the BOJ's major allocative weapons from the 1930s to the 1980s: from financing aggression in 1937 to directing funds toward "emergency imports" that might cut Japan's massive trade surpluses in 1978 and again during the late 1980s.

The Temporary Funds Adjustment Law forced commercial banks to get BOJ approval for any long-term loan transaction and to set up an elaborate bureaucracy to review loan applications. This loan-review apparatus survived World War II and provided the basis for further quantitative, as well as qualitative, credit allocation. It remained until the third quarter of 1991 in the form of "window guidance," the BOJ's unique review of commercial loan portfolios, to be discussed in chapter 3.

The growing powers of the Bank of Japan to control the credit-allocation decisions of the private banks were formalized and expanded even further through the Bank of Japan Law of 1942, patterned after the Nazi German Reichsbank Gesetz. This law, discussed more fully also in chapter 3, left very little outside the bank's competence in the financial realm: powers largely unchanged until enactment of a new Foreign Exchange and Foreign Trade Control Law in 1980.

CONSTRAINING THE STATE: CORPORATIST CONSENSUS-BUILDING MECHANISMS

As the national authorities progressively concentrated formal control powers over industrial credit in the Bank of Japan during the decade before Pearl Harbor, they were simultaneously forced by political counterpressures to broaden the range of control and consensus ratification mechanisms around the BOJ. This constrained the bank's ability to operate alone, even if it had desired to do so. This network of countervailing organizations and restrictions provided a vehicle for Japan's cohesive private sector to limit the state's autonomous powers to arbitrarily direct the flow of industrial credit, and thus to ensure predictability in their relationships with state financial authority.

One key private institution mitigating state financial power that developed during the prewar control period was the system of *sanyo*, or councillors—established in 1937 at the strong insistence of private financial and industrial groups fearful of being isolated from the credit-allocation process by the military. This corporatist system provided that eight business leaders would meet periodically to review the specific allocative operations of the BOJ and offer suggestions for change. By the 1970s the *sanyo* system had become a mere ritualistic ratification mechanism, as the practical private-sector need to countervail the BOJ declined. But during the 1930s, 1940s, and 1950s it appears to have been a significant channel for interest articulation on questions of credit and also a means for keeping bureaucrats in check. Such advisory mechanisms are unusual in other nations, such as France, which have actively regulated credit flows for industrial policy purposes.

A second device restraining the BOJ was the comprehensive range of supervisory powers conferred by the Bank of Japan Law on the Ministry of Finance. MOF was, for example, authorized, upon concurrence of the cabinet, to remove the central bank's leadership. This power was actually exercised by MOF in 1944, when BOJ governor Yuki Toyotarō opposed a finance plan providing that munitions companies could secure financing with the sole approval of the munitions minister, without BOJ acquiescence.[47] The MOF was also given extremely broad powers to "order the Bank to undertake any necessary business," and even authorized to insist that the BOJ submit a detailed budget of its operations to MOF for approval. As Patrick points out, the BOJ is probably the only central bank in the world so required.[48] Yet MOF's ability to direct credit flows was impaired by its own lack of direct operating responsibilities in relation to the private banks; it lacked strong bureaucratic incentives to do so, in any case.

The Bank of Japan was constrained by the private banks finally through the structure for formulating and implementing credit-allocation plans, set up just two months after the Bank of Japan Law was promulgated. The Finance Control Association (Kinyū Tōsei Kai), set up to mediate between the BOJ and the banking community, might best be described as an instrument of "indirect rule." The BOJ governor, as chairman of the Finance Control Association, had final authority to approve plans by the banks as a group to raise and allocate funds. But their specific objectives were to be established by the members (mainly commercial bankers) of the association itself. Such a powerful role for the bankers' associations, the postwar descendants of the Kinyū Tōsei Kai, has to this day remained an offsetting factor to any decisive strategic impulse from the BOJ.

Local authorities, just as MOF, bankers' groups, and businesspersons, developed as checks and balances to constrain the centralization of allocative powers in the BOJ. Beginning in 1942, regional "review boards" (formally, Provisional Capital Investigation Committees) were delegated authority to determine the consistency of local loan decisions with overall BOJ guidelines. These bodies won a de facto role in credit allocation at the grass-roots level, again continuing into the postwar era to become part of the complex "heritage of control."[49]

FINANCIAL CONTROLS AND
THE OCCUPATION INTERLUDE

By 1945, under the pressures of financial crisis and ensuing war, the formal profile of Japanese financial controls—intrusive but somewhat complex, administratively decentralized, and potentially vulnerable to private-sector co-optation—had largely emerged. The Allied Occupation, despite its market-oriented ideology, did not change this pattern much. It did dismantle many of the existing government financial institutions as war related, thus setting the stage for a partial return to private-sector dominance in industrial finance. It also, through the efforts of Joseph Dodge, gave birth to an elaborate new system of off-budget government finance, the Fiscal Investment and Loan Program, which is described in chapter 4, simultaneously contributing to its fragmented, complex oversight structure.[50] The program remains important to this day, although the very complexities of its early oversight structure, exacerbated further by political intervention to create more and more government financial institutions over the years, circumscribe its role as a tool of industrial strategy. But FILP certainly did not succeed in changing the central role of private banks in industrial finance, or in altering the extensive formal controls that bound them to the financial bureaucracy. Overall, the Occupation aided emergence of a Japanese capitalism based on indirect regulation in industrial finance, dominated by a group of private financiers and their regulators, rather than by state industrial strategists. Chapter 5 considers the operation of this Bankers' Kingdom in detail.

From the beginning the Allied Occupation faced handicaps in reshaping the formal profile of Japanese financial controls. World War II ended abruptly, before economic planning for the Occupation of Japan was complete. Planning document SWNCC (State-War-Navy Coordinating Committee) 150 declared the economy, including the process of organizing for economic recovery, to be a Japanese responsibility; the intention was to force Japan, as the initiator of the war, to pull itself up by its own boot straps. Consequently SCAP ignored financial policy until after the abortive February 1947 general strike, except insofar as finance related to *zaibatsu* dissolution. This interlude provided opponents of reform with a valuable tactical opportunity to regroup their forces and to plan strategy at war's end.

An ad hoc mixture of theory and improvisation gradually developed within SCAP regarding financial reform. Initially SCAP supported five major reforms relating to credit allocation:

1. General democratization of the economic structure, including the broadening of ownership of securities and access to capital markets.

2. Creation of a market-oriented financial system.

3. Creation of a financial system based, like that of the United States, on direct finance via stable and liquid securities markets.

4. Reduction in the powers of the bureaucracy over the financial system. This was to be accomplished through deregulation or decentralization of regulation, and via the establishment of independent regulatory commissions analogous to the U.S. Federal Trade Commission, Securities and Exchange Commission, and Federal Reserve Board.

5. Reduction of the role played in the Japanese financial system by government banks and other public institutions, particularly those formerly associated with the military.[51]

By 1948 the coincidence of domestic U.S. political pressures to make Japan self-supporting and strategic concerns relating to the cold war helped dampen Occupation enthusiasm for social reform. The practical implications of this "reverse course" for financial policy came in the findings of the Draper-Johnson Mission, which arrived in Japan during March 1948. This mission, headed by a former vice-president of Dillon, Read (Army Under-Secretary Williams H. Draper) and the chairman of Chemical Bank (Percy H. Johnson), recommended definitively to the War Department on April 26, 1948, that Japan's banks be taken off the deconcentration list prepared under the *zaibatsu*-dissolution program. This move also helped forestall the dissolution of the Industrial Bank of Japan, wartime coordinator of industrial finance; by April 1950 the IBJ returned to regular banking status, with no greater alteration in its wartime standing than a cut in the number of its branches.[52] The IBJ's important role in postwar industrial finance will be considered fully in chapter 5.

A powerful desire to rationalize the Japanese economy as fully as possible (consistent with the stability imperative) became strongly dominant in SCAP by late 1948, epitomized by SCAP's stiff nine-point memorandum of November 1948, calling on the Japanese government to undertake strict credit rationing. This would fund only business contributing directly to Japan's economic recovery.[53] The

[handwritten margin note: IBJ spared in dissolution campaign]

austere SCAP economic adviser Joseph Dodge, architect of currency reform in early postwar Germany and a strong foe of government-induced inflation, presided over the Japanese economy from 1949 to 1952.

Dodge insisted that Japan cut off massive, direct general-account subsidies to basic industry, orienting both industry and finance as much as possible to the market. This faced a mixed reaction in the Japanese bureaucratic and political worlds,[54] with the upshot that Japan combined sharp cutbacks in public enterprise and general account subsidies with an internationally distinctive Fiscal Investment and Loan Program. This provided off-budget support for industry and other sectors through an elaborate network of government banks. To obviate inflationary pressures, these were funded through a highly developed postal-savings program rather than through the national budget.

SCAP won its greatest short-term victories in the financial area on the battlefield of regulatory decentralization, which tended to make centralized control of credit flows more diffiult. In that field a technically proficient and insistent head of the Securities Division of the Economic and Scientific Section (ESS) of SCAP secured a revision of the Securities Exchange Act in early 1948, transferring regulatory authority over securities from MOF to a U.S.-style Securities Commission, while at the same time banning banks from trading in or underwriting securities.[55] An analogous partial success also occurred at the Bank of Japan, where Governor Ichimada was forced to agree against his wishes to share power with a Policy Board patterned after that of the U.S. Federal Reserve.[56] But even these partial gains were eroded with time. The Securities Commission, for example, was abolished and its functions transferred back to MOF just three months after the Occupation ended. Ultimately, SCAP failed to decisively reorient the Japanese financial system toward markets and toward diffused administrative responsibility on the American pattern.

In perhaps the Occupation's most portentous failure, SCAP failed to reorient Japanese corporations from their newly developed system of indirect finance toward the direct finance, based on capital markets, then prevailing in the United States; it thus implicitly affirmed the dominance of banks as financial intermediaries in Japan. To be sure, SCAP succeeded in making technical changes in the functioning of Japanese securities markets that moderated their volatility—by eliminating the highly speculative futures trading system, for example, which did not reappear in Japanese financial markets again until

1988. But SCAP failed to create the capital-cost incentives that could induce Japanese corporations to resort with confidence to the markets for their prime financing. Nor did it create the incentives for investors that would make holding securities attractive.

In sum, the Occupation focused narrowly on technical and ideological questions, such as "democratization," remaining for the most part blind to the deeper issue of incentives that might stimulate a thoroughgoing transformation of established practices. Such an emphasis was a major reason that SCAP failed to make really fundamental changes in the structure of Japan's financial system, although it contributed through its political reforms to a pluralist ferment in Japanese society that complicated strategic, state-dominated credit-allocation processes.[57] Internal SCAP divisions, MOF's internal cohesion (only nine of its officials had been purged),[58] and the astuteness of MOF lobbying efforts, led by such experienced English-speaking financial diplomats as Watanabe Takeshi, also reduced the prospects of major change in the status quo structure of financial controls, apart from the innovations introduced by Joseph Dodge.

Thus, for a complex of reasons, the American Occupation failed to produce an American system of finance in Japan, despite initial aspirations to do just that. But it did significantly modify the postwar dynamic of government-business relations, even as it left financial controls themselves in place. It left a state with important internal divisions, countervailed by a private sector newly vitalized by competitive forces within and outside Japan. The Occupation thus laid the basis for the subtle, interactive process of public and private negotiation that distinguished the Japanese selective credit programs of the past four decades, a crucial aspect of "strategic capitalism."

CHAPTER 2

The Strategists and Their Tribulations

THE GENERAL CAPACITY of nations to formulate and implement coherent, consistent policies is mortgaged to the quality and aptness of
the institutions through which they perceive problems and resolve
them. State structure also shapes profoundly the ability of government to impose its will on the private sector. Across the tremendous
range of cross-national variation, Japan is considered to have particularly efficient and well-coordinated state institutions, unusually capable of pursuing strategic objectives and causing public interests to
prevail. But while the strategic orientation and political capability of
some individual ministries has been documented,[1] how different
ministries coordinate their concerns in a single policy area where
several have interests remains poorly explored.

This chapter approaches the problem of coordination and strategy
in Japan's political economy by focusing on the strategists themselves as they address problems of industrial finance, within a complex institutional framework inherited from the past. John Zysman
has characterized policy finance in Japan as "the eyes and hands for
the state's industrial brain";[2] this chapter considers the appropriate-
ness of this formulation and others by looking at both bureaucratic
aspirations to be strategic and the inevitable political and institutional constraints on those efforts. The argument is that bureaucratic processes and internal divisions, together with complex interpersonal networks and a political context that strategists cannot
consistently dominate, create a strong bias toward status-quo policy
patterns, despite the desire of industrial strategists to transform the
political economy in more decisive fashion. This bias makes the Japanese state cautious both where it allocates resources and how it
regulates innovation in finance, often leaving the initiative to the
private sector. Government industrial strategists are thus forced to
struggle continually to enforce a forward-looking, strategic orientation in industrial-credit policy. The struggle for strategy is further
complicated by growing complexity in the government apparatus
through which strategy is implemented. Their political and institutional situation is suited to passive stabilization roles that may be
important to economic development in an overheated, high-growth

economy, but are hardly suited to entrepreneurial, state-led transformation of the economy as a whole.

THE CONTOURS OF NATIONAL CONSENSUS

Any analysis of Japanese policymaking must concede from the outset a broad, internationally distinctive commonality of general purpose, pervasive across most of Japan. Throughout the 140 years since Japan was thrust brusquely into international affairs after two centuries of isolation, its underlying mass sentiments have worked strongly for national unity. The Japanese are among the world's most homogeneous people, with 700,000 Koreans and 150,000 Chinese the only appreciable ethnic minorities. The Japanese have undergone long cultural and economic separations from the rest of the world, and share both a deep sense of distinctiveness from the rest of the human race and a pervasive sense of vulnerability in relation to the broader world, stemming from the material poverty of the home islands and their close proximity to historically formidable great powers.

Commonality of purpose is enhanced by the broadly common processes of education and selection that Japan's officials have undergone. Virtually all of the higher civil servants are graduates of Tokyo University, and most of its Faculty of Law. At the Ministry of Finance, half of all incoming officials are from the Tokyo University Faculty of Law alone,[3] where many of them formed close associations during their undergraduate days with future officials of MITI and the other major government ministries.

Japanese officials, then, confront problems of economic policy with a common esprit de corps and sense of their nation's beleaguerment vis-à-vis the broader world. But their success in confronting such problems cohesively is by no means foreordained. The contours of Japanese national consensus have always been vague. More important, the Japanese state has unusually complex internal divisions, limited staffing, and a powerful private sector to confront. And all this lies within a political tradition that makes overt state action in the absence of broad agreement difficult.

THE PROBLEM OF ADMINISTRATIVE
COHESION IN JAPAN

For all the underlying cultural and educational homogeneity of the Japanese civil servants, and their deep common sense of international beleaguerment, the Japanese state is also fraught by deep divisions, which are no less real for being purposely obscured before the outside world. Japanese bureaucratic conflict is certainly not unique in advanced industrial society; there is a rich and growing literature examining this phenomenon in the United States, Britain, France, and other major nations of the West.[4] It flows from the classic organizational dilemma that Graham Allison describes: "Governmental action requires decentralization of responsibility and power."[5] But problems do not fit neatly into separate domains. Each organization's performance of its job has major consequences for other departments. Important problems overlap the jurisdictions of social organizations; thus, the necessity for decentralization runs headlong into the requirement for coordination. Important characteristics of Japanese government ministries, Japanese employment systems, and the unusual configurations of Japanese regulatory policy have made the impulse to bureaucratic conflict unusually sharp in Japan.

The "organizational process" imperatives moving Japanese bureaucracies toward autonomy are stronger than in most comparable countries, mainly because the internal procedures of Japanese organizations tend to be extensively routinized and arcane—a tendency promoted by the lifetime employment system. Given a remarkably fixed thirty years to master specialized knowledge relevant only to one's organization, ministries and firms alike go to considerable effort to teach and employ distinctive internal operating procedures. As a result, organizations apparently similar can experience comically extraordinary difficulties in finding appropriate common routines.

An example graphically illustrating this dynamic at work was the remarkable "Army submarine case" of World War II. By mid-1943 the Imperial Army was having difficulty supplying its garrisons in outlying areas throughout the Pacific, due to American naval supremacy, and concluded that submarine resupply of these bases was inevitable. Already involved in bitter rivalry with the Navy over aircraft and munitions allocation, the Army could not stand to be dependent in the area of marine transport when the welfare of its troops was involved. Over Navy protests, the Army proceeded to develop a submarine itself. After initial reflection, the Navy offered to help, explaining that building submarines was difficult. But the Army rejected naval assistance and designed a submarine that became operational well before the end of World War II.[6]

Passive-aggressive routinization, leading to the sort of obliviousness to external coordination prospects manifest in the submarine case, has long been pronounced in the Japanese financial sector. There key organizations operated from the 1920s through the 1970s with virtually no changes in administrative structure and procedure, despite growing flux in financial markets themselves. At the Ministry of Finance in the late 1970s, a section chief (*kachō*) in the Banking Bureau decided problems in accordance with five volumes of formalized standard operating procedures (*tsutatsu*) and one volume of relevant laws—with all of which he needed to be alarmingly conversant. There were changes in the 1980s and early 1990s, but only minor changes of degree. This high degree of arcane—to outsiders often inaccessible—structure in organizational processes has made Japanese financial bureaucracies, like the wartime Imperial Army, highly resistant to uncertainty and outside interference in their internal functioning. It has also made Japanese ministries notoriously protective of what they consider to be proprietary "turf" (*nawabari*) and relentlessly expansionist in areas where jurisdiction is ill defined.

Running battles for autonomy in international operations among the Ministry of Finance, MITI, the Ministry of Foreign Affairs, and the Bank of Japan are legendary. Even in the early 1990s, Ministry of Finance representatives cabled Tokyo in code from the Washington embassy via a special transmission facility, to avoid dependence on the Ministry of Foreign Affairs, and kept an independent outpost in the U.S. capital at the semipublic Japan Center for International Finance (JCIF). To avoid Foreign Office supervision, MITI conducted its most sensitive political operations in the United States through special representatives based in New York; it likewise used Japan External Trade Organization (JETRO) and Manufactured Imports Promotion Organization (MIPRO) offices throughout the world to maintain its own autonomy in foreign economic relations. The Ministry of Finance often used the Bank of Tokyo in a similar way.[7]

Domestically the drive for autonomy shows itself in the proliferation of essentially redundant investment-behavior surveys with which the Japanese government and affiliated agencies shower the private sector. The Bank of Japan, the Japan Development Bank, and the Industrial Bank of Japan, for example, all conduct independent quarterly surveys of private-sector investment expectations, asking essentially the same questions. But they do not coordinate these parallel surveys; they must have independent sources of information.

The profound impulse of Japanese bureaucratic organizations for autonomy has an obverse side: organizational imperialism. For many reasons of process and parochialism that make ministries fight any authority exercised over them, such ministries often seek, in turn, to impose their will on those less powerful, where jurisdictions collide. Clashes are particularly frequent when those notoriously imperialistic agencies of economic policy, the Ministry of Finance and MITI, are at swords' point, as they have been over consumer credit, antitrust policy, service-trade development, foreign-exchange allocation, and the operation of government financial institutions.

Driven by insatiable desires at all levels for organizational autonomy, and by an ever more sophisticated economy with growing links to the broader world, the Japanese bureaucracy of the postwar period has been growing steadily more complex. This growing complexity *crunch* has likewise complicated the struggle for strategy among those bureaucrats intent on state-directed industrial transformation. Faced with small staffs and broad responsibilities, senior officials have lacked the resources effectively to oversee and direct the proliferating multitude of semipublic bodies concerned with industrial credit flows.

KEY GOVERNMENT ACTORS

To get a concrete sense for the complex tensions running beneath a facade of bureaucratic unity in Japanese industrial credit policy formation, it is important to look concretely at the relevant actors involved and at their divergent ideology and interests. The major institutional actors are MITI, the Ministry of Finance, and the Bank of Japan, together with the complex network of governmental and semigovernmental financial institutions. They can be roughly divided, by objective, into strategists and regulators: the central protagonists in the drama of Japanese credit allocation. Strategists will be considered in this chapter and the less proactive regulators in chapter 3.

The Chief Strategist: MITI

Chief among Japan's industrial strategists has long been the Ministry of International Trade and Industry and its predecessors, the Ministry of Agriculture and Commerce (1881–1925), the Ministry of Munitions (1943–1945) and the Ministry of Commerce and Industry (1925–1943 and 1945–1949). As Chalmers Johnson points out, the emergence of self-conscious industrial strategy at MITI was an evolutionary process, with deep roots in the turbulent Depression and mobilization for World War II. Through an ad hoc process of bureaucratic adaptation to events that challenged Japan's very prospects for national survival, the neo-Marxist view gradually evolved within MITI's pre-1945 predecessors that it should serve not simply as regulator, but also as proactive agent of industrial transformation. In doing so it could encourage the emergence and expansion of priority sectors and inhibit those less important from a national perspective.[8]

The approach of MITI to industrial strategy was never codified, or even identified explicitly as industrial policy until near the end of the high-growth period around 1970.[9] But an influential vision of how industrial transformation should be pursued flowed from a central formative experience of many of postwar Japan's elite industrial bureaucrats: the forced creation of a formidable industrial base in Manchuria during the 1930s and early 1940s. This vision of a unitary, regimented industrial state, beyond politics, which could marshal resources flexibly to meet any threat to national goals, deeply inspired not only military leaders such as Ishiwara Kanji, operations officer of the Kwantung Army during the Manchurian invasion and a key section chief on the General Staff during the mid-1930s, but also many of the industrial bureaucrats who served there, such as Kishi Nobusuke (prime minister, 1957–1960), Shiina Etsusaburō (foreign minister, 1964–1966), and Sahashi Shigeru (administrative vice-minister of MITI, 1964–1966). Many of them saw Manchuria, in Shiina's words, as the "great proving ground" for Japanese industry.[10] Their inspiration could be termed the Manchukuo Model, because that vision most fully, albeit incompletely, corresponded to the course of credit and industrial policy pursued by Japanese industrial planners in Manchukuo during the 1930s and the 1940s.[11]

The underlying premise behind this model was common with that of Meiji Japan—that economic vitality and national security were inseparably linked. The model had three central tenets: (1) control over credit and nonfinancial resource allocation must be centralized in the hands of the industrial planner, thus cutting out the banker, (2) adequately directed growth could be achieved only through an alliance of the state with emerging, nonestablishment economic forces; and (3) coherent, planned economic growth could be brought about efficiently only in an environment devoid of pluralist politics. The blueprint implicit in the Manchukuo Model was expressed through such actions by the Manchurian planners as expelling the *zaibatsu* and their banks from Manchuria, aligning state policy with such nonestablishment groups as the Nissan konzerne of Aikawa Yoshisuke,[12] and the suppression of trade unions and political parties that might otherwise challenge or complicate the process of industrial management.

Strategists at MITI had very concrete ideas, drawn from the French theory of the *economie concertée* as well as from Manchurian and wartime Japanese home-island experience, as to how they wanted to transform the Japanese economy. But MITI's capacity within the Japanese political economy as a whole to achieve its strategic ends was incomplete, despite substantial formal powers for much of the high-growth period with respect to raw material imports, foreign exchange, and technology licensing. Subtle differences emerged within MITI itself from time to time regarding strategic emphasis, driven both by differing institutional stakes within the ministry and also by complex human networks linking MITI to the corporate world. Even more important, MITI's regulatory authority with respect to industrial credit, and its broader political leverage within Japanese society as a whole, were so circumscribed as to make implementing MITI's strategic, developmental approach to the Japanese economy a continual, uncertain struggle.

The major strength of MITI's position in the credit field throughout the early postwar period was that from 1949 to 1964 it controlled foreign-exchange allocation. This role allowed it to influence the financial behavior of corporations directly and thus to "short-circuit" the considerable influence of banks in relation to Japanese industry. It created particular leverage against the heavy industrial firms that MITI was trying to promote, such as steel and petrochemicals, since these still uncompetitive firms were heavily dependent on imported coal, oil, and other raw material inputs. Indeed, after quantitative allocation of raw materials ended in the late 1940s, MITI's main leverage over corporate raw material supplies was via foreign-exchange controls.

The Foreign Exchange and Foreign Trade Control Law sharply restricted corporate access to convertible currencies, requiring, for example, that exporters remit their foreign proceeds to the government within thirty days of contract settlement. Accordingly, businesspersons came constantly and in droves to the International Trade Bureau (ITB) on the third floor of MITI's headquarters in the Toranomon section of Tokyo for the indispensable foreign-exchange authorizations. It became known as the "Toranomon Ginza" because of the crowds of businesspersons gathering there daily to seek dollars and sterling for imports, as well as export permits.[13]

Despite the sharp imbalance between supply and demand for convertible currencies during the early postwar period, control of foreign-exchange allocation translated into surprisingly little consistent leverage for MITI over the process of industrial structure transformation. During early postwar years, the period of greatest foreign-exchange scarcity (and therefore prospectively greatest leverage for MITI), the International Trade Bureau controlling the allocation was run by Foreign Ministry bureaucrats. Its first four directors, Takeuchi Ryūji, Oda Takeo, Ushiba Nobuhiko, and Itagaki Osamu, were all famous diplomats. They were also political allies of Prime Minister Yoshida Shigeru, himself a Foreign Ministry alumnus. Although nominally held within MITI, the foreign-exchange allocation function was thus effectively in other hands. It was not until 1956 that a "native-born" (haenuki) MITI official became head of the ITB, linking its foreign exchange allocation function more closely to industrial policy.

Even between 1956 and 1964, after which general trading companies gained a right to hold foreign exchange that undermined the control system, foreign-exchange allocation controls were a blunt tool of industrial policy. In the case of bank loans, interest rates could be varied in accordance with the priority of the project or the cooperativeness of the prospective borrower. But foreign exchange rates were fixed, and overall national shortages placed general constraints on quantities available. More detailed terms of availability were a matter for negotiation between individual firms and their banks, beyond the control of MITI. For some sectors, such as oil refining, petrochemicals, and to a lesser degree iron and steel, availability of foreign exchange was, to be sure, a major concern. But for domestically oriented sectors such as distribution, coal mining, and nonferrous mining, it was largely irrelevant. In any event, a foreign-currency black market remained, allowing firms that needed dollars or sterling to obtain convertible currencies for a price, even without MITI approval.

Apart from its control over foreign exchange allocation, which expired during the mid-1960s, MITI has had some major operational influence over the government financial institutions throughout the postwar period. It has had, for example, the duty of screening all loan applications at the Japan Development Bank, making annual estimates of the shortfall between available and needed capital,[14] and placing some of its important retired officials on the JDB's board.[15] Some of these responsibilities gave MITI significant leverage for implementing its strategic designs until the late 1960s. But the importance of these designs has been undermined by the persistent excess liquidity and slack private-sector demand for industrial credit over the past two decades.

Jurisdiction over special autonomous financial accounts (tokubetsu kaikei), whose income is not subject to dispersal through the normal budgetary processes, has afforded MITI some marginal enhanced leverage in shaping national credit flows. In the mid-1980s MITI held sole jurisdiction over only three of thirty-five special accounts, those dealing with alcohol sales, export insurance, and patents.[16] In addition, MITI shared control with MOF and the Labor Ministry over the relatively large Coal, Oil, and Alternate Energy Countermeasures Special Account, which disbursed ¥123.5 billion in 1986, derived from a special tax on oil imports, to a range of alternate energy programs, including solar energy.[17] The Ministry of International Trade and Industry also shared jurisdiction with MOF over the Electric Power Development Company (Dengen Kaihatsu K.K.), which builds power-generating and transmission facilities and supplies electricity to the electric companies. Finally, MITI traditionally supervised the Industrial Investment Special Account, established with U.S. counterpart funds in 1953, together with the MOF.

The special account that the strategically oriented planning sections of MITI, in contrast to the operational sections, were happiest about was the Industrial Investment Special Account (Sangyō Tōshi Tokubetsu Kaikei). It was set up on August 1, 1953, with income from U.S. counterpart funds that were drawn from sale of U.S. surplus food.[18] During the early and mid-1950s, the Industrial Investment Special Account served as a vast discretionary pool of finance for MITI to loan as it wished to key sectors. In 1953 this account disbursed 13.2 percent of all government loans and investments in Japan.[19] This ratio was 9.2 percent in 1957 and 6.1 percent as late as 1964,[20] despite the massive growth in government investment funds during the early 1960s. The fund was able to expand its resources by floating bond issues overseas, beginning in 1958, due to strong pressures exerted by Prime Minister Kishi, a MITI alumnus, on MOF.[21] But after Kishi's political star began to wane, MOF pressures on MITI's private fund began to increase. Its share in total government investment and loans fell to 1.2 percent in 1973,[22] and to only 0.2 percent in 1990.[23]

The fate of the Industrial Investment Special Account, a general-purpose fund, is significant when it is set against the pattern of proliferating new special-purpose accounts and the rapid growth rate of resources available to the major existing ones, such as the Coal and Oil Countermeasures Special Account. It suggests that MITI, when not in coalition with interest groups, is losing its power to pursue strategic industrial policies independent of MOF, at least in the special budget accounts sector. Its planning sector has lost much of its control over credit flows, with the crucial decline in influence coming during the late 1960s.

A final source of MITI influence with respect to industrial-credit flows is the Japan Bicycle Promotion Association (Nihon Jitensha Shinkō Kai). Managed by the Vehicle Section (Sharyō Ka) of MITI, this body is in no sense responsible to MOF. Its income flows from a monopoly on the gambling proceeds of bicycle races in Japan, and its resources are dispersed at the discretion of MITI officials, with the ultimate accounting known only to them.

When MITI has lacked strong backing in the political world, it has often failed in efforts to create organizations to serve its financial purposes even when its overall administrative responsibilities have been large. During 1955–1956, for example, it was unable to set up a Machinery Industry Promotion Corporation (Kikai Kōgyō Shinkō Jigyōdan), which would have allocated funds to the auto, capital goods, and telecommunications industries. Authorization required Diet approval, which created a need for strong political sponsorship, even though MITI was generally independent of the political world in its day-to-day operations. But by the late 1950s MITI's leverage in the political world had increased, with the ascent of its prominent alumnus Kishi Nobusuke to the prime ministership, and greater autonomy from MOF became possible.

Founded on October 1, 1957, shortly after Kishi became prime minister, the Japan Bicycle Promotion Association (BPA) was set up, as its foundation law stated, "to promote the development of the bicycle and other machinery and recreation industries." The provisions governing the operation of the association were strikingly broad and vague. Furthermore, the new association was excepted from public reporting requirements concerning disposition of its income from betting on professional bicycle races.

Since the balance sheet of the Bicycle Promotion Association is classified, the scale of its operations is difficult to gauge with precision. Subsidies granted in fiscal 1990 appear to have been around ¥55 billion, or four times greater than in 1978.[24] Around 46 percent, or about ¥25.5 billion in 1990, went to "promotion of the machinery industry."[25] Another 46 percent went to "promotion of activities of public worth," and only around 8 percent to the administration of bicycle racing itself.[26]

Funds from the BPA reportedly have helped MITI to develop a more strategic orientation by providing it with funds for staff research positions and analysis of long-run issues such as the so-called "English disease" in the advanced industrial world, prospects for service-industry evolution, and analysis of post–cold war superpower relationships that the Ministry of Finance could well have considered unnecessary or redundant. They assisted such activities as establishment of the MITI Research Institute, founded in 1987 to examine long-range trends in industrial evolution and global economic development. The BPA's reported technical aid to the medical equipment and the software industries, together with its support during the late 1970s for reorganization of industries in structural recession and its backing in the early 1990s of studies on how to promote American industrial recovery, also fits a strategic, farsighted model of Japanese policy finance. But much of the BPA's effort also reportedly goes into interagency warfare without clear national strategic application, such as support for MITI's special representatives in the United States in their turf wars with the Ministry of Foreign Affairs.

The BPA, important as it appears to be for MITI's strategic role in the Japanese political economy, is only the smallest of three such autonomous ministry-controlled discretionary funds in Japan. The other two ministry-controlled discretionary funds do not have nearly the strategic orientation of the Bicycle Promotion Association, and they clearly undermine the coherency of MOF leadership in policy finance. The Japan Central Racing Association (Nihon Keiba Kai), founded in 1954, and the Japan Shipping Promotion Association (Nihon Senpaku Shinkō Kai), established in 1962, are the exclusive affiliates of the Ministry of Agriculture and the Ministry of Transport, respectively.

Under the provisions of the Foreign Exchange and Foreign Trade Control Law (December 1, 1949), MITI assumed regulatory control of trading companies, with potentially important trade and investment financing functions. But the trading companies were for the ensuing decade mostly weak and fragmented: the *zaibatsu* dissolution of the late 1940s hit them harder than any other elements of the prewar industrial groups save the holding companies. The trading companies were incapable of any major role in the financial system other than arranging lease financing and playing a marginal arbitrage function that undermined rather than strengthened the force of financial controls. The regulatory powers MITI exercised over the trading companies thus afforded it little additional influence with respect to finance.

The Economic Planners

Apart from MITI and its predecessors, Japan has also had an independent economic-planning apparatus since the mid-1930s. Originally established to aid in the systematic development of Manchuria and to transform Japan into a "national defense state" in preparation for World War II, the economic-planning mechanism provided an intellectual support base for both the reconstruction policies of the late 1940s and the high-speed growth that followed. Although Japanese economic planning has been less interventionist than in France, South Korea, or other so-called developmental states, at certain periods, such as the late 1940s and the early 1960s, it provided a series of optimistic parameters endorsing rapid development of capital-intensive sectors that gave strong impetus to Japan's transformation into a high-growth heavy industrial nation during the 1950s and 1960s.

Although there were military-oriented planning bodies with specialized functions as early as 1927,[27] Japan's first comprehensive economic-planning body was the Cabinet Research Bureau (Naikaku Chōsa Kyoku), established in 1935. This elite body was a central coordinating entity drawing its staff from agencies across the Japanese government and attached directly to the cabinet.

Two years later the Cabinet Planning Board, otherwise known as Japan's "economic general staff," was created by merging the Cabinet Research Bureau and the older, military-oriented Resources Bureau.[28] This body brought together officials from the Army, Navy, Home, Finance, Commerce, Agriculture, and Communications ministries, and had major influence in drafting sectoral legislation in such areas as petroleum and electric power, while also performing broader macroeconomic analytical functions.

The wartime planning apparatus was dismantled, of course, in 1945, but a strategically oriented civilian planning mechanism to assist in the reconstruction effort promptly appeared in its stead. Created to supervise the enforcement of controls over prices, transportation, and finance, as well as the national public works budget, the Economic Stabilization Board (Keizai Antei Honbu) was established in August 1946. Seven months later, in March 1947, it assumed consolidated control over all economic-planning activities in Japan, expanding its staff to two thousand.

Despite a relatively short life (1946–1952), the Economic Stabilization Board (ESB) was arguably the most powerful and effective economic planning mechanism in Japanese history. It was small compared to major ministries, simple organizationally, and had strong esprit de corps. It drafted several historic reconstruction plans and in July 1947 inaugurated Japan's Economic White Paper. The ESB played a particularly key role in the recovery of Japan's basic industries in the immediate postwar period with its priority production program (keisha seisan hōshiki); this program realistically assessed the war-induced bottlenecks in a Japanese economy operating at 30 percent of prewar capacity in 1946 and directed resources toward them. The ESB's early leverage in this process was substantially increased by the existence of the Reconstruction Finance Bank (Fukkō

Kinyū Kinkō), a government institution established in early 1947 to aid rebuilding. The availability of subsidies to cover the gap between producer and consumer prices also helped.

The credit-allocation structure the ESB created clearly had perverse long-run consequences, as will be seen, including clientelism induced by the subsidy system and rampant inflation generated by financing RFB aggressively through the general account budget. As Chapter 5 suggests, many of the early postwar priorities established by the ESB, such as an emphasis on loans to the shipping industry, continued to dominate government lending over forty years later. (Indeed, the Japan Development Bank continued to provide interest-rate subsidies for shipping until 1988.) But in the short run the tools at the ESB's command during the late 1940s gave it an unusual leverage that its predecessors and successors never had, reinforced by SCAP's strong interest in Japanese economic recovery. Even when the Economic Stabilization Board was dissolved in 1952 and much of its gifted staff dissipated, a tight, cohesive network of alumni remained to play a key coordinating role in Japanese economic transformation throughout the high-growth decades just then dawning.[29]

In contrast to the formidable ESB, its successors have been much more macroeconomically oriented, with sharply less political ability to mastermind the complexities of economic transition than ESB commanded. With the end of the Occupation in April 1952, the ESB was supplanted by the purely advisory Economic Deliberation Agency, renamed the Economic Planning Agency (EPA) in 1955. From their inception the economic planning bodies were handicapped by Prime Minister Yoshida Shigeru's vehement opposition to planning and their identification with the Socialist Katayama cabinet, under whose auspices the Economic Stabilization Board had originally flourished during 1947–1948. Apart from political weakness, the planners were also handicapped for many years by "colonization" efforts of more powerful agencies such as MOF and MITI, which monopolized all the top administrative posts in EPA through the 1960s. It was only in the 1970s and the 1980s that the Economic Planning Agency came into its own once again—this time as a neutral, politically unattached technical forecasting agency with little systematic ability or inclination to strategically transform the Japanese economy.

Although institutional prerequisites (especially centralization of authority and a cohesive private sector) have been necessary conditions for effective industrial strategy in Japan, they have not been sufficient. Some sort of vision, individual or collective, has been required. Certainly there have been brilliant independent strategists with clear conceptions of Japan's industrial future: Arisawa Hiromi, the scholarly architect of the production-priorities scheme and a firm believer in a controlled economy along neo-Marxist lines; Okita Saburō, a visionary internationalist who stressed the importance of Third World linkages; and especially Shimomura Osamu, the apostle of high-growth economic transformation, the close confidant of Prime Minister Ikeda Hayato, and a principal architect of the Income Doubling Plan. There were also the great bureaucratic strategists, such as the MITI vice-ministers Sahashi, Morozumi, Konaga, and Fukukawa. Yet all these, like the institutions within which they worked, could provide only an image of the future and were themselves often prisoner to economic events.

Government Financial Institutions: Omnipresent Complexity

Complexity and specialization are the major hallmarks of Japanese government finance, aggravating the difficulties of Japanese economic bureaucrats in their struggle for strategy. The dilemma is apparent in comparative perspective. Although the share of overall financial flows channeled through public intermediaries in Japan is broadly comparable in scale to those in continental Western Europe, Japan's government financial system appears to be far more differentiated, with individual government banks much more specialized in their activities than counterparts in Europe.[30] Most government financing activities in France, for example, are handled by a single institution—the mammoth Crédit Nationale, which is empowered to undertake general commercial banking activities as well as a broad range of policy financial functions.[31] So is the Crédit Nationale's analogue in Germany, the KVW. But in Japan Trust Fund Bureau resources are allocated through eleven government financial institutions, together with nine special accounts, nine special companies, nine mixed public-private enterprises, one local public body, and thirty-six other semipublic intermediaries. Each is restricted by specific legislation authorizing only a narrowly stipulated range of functions.

Japan began to develop a relatively complex network of government financial institutions during the 1930s and the early 1940s in the course of mobilization for World War II.[32] But almost all the wartime institutions disbursing government credit—save only the Teitō Rapid Transit Authority, which manages Tokyo's subway system— were disbanded after August 1945. The problems of administrative complexity that now so plague the Japanese government financial system are thus a creature of the pluralistic postwar policy process.

The major early postwar government financial institution was the Reconstruction Finance Bank, founded in January 1947 and disbanded, under severe pressure from the conservative SCAP financial adviser Joseph Dodge, in January 1952. The RFB's central role was supporting reconstruction-oriented plant and equipment investment in the coal, steel, fertilizer, shipping, and electric-power sectors—largely through bond issues monetized by the Bank of Japan, rather than through reliance on actual national savings. This highly inflationary modus operandi, and SCAP's severely critical response, led to creation of an off-budget system of government financing funded by postal savings rather than government bonds—the Fiscal Investment and Loan Program, which was finally consolidated in fiscal 1953. This bears important similarities to the French Treasury circuit system, under which reserves on which the state could draw were created and redeposited in postal accounts.[33]

Precisely because of its insulation from the macroeconomic policy process, since its activities did not influence money supply, the Japanese FILP system lent itself to rising complexity and an increasingly political orientation. Off-budget financing through the FILP threatened no inflationary dangers and until 1973 was not subject to public review. The government financial institutions that served as the intermediaries for FILP funds provided postretirement sinecures for former officials, and the establishment of new ones provided tangible rewards to powerful pressure groups, while being legitimized through their broader formal purposes.

The original policy rationale for establishing an elaborate system of off-budget government financing funded through public savings programs was to create a powerful weapon of industrial strategy. This would simultaneously serve developmental purposes and avoid the inflationary excesses of the Reconstruction Finance Bank experience.[34] Joseph Dodge, MITI industrial strategists, and Minister of Finance Ikeda Hayato all agreed on this overall concept, although they had somewhat divergent views of the appropriate oversight structure and the relative importance of developmental transformation and inflation control.[35] With these potential contradictory objectives in mind they established the Japan Export (later Export-Import) Bank (1950) and the Japan Development Bank (1951), while also drafting legislation to provide them with secure funding sources in the public savings programs (1951).[36] But in the turbulent political climate of the times, before the conservative preeminence that was to continue for forty postwar years and more had been assured, polit-

TABLE 2-1
Strategy versus Politics at the Japanese Government
Credit Institutions (in ¥ billions)

Institution	FILP Budget (1991)	Date Founded
Housing Loan Corp. (Jūtaku Kinyū Kōko)	¥559	1950
People's Finance Corp. (Kokumin Kinyū Kōko)	212	1949
Small Business Finance Corp. (Chūshō Kigyō Kinyū Kōko)	192	1953
Finance Corporation for Local Public Enterprises (Kōei Kigyō Kinyū Kōko)	115	1957
Japan Development Bank (Nihon Kaihatsu Ginkō)	109	1951
Japan Export-Import Bank (Nihon Yushutsunyū Ginkō)	101	1950
Agriculture, Forestry, and Fishery Finance Corp. (Nōrin Gyogyō Kinyū Kōko)	41	1953
Environmental Sanitation Business Finance Corp. (Kankyō Eisei Kinyū Kōko)	22	1967
Hokkaidō-Tōhoku Development Corp. (Hokkaidō-Tōhoku Kaihatsu Kōko)	14	1956
Okinawa Development Finance Corp. (Okinawa Shinkō Kaihatsu Kinyū Kōko)	13	1972
Small Business Credit Insurance Corp. Corporation (Chūshō Kigyō Shinyō Hoken Kōko)	8	1986

Source: Zaisei Tōyūshi (Fiscal Investment and Loans Program), 1990 ed. (Tokyo: Tōyō Keizai Shinpōsha, 1990), 234.

Note: Apart from the foregoing, the Medical Finance Corporation (Iryō Kinyū Kōko), established in 1960, provided special government financial assistance to the medical profession until January 1985, when it was absorbed into the Special Welfare and Medical Facilities Corporation (Shakai Fukushi Iryō Jigyōdan).

ical pressures provoked the creation of a much more elaborate and specialized system of government financial institutions than the industrial strategists at MITI had originally envisioned. By 1990, as noted in table 2-1, the two government financial institutions originally seen by strategists as the heart of government financial operations (the JDB and the Exim Bank) were only the fifth and sixth largest recipients of FILP funds. They were dwarfed in scale by other politically inspired banks devoted to housing and small-business credit.

Even more striking than the proportion of government loan funds received for dispersal by the four early "political" government financial institutions has been their share of government subsidies. The huge subsidy shares of the "political" banks is a recent phenomenon, dating particularly from the "crisis" for the ruling conservatives of the early 1970s.[37] In 1965, for example, only JDB and Exim received subsidies. But by fiscal 1985 the four "political" banks received 92.5 percent of the total subsidies provided from the general account of the national budget to *all eleven* government financial institutions, allowing them to lend at much lower interest rates than the more "strategic" banks such as JDB and Exim were able to do.[38] Especially notable were the rapidly rising subsidies to the Housing Loan Corporation, which grew eighteenfold between 1973 and 1985, after long years of public delay in coping with the steady deterioration of Japan's living environment.

Over the course of the 1950s, and especially the 1960s, Japan's system of off-budget government finance grew steadily more complex, driven more by political than strategic considerations. New banks were established to accommodate doctors, lobbyists for prefectural concerns, and depressed regions such as Tōhoku, Hokkaidō, and Okinawa. In perhaps the most notoriously political case of all, the Environmental Sanitation Business Finance Corporation was created in 1967, reputedly in a single night of furious bargaining between Tanaka Kakuei, secretary general of the Liberal Democratic party (LDP), and the top leaders of the Japan Innkeepers' Association, as compensation for their prospective support in the 1967 general election.

Apart from the government banks, a complex structure of ambiguously defined off-budget public "units" (*kōdan*) expanded rapidly during the 1960s, as indicated in table 2-2. They were complemented during the late 1980s by a proliferation of hybrid mixed public-private enterprises. A few of these new creations, such as the Information Processing Promotion Association (Jōhō Shōri Shinkō Jigyō Kyōkai) or the Telecommunications and Broadcast Satellite Association (Tsūshin Hōso Eisei Kiko), both established during the 1980s, had clear strategic objectives. But these, ironically, were few in number and received relatively little funding.

The vast majority of the new entities supported by the FILP—receiving 94 percent in 1990 of total FILP funds not allocated to the government banks described above in table 2–1—specialized in supporting the operation of local post offices (25 percent of funding),

TABLE 2-2
Increasing Institutional Complexity in the Fiscal Investment
and Loan Program, 1953–1990

Type of Organization	Number of Organizations Participating in FILP							
	1953	1955	1960	1965	1970	1975	1985	1990
Government financial institutions (kōko)	5	6	10	9	10	11	11	11
Special accounts (tokubetsu kaikei)	2	3	3	5	5	7	7	9
Public corporations (kōsha)	2	2	2	2	2	2	2	—
Public units (kōdan)	1	2	8	25	27	28	28	36
Local public bodies (chihō kōkyō dantai)	1	1	1	1	1	1	1	1
Mixed public-private enterprises (tokushū kaisha)	3	6	8	6	5	3	4	9
TOTALS:	14	20	32	48	50	52	53	66

Source: Ishikawa Itaru and Gyohten Toyoo, eds., *Zaisei Tōyūshi* (The Fiscal Investment and Loan Program) (Tokyo: Kinyū Zaisei Jijō Kenkyū Kai, 1977), 106; and Ministry of Finance Financial Bureau, *Zusetsu: Zaisei Tōyūshi* (The Illustrated Fiscal Investment and Loan Program), assorted issues.

construction (21 percent), local government (20 percent), and pension subsidies (18 percent). Some of this spending, especially the construction-related aspect, bore tenuous relationship to industrial-policy purposes, but the overall objectives were primarily political. Only around 2 percent of government off-budget spending beyond the eleven government banks had a clear, strategic industrial-policy referent.[39]

During its early years of operation in the 1950s, the Fiscal Investment and Loan Program was a relatively simple body, organized around government financial institutions, with the Japan Development Bank and the Japan Export-Import Bank at its heart. By 1990 the number of constituent units had proliferated more than fourfold, as indicated in table 2-2, and JDB/Exim allocations combined had fallen to only 6 percent of the FILP total.[40] The institutional framework through which Japanese government credit policies are administered, in short, has become steadily more complex, segmented, and vulnerable to political influences, thus intensifying the challenge confronted by industrial strategists pursuing developmental objectives.

TRIBULATIONS FOR THE STRATEGISTS

Despite their vision and entrepreneurship, the bureaucratic strategists of postwar Japan, including those at the supposedly all-powerful MITI, have frequently lacked the power to realize their developmental conception of how the Japanese political economy and its industrial strategy should be configured. Their particular trials in the industrial-credit area have been fivefold: (1) weak centralization of government credit-allocation powers, with important levers in the hands of those lacking strategic vision; (2) private-sector cohesion and influence with the bureaucracy; (3) weak MITI and EPA alumni networks in the Japanese political world; (4) political clientelism; and (5) rising liquidity in the Japanese financial system, undermining the leverage of state allocators. In all five respects the institutional and sociopolitical obstacles confronted by Japanese government industrial strategists have been significantly greater than in other so-called "developmental states" such as France, South Korea, Taiwan, and Singapore, making the Japanese struggle for strategy correspondingly intense,[41] and suggesting the merits of a separate paradigm for the Japanese case.

These broader conceptual issues will be more fully developed in chapter 8. Comparative analysis is employed here only to illustrate the structural obstacles that make the struggle for strategy intense and frustrating in the policy finance area for the Japanese government officials concerned.

Weak Centralization of Credit-Allocation Powers

Despite a wide variety of tools to deploy in influencing the distribution of industrial credit, the industrial strategists—including MITI, the government financial institutions, and at times the Economic Planning Agency—have always suffered in the struggle for strategy from their total lack of regulatory jurisdiction over banks and securities companies. This pattern contrasts strongly to that of other political systems regarded as developmental states, such as France and South Korea. In France industrial strategy and financial regulation have long been concentrated tightly in a single small institution of slightly more than one hundred elite members: the Trésor. In South Korea the Economic Planning Board (EPB), whose director doubles as deputy prime minister, exercises sweeping authority over both industry and finance.

Under cover of war, Japanese government industrial strategists had on occasion been successful in bringing the private banks to heel. During the latter stages of World War II, for example, the Ministry of Munitions, MITI's predecessor, engineered a cabinet decree that commercial banks discount all war-related bills approved by the Ministry of Munitions. The governor of the Bank of Japan resigned in protest, but to no avail.

Controlling private banks proved far more difficult for industrial strategists after 1945. Perhaps the most ambitious and celebrated MITI attempt was that of Enterprise Bureau chief Sahashi Shigeru in the early 1960s. Sahashi had confirmed a belief in centralized state industrial leadership in prewar Manchuria and in wartime industrial planning within Japan proper. During 1962–1963 he proposed a law (the so-called "Tokushin Hō," or Draft Law of Special Measures for the Promotion of Designated Industries) that would have introduced a system of comprehensive credit and other controls in Japan.

These controls, roughly parallel to those employed during the 1960s in Fifth Republic France,[42] would have effectively subjected private banking decisions throughout Japan on capital-investment projects to MITI approval.[43] Sahashi proposed to establish committees across a wide range of strategic industries—including electronics, autos, machinery, and oil refining—to be composed of MITI, MOF, banking-sector, and industry representatives, along the lines of industrial councils in France. Sahashi's proposed committees, operating under the supervision of the "responsible minister" for the industry in question (MITI for virtually all major industrial sectors except shipbuilding), would determine firm-by-firm levels of investment spending, with the objective, explained Sahashi, of limiting oligopolistic *keiretsu* rivalry and consolidating the fragmented structure of industry—measures allegedly necessary to prepare for onslaught by foreign capital anticipated after Japan accepted International Monetary Fund (IMF) Article 8 status and joined the Organization for Economic Cooperation and Development (OECD) in 1964.[44]

From the very first, the Tokushin Hō proposal was bitterly opposed by the large commercial banks, particularly *keiretsu* leaders such as Mitsubishi, Fuji, Sumitomo, and Mitsui banks.[45] These institutions, increasingly powerful elements of the Japanese political economy from the late 1940s on, faced the most drastic constraints on their freedom of operation from the proposed legislation. In the forefront of opposition was Usami Makoto, president of the Japan

Bankers' Association and also chairman of the Mitsubishi Bank until 1964, when he became governor of the Bank of Japan.[46] Not far behind came the Ministry of Finance and the Fair Trade Commission, which has for over a generation named to its leadership substantial numbers of former MOF officials.[47]

Almost as crucial to Tokushin Hō's ultimate frustration as the determined opposition of the financial community was the division within MITI and the industrial world. The Enterprise Bureau of MITI, charged with overall industrial planning, might support the measure, as did some major firms threatened by potential foreign competition, such as Toyota and Nissan. But against it stood the dominant element in Keidanren, Japan's preeminent big-business federation, led by its chairman, Ishizaka Taizō, and the Heavy Industry and Chemical Industries bureaus of MITI.

Politicians, including Prime Minister Ikeda Hayato, by and large maintained an aloof neutrality and refused to force the Tokushin Hō issue. Ikeda was in an especially delicate spot, as a Ministry of Finance alumnus who had also recently headed MITI, and found it inopportune to act decisively. Despite substantial concessions by Sahashi,[48] introduced into the forty-third, forty-fourth, and forty-sixth sessions of the Diet (1962–1964) the Tokushin Hō measure never came to a vote.[49] Thus failed the most determined effort ever by Japan's industrial strategists to assume comprehensive credit-allocation prerogatives—one that reconfirmed contrasts between Japanese and French lines of industrial development.

After the defeat of the Tokushin Hō, industrial strategists used industry-specific legislation to extend their influence marginally into the financial sphere, after they found legislation conferring French-style powers of comprehensive industrial guidance politically difficult to obtain. As a substitute for direct control over lending decisions of banks, MITI has sought control powers over capital investment decisions by industry in key sectors. In oil refining and electricity generation, for example, MITI has usually wanted to suppress retail prices to benefit heavy industrial consumers.[50]

To generate the necessary leverage to control industrial credit on a sector-specific basis, MITI pressed for highly detailed, industry-specific laws. These laws required the licensing by MITI of all capacity expansion, thus indirectly allowing it to allocate capital-investment credit within the sectors in question. In addition, MITI sought analogous powers in the electronics and machinery sectors, with only partial success. Such capital-investment licensing powers as MITI obtained, however, permitted it only to regulate the flow of investment funds *within* specific industries and did not provide any capacity to allocate across sectors. As detailed analysis in chapter 4 will show, the industrial strategists had enormous trouble regulating industrial credit even *within* major sectors due to their lack of leverage over the private-sector banks.

Periodically, as in the late 1970s, a coincidence of interest in restructuring depressed industries brought the banks and the industrial strategists together for short periods. The banks, for example, supported the Recession Industries Bill of 1978, which established a public fund to finance scrapping of excess capacity in MITI-designated industries.[51] But these alignments were simply temporary expedients and limited to unattractive sectors. Japan's industrial strategists have always had trouble controlling its banks, especially in their entry strategies for attractive sectors of the future.

Limited Political Leverage

On routine administrative matters or the generation of detailed new technical proposals for government action, bureaucrats indeed do generally rule in Japan. But in the complex, delicate proceedings of the Diet—through which all major proposals for centralization or other reform of the fragmented Japanese credit-allocation system have had to pass throughout the postwar period—the politicians have had career officials at their mercy. There have consistently been a large core of former government officials in the Diet itself. But most of these have been from agencies oriented toward regulation, brokerage, and clientelism, with ex-industrial strategists only a small, relatively junior minority.

As indicated in table 2-3, there were only eight MITI alumni in the Diet during the mid-1960s—six in the Lower House and two in the Upper. Only two of them—former Prime Minister Kishi Nobusuke and faction leader Shiina Etsusaburō, who had succeeded Kishi as MCI vice-minister—could be considered politically influential. Only a single member of the Diet hailed from the Economic Planning Agency.

As table 2-3 also shows, during the 1970s MITI's Diet strength fell below even the minimal level of the mid-1960s. Following the retirement of Shiina Etsusaburō and Kishi Nobusuke in 1979, no senior MITI alumni with major influence in the Japanese political world remained at all. There was, to be sure, a modest comeback in the 1980s. The ministry doubled its representation in the Lower House

Table 2-3

The Persistent Prominence of MOF Alumni in the Diet
Membership of Ex-Bureaucrats in the Diet by Ministry, 1966–1992

	Lower House				Upper House				Total 1966	% of Total	Total 1979	% of Total	Total 1986	% of Total	Total 1992	% of Total
	1966	1979	1986	1992	1966	1979	1986	1992								
Home Ministry (defunct)	21	10	4	4	6	7	5	3	27	23.2	17	18.9	9	7.8	7	6.3
MOF	14	20	26	27	6	7	8	1	20	17.1	27	30.0	34	29.3	28	25.2
Agriculture	9	1	7	9	8	7	9	3	17	14.7	8	8.9	16	13.8	12	10.8
MITI	6	6	8	13	2	—	1	0	8	6.9	6	6.7	9	7.8	13	11.7
Transportation/Railway	5	4	3	1	5	2	5	2	10	8.6	6	6.7	8	6.9	3	2.7
Welfare	3	3	5	2	5	—	2	3	8	6.9	3	3.3	7	6.0	5	4.5
Foreign Affairs	3	3	3	3	3	—	1	1	6	5.2	3	3.3	4	3.4	4	3.6
Communications (defunct)	4	—	—	—	3	—	—	—	7	6.0	—	0.0	—	0.0	0	—
Labor	2	4	4	2	1	2	4	2	3	2.6	6	6.7	8	6.9	4	3.6
Construction	1	1	6	6	4	7	5	11	5	4.3	8	8.9	11	9.5	17	15.3
Postal	1	1	1	1	1	2	4	4	2	1.7	3	3.3	5	4.3	5	4.5
Economic Planning	1	—	—	—	—	—	—	—	1	0.9	—	0.0	—	0.0	—	—
Autonomy	1	—	6	1	—	—	5	9	1	0.9	—	0.0	—	0.0	10	9.0
Defense Agency	—	—	1	1	1	2	2	1	1	0.9	2	2.2	3	2.6	2	1.8
Education	—	—	—	—	—	1	2	1	—	0.1	1	1.1	2	1.7	1	0.9
TOTAL	71	53	75	69	45	37	52	41	116	100.0	90	100.0	116	100.0	111	100.0

Source: Fuji Seikei Shimbun Sha, *Kokkai Yōran* 1967 and 1979 ed. (Tokyo: Fuji Seikei Shimbun Sha, 1967, 1979); Asahi Shimbun Senkyo Honbu, ed., *Asahi Senkyo Kaikan* (Asahi Electoral Almanac), (Tokyo: Asahi Shimbun Sha, 1986), 19; and *Asahi Shimbun*, various issues.

Notes: Diet members are counted as alumni of the first ministry they joined, except in the case of defunct ministries. In such cases, they're counted as members of the last ministry in which they served. Home Ministry and Autonomy Ministry figures are combined in calculations for 1979, 1986, and 1992. Figures for 1986 are as of September 26, 1986, following the double election of that year. Those for 1992 are for August 1992, following the Upper House election. Home Ministry figures for 1986 include police.

between 1979 and 1992, mainly in outlying prefectures enamored with its regional and small-business policies. But it remained far behind MOF in overall Diet strength. Able middle-ranking MITI alumni in the Diet, such as Hayashi Yoshirō, who chaired the LDP Commerce and Industry Committee, also slowly began gaining leadership credibility during the 1980s. By 1993 Hayashi had risen to become Minister of Finance in the second Miyazawa Cabinet. But he still did not head a major faction within the ruling party, and lacked crucial behind-the-scenes political influence. The Economic Planning Agency had no representatives in the Diet whatsoever throughout the late 1980s and early 1990s.

Contrasting sharply with the political weakness of industrial strategists in the postwar Diet has been the substantial and rising strength enjoyed by the "regulators," especially alumni of the Ministry of Finance. For a full discussion of the orientation and role of "regulators" in the Japanese policy process, see chapter 3. The distributive, clientelistic character of Japanese politics, in which a strong premium is placed on the ability to secure regulatory dispensations, budget allocations, and abatements through one's representative, is the central reason for the Diet strength of these MOF alumni; "industrial strategists" from MITI are few both because they have attractive opportunities in the business world and because their agencies dispense relatively few distributive benefits of concern to interest groups, compared to those of the regulators. As table 2-3 points out, there were more than twice as many MOF alumni in the Diet during the mid-1960s as MITI alumni; by the late 1970s there were more than four times as many. Indeed, by 1979 there were more Diet members with prior careers in the Ministry of Finance than with any other ministry—nearly one third of all the ex–civil servants.

These ratios generally persisted into the 1990s, with only a slight decline in MOF preeminence. Between 1966 and 1979 the number of former MOF officials in the Diet rose from twenty to twenty-seven, while the number from every other major ministry declined. By 1986 thirty-four Finance men had constituencies, although several other ministries, most notably Agriculture and Construction, showed a faster relative increase in representation. Of the dominant bureaucratic alumni networks in the Diet by the late 1980s, only one (that of MITI) was preoccupied with industrial strategy. The other four (MOF, Construction, Agriculture, and Home Affairs/Autonomy) had a much more static "regulatory" orientation and a clientelist bias in their dealings with interest groups.

Constraining Business-Government Networks

The flow of retired Japanese government officials from government to the private sector (the so-called "descent from heaven," or *amakudari* as it is known in Japanese) has often been seen as a mechanism for enhancing government dominance over the private sector.[52] But when the flow of such officials is precisely charted by size of firm, and when the actual activities of such retired officials are examined in detail, a more complex picture emerges.[53] In contrast to patterns in France and Korea, relatively few former officials flow to the largest industrial or trading firms; neither do they move to the most powerful industrial groups, such as Mitsubishi, Mitsui, and Sumitomo. Virtually none—especially from the ranks of the industrial strategists—flows to the largest banks.[54] Significantly smaller numbers go to the largest *keiretsu* rather than to other less economically powerful firms. *Amakudari* thus operates to *broaden* the access of the less-connected portion of the corporate world to government information, and frequently to *co-opt* and to *undermine* bureaucratic efforts at strategic dirigisme. It often constrains the bureaucrats, and thus complicates rather than reinforces their struggle for strategy.

Pressures toward Clientelism

Japanese politics throughout the postwar period—especially since the onset of rapid growth during the early 1950s—has had a consistently pronounced distributive orientation, although the magnitude of the benefits conferred has fluctuated cyclically in many sectors.[55] The bias of both the electoral system and the political culture toward cultivation of small, intense support groups with material benefits has also encouraged politicians to aid industry—especially mature, noncompetitive industry—in pursuing regulatory capture. However strategic the bureaucracy may desire to be in reordering sectors of the past, the bias of a political system in which strategists lack dominant influence is against such forceful, dirigiste reordering.

Cross-national comparison helps in understanding the systemic bias of the Japanese political economy toward clientelism. Japan's multimember district electoral system for its dominant Lower House, which strongly intensifies the bias toward cultivation of small, intense special-interest groups, is highly unusual internationally; it has close analogies only in Ireland and in Finland.[56] Both France and Germany employ variants of a list system, which unlike the dominant portion of Japan's arrangement strengthens parties and provides some autonomy for the politician from small, intense pressure groups. Britain and the United States employ single-member district approaches that force appeals to broader electorates, again providing more autonomy from the demands of small-scale pressure groups. Patterns of political culture reinforce these general differences among nations, making pressures toward clientelism and patron-client relationships much more salient in the politics of Japanese policy formation than in any Western political economy except possibly that of Italy.[57]

Rising Liquidity in Japanese Finance

As the Japanese economy struggled to recover from World War II, demand for capital was huge, since so much physical plant needed to be rebuilt or refurbished. Direct and indirect losses came to 34 percent of national wealth as of 1935 and set the Japanese GNP back to 1935–1936 levels, wiping out a decade of effort.[58] Around 20 percent of chemical and pig-iron capacity, 50 percent of thermal-electric-power capacity, and over 60 percent of oil-refining and shipping capacity had gone down to the bombers.[59]

Technological obsolescence also generated urgent capital requirements in an early postwar Japan where sadly little capital was available. At war's end Japan found itself nearly twenty years behind the West in heavy industrial technology, due to its isolation from most world technological developments during the militarist period. Obsolescence was especially pronounced in the steel industry, where it resulted in Japanese steel production costs nearly double those of the United States during the late 1940s. To compete internationally, Japan would need almost to totally refurbish its mills, requiring billions of dollars more capital.

Demand for capital to fuel new investment increased further following the onset of the Korean War and the beginning of U.S. military procurements. It accelerated during the late 1950s and early 1960s due to the rapid expansion of capital-intensive sectors such as petrochemicals and shipbuilding, in addition to steel. Artificially low interest-rate policies further stimulated corporate demand for funds, initially strengthening the position of allocators in the control-oriented institutional framework remaining from war and reconstruction.

Over the course of the 1960s and especially following the Oil Shock of 1973, however, corporate liquidity began to rise, due to favorable depreciation policies, export profits, and declining capital requirements as growth rates declined and industrial structure shifted from capital-intensive heavy industries such as steel toward sectors such as electronics, which require less capital. This shift toward easy money was further stimulated by expansionary monetary and fiscal policies, especially under Prime Minister Tanaka Kakuei (1972–1974). The result of this rising liquidity was declining leverage for Japan's state industrial strategists, whose capacity to direct the Japanese economy was already being compromised on numerous fronts, as noted above.

The strategists, despite their frequent brilliance and foresight, have faced structural and, increasingly, macroeconomic obstacles that have made developmental policymaking difficult. Their political weakness, which has been persistent over time, has reduced the industrial-policy process to a much more pluralistic one than generally recognized. It is divided among three groups: the strategists, the regulators, and the dynamic, organized private sector. The role of these latter two groups in industrial-credit policymaking is considered in detail in chapters 3 and 5.

CHAPTER 3

The Regulators and Industrial Credit

THE BUREAUCRATS of twentieth-century Japan have been by no means unified in their conception of how government should relate to industrial credit, or to the process of industrial transformation more generally. MITI and its predecessors, as noted in chapter 2, have often considered government's appropriate role to be strategically transforming industrial structure; they have struggled—with occasional success amid frequent futility—to achieve this end. Their struggle for strategy has been shared by an assortment of economic planners and intellectuals. But both skeptics on intellectual grounds and opponents of MITI's institutional dominance have been legion.

Contrasted to the strong developmental prescriptions of the industrial strategists has been a more cautious conception: that stability is the great imperative for the Japanese political economy, and that government's role is to ensure stability and order rather than to spearhead transformation. Where transformation is inevitable due to outside market or political pressures, continuous administrative oversight should be perpetuated in the public interest. Stressing the *regulatory* functions of the state, this latter conception is philosophically similar to the notions of governance that began emerging in the United States toward the end of the nineteenth century, inspiring the U.S. Interstate Commerce and Federal Trade Commissions, although the Japanese conception of the regulatory state, it should be emphasized, assumes an organic conception of society and less independent legitimacy for the market than would be true in the West.[1]

Ministry of Finance Banking Bureau Director Aichi Kiichi, ultimately to serve as a distinguished minister of finance and chief strategist for the activist Tanaka Kakuei in Tanaka's 1972 campaign for the prime ministership, outlined the regulatory conception of industrial finance in an influential 1950 address.[2]

Aichi made the following points:

1. Hardheaded economic rationality is the primary requisite for Japan's economic survival in an inhospitable and unforgiving world. Rationality implies that banks should not extend funds adventurously to firms in deficit, regardless of the character of their business operations or the social utility thereof.

2. Access to credit should not be determined by quotas (*waku*) or political appeals (*chinjō*). Finance is not social assistance, but borrowed money from depositors. Clear repayment plans are needed, and collateral is imperative, especially if the borrowing firms in question are not in the black.

3. Stock markets are highly speculative and unreliable.

4. The highest priority for government in the financial area is to ensure the soundness of the banking system.

Ichimada Naoto, longtime (1946–1954) governor of the Bank of Japan whose considerable influence led contemporaries to call him "the Pope," further amplified the viewpoint of this regulatory school.[3] Like Aichi and many of his Ministry of Finance colleagues, Ichimada's fundamental concern at the BOJ was avoiding instability rather than transforming the economy in developmental fashion. Indeed, Ichimada saw the integrity of the banking system, and the related imperative of avoiding unsound loans, as fundamental to the maintenance of broader social order. Heavily influenced by his formative experiences as a young Bank of Japan official in Weimar Germany amid the ruinous hyperinflation of the early 1920s, Ichimada likewise saw counterinflationary policies as a strict imperative. He favored credit allocation in the early postwar period, but as a means of arresting inflationary price spirals rather than as a tool for transforming industrial structure. Ichimada felt that such credit as was provided to industry should be concentrated narrowly on sectors critical to recovery, such as textiles, coal, and fertilizer, principally through quantitative allocation.[4] The aggressive expansion of heavy industry beyond the requirements of gradual economic recovery seemed to Ichimada a waste of resources; he did not share the vision of the strategic transformation of Japan's comparative advantage through industrial policy that is often attributed to Japanese planners.

Ikeda Hayato, author of the Income Doubling Plan of 1959–60, presided over much of Japan's rapid growth and structural transformation as MOF minister (1949–52), MITI minister (1952 and 1959–60), and as prime minister (1960–64). Some present him as a prominent architect of the developmental state.[5] Yet Ikeda's central concerns were primarily macroeconomic in character, and his well-known involvement in fostering off-budget finance (the Japan Development Bank, Japan Export Bank, and the Fiscal Investment and

Loan Program)[6] flowed more from a macroeconomic search for low-inflation growth than from an explicit developmental perspective.

Ikeda, a career MOF official before entering politics, also contributed to the "regulatory" vision of the Japanese economy. In his classic *Kinkō Zaisei* (Balanced Finance), published on the heels of the Occupation in August 1952, Ikeda inveighed strongly against inefficient and inflationary aspects of government finance in the early postwar period, as practiced by the Reconstruction Finance Corporation (Fukkō Kinyū Kōko). Ikeda's views in this respect were very similar to those of longtime SCAP financial adviser Joseph Dodge, with whom he worked closely during the Occupation. His principal concerns were savings, the savings-investment balance, and stable economic growth, rather than industrial transformation per se.[7]

THE KEY INSTITUTIONAL ROLE OF REGULATORS IN JAPANESE INDUSTRIAL CREDIT

Chalmers Johnson argues that a "regulatory" view of the state's role in economic life is characteristic of the United States, but that a "developmental" orientation toward private economic activities is broadly typical of Japan.[8] Upon close examination, it appears that in the industrial-credit area, at least, a variant of the "regulatory" approach—albeit one more sensitive than that of the United States to broad national economic welfare—has been well developed, politically influential, and on significant occasions even dominant in the Japanese government. This was true even for the pre-1970 high-growth period when "developmental" industrial policies were most influential among MITI bureaucrats in Tokyo.[9]

As is suggested in figure 3-1, several government bodies other than MITI have had important oversight relationships with respect to private-sector industrial credit. Most salient among these have been the Bank of Japan, the Ministry of Finance, the Ministry of Post and Telecommunications (MPT), and the Ministry of Transportation (MOT). The Ministry of Agriculture, the Ministry of Construction, and the Ministry of Health and Welfare, among others, also have important advisory roles in the allocation of some specialized government credit. Yet for complex reasons of institutional history and structure, none of these bodies has had a strong developmental orientation. Their concerns, particularly at MOF and the Bank of Japan, have been primarily with regulation—that is, "preoccupation with the rules by which private firms conduct themselves"[10]—rather than with industrial transformation.

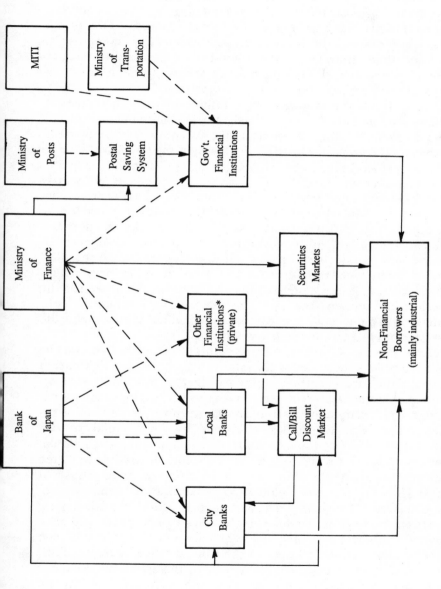

Figure 3-1. Fragmented Oversight Relationships in Japanese Industrial Finance. Solid lines indicate flow of funds; dashed lines denote regulatory relationships.

*Major lenders in this category include: insurance companies, agricultural financial institutions, long-term credit banks, trust banks, and mutual savings banks.

In cases of institutional conflict, the regulators have frequently also had the political influence to carry the day against the strategists. As was noted in chapter 2, Ministry of Finance alumni have consistently been far more numerous and powerful in the Diet than those of MITI; four MOF alumni (Ikeda, Fukuda, Ōhira, and Miyazawa) reached the postwar prime ministership, compared to only one (Kishi) from MITI. More than thirty MOF alumni have consistently served in the Diet for most of the past generation—compared to less than one-third as many from MITI.

The MPT and the MOT also have important roles in industrial-credit policymaking—through oversight of postal savings, on the one hand, and shipbuilding, shipping, and private railway development, on the other. Both ministries likewise have stronger traditional ties to the political world than does MITI. Although few Bank of Japan officials have ever served in the Diet, the BOJ once had extraordinarily strong ties with the Allied Occupation through its early postwar governor Ichimada. International links forged then have continued to give the BOJ leverage within the Japanese domestic political economy.

To understand the role of government "regulators," as opposed to government "strategists," in the political economy of Japanese industrial finance, it is useful to look in detail at the institutions involved, their histories, and their incentive structures, as well as the broader environment that gives the regulators leverage in policymaking. This means, in particular, understanding the role of the Ministry of Finance and the Bank of Japan.

Careful analysis illustrates three points. First, both MOF and the BOJ have been preoccupied with stability rather than transformation in industrial finance, thus complicating the task of strategists, notably those at MITI, who were trying to accomplish the latter.[11] Second, the administrative structure of government banks and semipublic financial institutions presided over by the financial authorities in Japan has been highly complex, compounding their implementation of even regulatory tasks. This complexity has rendered government finance a blunt instrument for achieving industrial transformation, even when policymakers have unified behind strategic objectives. Third, the risk adversity implicit in bureaucratic functioning has compounded the obstacles to government finance serving as a developmental tool. The MOF and the BOJ have been grossly undermanned relative to their broad range of responsibilities, thus affording considerable leeway in the actual allocation of industrial credit to Japan's aggressive and well-organized private sector.

THE BANK OF JAPAN AND
CREDIT ALLOCATION

Customary analysis has long placed the Bank of Japan at the heart of developmental efforts to transform Japanese industry through credit allocation, from at least 1945 into the 1970s. A respected observer in 1977 described the Japanese banking system, for example, as "among the most centralized and controllable in the world," noting that "at the top of the hierarchy stands the Bank of Japan, . . . the single tap through which virtually the entire Japanese monetary and credit supply must flow," an organization that "controls almost the entire credit supply."[12] Yet there has been little detailed empirical consideration of actual Bank of Japan involvement in qualitative credit allocation. The only major work originating in English on Japanese central banking has been that of Hugh Patrick, who does not consider credit allocation in detail;[13] parallel analysis in Japan has likewise focused on the central bank's economic role in monetary policy and macroeconomic stimulation,[14] with its emphasis shifting only slowly to the specifics of institutions and of qualitative allocation patterns themselves.[15] Apart from the *Nihon Ginkō Hyaku Nen Shi*,[16] the official centenary history of the Bank of Japan, all major studies have been completed by economists.

This analysis considers a proposition commonly set forth in current literature on Japanese financial policy: that the Bank of Japan has directly and actively controlled private-sector lending, particularly before 1970, with a view to strategically transforming industrial structure. The analysis also entertains the possibility that the BOJ played other indirect roles in allocating credit, through its operations in short-term call and bill-discount markets or by imposing restrictions on the terms and cost of its credit. Through such an examination the role of the BOJ as a "regulator" rather than a developmental "strategist"—or as a subordinate tool in a MITI-dominated strategic order in industrial finance—becomes clear. Tellingly, the "regulatory" orientation—and the BOJ's problems controlling the private sector even in that unambitious capacity—are clear for the high-growth period of supposedly tight controls (1955–1973), as well as for the post–Oil Shock period, when excess financial liquidity and large-scale government bond issues were universally recognized to have forced an increasing market orientation in Japanese industrial finance.

Special status.

direct short capit

? ask Cowley or whins

Formal Powers

The Bank of Japan is not legally a government institution, but rather a special corporation standing outside the framework of the government.[17]

Yet the Bank of Japan, despite its deep linkages with the private sector, has long held substantial formal powers, which continue to be based on the wartime Bank of Japan Law (1942). The extreme generality of this law is conveyed in Article 1:[18] "The Bank of Japan (BOJ) has for its object the regulation of the currency, the control and facilitation of credit and finance, and the maintenance and fostering of the credit system, pursuant to the national policy, in order that the general economic activities of the nation might adequately be enhanced."

The specific statutory powers of the BOJ were also defined in a broad and general way that did not force an activist role on the bank but, at the same time, did not preclude one. In Article 20 of the 1942 Bank of Japan Law, for example, the BOJ was empowered to engage in bill discounting (type of bill and issuer unspecified), buy and sell bullion, receive money for deposit (lender unspecified), make loans against collateral (recipient unspecified), "deal in domestic exchange" (content of transactions unspecified), and "perform other business incidental to the business enumerated in the preceding items."[19] Such a broad mandate could, but need not, concentrate within it truly massive allocative powers vis-à-vis the private banks. The less such power was in fact centralized, the more it fell into other hands—particularly those of the private banks—and the less potential the BOJ had to play an activist developmental role.

Ichimada as "Pope": An Interventionist BOJ and Industrial Credit

It is often observed that the high point of the Bank of Japan's influence over the disposition of credit came during the governorship of Ichimada Naoto, dubbed "the Pope" for his reputed powers, if not his infallibility. Ichimada served as governor for eight and a half years (1946–1954), outlasting seven cabinets and nine ministers of finance. Then he spent three years, divided into two terms, as minister of finance himself—from December 1954 to December 1956, and from July 1957 to June 1958.[20]

As Ichimada's former assistant Yoshino Toshihiko points out, Ichimada's powers, both personal and institutional, had at least six forces working for them in these years:

1. Ichimada was close to American Occupation officials.[21]

2. His most explicit rivals for political and economic power, such as Kishi Nobusuke, Shiina Etsusaburō, Ishibashi Tanzan, and Hatoyama Ichirō, were purged from active public life.

3. The commercial banks that the BOJ regulated were weak, due to the dissolution of the *zaibatsu*.

4. The foreign exchange banks (Yokohama Specie Bank, now the Bank of Tokyo, together with the Chōsen Ginkō and Taiwan Ginkō) were closed after the war, so there passed to the BOJ great new foreign-exchange responsibilities.

5. The rivals among the special banks lending domestically, such as the Industrial Bank of Japan and the Nippon Kangyō Ginkō, were also destroyed or handicapped. Until August 1945 these special banks, in which the state generally held a minority share, had played key roles in funding strategic industries at home and extending loans to important political clients of Japan abroad, particularly on the Chinese mainland.

6. Japan faced an overall capital shortage. Under administered interest rates this generated substantial demand on the part of both industrial and commercial enterprises against private banks for funds. It also consequently intensified the demands of private banks against the Bank of Japan for credit, due to the liquidity shortages that heavy industrial borrowing created for those private banks.

An additional factor strengthening the leverage of the BOJ during the immediate postwar period was the large holdings of wartime government bonds by the city banks. Lacking a market for such obligations, the city banks were at the mercy of the BOJ to redeem them.[22] National bonds outstanding amounted to twice the national income in 1945, a ratio that declined to 10 percent by 1951 due to the ravages of inflation.

Short-Term Finance

In the early postwar years the allocative powers of the BOJ were at their strongest and most fundamental in short-term finance, where virtually the only private-sector participants were commercial banks and trading companies. The latter were weak and fragmented due to *zaibatsu* dissolution and the collapse of Japan's foreign trade, whereas the former confronted a chronic and insistent private-sector demand for funds beyond their capacity to supply; private banks were hence heavily reliant on the Bank of Japan.[23] The only alternative to the BOJ for financiers in search of funds to supply clients was the black market, whose rates were much higher than those the BOJ offered.

The BOJ's most basic control over short-term finance was exercised through its regulation of the rediscounting on short-term notes. The precedent of extensive central bank provision of funds to the private sector through rediscounting had been set during World War II, when the central bank rediscounted munitions company bills. On March 27, 1946, it established a special discount system for civilian commercial paper, just fourteen days before Japan's first postwar election. This new system provided for rediscount significantly below even the rate on bills secured by national bond collateral,[24] and was made even more specific and discriminatory in August 1946, after Ichimada became governor.

Ichimada's initial rediscount plan balanced the interests of farmers and small businesspersons against those of large-scale industry, discriminating far less than originally anticipated. It failed to serve the goal of economic transformation favored by industrial strategists. At the heart of the program was a "stamped bill system," designating certain types of paper as preferred collateral, to be rediscounted at concessionary rates. The special rates had much more of a political than a strategic rationale: they went initially to the coal industry (a favorite of both business and Diet members, Socialist as well as conservative), fertilizer manufacturing (well liked by farmers and business), textile fabrication (small business and trading companies), and special regional industries.[25] At the same time that the stamped bill system was inaugurated, the BOJ also set up discount systems for export trade bills and for "industrial bills" financing producers' purchases of raw materials. All these discount measures were strongly desired by large-scale industry, including producers of both light and heavy manufactured goods.

Pressures for further rediscount systems did not subside—precisely because the original system was discriminatory, albeit not to the degree that BOJ governor Ichimada had originally wished. Some groups never secured redress. But an "agricultural bill system" was established to provide preferential credit through the BOJ for purchases of fertilizer, agricultural chemicals, and farm machinery. In January 1949 the fishing industry secured similar privileges. By the end of 1949, two-thirds of the total volume of funds borrowed from the BOJ consisted of loans within the "preferred" category, among which there was little, or sometimes no, differentiation.

Broadly speaking, the BOJ during the late 1940s and the early 1950s favored continuation of support for light industries such as textiles rather than aggressive, risky promotion of heavy industries such as steel and machinery, which involved huge construction expenditures and demands on scarce foreign exchange reserves that threatened both inflation and international insolvency. The latter were favored by developmental strategists at MCI and then MITI. The BOJ was supported in its cautious approach by SCAP, especially in the dark early days of the Dodge Line (1949–1950), when the long-term prognosis for the Japanese economy was by no means clear.[26]

Many BOJ policies, such as the industrial and export trade bill systems, indeed benefited both heavy and light industry, but the primary emphasis was on the established lighter sectors rather than on developmental transformation toward heavy industry.[27] The preferential rediscount rates for raw wool and cotton imports (from June 1950), textile fabrication (August 1946), and general exports (August 1946), of which textiles were a heavy proportion, all display this pattern of cautious BOJ preference for lighter, established sectors. The system's only real benefit for steel was a preferential rate on imports of steelmaking raw materials. But this was established much later (March 31, 1951) than the textile measures, after Korean War imperatives made development of a Japanese steel industry a military priority for SCAP. It was in no sense the product of any clear developmental vision.

This preponderant light-industry bias at the BOJ reflected in part short-term preoccupation with a precarious foreign-exchange position; sectors such as textiles and cheap domestic goods were proven foreign-exchange earners in the early 1950s, while the potential of steel, automobiles, and even shipbuilding remained largely untested. Political forces acting on the Bank of Japan as well as the governor's personal inclination appear to have pushed the BOJ in this direction: when the Bank of Japan Policy Board was founded in 1949, its most powerful member—and the one reputedly closest personally to the governor—was Miyajima Seiichirō, a major textile industry and *zaikai* (organized business world) leader, president of Nisshinbō Spinning Company. Many of the principal political confidants of Prime Minister Yoshida Shigeru were affiliated with the industry, including Oya Shinzō, finance minister when the Dodge Line was imposed and president of Teijin Limited.[28]

SCAP, with whom Ichimada was friendly, likewise wanted to see

Japan promote textiles. That sector readily generated foreign exchange and industrial employment, while also promoting expansion of American exports.[29] Ichimada himself felt that the promotion of labor-intensive light industry was far better suited to Japan's factor endowments (large population, few raw materials, little capital) than to heavy industry. Many other economists of the day agreed with him.

Separate from the bill-discount system, but working closely in tandem with it, was the BOJ's chief tool for controlling the short-term financial behavior of private firms: the "higher rates application system." Essentially this was a structure of variable penalty rates on borrowing from the Bank of Japan that exceeded BOJ guidelines yet did not fall within the priority categories outlined under the bill-discount system.[30] When the penalty rates went up, they strengthened the incentives for a private bank either to cut back its lending or to direct it more narrowly toward the priority categories. Declining rates increased the private banks' willingness to broaden their lending pattern and expand loan volume. To reinforce their caution in overall lending, the central bank kept secret its formula for calculating penalty rates.

The "higher rates application system" appears to have effectively restrained short-term credit expansion during the late 1940s. It also helped to enhance BOJ independence of the Ministry of Finance, since MOF had power only to regulate changes in the basic BOJ discount rate, but not to make alterations in the penalty rate system. Nevertheless, the constraints on commercial bank borrowing lost effectiveness with the years as new sources of funds developed and financial penalties lost their sting for the growing and increasingly cohesive industrial groups, leading to the development of "window guidance" in the 1950s.

The higher rates application system was primarily a means of quantitative rather than qualitative restraint, only able to affect allocation of credit among industries insofar as it encouraged credit to flow into "preferred sectors." And as preferred sectors came to be defined so broadly, penalty rates proved a blunt tool indeed—incapable of spearheading developmental transformation of industrial structure even had the BOJ desired such an outcome.

Loan Guidelines

Together with its controls over short-term credit flows, the early postwar Bank of Japan also employed loan guidelines (*yūshi junsoku*) by industry, a continuation of wartime practices authorized by the

TABLE 3-1

Japanese Government Loan Guidelines, 1947 (defined by MOF; administered by BOJ)

Category A (highest priority): coal, iron and steel, shipbuilding, electric power, electric cable, railroads, chemical fertilizer, housing, machine tools, warehousing, transport (equipment investment only).

Category B (secondary priority): paper (working capital only), transport (working capital only), textiles, most other manufacturing industry not included in *A*, retail trade, agriculture, educational institutions, construction (case by case), broadcasting (case by case).

Category C (proscribed): real estate, department stores, hotels, restaurants, cameras (equipment investment and working capital), securities, commercial trading, entertainment (including movies production), paper (equipment investment), publishing (equipment investment), alcoholic beverages.

Source: Bank of Japan data.

Temporary Funds Adjustment Law of 1937.[31] Among the most favored sectors were coal, fertilizer, housing, and fabricated steel products. This portfolio of favored industries was clearly driven by the exigencies of reconstruction; there was no clear effort through the guidelines to transform industrial structure.

Formally speaking, the guidelines themselves were drafted by MOF, under Ichimada's rival Ishibashi Tanzan, although formal consideration of applications for credit was left to the bank's Capital Adjustment Bureau (Shikin Chōsei Kyoku). The MOF prepared the "Regulations about Funds Supplied by Financial Institutions" (Kinyū Kikan Shikin yuzuru Junsoku), promulgated March 1, 1947. This ordinance divided Japanese industries into three groups, separately for working capital and equipment investment, according to the presumed value of loans to them for the Japanese economy as a whole, as indicated in table 3-1. The full categorization ran to twenty pages and became much more complex over time as amendments and exceptions were added. These emerging qualifications steadily eroded such limited discriminatory potential as the guidelines had in the beginning.

Interorganizational conflict over implementation also eroded the force of the controls. From the first, the Bank of Japan placed relatively low priority on enforcing even those parts of the guidelines that did not conflict with its own objectives. These guidelines had been prepared by MOF, whose attempts at controlling the whole Japanese financial system were resented by the BOJ. Implementation of the guidelines was assigned by the BOJ to a section of its Capital Adjustment Bureau with only eight to ten employees. This section was already charged with responsibility for a number of priority anti-inflation programs as well as administration of frozen bank accounts from the wartime period, in *addition* to the complex loan guidelines. The section simply lacked the staff to enforce the guidelines actively. Persistent interest-group pressure also eroded the effectiveness of loan guidelines in actually affecting the course of credit, as chapter 6 points out in detail.

In August 1949, following the Dodge Line and the coming of deep recession, the Bank of Japan stopped its lukewarm enforcement of loan guidelines, which had been motivated in any case by inflationary fears rather than a desire for strategic industrial transformation. In 1954 the BOJ abolished the Capital Adjustment Bureau, which had administered the guidelines. The MOF continued to use the controls to coerce or gain favors from industry through "moral suasion," and only gradually liberalized them on paper. When it came to building hotels and other marginal but popular uses of credit, MOF frequently put such valuable means of bargaining for mass political support to nakedly political use.

In October 1955 the guideline ordinance was amended to give categories *A* and *B* equal priority and to permit a higher percentage of loans to be devoted to category *C*. The MOF, with a regulatory but highly political bias, continued to use the ordinance to pressure industry (and to reinforce MOF Diet members' "brokerage" role) during periods of credit restraint. Finally, on July 22, 1963, the loan guidelines formally passed out of existence when the Emergency Financial Order (Kinyū Kinkyū Sochi Rei), on which they were based, was repealed. This step was taken as an element in Japan's economic liberalization preparatory to joining the OECD in April 1964. To the very end, banks were required by MOF to submit monthly figures on loans to category *C* firms, even though such loans were automatically approved.

Long-Term Finance

Bank of Japan efforts to influence long-term credit flows took three forms: (1) attempts to control the Reconstruction Finance Bank, established in 1947 to channel long-term funds into priority industries (2) dominance of the Bond Committee (Kisai Kai), which was located physically within the Bank of Japan during 1947–1949; and (3) activities of the BOJ Loan Mediation Bureau (Yūshi Assen Bu). Taken together, these operations had an enormous potential for systematically shaping the long-term evolution of Japanese industrial structure. But even before the Dodge Line was established, complex personal and institutional conflicts prevented the Bank of Japan from assuming a decisive coordinating role in any of these areas; the dissolution of the Reconstruction Finance Bank, the reemergence of long-term credit banks, and the gradual reconstruction of institutionalized *keiretsu* ties between banking and industry during the early 1950s deprived the BOJ of such opportunities for preeminence in long-term finance as still remained.

The political shift as the Occupation ended from a price-stability-oriented regime (that of Joseph Dodge) to the more growth-oriented bias of heavy industry and the ruling conservatives also complicated the BOJ's prospects for dominating economic policy processes.[32] The Reconstruction Finance Bank, conceived by the expansionist finance minister Ishibashi Tanzan as a vehicle for financing heavy industrial recovery through aggressive credit expansion, commenced operations in January 1947. The first chairman was Itō Kenji, formerly president of the Industrial Bank of Japan and an ally of Ishibashi. Over Itō was the Reconstruction Finance Committee, chaired by Ishibashi himself and including BOJ governor Ichimada only as one of five members. Despite the subsequent purge of Ishibashi and Ichimada's dispatch of his vice-governor to the RFB as a "loan adviser," the Bank of Japan was never able to gain full control of the RFB and restrain its expansionist policies. But ultimately this strategic vehicle of developmental transformation toward heavy industry was dismantled through the intervention of SCAP adviser Joseph Dodge. Dodge feared inflation and distrusted Japan's more expansionary industrial strategists—much as the Bank of Japan did.

The BOJ's control over corporate bond issues was likewise intermittent, incomplete, and regulatory rather than developmental in orientation. Prior to World War II the Bond Committee (Kisai Kai), with ultimate discretion regarding corporate bond issues, had been essentially a private-sector body, coordinated by the Industrial Bank of Japan. Under the January 1947 Temporary Law for Credit Allocation, the Kisai Kai was moved to the Bank of Japan, although representatives of the Ministry of Finance and the Economic Stabilization Board (Keizai Antei Honbu), as well as private banks and securities companies, were included as committee members. In 1949 the Temporary Law for Credit Allocation was rescinded and the Bank of Japan lost direct supervisory responsibilities over corporate bonds, although it maintained some indirect influence over the terms of bond issues until 1955.

Perhaps the Bank of Japan's most important uncontested activity in long-term finance was through its Loan Mediation Bureau (Yūshi

Assen Bu). This organization was set up in August 1946 as an autonomous division of the Bank of Japan to channel surplus funds from banks, mainly in rural areas that lacked sufficient borrowers, toward purposes consonant with national policy guidelines and, at all costs, away from the black market.

The mediation system had been initiated in March 1946 and placed under the jurisdiction of the Business Bureau, which was responsible for dispersing direct BOJ loans to banks. But the work proved to be so complex that it could be handled only by a separate organization. The Loan Mediation Bureau (LMB) was set up next door to the Business Bureau, but gradually developed almost total independence, due to its complex standard operating procedures and independent political constituency. The formal objective was to have the surplus-funds banks subscribe to RFB, local, and national government bond issues and have them help fund priority small businesses, which were desperately short of capital. The volume of loans mediated through the bureau was substantial—12 percent of total loans and discounts nationwide in 1947, 18.1 percent in 1948, and 23.9 percent in 1949.

Because of the BOJ's lack of leverage against the surplus-funds banks, its role quickly dwindled to one of mediation and cajolery rather than domination, and was frankly reduced to making markets to replace banker-industry connections dislocated by the war. It allocated funds more in line with the demands of private-sector banks, industrialists, and politicians than in conformity with any abstract, autonomous norms of its own choosing.

These conclusions are verified by an examination of the pattern of loans made under the "mediation" system. Contrary to the initial formal plan to direct such "mediated" finance into small business, loans went overwhelmingly to large firms. Within the big business community, the distribution was also skewed in a way that seems to reflect the period's market imperfections and political realities more than any systematic BOJ planning.

By far the largest proportion of loans overall was granted to affiliates of either the Fuji (formerly Yasuda) Bank or the Industrial Bank of Japan. These banks had been the two most severely hurt by SCAP's antimilitarist and anti-*zaibatsu* measures. They were also the two with the best and most longstanding political connections with the "growth faction" in the bureaucratic and political worlds, which was estranged from the conservative, anti-inflationary orientation of the BOJ and SCAP. Of the ¥20.1 billion in loans arranged nationwide in 1947, Fuji alone got ¥2.6 billion. This total rose to ¥7.3 billion, or 10.6 percent of a much larger total, by 1948—by far the highest proportion obtained by any of the "Big Five" city banks. The IBJ and its affiliates amassed an even larger share. In 1949 all of the four largest borrowers under the mediation program (Nippon Kōkan, Nihon Seitetsu, Nihon Hassōden, and Chisso) were affiliates of the IBJ or Fuji—three of the former and one of the latter.[33]

Other patterns discernible in the Loan Mediation Bureau's financing accentuated its overtones of particularism and political alertness. There were far more loans to Kantō (eastern Japan) firms, which were traditional favorites of the bureaucracy, than to Kansai firms. Trading companies affiliated with the former zaibatsu, as a result of SCAP's deconcentration efforts, got hardly any loans, despite their desperate straits. Toshiba, with good postwar zaikai connections, and Shōwa Denkō, deeply involved in politics, were frequent loan recipients.

An examination of the LMB's decision making, based on extensive participant interviews, also confirms the sense of ad hoc decisions oriented more toward bailing out distressed firms than establishing consistent, long-term guidelines for industrial transformation. The LMB's ad hoc character was clear from its elementary lack of an overall allocation plan. It simply waited for banks to introduce clients. The lack of coordination with other bodies can be seen in its slight contact with the BOJ's General Affairs Department, which planned discount-bill-allocation policy, or the Business Bureau, which allocated other forms of direct loans. The LMB was a highly autonomous part of the BOJ, vigorously supported by Governor Ichimada, who wanted to expand the central bank's allocative role. But it was disliked by other bureaus. In the same year that Ichimada left office (1954), the Loan Mediation Bureau was abolished.

Window Guidance

One of the Bank of Japan's few intensive involvements with other organizations in Japanese society that continued throughout the 1950s and 1960s—indeed, perhaps its most authoritative formal role—was its shepherding of private-sector financial institutions in their lending operations. This madoguchi shidō—literally "guidance at the window opening," which Japanese often translate as "official guidance"—alludes to the bank's power over other organizations through its discount window. This form of extralegal credit rationing is by no means traditional in Japan: it originated in the early 1950s and was not used extensively until after the more formal structure of financial controls was dismantled during the mid-

1950s.[34] Like the longerstanding patterns of administrative guidance (gyōsei shidō) of which it is a manifestation, window guidance served in many ways as a functional substitute for formal controls after their political support and economic rationale began to erode with rising national affluence and corporate liquidity. It involved the application of central bank quotas and guidelines directly to the lending programs of city banks and, on occasion, to other types of financial institutions as well. Window guidance declined in importance after the mid-1970s, as the Japanese financial system became steadily more market oriented, and was finally abolished from the July–September quarter of 1991.[35]

The window guidance system, even at its acme, had no formal basis in law. Its efficacy rested entirely on two forces—the desire of city banks and other financial institutions to supplement their own resources through borrowing from the central bank, and on parallel desires for the bank's cooperation in the short-term and bill-discount markets, where its presence was pervasive. From the late 1940s to the 1960s, city banks without a deposit base large enough to meet their loan demands came to the central banks for credit; they were therefore often in a state of "overloan," with a commensurate need to "overborrow" from the BOJ. The Mitsui Bank, with a peculiarly small deposit base for a city bank—its directors for most of the first postwar generation failed to emphasize deposit expansion because they envisaged Mitsui as the Morgan Guarantee Trust Company of Japan—and the Mitsubishi and Sumitomo banks, all under heavy keiretsu-related demands for industrial funds, were especially reliant on the BOJ. The city banks as a group borrowed on average well over 10 percent of their total funds from the BOJ throughout the 1950s and the early 1960s.

In contrast to cumbersome credit controls, central bank loans have always offered private institutions, especially city banks, positive incentives to cooperate. Most important, borrowing from the BOJ has been profitable for private banks. Throughout the 1950s and 1960s the BOJ artificially pegged its discount rate below private-sector short-term rates, so that borrowing banks could make money by lending elsewhere. The prospect of an emergency credit line from the central bank was also reassuring to the private sector in the light of the periodic credit crunches that wracked the Japanese financial system of this period.

Throughout the postwar years the BOJ has liked the extralegal character of both window guidance and the penalty rate system, due to the organizational autonomy these mechanisms provided it. Whereas MOF can by law determine the central bank's discount rates, it cannot determine the content of window guidance. Nor can politicians or business executives easily intervene. Secrecy, which the bank invokes in the exercise of both window guidance and penalty rates until some months after policy is implemented, also keeps MOF at arm's length. The particular organizational context in which the BOJ has found itself (scant political leverage, danger of dominance from MOF) appears to have determined its choice of major policy tools.

The procedures for the usual form of window guidance during their period of most frequent usage in the late 1960s were as follows: a section-chief-level official (*kachō*) of the Bank of Japan's Business Bureau visited each commercial bank subject to guidance once a month, meeting for an hour or so with the Accounting Bureau head (*shinsa buchō*) of the bank under guidance, a slightly more senior official than his BOJ counterpart. Discussion focused on the deposit base of the bank under guidance—how much it had grown in the previous month and how much it was to grow in the future. This was because the Bank of Japan's regulatory efforts were primarily directed toward regulating deposit bases, so that no bank grew appreciably faster than any other, and interfirm uncertainty was thus minimized.

Apportioning credit was a secondary concern. The commercial bank official was asked for estimates of funds demand at his bank. After being given this information and comparing it with his own confidential calculations of what seemed reasonable, the BOJ *kachō* laid down a numerical ceiling for deposit levels and, in periods of credit restraint, for loan levels as well. There was no discussion of how this level compared to that of other commercial banks. The BOJ kept such information confidential to strengthen the efficacy of its window guidance.

Following discussion of these aggregate issues, the BOJ officer embarked on detailed scrutiny of individual changes in the target bank's loan portfolio. His attitude tended to be one of constant probing for justifications, apparently for informational rather than immediate policy purposes. But it apparently went little further than that, in contrast to the much more active intervention of the early 1950s, described in chapter 5.[36] Contrary to the prevailing view among many Western analysts, window guidance apparently did *not* typically serve as a vehicle for qualitative credit allocation by the BOJ. Through window guidance the Bank of Japan limited only deposit increases and, in times of credit restraint, overall loan levels; it did not seek to impose a particular pattern of allocation even in times of restraint. That was the responsibility of individual banks. The Japanese state, in short, abdicated day-to-day regulatory control of industrial-credit decisions to the organized private sector.

There were forms of window guidance supplemental to the monthly meeting, but usually only in periods of credit restraint. The most common form was for the BOJ's Business Bureau director general (*eigyō kyokuchō*) to summon managing-director-level executives (*jōmu*) of the city banks—and later executives of the larger local banks and long-term credit banks—to quarterly meetings at the head office in the Nihonbashi section of central Tokyo. There he outlined loan targets for the economy as a whole. The discussion covered almost exclusively macrofinancial issues. Questions involving loan ceilings for individual banks were a matter for the monthly meetings.

No matter what the actual form of window guidance was, there is no denying that its scope was more limited than generally recognized, even at the high point of interventionism. Bank of Japan data indicate that guidance involving quantitative restriction of the overall volume of city bank loans was in effect only about 37 percent of the time, or 15 of 41 years, between the time window guidance was set up in 1950, and when it was abolished in 1991, and about 22 percent of the period after 1968, as the system of credit controls was waning. (See figure 3-2.) Only certain institutions came under window guidance, and it was applied even to them only intermittently. The trading companies and insurance firms, while performing many of the functions of banks, were never subject to BOJ controls. Agricultural financial institutions and mutual savings banks were subject only rarely, and even then were committed only to observe guidelines on a voluntary basis.

Toward a Market-oriented Central Bank

In December 1954 Ichimada Naoto left the Bank of Japan to become minister of finance, accelerating the slow retreat from the abortive control policies that had begun in 1949 with the BOJ's withdrawal from enforcement of loan guidelines. Ichimada's successor, Araki Shinichi, had just returned from service as ambassador to Washington, expounding market allocation of credit and a relatively restrained, market-oriented role for the bank similar to that of the Federal Reserve Board in the United States. Araki felt that BOJ dealings, as those of the bankers' bank, should be only with banks and that Ichimada's practice of attempting to control industrial corporations

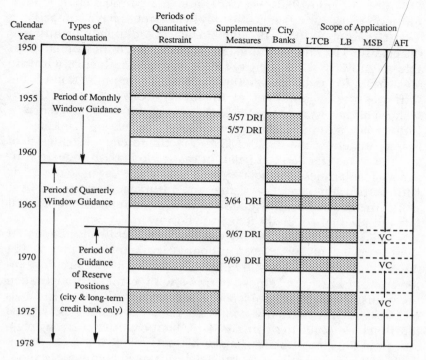

Legend:
1. DRI = Discount rate increase
2. LTCB = Long-term credit bank
3. LB = Local bank
4. MSB = Mutual savings bank
5. AFI = Agricultural financial institution
6. VC = Voluntary cooperation

Figure 3-2. The Limited Application of Window Guidance. From early 1979 until the third quarter of 1979, general window guidance was imposed over city banks, long-term credit banks, and local banks for purposes of currency management. After 1982 window guidance involved, in concept, full respect for private banks' own lending plans. Effective with the third quarter of 1991, window guidance was formally abolished.

Source: Bank of Japan internal data.

through credit allocation should be abandoned. Araki soon cut back sharply on the highly differentiated and discriminatory rediscount system, despite the predictable delaying actions from affected interest groups. The last preferential rediscount system to be scrapped, aside from strategically significant general export rediscounts that were retained, was the agricultural bill system. It survived in part until 1959, four years after the bulk of the rediscounts were abolished.[37]

During the mid-1950s, the economic and political environment surrounding the BOJ changed in ways that would have compelled a retreat from pretensions of control even if Araki had not initiated the change. The private commercial banks, which the BOJ had been able to partially dominate, rose in stature and influence with the recovery of the industrial group structure. The culmination of this shift was the appointment of Mitsubishi Bank chairman Usami Makoto as governor of the Bank of Japan in 1964, in preference to various BOJ alumni. Other power centers in private banking appeared, including the Bank of Tokyo in the foreign-exchange field and the Industrial Bank of Japan in that of long-term industrial finance. The Japanese financial system as a whole began to diversify, with institutions such as trading and insurance companies, over which the BOJ had no direct control, playing an increasingly central role in the supply of credit to private borrowers.

Since the mid-1950s, in sharp contrast to the Ichimada period that went before, the Bank of Japan has only very rarely been involved in direct credit-related allocation dealings with industrial firms. Its interactions have been almost entirely with banks, through such mechanisms as window guidance. The central bank did extend a direct loan to the virtually bankrupt Yamaichi Securities, Japan's fourth largest securities firm, in 1965,[38] but only under strong pressure from Finance Minister Tanaka Kakuei.

Similarly, in the fall of 1973 the electric power companies experienced severe cash flow problems because of the first Oil Shock, combined with MITI's reluctance to allow them to pass on costs. Quite unencouraged by the BOJ, representatives of these firms and their industry association begged for a direct loan from the Business Bureau, but the bureau, unwilling to be drawn again into the uncomfortable, politicized decision making of the Yamaichi affair, refused. Still, the Bank of Japan did arrange for special-impact loans to the electric power firms through the foreign banks in Tokyo, and for special loans from the Industrial Bank of Japan. But from the numerous serious bankruptcies or near bankruptcies of the 1975–1978 recession period, such as Kōjin, Eidai, Tōyō Value, and Sasebo Heavy Industries (SHI), the bank simply kept its distance. By the early 1980s it conceived itself clearly to be a market-oriented central bank, comparable to its counterparts in Britain and the United States.

Aside from the cases cited above, the only qualitative discriminatory credit allocation in which the Bank of Japan has explicitly engaged since the agricultural bills system was finally abolished in 1959 has been that designed to aid the balance of payments. And such assistance, in the form of favorable rediscounts, has been to exporters and importers as *categories*, rather than to specific firms or industries. Thus it did not force the BOJ into making politically delicate distinctions among individual claimants or pronouncing on clear-cut matters of industrial strategy.

Special aid to exports, which had been suspended during the general dismantling of control measures under Governor Araki, resumed in May 1957, its occasion being the onset of a credit-restraint period brought about by among the most serious balance-of-payments difficulties confronted by Japan during the entire post-Occupation period. Twice during the summer of 1957 Japan was forced to draw major emergency loans from the IMF, totaling $125 million.[39] Given the cause, the BOJ wanted at all costs not to weaken exports and consequently granted them preferential treatment. Such concessionary export financing continued until 1971–1972, more than two years after the OECD pronounced the Japanese economy to be in structural surplus.

Two types of concessionary export financing were in fact suspended at different dates. As of August 10, 1971, five days before Richard Nixon abruptly imposed a surcharge on U.S. imports to correct rising trade imbalance, the interest rate on export credits was raised to the same level as the basic Bank of Japan discount rate. (The export credit rate had generally been about 1.75 percent lower than the discount rate until 1970, when it gradually began to approach it.) Automatic granting of central bank credit for exports was abolished between March and September 1972.[40]

The Bank of Japan has also provided some modest qualitative support for imports. Preferential import finance had begun in 1950 and lasted through 1965. In May 1978 the BOJ announced a resumption of preferential import finance to help cut the burgeoning trade surplus. After a hiatus following the 1979 Oil Shock, preferential rediscounting of import bills resumed in the mid-1980s, as Japan's trade surpluses began once again steadily to rise.

Since the mid-1950s the Bank of Japan has, in line with its growing market orientation and its desire to avoid social conflicts that it cannot easily win, consciously avoided the politically controversial credit-allocation issues, even when they have related directly to the regulation of banks. The BOJ has, for example, refused to confront the question of regulating compensating balances[41]—an issue that has deeply engaged more politically connected entities such as the Fair Trade Commission (a favorite of consumer groups with strong MOF ties) and MOF's Banking Bureau, as well as the Diet. The BOJ has been equally reluctant to attempt qualitative credit allocation, an unavoidably controversial activity, as was suggested earlier.

The bank's "isolationism" has extended to Diet membership (no BOJ members since 1960 versus twenty-eight for MOF in 1992), to personnel interchange with other government organizations (virtually none at the critical midcareer levels), and to avoidance of decisive involvement in almost all the great economic policy decisions of the past generation, even when a central element has been monetary policy. Conspicuously it has dodged:

1. Formulating of the landmark economic plans of the past thirty years—Ikeda Hayato's Income Doubling Plan (1960) and Tanaka Kakuei's Plan for Remodeling the Japanese archipelago (1972)—both basically the creation of MITI bureaucrats.[42]

2. Responding to the Nixon Shock of 1971. Japan's initial abortive decision to defend the ¥360 = $1.00 exchange parity and the ultimate decision on August 27, 1971, to float the yen were both made by MOF's vice-minister for international affairs, Kashiwagi Yusuke. The BOJ's hesitantly given advice was ignored, even though Governor Sasaki Tadashi had spent years as BOJ's London bureau chief and was perhaps the foremost international monetary specialist in Japan.[43]

3. Handling the 1972–1974 inflation. The huge expansion of the Japanese money supply in the fall of 1972, which triggered the grave inflation of the following years, was reportedly ordered by top MOF officials and politicians,[44] especially Prime Minister Tanaka Kakuei and MOF Administrative Vice-Minister Aizawa Hideyuki, subsequently a Tanaka-faction Diet member. They encouraged this expansion so as to monetize the huge increases in the Japanese general account budget required to fund Tanaka's expansionary, construction-oriented Program for Remodeling the Japanese Archipelago (Nihon Rettō Kaizō Ron).[45] The BOJ's reservations and requests for higher interest rates were rejected. Following the Oil Shock, MOF Minister Fukuda Takeo, rather than the Bank of Japan, took charge of the anti-inflation effort.

THE JAPANESE TREASURY: PREOCCUPATION WITH REGULATION, CENTRALIZATION, AND STABILITY

Like the Bank of Japan, Japan's Ministry of Finance has long had major responsibilities with respect to industrial finance. And also like the BOJ—and in contrast to MITI—MOF's approach to such matters has been primarily regulatory rather than developmental.[46] With perhaps the broadest span of control of any ministry in Japan, MOF has understandably been preoccupied with issues of internal coordination. This enormous span of control, coupled with strong political leverage, as outlined in chapter 2, has allowed it to remain passive and reactive without losing significant influence; a more precarious power base has forced MITI to be incessantly aggressive and strategic. The MOF has, however, faced internal difficulties in maintaining strategic cohesion; it has been confronted with cross-cutting external interests, such as banking and securities, that accept MOF's overall prerogatives but align with different bureaus within the ministry.

For many top Ministry of Finance bureaucrats in Kasumigaseki during the 1950s and 1960s, the centralized French financial structure represented something close to an ideal, as France's developmental industrial policies also did for MITI. Overwhelming influence over the entire French financial system was concentrated in the tiny Trésor, with a staff of only one hundred.[47] This government body had a central role in the money market, bonds, and foreign exchange. Its human network extended via its alumni into the largest banks in France.[48] In 1980 former Trésor officials held top positions in all three of France's largest banks—Crédit Lyonnais, Banque Nationale de Paris, and Société Générale. Through this human network it was able to transcend institutional rivalries, thus enhancing its coordinating powers. Further, the Trésor directly controlled investment by government departments, which constituted a substantial portion of total investment in France, with its large number of state firms. The Trésor also had discretionary control over major semiprivate financial institutions, such as the Crédit Agricole.

Ministry of Finance officials, like those at MITI, waxed envious about the French system. They dispatched many subordinates to Paris to study its intricacies. But they could never duplicate it in the Japanese political context, despite MOF's considerable influence in the Diet.

It is true that in the 1950s and 1960s the MOF held fairly formidable powers for a national treasury. It controlled bank branch expansion, taxation, securities regulation, foreign-exchange operations, and authority to draft Japan's four national budgets. Together with the Bank of Japan, it exercised firm control over foreign banks operating in Japan, which consistently provided around 15 percent of the total funding available for domestic bank lending in Japan.[49] MOF even enjoyed the power, actually exercised in 1944, to fire the governor of the central bank. In the United States its broad functions are split among the Treasury, Securities and Exchange Commission, Office of Management and Budget, Federal Reserve Board, and other agencies. In contrast to the Bank of Japan, throughout the high-growth period MOF consistently and forthrightly tried to exercise its formal power, even when this led to confrontation with the private sector.

Yet MOF could not match the centralization of bureaucratic authority at the French Trésor, even given its influence with the political world. In the Japanese money markets, the Bank of Japan and the Kisai Kai, chaired by the private Industrial Bank of Japan, preempted functions occupied by the Trésor in France. Japan, unlike France, had few government enterprises whose financial plans could be shaped by the MOF. The largest one, Nippon Telephone and Telegraph (NTT), was financially self-sufficient due to revenue from bonds that telephone subscribers were required to buy when they first obtained service; NTT was thus largely beyond MOF control.

The Ministry of Finance had little authority over the nonbank financial institutions, such as those in agriculture and small business, and wielded no control at all over the important general trading companies (sōgō shōsha). These have no direct analogue in the industrialized West and are regulated by MOF's rival MITI. Finally, MOF was unable to infiltrate its alumni into executive positions with the largest private banks, which thus were able to retain considerably more autonomy than their counterparts in France, even before the widespread French banking nationalizations of the early 1980s.[50] Even though MOF placed prominent alumni with the Bank of Tokyo, Sanwa Bank, Taiyō Kōbe, Tōkai, Saitama, Yokohama, and Hokkaidō Takushoku banks—seven of the thirteen large city banks—it was unable to place any alumni with the five largest and most important ones.

Problems of Centralization at MOF

MOF's difficulties in centralizing control over the whole pattern of credit allocation in Japan stemmed, first, from its own decentralized nature. "All bureaus, no ministry" is the stereotype of MOF in the Japanese bureaucratic world. As table 3-2 indicates, only 2.1 percent of total MOF personnel in 1992 were employed in the secretariat, the primary body responsible for coordination throughout the ministry; the 471 so employed were over 20 percent fewer than in 1964. By the late 1980s MOF had the smallest secretariat of any major government organization in Japan, relative to overall personnel levels. Its secretariat in 1992 was less than one-third the relative size and slightly over half the absolute size (471 compared to 773) of MITI's secretariat.

TABLE 3-2
All Bureaus and No Ministry: MOF'S Small Secretariat
(percentage of secretariat personnel)

	1964	1969	1973	1978	1983	1988	1992
Ministry of Local Government	26.4	23.9	27.0	25.7	24.8	21.1	25.6
Ministry of Foreign Affairs	26.4	26.9	25.5	22.4	20.7	19.9	18.7
Economic Planning Agency	21.9	20.5	25.0	26.6	25.2	24.5	24.2
Prime Minister's Office	10.8	11.1	11.7	12.6	13.2	57.5	57.7
MITI	8.8	.9	8.7	8.5	8.9	8.6	8.4
Ministry of Finance	**2.4**	**2.2**	**2.2**	**2.3**	**2.3**	**2.1**	**2.1**
Ministry of Agriculture	1.8	1.9	2.0	2.1	2.2	2.4	2.4
Ministry of Construction	0.8	1.6	1.8	1.9	2.2	2.3	2.4

Source: Administrative Management Agency, *Gyōsei Kikō Zu* (Diagrams of Administrative Structure), 1964, 1969, 1973, 1978, 1983, 1988, and 1992 editions. (Tokyo: Gyōsei Kanri Kenkyū Center, 1964–92).

Note: The absolute number of MOF secretariat personnel declined steadily from 610 in 1964 to 471 in 1992.

Compared to most entities of the Japanese government, MOF's secretariat is limited, for reasons largely historical, not just in numbers, but in assigned functions. The constituent bureaus of MOF are old, even if not as old as the private banking system; MOF's basic bureaus (Budget, Tax, Banking, and Tariff) all date from the founding of the ministry in 1886, with the other major bureau, Financial Affairs, dating from 1897.[51] All have well-established private-sector constituencies that join the bureaus themselves to resist any effort at centralization of control. Significantly, MOF is the only ministry in which the function of compiling the intraministerial budget from the various departments is not centralized in an accounting section within the secretariat; instead, each appeals directly to the examiners within the Budget Bureau. Such collegiality entails a dispersion of power and initiative throughout the ministry that would render a strategic, developmental orientation ineffective even should senior officials seriously desire to pursue such a course. This pattern of clientelism in a highly regulated system has important parallels to France and to aspects of Japanese agricultural, small-business, and welfare-related policymaking.[52]

An attempt has been made to unify MOF functionally by establishing patterns of promotion that entail bureaucrats with top-level experience in one bureau being advanced on their next move to top positions in another. The director general of the Financial Affairs Bureau (Rizai Kyoku), for example, often subsequently becomes director general of the Budget Bureau. Similarly, the head of the Securities Bureau likewise normally succeeds to leadership of the Banking Bureau.

These attempts at unification of policy through personnel transfers generally fail, however, for two reasons: (1) the highest level of officials are increasingly unable to control the organizations under them, if only because of their transience; intensifying pressures of competition cut bureau-chief tenures from nearly six years in the immediate postwar period to two years or less by 1990. The real mandarins hardly have time to familiarize themselves adequately with their new bureau, or to develop networks that could effectively coordinate the activities of various bureaus. (2) Furthermore, interest-group pressures from regulated industries (securities-sector pressures against the Securities Bureau, for example) also impede close coordination of these highly autonomous bureaus, which often reflect the divergent concerns of the industries they regulate.

Small Staff and Large Tasks

Even when MOF's bureaus are able—and they often are—to coordinate smoothly with one another, they face difficulties in regulating the private sector, forcing reliance on private cooperation and initiative. Asymmetry between the complex, personalistic character of their regulatory tasks and the small number of MOF officials available to do the regulating makes this inevitable. The ambiguity of their tasks, the fragmentation of the Japanese state regulatory structure, and the delicate, time-consuming obligation to build consensus in and with any large Japanese enterprise encourage this small staff to balance existing private interests, after hearing them in detail, rather than impose dirigiste solutions, however strategically farsighted they might be.

As indicated in table 3-3, the MOF supervisory force directly overseeing all of Japan's financial institutions, public as well as private, with assets of well over ¥200 trillion in 1978 and nearly quadruple that level by 1992,[53] included only slightly more than 150 people. Even counting the entire staffs of the Banking, Securities, International Finance, and Financial Affairs bureaus, including those engaged in research, in internal administration, and as regulatory

TABLE 3-3
MOF's Small Regulatory Staff

Organization	1968	1973	1976	1978	1992
Banking Bureau	221	212	210		211
Special Financial Section (government financial institution)	8	10	12	10	11
Small Business Finance Section	10	11	11	11	15
Banking Section	10	11	11	11	13
Insurance Division	31	36	32	33	42
Inspection Division	68	92	65	78	85
Financial Examiners in Inspection Division	16	72	44	60	65
Securities Bureau	139[a]	135	180		136
Financial Affairs Bureau	384[a]	384	377		371
General Affairs Section	13	11	14	15	22
Capital Section	12	12	11	11	34
Government Financial Corp. Section	12	12	11	11	—
Capital Management Section	9	12	12	12	15
Local Capital Section	13	12	11		15
International Finance Bureau	162[a]	157	152		151
TOTALS:					
Key Regulatory Sections	109	115	86		152
All Personnel—Regulatory Bureaus	906[a]	888	919		869

Sources: Ministry of Finance, *Bessatsu Ōkura Yōran* (Addenda to the Financial Handbook), 1968–78 eds. (Tokyo: Ōkura Zaimu Kyōkai, 1968, 1973, and 1976; and Ōkura Zaimu Kyōkai, *Ōkurashō Shokuin Roku* (Ministry of Finance Employees Record), 1992 ed. (Tokyo: Ōkura Zaimu Kyōkai, 1992).

Note: Figures are for all MOF personnel engaged in regulating financial institutions (public and private).

Totals for Insurance Division and the Capital Management Section have not been included in those for "Key Regulatory Sections."

1992 totals for the Financial Affairs Bureau, Capital Section, represent those for the Banking Bureau and the Securities Bureau, as the previous section was split.

[a] Denotes 1969.

personnel, in 1992 MOF's supervisory force came to only 869 people—only 0.5 percent of the 159,969 employees of the city banks alone[54]—not to mention the trust, long-term credit, and mutual savings banks, which MOF also supervises.

The French Trésor, it has been argued, functions well precisely because of its small size, and the possibility for flexible coordination that flows from it. One might wonder why the same dynamic would not operate in Japan. Although to a point compactness also breeds efficiency there, the unusually great reliance on labor-intensive person-to-person contact and the aversion to abstract, general solutions that prevails in Japan generate unusually great demands, unique to the Japanese policy process, for regulatory personnel. The rapidly growing scale and complexity of the Japanese economy and its regulatory processes also imposed heavy and growing demands on career bureaucrats over the high-growth period, as evidenced by the hours they kept.

The shortage of MOF regulatory personnel has been particularly striking with respect to the government financial institutions. Only one section of MOF keeps day-to-day contact with those eleven organizations, not to mention the numerous public enterprises with financial functions: the Special Financial Section of the Banking Bureau, with a staff of just over ten career officials. Two other sections—the Capital Section and the Government Financial Corporation Section—were also involved in planning the annual supply of funds to the government financial institutions, but were not concerned with the pattern of specific loan decisions. They had fewer than thirty-five career staff members between them.

MOF's regulatory capabilities were consistently inadequate to active dirigisme throughout most of the Bankers' Kingdom. In 1964, for example, despite the complex administrative demands imposed by a highly regulated financial system, the personnel strength of MOF's Banking Bureau was only 6.7 percent greater than in 1978; the *genkyoku*, or operational, industry-oriented divisions of MITI most nearly equivalent functionally to the Banking Bureau in MOF, were 50.9 percent stronger in 1964 than in 1978.[55] Such consistent understaffing at MOF inevitably forced the ministry to leave the initiative on a wide range of working-level decisions to the private financial sector.

THE INDUSTRIAL REGULATORS

By no means all of the Japanese bureaucracy supervising industrial development is preoccupied with strategic industrial transformation. Much of it, in fact, could be categorized in the "regulatory" camp, together with MOF and the Bank of Japan. The range of organizations involved is huge and their collective influence substantial. Several "industrial regulators" have major influence over the evolution of economic structure and deserve independent mention.

Most obviously in the regulatory camp are Japan's independent regulatory commissions, explicitly established by the Allied Occupation forces in the early postwar period to fill regulatory functions parallel to those undertaken in the United States. The independent policy review boards and Securities Commission set up in the immediate aftermath of World War II disappeared with the Allied Occupation in 1952, but the Fair Trade Commission, sustained by the Ministry of Finance and parts of the political world, has steadily increased its influence, especially since the early 1970s. Shortly after its foundation in 1947 the FTC, in one of its first decisions, overruled efforts by the bankers' association to set interest rates, paving the way for MOF administrative guidance to become an increasingly central element in determining the corporate cost of capital. The FTC has also played a significant role in inhibiting cooperative efforts by the banking sector to set criteria and levels for compensating balances on industrial loans, thus keeping interest rates down. The FTC's role in the Japanese political economy has clearly risen in the past two decades, in significant part due to the transnational political support it invariably gets from U.S. trade negotiators.

The distinction is frequently drawn in Japan between *seisaku kanchō*, or "policy ministries" such as MITI, and *kisei kanchō*, or "regulatory ministries." Among the latter, more or less explicitly regulatory ministries with some relationship to industrial activity are the Ministry of Health and Welfare (MHW), the Ministry of Transportation, the Ministry of Construction (MOC), and the Ministry of Post and Telecommunications. Although the MPT has been trying to transform itself into a *seisaku kanchō* with strategic pretensions since the deregulation of Japanese telecommunications began in 1985, it retains a generally regulatory orientation. And the other three ministries, which administer such industrially important sectors as shipbuilding, pharmaceuticals, and construction, have not even begun to change their relatively static and passive approaches to economic activity.

The four major *kisei kanchō* with importance for industrial development share some significant common traits. All have relatively large, nationally dispersed ministerial staffs and extensive regulatory controls over the sectors that they administer. The MHW, for example, regulates authorizations of new drugs and medicines, as well as their pricing, with major industrial implications. It also supervises the heavily regulated national health insurance and government pension programs. The MPT controls the full range of telecommunications authorization, including many that in the United States would lie in the hands of local authorities. The MOT is responsible for airline, railway, and sea routings and related fares, whereas MOC regulates land use and the construction industry.

At the same time that they enjoy extensive regulatory operations and a nationwide sweep of activities, the *kisei kanchō* also each have complex histories of institutional fragmentation. None was among Japan's earliest ministries; all have been significantly reorganized since 1945. The MPT, for example, is an offspring of the prewar Communications Ministry, newly established in 1950. The MHW was formed in 1938 from a bureau of the Home Ministry. The MOC also sprang from the Home Ministry, being founded on its December, 1947 dissolution. The MOT was founded in 1920, but with significant functions, including critical activities related to shipbuilding, shipping, and railroads, that were added with the demise of the Railway Ministry after World War II.

As a consequence of their large, high-stakes span of regulatory controls, and their fragmented institutional histories, the *kisei kanchō* have, not surprisingly, all been clientelized to a significant degree by the political world and the industries that these ministries regulate. Most of these industries receive substantial government assistance, but not in any strategic fashion. None of these industries is competitive internationally. Clearly this portion of the Japanese political economy cannot readily be considered part of any "developmental state."

In our search for the dynamic center of the Japanese political economy, we have explored in detail the aspirations and structure of Japan's public sector. We have found fragmentation and a clear internal split between "strategists" and "regulators." How do these divisions play themselves out in the actual conduct of government industrial-credit policy? How effectively is the Japanese state able, given its internal divisions and the impact of domestic politics, outlined above, to direct resources toward sectors of the future so as to effect developmental, state-led industrial transformation? It is to such issues that we now turn.

CHAPTER 4

Profiles of Public Action

SINCE THE COMING of Perry's black ships to Shimoda nearly a century and a half ago, and especially since the mobilization for war of the 1930s, Japan's political economy has undergone a profound transition. The state's role has undeniably been great, especially in contrast to the Anglo-Saxon nations. But the Japanese government has not been omnipotent, nor has it been unified in its view of the development process. Strategists, often politically outnumbered and confronting a complex policy apparatus, have been forced to struggle with both public and private foes to implement their dynamic vision of industrial transformation.

The last two chapters have outlined the institutional context confronting Japan's industrial strategists, even at the acme of their influence: a fragmented state, including numerous independent agencies with concerns other than strategy. The very real question arises as to how capable such a divided state can be of spearheading industrial transformation. Yet in view of the strong arguments made by Johnson and others regarding the developmental qualities of the Japanese state, an empirical survey of actual policy outputs—more systematic than a series of historical anecdotes—is in order. This chapter examines first the cross-sectoral profile of Japanese government lending and then state efforts to allocate private-sector industrial credit flows. The analysis places considerable emphasis on microanalytical perspectives, since it can only be through individual institutions such as the Japan Development Bank, and in the context of particular industries, that the Japanese state can attempt to shape such credit flows.

GOVERNMENT LENDING DECISIONS:
A CROSS-SECTORAL ANALYSIS

The hypothesis with which we begin flows from both bureaucratic theory and the structural analysis of previous chapters: that the Japanese state in its credit allocation behavior will be rigid, cautious, and reactive, rather than entrepreneurial. Divided from within and seeking in any event to routinize transactions as any bureaucracy would,[1] it will pursue a conventional course, mandated largely by the past, rather than blaze new frontiers. Major changes in allocative patterns will be provoked from outside the state, rather than strategically generated from within.

As table 4-1 points out, loans to basic industry, traditionally considered the Japanese state's main concern, made up only 7.8 percent of total government credit extended in 1965, at the height of the high-growth period; this share subsequently declined sharply to only 2.9 percent of the total by 1990. Housing, public works, and small business, by contrast, were larger recipients of government credit than basic industry even in 1965; their combined share had nearly doubled by 1990 to a combined 55.9 percent of all government credit outstanding. As previously noted, these sectors also absorbed a disproportionate share of the general-account subsidies allocated to government credit programs. Some small-business support, particularly in the precision-machinery area, was clearly strategically oriented. But the bulk of it, concentrated since the mid-1970s on no-collateral loans to inefficient distributors and service establishments politically connected to the ruling LDP, could not be justified on industrial-policy grounds.[2] Neither could most of the huge government housing expenditures. By the early 1990s Japan's government credit programs had thus become primarily welfare oriented, with their strategic support function clearly secondary in quantitative terms.

Just because large amounts of government credit are directed toward welfare purposes does not mean, of course, that some smaller share of Japanese government lending may not be highly strategic. One way of focusing more narrowly on the question of strategy, and also gaining more insight into the functional role of government credit within the broader Japanese political economy, is to examine the share of loans from government financial institutions in total borrowing of particular economic sectors. This ratio provides a measure of the reliance of specific sectors on government credit as opposed to other sources of finance; if we assume that government credit is generally desirable for private firms (on grounds of price, lack of compensating balances, and so on), this indicator provides us with a measure of governmental discrimination for or against particular sectors as the decision on ultimate private-sector borrowing magnitudes would then lie in the hands of government. Comparing cross-sectoral profiles of dependence on government credit at different points in time can also provide insights into how the sectoral bias of government policies changes or fails to do so.

TABLE 4-1
Shifting Sectoral Distribution of Government Credit, 1965–1990
(percentage change in 1965 Share)

	1965	1973	1978	1983	1990	Share
Categories with Rising Shares						
Housing	13.9	18.1	24.7	25.6	30.3	+118.0
Small business	12.6	14.8	16.1	19.0	15.8	+25.4
Roads	7.9	9.4	7.1	7.6	9.8	+24.1
Categories with Declining Shares						
Regional development	7.0	3.9	2.5	2.5	2.5	−64.3
Basic industry	7.8	3.6	2.7	3.0	2.9	−62.8
Land conservation and disaster reconstruction	3.1	2.3	1.6	1.6	1.3	−58.1
Agriculture	7.2	4.6	4.8	4.7	3.1	−56.9
Transport/communication	13.9	13.1	10.8	9.3	8.3	−40.3
Education	3.1	2.0	4.7	3.8	2.0	−35.5
Foreign trade/economic cooperation	7.5	8.9	6.8	6.4	5.8	−22.7
Welfare	3.6	2.9	3.3	.1	3.1	−13.9

Source: Ministry of Finance Budget Bureau Research Section, *Zaisei Tōkei* (Financial Statistics), 1983 ed. (Tokyo: Ōkurashō Insatsu Kyoku, 1983), 41; 1990 ed., 41.

Note: Figures indicate shares of total FILP expenditures, apart from interest payments.

Figure 4-1 presents two snapshots across a more than thirty-year interval in the cross-sectoral allocation of Japanese government credit. The two benchmarks are the years 1953 (at the high point of bureaucratic controls just after the Japan Development Bank was founded) and 1986 (after the financial system had been fundamentally liberalized, but before the emergence of commercial paper markets in 1987). The indicators are a scale of overall sectoral dependence on government credit, designed to show which sectors are most and least reliant on such support and how their dependence changes over time. The choice of sectors was unfortunately constrained by data availability, since changes in Bank of Japan definitional categories restricted the range of alternate sectors that could have been examined. But there is sufficient continuity to make some provocative initial generalizations about the intersectoral evolution of Japanese government lending.

One of the most striking conclusions when one compares patterns of sectoral government credit support in the 1950s to those of the

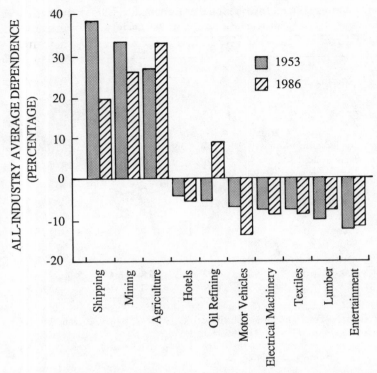

Figure 4-1. The Intersectoral Profile of Japanese Government Credit, 1953–1986.
(1) "All-industry average dependence" is the mean percentage of government credit in total loans outstanding of the twenty sectors of the Japanese economy (BOJ classification) for which categories are comparable across the 1953–1986 period. (2) The total of JDB, Small Business Finanace Corporation, Agriculture and Forestry Finance Corporation, and Japan Export-Import Bank loans are taken as a representative proxy of government credit, due to data availability for some of the other small institutions. (3) Divergence from average dependence for a given sector is equal to the dependence of the sector on government credit minus average dependence. (4) Sectors were selected in terms of historical or present importance in Japanese economic and social life.

Source: Bank of Japan, *Hondo Keizai Tōkei Nenpō* (Economic Statistics Annual of the Home Islands), 1955 ed., 87–90, 141–44; 1986 ed., 131–34, 140–43.

1980s (figure 4-1) is *how little actually changed*. Both the Japanese economy and Japanese society were transformed massively in the interim—the agricultural share of Japan's working population, for example, fell from 48 to under 8 percent between 1950 and 1990, while manufacturing and services have risen sharply in importance.[3] Yet intersectoral patterns of reliance on government funds have hardly shifted at all, despite the developmental pretensions of government to engineer industrial transformation. The only significant change was increased dependence of the oil-refining sector on government funds to finance the enormous structural transformation that the industry was forced to undergo after the two Oil Shocks of the 1970s.

Particularly graphic were the circumstances of shipping, mining, and agriculture. In both 1953 and 1986 they were disproportionately reliant on government funds—indeed, among the most heavily reliant of any sectors, as figure 4-1 suggests. They continued to receive extensive support over the decades, even as their economic role declined, especially relative to growing high value-added industries such as electronics and automobiles. The justification for support also became more tenuous from a national economic-security standpoint, as Japan's foreign-exchange reserves rose and multiple foreign sources of agricultural products, raw materials, and shipping services emerged. By the mid-1980s government lending to shipping, mining, and agriculture was thus difficult to construe as "strategic." Yet heavy dependence continued, as these noncompetitive wards of the state found it difficult to raise other sources of funds and government indulged them in their dependency.

The consistently low overall dependence of Japan's most dynamic industrial sectors on government credit—even in the 1950s—is also instructive. Motor vehicles and electrical machinery—two of the great success stories of Japanese industry—*never* relied heavily on government funding. Whatever "developmental" shifts occurred in intersectoral government lending appear to have been nuances at the margin.

Also striking is the persistent tendency over time toward clientelism—not only in preserving the prerogative of once-strategic sectors such as shipping and mining, but also in subsidizing once-independent, prosperous sectors as they began to decline. Textiles and lumber, for example, relied little on government credit in 1953— even less relative to all-industry average dependence than motor vehicles. Yet the dependence of both textiles and lumber had risen by the 1980s, with political intervention and resulting clientelism clearly important in the case of lumber.

Energy industries such as oil refining and electric utilities also greatly intensified their dependence on government credit over time, with oil refining becoming the only sector surveyed to join shipping, mining, and agriculture in heavy reliance on government funds by the mid-1980s as was noted earlier. As in the case of shipping and mining in the late 1940s, the initial impulse to this heavy new energy lending was no doubt strategic. In this instance, MITI had strong control in the sector, through such mechanisms as the dirigiste Petroleum Law (Sekiyū Gyōhō) of 1962. It faced clear outside challenges, such as the dominance of the foreign Seven Sisters (1960s) and the Oil Shocks (1970s), which both galvanized MITI to action and caused others to accept its strategic designs. But in the end government controls and developmental policies bred clientelism, rigidity, and a government bailout. It is hard to explain in strategic terms the heavy reliance of the depressed, inefficient oil-refining sector of 1986 on the state. And there is plenty of evidence, such as heavy employment of senior ex-MITI bureaucrats in the sector, to suggest that clientelist pressures were in fact the driving forces at work.[4] Once a "circle of compensation" has been established to aid state developmental purposes early in a product life cycle, it can easily be used later to perpetuate clientelism, as the Ministry of Transportation's planned shipbuilding (keikaku zōsen) program also made clear at the same period.[5]

GOVERNMENT LENDING: HISTORICAL PROFILES

In thinking more systematically about patterns of government lending to the Japanese private sector and why they take the forms that they do, it is useful to return briefly to the basic typology and set of analytical questions with which this book began. Our concern throughout has been to understand, first, the degree to which the Japanese state has been strategic, or developmental, in its industrial credit policies and, second, why policy outputs have diverged from the developmental state paradigm. Applied to the question of government lending to the private sector, our original typology explaining the divergence of actual Japanese policy patterns from this paradigm could be reformulated as suggested in figure 4-2. The typology is a conceptual one, but the empirical basis for the sectoral judgments is the same Japanese government statistical data used in preparing both the key figures in this chapter and the sectoral case studies elsewhere in this volume.

Historical analysis of how government lending toward particular sectors evolves over time helps us to assess how strategic and proactive government has been in its lending at key junctures in sectoral development. Figure 4-2 suggests four separate patterns of government financial support for Japanese industry, appearing at different stages in the industrial life cycle:

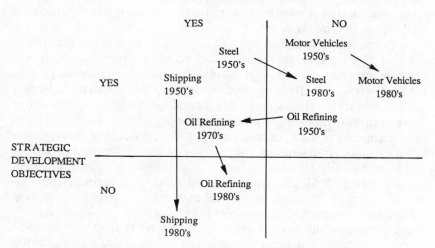

SUBSTANTIAL GOVERNMENT SUPPORT
(Shares of Corporate Funding)

Figure 4-2. Strategic Imperatives and Patterns of Government Lending

1. Strategic state response. The conventional wisdom is that the Japanese state strategically develops infant sectors. What appears much more common is strategic reaction to external events. This pattern appears in the intermediate stages of computer industry development, where government lending to that sector was initially low but rose sharply following the dramatic acquisition of the prominent French computer manufacturer Machines Bull by General Electric in 1964, and the rising sense of foreign challenge to Japan's technological independence that MITI subsequently began to sense during the late 1960s. Japan Development Bank loans to the computer industry, which had been only ¥2.5 billion in 1964, nearly tripled to ¥7 billion by 1966, and doubled again to ¥15.5 billion by 1969.[6] Oil refining presents a parallel case. Government lending was initially low, but MITI tried to develop national refiners such as Kyōdō Oil to compete with the multinational Seven Sisters during the 1960s. The ministry then threw funding at the industry to achieve rationalization in the wake of the two Oil Shocks of the 1970s.[7] This fostering of sectors with future promise is explicable under the well-known logic of the developmental state, which needs little further elaboration. It is, however, instructive that in such important sectors as computers and oil refining, the Japanese state's strategic response was *reactive* to external shocks rather than proactive—perhaps reflecting the obstacles enumerated in chapter 2 that confront state strategists.[8] That MITI was able to more proactively restructure the auto-parts industry is an anomaly to which we will return in chapter 6.

2. *Corporate-led strategic capitalism*. This pattern, represented in figure 4-2 by the consumer electronics sector, is one of minimal reliance on government credit. It involves converse reliance on private institutions, especially long-term credit banks, *keiretsu* main banks, and occasionally even capital markets and foreign investment, and is more common early in the product cycle of globally successful Japanese competitors than generally supposed. In the case of SONY, development was so independent that MITI even reputedly tried to deny it funds in the early 1950s for licensing the transistor. Consumer electronics maverick Sharp Corporation similarly had periodic confrontations with government industrial strategists, particularly during its dynamic, sustained expansion of the 1960s.

Despite more substantial aid in its early days than consumer electronics received, and some government aid in restructuring during the mid-1960s, the auto industry's evolution belongs largely in the corporate-led development category.[9] Toyota Motors, like SONY during the same period, confronted substantial opposition to its early postwar development from central government authorities. Ichimada Naoto, governor of the BOJ, went so far as to bluntly declare in 1950 that domestic automobile development in Japan did not make much sense.[10] But the Nagoya district office director of the Bank of Japan, Takahashi Takeo, engineered a crucial syndicate loan for Toyota responsive to the entreaties of that straitened firm, against the initial opposition of higher government authority.[11] World Bank loans guaranteed by the Japan Development Bank were also important in aiding facilities investment by the top four auto producers between 1951 and 1956,[12] and Export-Import Bank loans aided exports during the Korean War procurement boom.[13] But the overall scale of government financial support was minor compared to that extended to sectors such as steel. At least with respect to finance, the private sector clearly determined the contours of sectoral development. In several important cases, such as motorcycle producer Honda's persistent and ultimately successful efforts to become a major auto manufacturer, government actually tried to curtail private financial support, to no avail.

Industrial policy, to be sure, can indirectly benefit sectors such as consumer electronics and autos, as through state support for the development of components such as integrated circuits, or of infrastructure such as railways, ports, and electric power facilities. But in

PROFILES OF PUBLIC ACTION · 111

general such externalities are much more important in heavy industrial sectors than in the consumer industries, where Japan has shown its strongest recent competitiveness. Most key initiatives in sectoral development, especially in consumer-oriented sectors, have been made by the private sector, albeit in highly strategic fashion. In general the role of private long-term credit banks in strategic resource allocation has been large under this paradigm, as chapter 5 suggests in detail, whereas the role of MITI and other government ministries has been conversely small. This general subject is a pressing one for further interdisciplinary research on the origins of competitiveness,[14] to which we will return in chapter 8.

3. *Incipient clientelism.* This pattern normally appears at mature stages of the industrial life cycle. As figure 4-1 made clear, many of the original government strategic lending targets in the early postwar period—especially those that were priorities of the highly interventionist priority-production policy (*keisha seisan hōshiki*)—have remained heavily dependent on government funds, even though they do not remain strategic priorities by any stretch of the imagination. Apart from shipping, mining (especially coal mining) and agriculture clearly also fall into this category. Agricultural reliance on government credit actually *increased* from 1953 to 1986, even as the sector became more and more abysmally noncompetitive. Oil refining, where state decision making was highly strategic during the high-growth era, joined clientelist ranks during the 1980s.

In the case of all four clientelized sectors (shipping, mining, agriculture, and recently oil refining) three catalysts to clientelism appear to be have been consistently at work. First, the sectors have long been highly regulated—increasing the incentives of the private-sector interest groups involved toward regulatory capture.[15] Second, the sectors in question have a strong local geographical base, generating intense multipartisan political support in the Diet. Each of these industries, for example, has major backing from the Opposition, as well as from the ruling LDP. Third, each sector has important personal networks that link it tightly with the government financial institutions supplying credit. In most cases, major firms in the sector accept retirees from the government banks, or from the ministries supervising the banks, into their enterprises as senior executives.[16] In 1990, for example, there were eight former senior officials of the Japan Development Bank serving as directors of major Japanese shipping firms.[17] These catalysts to clientelism—especially the personal networks and political ties—make it difficult for government to terminate lending commitments to such sectors, even when the imperatives of industrial strategy change.

4. Devolution to the private sector. In probably the most analytically compelling case type in the politics of Japanese government credit, a small number of sectors evolve from relatively high initial dependence on the state toward a stronger private-sector orientation. Steel, as suggested in figure 4-2, fits this pattern in Japan, although this may be a distinctive pattern among steel industries cross-nationally, where clientelistic reliance on the state is often chronic.[18] Machine tools and some subsectors of electronics, particularly computers, also appear to fit this devolutionist pattern. Because the overall sectoral patterns do involve government credit in a central way, and also because the sectoral nuances have broader import for an understanding of Japanese government-business relations, we include product life-cycle case studies on government financial support to these industries.

STEEL

The steel industry was a relatively mature and established sector of the Japanese economy at the creation of the present-day government financial system in Japan after World War II. To both Japan's private sector and its industrial planners at that time, the need for the industry's reconstruction, as a central element of the Japanese economy's overall revival, was self-evident, so few complex strategic calculations were required. The industry had an enormous network of supporters within the Ministry of Commerce and Industry, as well as other parts of the government; indeed, the largest firm in the industry, Yawata Steel, had been operated continuously by the government since 1901. Support for steel seemed natural to almost all of Japan, although differences existed on whether marginal firms should receive it, as will be seen in chapter 6.

Under the priority-production policy of the early postwar period, the government-owned Reconstruction Finance Bank supplied the overwhelming share of capital for steel industry investments, as well as a producer subsidy equal to the difference between the cost of production and the decreed maximum price to consumers, generally less than production cost during this period.[19] Of the total capital invested in the steel industry during fiscal 1948, for example, nearly 80 percent was supplied by the RFB.[20] This constituted more than 40 percent of RFB loans to all industries combined.[21] Support to a national steel industry was, of course, nothing unusual, comparatively speaking, at this period. The British, French, Dutch, Belgian, and Italian governments all subsidized steel heavily after World War II. Even the United States used the government's Reconstruction Finance Corporation to make 380 loans, totaling $200 million, to the American steel industry from 1950 to 1953.[22]

After the demise of the Reconstruction Finance Bank from 1949 to 1952, levels of government support for the Japanese steel industry fell sharply, even though the sector's strategic importance to the nation as a whole had not changed. As figure 4-3 suggests, government funding from the Japan Development Bank, virtually the sole source of government financing for steel, provided only 8.2 percent of the funds for the first steel modernization program (1951–1955), and less than 6 percent for the second (1956–1960). Long-term credit bank funding was the largest single source of banking support for steel throughout the 1950s, although it fell significantly by 1960. As the steel industry moved out of direct reliance on government and long-term credit-bank funds, foreign-exchange loans, equity issues, and internally generated funds—all forms of private finance whose accessibility was a clear mark of industry maturity and stability—became correspondingly more important.

Support for the steel industry devolved to the private sector not due to any explicit government decision that the industry was no longer strategic, but due to the industry's increased ability to raise

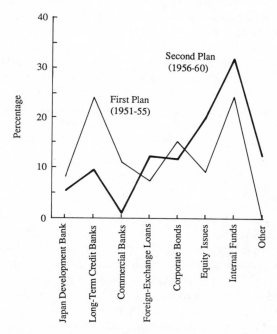

Figure 4-3. **Funding Sources for Steel Industry Modernization**

capital on its own and the attractiveness of autonomy to the private firms involved, once they had that capacity. The support of long-term credit banks made this transition easier in its early phase. The rising importance of private trust and insurance companies was also an important, if little noticed, factor. During the first two rationali-zation programs (1951–1960), loans from public and private sources combined had constituted roughly 50 percent of total funding for capital expenditures; during the third rationalization program (1961–1965), this share fell to 32 percent, with equity issues provid-ing nearly 27 percent of total financing. Thereafter internal funds and private loans grew in importance, and the government share of steel-industry funding declined into insignificance by the late 1960s.

In the steel industry's early post–World War II development, gov-ernment credit smoothly performed both strategic and indicative functions, in relation to established firms well known to govern-ment—to members, in other words, of its existing support network, or "circle of compensation."[23] It took little foresight for the state to see that steel in the 1950s and 1960s was important for the Japanese economy. Nor did it take much political effort to encourage state and private institutions that had been lending to Japan's established firms for a half century to continue to do so. Strategy in this sector simply amounted to routine action, involving little challenge to state organizational or political capacity. But government displayed less insight in dealing with smaller, yet technologically innovative firms with whom bureaucrats were not acquainted; one of Japan's most innovative oxygen producers, Amagasaki Steel, for example, went into receivership in 1954 as a result. Similarly, government ambivalence toward efficient new, would-be integrated producers beyond its established "circle of compensation," such as Kawasaki Steel in the early 1950s, also proved nearsighted, as chapter 6 suggests.

MACHINE TOOLS

Government lending policies in this sector, where state intervention has been considered crucially influential,[24] do not, in reality, as clearly recommend the strategic capabilities of the Japanese state as do its lending policies toward steel, although the political challenge confronting strategists was clearly a keener one. Government finan-cial assistance to the machine tool industry was, as in steel, propor-tionately higher, relative to total capital investment, in the very early stages of the industry's development than later on; a process of devolution to the private sector also occurred there over time.[25] In

1957, the year MITI's machine-tool rationalization program was introduced under the previous year's Extraordinary Measures Law for the Promotion of the Machine Industry (Kishin Hō), the government-run Japan Development Bank provided 33 percent of total industry financing.[26] The JDB supplied a ¥1.8 billion loan to the industry, to organize twenty-two companies into a rationalization cartel to increase specialization and upgrade products.[27] The industry thought the funds inadequate, and they fell sharply as a proportion of the industry total thereafter.

To a greater degree than in steel, there has been a pronounced *cyclical* flavor to government involvement in machine-tool corporate finance, driven in part by the cyclical character of capital spending in the industry as a whole. There was a second surge of sectoral reliance on government loans in 1962–1963, as an export drive in machine tools began to gather momentum; both MITI and the Japanese private sector saw export expansion as vitally necessary, since the import liberalization consequent on joining OECD was expected to hurt the balance of payments. The critical transition to numerical controls and robotics during the early 1970s, which involved fusing mechanical and electronics technologies and commercializing the mechatronic hybrid, was aided by expanded Japan Development Bank loans under the 1971 Kiden Hō.[28] But late 1970s government loans to machine tools were virtually zero. Although they did increase modestly again in the early 1980s, private expenditures surged much faster. In machine tools, as in steel, a process of devolution to the private sector took place.

Government finance had an important role in promoting the infant-industry development of machine tools in two respects. First, it was apparently used effectively to induce *strategic changes in industrial organization*, particularly to underwrite the 1957 rationalization cartel. This pattern seems to parallel that in the auto parts industry of the same period, as discussed in chapter 6, but to contrast that of steel, where firms were often too large and self-sufficient to be affected by such government efforts. In machine tools government loans were also used to direct the attention of small firms to the production of clearly defined specialty products, thus optimizing economies of scale throughout the industry, and to new products fusing established industrial technologies, as in the case of mechatronics.

Government lending also apparently played an *indicative function* for private-sector lending in the early stages of industry development, although the private sector typically did not expand its lending immediately after the government made its commitments.[29]

The major surges in private lending to machine tools appear to have followed two to three years after each major expansion of public financial commitments—during 1961 and during the late 1960s and early 1970s—with the government's macroeconomic policies, as well as broader economic prospects, strongly influencing how rapidly the private sector would follow the state's indicative lead. Thus government seems to have retained some capacity to influence strategic decisions of machine-tool firms, even as its share of total corporate funding declined. But the overall initiative in industry development—especially in expanding capacity and market share during cyclical upturns—lay with the private sector, especially as the industry matured.

COMPUTERS

Unlike steel, and to a lesser degree machine tools, the Japanese electronics industry did not clearly belong to the "circle of compensation" of the industrial-policy bureaucracy during early postwar days. Neither did it have strong ties to the prevailing *keiretsu* or long-term credit-bank structure, which dominated the allocation of private credit in Japan during the 1950s and the 1960s. As a consequence of its early outsider status, electronics was often forced to struggle for technology licenses, foreign-exchange authorization, tax benefits, and government credit, despite the considerable promise it was ultimately to demonstrate. Whereas the state often spontaneously introduced measures to support steel, shipbuilding, shipping, fertilizer, and even mining during the late 1940s and the 1950s, most early government support for the electronics industry emerged through private initiative.[30]

Until well into the late 1950s, the electronics industry had to struggle against a range of government measures intended to suppress it and redirect its financial resources elsewhere. Electronics was *not*, in short, a strategic priority of MITI from the very beginning, as evidenced by MITI's ambivalence about SONY's application for foreign exchange to obtain transistor patents in the early 1950s. The days of electronics in the orbit of state strategists came later.

In 1954, following the first American computer exports to Japan and the onset of licensed Japanese transistor production, private electronics manufacturers urged MITI to accelerate the development of indigenous computer technology. But it was not until 1957 that the first legislation specifically affecting computers, the Electronics Industry Development Provisional Act, became law. This law provided for research and development subsidies to promising technologies, government loans for products just entering production, and loans and accelerated depreciation for plant and equipment investment to rationalize production. But the total subsidies provided computers during the first five years (1957–1961) were less than $1 million;[31] the industry's cumulative total of loans, subsidies, and tax savings through accelerated depreciation to the computer industry came to less than $25 million even in 1970.

As in automobiles, the one early form of government leverage that was actively and effectively used in the early days of the Japanese computer industry was trade protectionism, although Japan's precarious current account position and the residue of early postwar exchange control meant that such protection required little active vision about the future of computers on the part of MITI itself. In 1961 IBM was allowed to set up manufacturing operations in Japan, in return for its extraordinarily generous agreement to cross-license basic computer patents to thirteen Japanese manufacturers, at no more than a 5 percent royalty,[32] and to yield to MITI administrative guidance with regard to production levels in Japan. The following year the Japanese private electronic makers once again approached MITI, to request help in offsetting IBM's highly successful computer leasing program with a similar program for Japanese-made computers, financed by the Japan Development Bank.[33] Thus was born, through private initiative, the Japan Electronic Computer Corporation (JECC), a joint venture among the six Japanese computer manufacturers to rent computers to end users. This venture was financed primarily by JDB funds, but they did not come in very large amounts until the mid-1960s.[34]

Although many early policy steps in the electronics industry were by private initiative, when a clearly definable external challenge appeared MITI moved reactively into strategic action. In computers, IBM's 1961 arrival in Japan and, more important, the sudden acquisition of France's preeminent domestic computer manufacturer, Machines Bull, by General Electric in 1964, together with the unveiling of the IBM 360 in the same year, were the catalysts for vigorous state action. Government loans from the Japan Development Bank to JECC to finance domestic computer purchases rose from ¥1.5 billion in 1963 to ¥7 billion in 1967, becoming the financial heart of this strategy for countering the IBM challenge.[35] In addition, in 1967 MITI encouraged the six domestic computer manufacturers and JECC to establish the Japan Information Processing Development Center (JIPDC). In 1969 MITI also pressed development of another joint undertaking, the Information Technology Promotion Agency, to promote software industry development, again with JDB funds.[36] With an initial capitalization of only $1.1 million, the venture made more than $30 million in debt financing possible to its clients during 1971, its second year of operation.[37]

JECC bought computers from the manufacturers (IBM was not invited to join) and sold them back to the manufacturers at JECC book value when returned by the end user. Throughout the 1960s JECC was by far the single largest form of government financial support for the Japanese electronics industry.[38] But during the 1970s devolution toward private-sector finance, paralleling trends in steel and machine tools, began to occur. As is indicated in figure 4-4, by 1980 JECC purchases, although continuously growing, had declined to just over 15 percent of total Japanese computer industry sales, and before 1990 they had fallen under 10 percent. The decline was triggered during the 1970s by the emergence of direct leasing to customers by the two major computer manufacturers, Hitachi and Fujitsu, insofar as the cash flow of those firms permitted. As a bureaucratic creation, JECC had a fixed-price policy; large users wanted better prices, and competitive pressures led the major producers to accommodate them, even though doing so undercut JECC.[39] Narrowing cost differentials between JDB and commercial funds as the Japanese financial system gradually began to liberalize further undercut JECC's competitive position, leading to rapidly declining corporate reliance on this government institution.

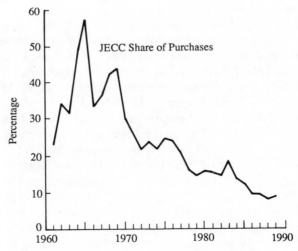

Figure 4-4. JECC Finance and Japanese Computer Sales

During the 1970s MITI tried to use government finance strategically to force reorganization of the Japanese computer industry into three large groups, specializing in such areas as mainframes and peripheral equipment. Although it had succeeded earlier with this strategy in auto parts, and to some degree in machine tools, it failed in computers.[40] Japan's large computer manufacturers were simply too powerful politically and had too many sources of alternate financing to be intimidated by bureaucratic sanctions. The rising liquidity of the Japanese economy in the 1970s also blunted the strategic efficacy for MITI of government finance.

Although government finance failed in computers as a tool of industrial reorganization, it was more successful in basic research, as it had been in stimulating market demand for domestic machines through JECC. This success was shown in such focused efforts as support for the VLSI memory chip and semiconductor production equipment projects of 1976–1980.[41] During the 1980s government loan/subsidy programs in the research area, whereby corporations would borrow money from public entities and repay them only if the research in question was commercially successful, became increasingly common. Indeed, this type of program became one of the most important mechanisms by which Japanese industrial policy sought to diffuse the risk of capital-intensive research projects in high technology. The role of government finance in Japanese computer industry finance has thus been gradually declining over time—devolving funding responsibility onto the private sector. But it has retained a niche in the research-and-development area, in intimate collaboration with private capital.

Considering government credit policies toward the steel, machine tool, and computer industries collectively, it is clear that devolution proceeded most smoothly in the case of a sector dominated by large firms that had relatively strong ties to private-sector long-term credit banks (for example, steel). Where the firms in question were small, with poorer financial ties of their own, as in machine tools, it was more difficult for government to disentangle itself from their financial activities. In technologically volatile sectors such as computers, research and development created a continuing rationale for government involvement. But none of these three sectors was geographically concentrated, intensively regulated, or otherwise structurally linked to politics and administration—in contrast to shipping, mining, railways, and oil refining. Only technological pressures sustained the state role. In the absence of clientelism this state role gradually declined, except where the technological rationale continued to provoke some state involvement.

The Problem of Venture Capital

The preceding pages have suggested that the ability of government credit to address industrial problems in Japan has depended profoundly on the nature of the problem being addressed and the sort of decision making capacity it demands of government. When the problem requires only passive, routine, status quo management, as occurred in relatively mature industries like steel in the 1950s, or when it involves neutrally providing externalities such as infrastructure and basic technology, government can do fairly well. When the national challenge is dramatic and threatening enough to galvanize a politically unified response even in an emerging industry—computers and oil refining are good examples—government has also done well.

The problems come when the issue is less clearly definable, more politically controversial, or requires complex organizational coordination—hallmarks increasingly of globally emergent infant industries. What Japanese government credit has never been able to do effectively, from the 1950s to the 1990s, has been to serve as a catalyst bringing capital into new, nonestablished industries, or to new, innovative firms within existing sectors, in venture capitalist fashion. Government, in short, has found it difficult to move flexibly beyond its established range of associations except in the event of grave, broadly recognized political or economic crisis that mandates broader inclusiveness.

The list of promising infant sectors and firms ignored in their earliest, most vulnerable days is a long one—Toyota Motors and Kawasaki Steel in 1950, SONY and the oxygen-furnace steel producer Amagasaki Steel in 1954, television producers as late as 1956, and Sharp in electronics in the 1960s. In 1990 the Japan Development Bank extended loans to only one major pharmaceutical manufacturer, Green Cross, despite the rising prospective importance of that sector in a rapidly aging Japan. Such relatively small but promising high-technology companies as Fanuc and Hitachi Seiki got no assistance at all from the JDB.[42] As late as 1984 Japan's entire biotechnology industry, a strategically important emerging sector, had yet to receive any financing from either the JDB or the Small Business Finance Corporation.[43]

This strategic blind spot of Japanese government finance toward many emerging sectors flows directly from a more general feature of Japanese social, economic, and political life: the importance of "circles of compensation."[44] These networks of reciprocal benefit and obligation bind both government officials and private businesspersons to established people and projects at the expense of the more entrepreneurial. Japanese government banks, perhaps even more than those of the private sector, have historically had great difficulty admitting new members to their circles of compensation, just as they have found it difficult to cast out those who have been accepted as a legitimate object of government attention. This has not been simply a matter of culture; more immediately and directly, it has been a result of structure and organizational mission. The difficulties are posed clearly in the case of the Japan Development Bank (JDB), which has been conventionally seen as a primary tool of the Japanese developmental state.

The JDB was born in the spring of 1951, a turbulent period of reconstruction, retrenchment, and speculation just after the onset of the Korean War. Japan was still under Occupation, and memories of the inflationary excesses of JDB's predecessor, the entrepreneurial Reconstruction Finance Bank, were still fresh in the minds of Finance Minister Ikeda Hayato and the conservative SCAP financial adviser Joseph Dodge, who oversaw JDB's creation.[45] Not surprisingly, its founding law, which powerfully configured the JDB's operations over the years, reflected the prudent, risk-averse bias of these two "regulators," Ikeda and Dodge. Article 18, for example, clearly states that "the making of loans . . . may be conducted only when the redemption of funds to be loaned . . . are deemed certain."[46] The law also mandates that the bank "make loan of funds which are difficult to obtain from other banks and financial institutions as necessary,"[47] but only subject to the recoverability clause. The JDB was further restricted in its operations by provisions that rates of interest be uniform for all loans in a particular category (Article 19), that the JDB not compete with other banks in conducting its business (Article 22), and that it be compelled to remit profits to the National Treasury as provided by cabinet order (Article 36). The JDB's parameters for lending have also been constrained by the reality that the framework for its policy loan categories is established by legislation. Although relevant laws are invariably drafted by the bureaucracy, they take time to prepare and pass through a sometimes fractious Diet,[48] inhibiting early JDB intervention in infant sectors.

The JDB lent overwhelmingly in its early days to manufacturing industries such as steel, together with such related basic sectors as shipping, electric utilities, and the private railway system. It lent *not* as a market-oriented private lender, but as an agent of government, giving authoritative signals upon which the private sector could expect to rely. But its mandate, to reiterate, was to do so only provided that public funds—ultimately flowing from the postal savings of the Japanese public—were not to be lost. In its earliest days, particularly under the first steel modernization program (1951–1955), the JDB relied surprisingly little on its own credit evaluation; IBJ personnel on secondment, together with MITI's *genkyoku*, provided some analysis, and the firms in question were in any event large, with well-established national reputations. IBJ credit evaluators continued to be dispatched via secondment to aid the JDB right down to 1970.

As a result of its own unique institutional history and its legal mandate, the Japan Development Bank—contrary to the conventional wisdom and despite a specific responsibility to socialize risk—became decidedly *risk averse rather than risk taking*. It abhorred the prospect of bankruptcy, no matter how noble the cause, and rarely lent to firms with any prospect of financial difficulty, no matter how innovative. Like MOF and the Bank of Japan, it came to behave as a "regulator" more than as a "strategist."

A review of microlevel incentives in operation is crucial to understanding JDB's behavior. As a bureaucracy, the JDB shared the generic impulse of bureaucrats toward uncertainty avoidance.[49] Its specific institutional responsibility of definitively judging long-term projects—the more uncertain the further their time horizon—accentuated its tendency toward caution and painful deliberation. And there was no easy way of rewarding JDB, as there was with a private bank, for the risks it took. The interest rates of the JDB were generally lower than those of private banks, and they were set by policy rather than by market criteria, as noted above, denying its leadership both financial rewards and politically important discretion. Furthermore, the JDB was prohibited from demanding compensating balances, which allowed private banks to vary their effective interest rates even when nominal rates were under government control.

So although the Japan Development Bank was created to foster strategic industries, including infant sectors, it found playing a venture-capitalist role difficult. Neither the Japan Export-Import Bank, the Housing Loan Corporation, nor any of the regional-development institutions played such a venture-capitalist role either. Japan has, it is true, three government banks established specifically to aid small business, but they fill largely political functions, or aid the subcontractors of major established companies. The bulk of People's Finance Corporation loans, for example, have since 1974 been tendered on an unusual noncollateralized basis to more than two million small, often unstable firms, on the mere recommendation of LDP Diet members and the formalistic recommendation of local chamber of commerce officials serving as a front for conservative

political interests.[50] The Small Business Finance Corporation con-
centrates on providing loans to existing big-business subsidiaries
and affiliates for modernization and rationalization. None of the established government banks was created to meet the need for venture capital, nor is any particularly suited to do so. These institutions thus compound rather than offset the dominant conservative
bias of the government ministries.

To be sure, MITI has abstractly recognized the potential of venture
capital to further the development of small high-technology firms in
Japan, at least since the mid-1960s.[51] Three semipublic small business investment companies (SBICs) were set up in Tokyo, Nagoya,
and Osaka under provisions of the Small Business Investment Law of
1963, inspired by the American Small Business Investment Act of
1958. But the SBICs, jointly owned by prefectural and local authorities, as well as large banks, have always been cautious and conservative in their operations.[52] They may only, for example, invest in div-
idend-paying enterprises and in those that intend to offer their
shares to the public. In 1975 MITI also established the Venture Enterprise Center (VEC) to guarantee loans for development and to dissem-
inate information on venture capital. But its scope of operations has
been small, with only ¥8.5 billion in guarantees extended over its
first ten years of operation.[53]

As Japanese technological levels moved closer and closer to the
global frontiers during the 1970s and early 1980s, and as foreign
firms became increasingly wary of the competitive consequences of
licensing to their Japanese counterparts, the national strategic need
to foster domestic research and development within Japan became
more evident and acute. Policy changes encouraged existing public
institutions to reflect this priority in their lending; the Japan Development Bank Law, for example, was revised in 1985 to authorize
financing for research and development costs in the precommerciali-
zation stages that were associated with product development. The
JDB's loans for the development of technology rose 32 percent between 1981 and 1985, to 7.5 percent of the total loans outstanding.[54]
But the overwhelming majority of these JDB loans, as at other government financial institutions, went to established companies for
the commercialization of existing, even if new, technologies such as
value-added networks, cable television, industrial production of
software, and transmission systems for communities with new
media facilities.[55]

With existing institutions becoming conservative, the Japanese
policy response to the new strategic challenge of technological development was, as in so many previous cases, institutional prolifera-

tion: the creation of hybrid public-private research support institutions, many established at private initiative. An early version was the Information Technology Promotion Agency (IPA), a special juridical affiliate of MITI established with funding from MITI, the Japan Software Association, the Japan Information Processing Center Association, the six largest computer manufacturers, and the three long-term credit banks. The structure and the funding procedures of the IPA are indicated in figure 4-5. Between 1970 and 1979 the IPA granted a total of ¥43.5 billion in software development loans, 75 percent of them to software houses themselves—generally small venture-type firms.[56] By 1992 its lending had expanded modestly to ¥5.6 billion annually, with special emphasis on supporting automation of software production and development of distribution-sector software applications.[57]

Mixed public-private ventures have also been active in the energy area. Born in 1980 in the shadow of the second Oil Shock in order to aid Japan in diversifying away from its heavy dependence on im-

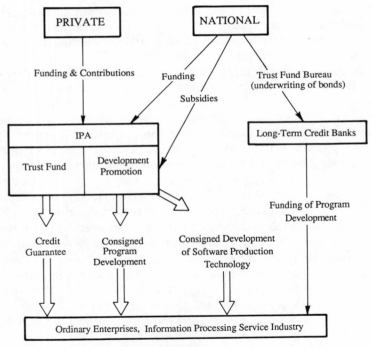

Figure 4-5. The Information-Technology Promotion Agency: Flow of Funds
Source: Japan Information Processing Development Center, *Computer White Paper* (Tokyo: JIPDC, 1980), 36.

ported oil, the New Energy Development Organization (NEDO) emerged from private-sector resistance to MITI efforts to establish a new public energy corporation.[58] Headed by private-sector executives on secondment from their firms, but with some funding from the government's FILP, NEDO engages in basic synfuels and other alternate energy research.

Potentially the most significant of the new public-private funding agencies for high technology is the Japan Key Technology Center, founded through private initiative. Following passage, in February 1985, of the Law for the Facilitation of Research in Fundamental Technologies, a broad range of private-sector business leaders combined, at Keidanren's suggestion, to formally propose this center's establishment to MITI and MPT. The center, which came formally into being on October 1, 1985, received funds from three sources: (1) sale of shares in public corporations, principally Nippon Telephone and Telegraph; (2) government financial institutions, especially the Japan Development Bank; and (3) private corporations. The Key Tech Center lends these funds to private firms, including startups, to support research and development projects in fields ranging from biotechnology and steel production to futuristic aircraft engines, with individual projects organized at private initiative. By the late 1980s Japanese subsidiaries of Digital Equipment, IBM, and Hoffman–La Roche, among other foreign firms, were involved in research consortia funded by the center, which had disbursed ¥32 billion ($256 million) in capital to research groups in the first three years after its 1985 inception.[59] In fiscal 1992, as noted in Appendix II, the Key Tech Center's budget was around ¥31.6 billion, with 82 percent of this coming from public sources. Interest on the loans disbursed is due only if a given research and development project is successful. The center's operational funding structure is presented in figure 4-6.

Whether mixed public-private funding and research supervision bodies such as IPA, NEDO, and the Japan Key Technology Center will be sufficient to meet Japan's grave strategic need to generate creative new technology is still unclear. The private venture capital market in Japan expanded rapidly during the early 1980s, its total investments rising from a stake of $260 million in less than eight hundred companies during 1981 to $1.06 billion in more than three thousand companies by the end of 1985,[60] continuing to surge throughout the latter half of the 1980s, until meeting the tight credit, falling stock prices, and ultimately recession of 1990–1992. But the Japanese venture capital market remained tiny compared to its U.S. counterpart, only one-fifteenth the U.S. scale in the mid-1980s, with few tax in-

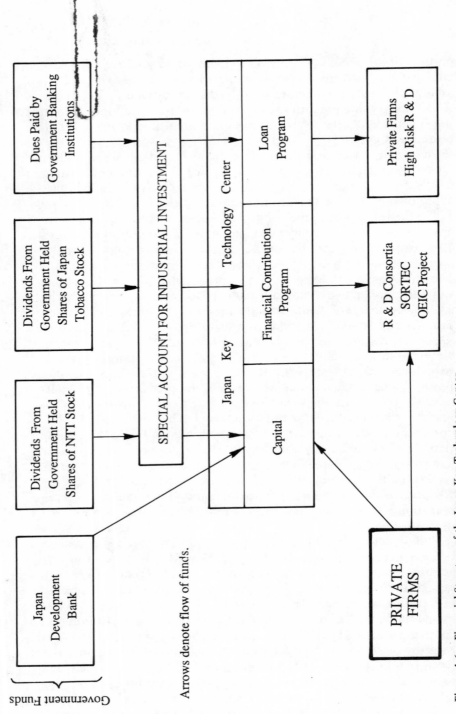

Figure 4-6. Financial Structure of the Japan Key Technology Center
Sources: Japan Key Technology Center, unpublished materials. National Science Foundation, Tokyo Office, Report Memorandum No. 91 (January 16, 1986), *Japan Key Technology Center.*

centives to encourage it and registration requirements in the local over-the-counter market (established in 1983) substantially more stringent than in the United States.[61] Whether public direction— even in the form of public-private joint enterprise—can do an efficient job of supplying capital to fledgling new firms at the research- and-development, as opposed to the commercialization, stage of industrial development remains questionable.

The Internationalization of Japanese Government Finance

In an era of declining capital investment demand and rising domestic liquidity, and with hybrid public-private bodies increasingly active in furthering public purposes in high-technology finance, Japan's government financial institutions have found themselves in ever more insistent search of a new role. The Japan Development Bank, for example, was originally established in 1951 to promote "economic reconstruction and industrial development"; by 1980 only 28 percent of its loans were going to manufacturing industry.[62] The Japan Export-Import Bank, founded originally to sustain the exports of a chronic deficit nation in the early 1950s, was directing only 39 percent of its financing to exports by 1978.[63]

In an era of both rapidly rising global economic interdependence and sustained expansion in the offshore operations of Japanese firms, government finance during the 1980s took on an increasingly international cast. A hand was extended to foreign firms in whose operations Japan had some political or strategic interest. Government finance also became progressively more closely integrated with Japan's foreign aid programs, which likewise served both political and strategic-industrial goals.

Japanese industrial policy, including strategic credit policy, long explicitly discriminated against foreign firms. For example, IBM and other outside computer manufacturers were pointedly not asked to participate in the government-supported computer leasing program (JECC) at its inception in 1961. Foreigners were also excluded from such government financed projects as FONTAC, VLSI, and the Fourth Generation Computer Subsidy project, all of which were designed to aid domestic electronics producers to catch up with IBM.

In the early 1980s, however, a new policy function began emerging for Japanese government financial institutions—helping foreign firms, particularly in high technology, to set up operations in Japan and assisting them in joint venture projects with Japanese firms that were of policy interest to Japan. Rising international trade tensions and a desire for continued access to foreign markets were making assistance to foreign firms attractive from a diplomatic point of view, and the opportunity to introduce new foreign technology into Japan through these foreign affiliates was also becoming increasingly attractive from the perspective of industrial strategy, as Japan moved rapidly toward global technological frontiers. Declining demand from Japanese firms for government credit, due to the increasing availability of alternate low-cost private funding, made such gestures toward foreigners less controversial within Japan. For foreign firms, cooperation with government institutions like the Japan Development Bank was conversely a significant way to enhance their legitimacy within Japan, totally apart from any possible financial benefits.

As excess liquidity within the Japanese economy grew, and alternative business opportunities with Japanese domestic firms began to decline, Japanese government loans and other assistance to foreign firms steadily increased. In 1981 the government indicated that foreign firms might be included in most government-sponsored research and development projects if they wished and could meet objective eligibility criteria. In 1982 the Japan Development Bank approved a major loan to Schlumberger-Fairchild for the building of an electronic components plant at Isahaya in Nagasaki prefecture. In fiscal 1983 the JDB initiated a special program of loans to help the subsidiaries of foreign firms finance plant and equipment investments in Japan, extending nine loans worth ¥5 billion. By 1987 JDB loans to foreign subsidiaries in Japan had nearly tripled, rising more than 100 percent in fiscal 1987 to the equivalent of $229 million.[64]

Among the major borrowers was Intel Japan, which used its loan to set up facilities for stocking imported integrated circuits in Tōyōsato-cho, Ibaraki prefecture. Other investments have been in such diverse fields as computers and semiconductors; pharmaceuticals; chemicals; and metal processing, with about 60 percent of the loans going to U.S. firms. The JDB has also strongly supported the Boeing 777 U.S.-Japan aircraft joint venture to develop an advanced 4200-mile-range, 400-seat wide-body passenger plane by 1995, financing around 20 percent of the development work for the project as a whole.[65]

Aside from lending more heavily to foreign firms operating within Japan, MOF also began in the late 1980s to support expanding transfers to developing nations, both directly from the Trust Fund Bureau and through loans from major government financial institutions. In March 1987 the ministry announced its intention to use ¥6 billion in such funds for fiscal 1987, and a total of ¥30 billion over three years, to purchase yen-denominated World Bank development assistance bonds, and to donate the proceeds back to the World Bank gratis as

Japanese foreign aid. The MOF also agreed to approve the issue in Tokyo capital markets of a total of ¥330 billion in World Bank development bonds, with the ¥300 billion not absorbed by MOF itself to be purchased by private investors.[66]

Even more significantly, Japan in 1986–1987 announced a program to greatly accelerate the flow of direct Japanese government lending to support projects being carried out in developing nations. At the World Bank-IMF annual meeting in the fall of 1986, Finance Minister Miyazawa Kiichi announced Japan's intention to encourage the flow of public and private financial resources to the middle-income countries through large-scale untied loans, including co-financing with the World Bank. Early in 1987 Prime Minister Nakasone Yasuhiro announced further details, including $12 billion in untied loans by the Overseas Economic Cooperation Fund and, most important, the Japan Export-Import Bank, over a three-year period. Six billion dollars of this money was to consist of untied Export-Import Bank loans co-financed with multilateral development banks such as the Asian Development Bank and the Inter-American Development Bank, while a further $3 billion was to be untied project-finance loans supplied through the Export-Import Bank in cooperation with private Japanese banks.[67]

Following the completion of this program in 1990, aid-related Japanese government lending continued to rise. In fiscal 1991 it reached ¥775 billion (well over $5 billion), or nearly 51 percent of Japanese overseas development assistance—this figure was more than triple the scale of such development lending in 1987.[68] Many of the project finance loans were directly linked to overseas investment projects of Japanese corporations or to associated infrastructure. Well over half of total FILP lending was committed in Asia, prime beneficiary of the post-1985 outward surge in Japanese foreign investment. But there were also numerous major projects under way throughout the world, including a $1 billion program for environmental assistance to Mexico announced by Prime Minister Toshiki Kaifu in 1989, and feasibility studies regarding multibillion-dollar Export-Import Bank loans for Sakhalin energy development, announced in 1992.

PUBLIC ACTION AND PRIVATE CAPITAL: AN ASSESSMENT OF ALLOCATION EFFORTS

The Japanese state has been ambivalent about trying to direct private capital toward "priority" sectors. The Ministry of Finance and the Bank of Japan, as good financial regulators rather than industrial strategists, have concerned themselves mainly with the solvency of the private banks, rather than with their portfolios per se. They have had little underlying interest in "developmental" transformation of the Japanese industrial base.

This has left MITI as the chief public agent of strategic industrial transformation. The ministry's principal advisory body on intersectoral industrial finance has been the Industrial Capital Subcommittee (Sangyō Shikin Bukai) of the Industrial Structure Deliberation Council (Sangyō Kōzō Shingikai). This group formally includes members from private business, journalism, and academia, although the staff work has always been done by MITI. From 1959 to 1969, the height of the high-growth, low-interest-rate period when qualitative credit allocation was most explicitly practiced, the Industrial Capital Subcommittee issued explicit, published recommendations regarding capital spending in key industries. These guidelines, compared with the sector-specific investment plans of the private sector before state intervention, are summarized in table 4-2.

Table 4-2 suggests several concrete generalizations about MITI's attempts to influence private-sector credit flows:

1. Efforts at explicit allocation continued only for a limited period of time. These efforts were most pervasive across sectors during the 1961–1964 period, while Sahashi Shigeru, a firm believer in state-led industrial mobilization, was serving as MITI's Enterprise Bureau director general. They were less pervasive before 1961 and after 1965; after 1969 explicit guidelines disappear entirely from MITI's major publications on capital investment and are generally conceded by specialists in such matters to have been relaxed.

2. The attempts of MITI to control the private sector were limited to *suppression* of what MITI believed was *excessive* capital spending: MITI apparently did *not* explicitly *encourage additional spending* in areas of special promise. Tax policies indirectly encouraged investment in some areas of special social priority, such as pollution-control equipment after 1970, but credit allocation itself was apparently not used for such purposes. Even tax policy was a relatively blunt and sporadically used tool for encouraging industrial transformation.[69]

3. Apparently MITI had remarkably little empathy in its industrial credit policies for clearly emerging sectors of the future, in many instances due to a preoccupation with its established circles of compensation. Private-sector investment in the automobile industry, for example, was systematically cut back throughout the 1960–1965 period, when that sector was first emerging as an international competitor. The thrust of MITI's control effort was to suppress smaller firms, such as Honda, Tōyō Kōgyō, and Isuzu, with which it had relatively distant

TABLE 4-2
Private Ambition and Public Restraint:
Proposed Allocation Cutbacks, 1959–1969
(percentage of private-sector projected capacity expansion)

Industry	1959	1960	1961	1962	1963	1964	1965	1966	1967	1968	1969
Petrochemicals	19.1	37.7	30.6	28.8	13.8	20.7	12.3	5.3	19.6	31.3	5.9
Synthetic textiles	19.0	13.4	1.7	27.2	10.5	11.1	5.8	—	5.2	—	—
Fertilizer	17.2	8.3	16.2	12.9	11.4	9.0	11.6	—	—	—	—
Automobiles	—	6.2	10.4	20.3	3.8	20.1	4.4	—	—	—	—
Steel	16.6	7.1	5.0	23.0	4.0	7.8	4.1	4.5	8.6	17.2	—
Oil refining	13.2	16.0	8.4	40.1	27.5	28.6	2.0	—	8.5	7.5	3.5
Coal	8.9	—	—	0.2	3.1	8.7	1.7	—	2.6	—	—
Paper/pulp	8.8	6.4	8.2	14.4	0.2	24.8	12.5	4.8	11.9	12.3	5.3
Electric power	1.8	0.7	0.2	8.4	1.2	—	—	—	4.8	4.0	1.5
Electrical machinery	—	7.1	—	—	—	—	—	—	—	—	—
Electrical industry	—	5.0	9.0	18.9	—	10.5	—	—	—	—	—
Cement	—	—	16.5	—	6.4	—	—	—	—	—	—
Nonferrous metals	—	—	3.2	16.9	15.5	28.0	2.5	—	—	14.5	
Electric cable	—	—	—	—	—	4.3	3.5	—	—	2.3	—

Source: MITI Enterprise Bureau, Shuyō Sangyō no Setsubi Toshi Dōkō (Capital Investment in Basic Industries), 1959–70 eds.

Note: "Electrical industry" refers to consumer electronics, whereas "electrical machinery" denotes computers and heavy electrical equipment.

relations and that it felt could not become competitive; these ultimately became some of Japan's most innovative producers. The parallels are striking to its earlier neglect of maverick outsiders in the steel industry, such as Kawasaki Steel, Sumitomo Metals, and Amagasaki Steel.

4. The ministry was also remarkably tolerant of some clear "sunset" sectors with which its officials had longstanding ties. By the late 1950s the need for a steady transition from coal to oil in Japan, for example, was clear.[70] Yet MITI did not begin actively suppressing coal-industry capital investment until 1962–1965, and cut it much less sharply than in the emerging auto sector, not to mention oil refining, where cutbacks were severe throughout the 1960s.

5. The sharpest cutbacks by MITI were reserved for industries, especially oil refining and petrochemicals, where the presence of major *keiretsu* (for example, Mitsubishi, Mitsui, and Sumitomo) and foreign capital—both relatively distant from the political and interpersonal network of the bureaucracy during this period[71]—was especially strong.

The overall role of MITI with respect to industrial credit thus appears to have been *less strategy*—that is, clearly picking winners and losers and discriminating between them—*than stability*, both within sectors and between them.[72] Across sectors MITI acted not so much to foresee the future—leaving that more to the private sector than generally appreciated—as to ease the transition to a future chosen by private firms themselves. Within major sectors MITI's overall role was typically curbing oligopolistic rivalry and slowing the ascent of newcomers, while also inhibiting the expansion of foreign affiliates. Whatever its developmental aspirations, MITI's actions, in short, were remarkably conservative—protecting its existing circle of compensation, while trying to inhibit outside efforts, both by Japanese *keiretsu* and foreign firms, to revise the status quo.

As a study in political analysis, the focus of this research is necessarily on government decision rather than economic outcomes per se. But it is highly relevant to our transcendent theme of private-sector initiative and influence on economic outcomes to note that MITI's credit-allocation efforts were often subverted or ignored. As indicated in table 4-3, actual capital spending in many Japanese industries during the 1960s well exceeded MITI's guidelines, even during a period generally agreed to be one of relatively pronounced MITI bureaucratic influence.

The divergence of actual capital spending from MITI's guidelines appears to have been greatest in the following sorts of cases:

1. Capital-intensive sectors characterized by oligopolistic rivalry and strong ties to private banks. During periods of economic expansion, such as 1959–1960 or the late 1960s, steel, cement, and petrochemical producers, for example, began to compete fiercely for future market share, ignoring MITI's investment guidelines in the process. This was the fabled "excess competition" (*katō kyōso*) of which MITI often complained. Such excess competition and associated violation of MITI lending guidelines were much less frequent in sectors such as electric power, where *keiretsu* ties were weaker and microeconomic expansionary pressures on industrial firms were less pronounced than in heavy industry.

2. Sectors combining weak historical ties to bureaucracy and strong long-term credit-banking relationships—automobiles, heavy electrical equipment, computers, and consumer electronics, for example. With strong, independent private-sector banking ties, these sectors could afford to treat MITI's conservative "balance"-oriented guidelines lightly and to expand in response to market forces even against MITI's wishes. Not surprisingly, these sectors are among Japan's most internationally competitive today.

This chapter's theme of public-sector conservatism leaves important questions unanswered. From whence did the demonstrable flex-

TABLE 4-3

The Limits of Government Restraint: Public Guidelines and Private Investment Behavior, 1959–1970 (percentage divergence of actual private investment behavior from previous year's Industrial Capital Subcommittee annual guidelines for that year)

	1959	1960	1961	1962	1963	1964	1965	1966	1967	1968
Petrochemicals	+1.1	−8.7	+4.0	−14.9	−16.9	−15.5	−8.7	−10.0	+0.1	+38.8
Synthetic textiles	−19.7	−1.1	−1.5	+3.3	+11.7	+47.6	−19.7	+12.0	+9.3	+13.1
Fertilizer	−14.2	−9.5	−5.4	—	−4.3	−2.4	−13.1	−8.6	−1.7	+3.3
Automobiles	+29.3	+27.2	−7.3	−4.4	−0.1	−1.7	−8.1	+0.7	+18.4	+13.6
Steel	−2.2	+21.4	−9.5	−2.1	−0.4	−5.9	−4.9	+15.5	+13.9	+22.0
Oil refining	+3.9	+32.0	−13.5	−7.2	−4.6	+2.4	−8.9	+0.0	+2.6	+4.8
Coal	−5.4	−8.6	—	—	−15.3	+5.2	+4.1	−5.1	+13.5	−4.9
Paper/pulp	+17.7	1.6	−21.2	−14.1	−8.4	—	+0.0	+6.5	−2.7	+11.5
Electric power	+4.5	+6.3	−3.9	−8.5	−6.6	−4.0	+0.4	+0.0	+1.2	+10.8
Electrical machinery	—	+37.4	+5.7	+7.9	−18.1	+60.6	−20.9	+5.2	−29.5	+40.4
Electrical industry	—	+19.5	−9.8	−12.9	−2.5	+4.1	−2.7	+29.5	+12.5	+24.0
Cement	—	+13.3	−11.9	−11.9	+5.7	−7.2	−20.0	+1.7	+13.7	+30.0
Nonferrous metals	—	+25.9	—	—	—	−19.9	−0.7	+11.1	+3.6	+21.5
Electric cable	—	—	—	—	—	−22.7	+4.9	−10.9	+3.6	+34.3
Auto tires	—	—	—	—	—	+21.8	−6.5	−15.9	+11.2	+28.6
All industries	+11.5	+6.9	+0.8	−1.2	−5.6	−1.6	−7.3	+2.7	+10.4	+17.2

Source: MITI Enterprise Bureau, *Shuyō Sangyō no Setsubi Toshi Dōkō* (Capital Investment in Basic Industries), 1959–70 eds.

ibility and farsightedness of the Japanese political economy, which positioned Japan deftly and consistently in high-growth, high value-added sectors of the future, arise? To the extent that key industrial-credit decisions originated outside the state itself, what sort of private institutions and processes were responsible for making them? How did a state more divided and passive and a private sector more cohesive and strategic than conventional wisdom suggests actually interact?

Is there an alternative to the hypothesis of state developmental leadership, which loses some plausibility when the concrete actions of the state itself are considered in detail? Such questions require detailed consideration of private-sector institutions and processes of industrial-credit decision making, to which we turn in the following two chapters. They are a crucial aspect of Japan's distinctive strategic capitalism.

Private Financiers and Public Functions

JAPANESE CAPITALISM has clearly done a remarkable job of promoting economic growth and structural transformation toward higher value-added industries. What needs further examination are the mechanisms that have been centrally responsible for this unexampled performance. Chalmers Johnson presents MITI as the central agent—indeed, virtually the sole orchestrator—of the Japanese economic miracle. Yet the foregoing pages, considering both government structure and actual public-policy performance in the area of industrial credit, have presented a different picture. They have portrayed an often hesitant, reactive Japanese state whose industrial strategists, despite their at times visionary instincts, lacked the power to unilaterally transform Japan, even at the high point of controls in the 1950s and 1960s.

If MITI's role as the catalyst for Japanese economic transformation—or that of the Japanese state more generally—has been overexaggerated, where shall we then look for explanations for a success that is so palpably obvious in narrowly economic terms? This work cannot answer that sweeping question in its entirety. But we can say that to understand how Japanese credit has been allocated over the fifty years and more since the earliest introduction of state controls—indeed, to grasp the most fundamental origins of Japan's remarkable economic growth and industrial transformation—it is vital to grasp the workings of the private sector and its relationship to public policy. Private institutions, as in West European corporatist democracies such as Germany, have often played important "para-public" functions,[1] in what often resembles, to return to the typology of our introductory chapter, a system of "corporate-led strategic capitalism" more than it does a "developmental state."

One particular contribution of the Japanese private sector deserves special emphasis—its ability, especially during the high-growth period, to identify promising sectors and firms in the capital-intensive portion of the economy and aggressively to mobilize the financial resources, the marketing skills, and the technology to foster international competitive success through large capacity increases and market-share gains at key moments in the industrial life cycle. This ability has been graphically evident in many of the sectors of greatest Japanese competitive success, such as automobiles and consumer electronics, where the role of state industrial policy has generally been quite limited.

Especially crucial in the financial dimension to this competitive success were the long-term credit banks, especially the Industrial Bank of Japan. As will be seen later in this chapter, the IBJ combined analytical capacities, long-term vision, strong networks of personal ties to borrower firms, extensive understanding of their potential, and the related capacity to raise large sums of "dedicated" capital, committed for long periods without clear short-term prospects of high return.[2] Government banks were more constrained in their operations, especially early in the product life cycle, by complex internal bureaucratic decision making, lack of technical expertise, and dependence for lending authorization on an established legal framework mandating policy loans for the sector in question, as had been noted. These flexible, farsighted qualities were crucial to the success of such diverse industries as steel, shipping, shipbuilding, petrochemicals, telecommunications equipment, and automobiles. In many of Japan's most competitive sectors, such as automobiles, IBJ's little-examined role was arguably both more farsighted and decisive than that of state industrial strategists at MITI.

The Japanese private sector as a whole was and continues to be unusually well organized and cohesive, with an articulate and mobilizing sense of its self-interest. With the partial exceptions of Sweden and Germany, there have been no close parallels elsewhere in the industrialized world to Japan's powerful private industrial groups and industrial banks, especially during the 1950s and 1960s.[3] Taken together with the powerful—if often passive—state institutions that evolved during the 1930s and 1940s, these cohesive private interests, together with the well-organized business federations and bankers' associations representing them, were at the core of Japan's "distinctive strategic capitalism," with corporate strategies unusually sensitive to long-range market logic and the concerns of the organized private sector. The deregulation and internationalization of the Japanese economy over the past two decades have only intensified this pattern of powerful private-sector influence in economic transformation.

To be sure, the major commercial and industrial banks of Japan have enjoyed important mutual interests with the state in the common ground of the broad national regulatory structure, as was true of the great steel, electric power, and other basic-industry firms.[4] At the microlevel this has frequently enabled them to order policy in certain directions uniquely beneficial to themselves. To this end they had at their disposal not only the political resources of the private-interest-group associations, but the information and operating expertise mobilized by the industrial group structure—often greater than that available to the state itself. The centrality and influence of these private institutions in the operation of the financial system—and beyond into the political economy as a whole—was such that we may speak of Japan from the early postwar years through the high-growth period as a Bankers' Kingdom.

THE BANKERS' KINGDOM: AN OVERVIEW IN COMPARATIVE PERSPECTIVE

The classical Japanese private-sector financial arrangments of roughly 1946–1970 had six distinctive systemic characteristics with special relevance for business-government relations: (1) the predominance of indirect financing, making bank loans the principal form of corporate finance, (2) controlled domestic interest rates, (3) exchange controls to prevent international arbitrage, (4) imbalance of liquidity between city banks and other elements of the financial system, (5) overloans from the Bank of Japan to the city banks to cover some portion of their funds shortage, and (6) a bifurcated system of private financial intermediaries, with city banks lending to large corporations and local or *shinkin* banks to small-scale industry. The major features of this Bankers' Kingdom are shown in figure 5-1.

Throughout the early postwar and high-growth periods, Japanese corporations were conspicuously more reliant on bank borrowings than was common in the other major industrialized nations. From 1966 to 1970, for example, Japanese corporations borrowed 49 percent of their entire funds demand from banks, compared to 29.6 percent in West Germany, 27.4 percent in France, 12.4 percent in the United States, and only 10.3 percent in the United Kingdom.[5] Reliance on equity and corporate debt issues in Japan was conversely much lower than in the West, due in part to regulatory constraints; the cost to the firm of these alternate modes of finance was in many instances actually less than that of bank borrowing. Tait Ratcliffe argues, for example, that corporate debt offerings would have been significantly cheaper for Japanese firms of this period than bank borrowings, particularly when compensating balances are taken into consideration.[6] Self-financing in Japan was also less developed than in any other major industrialized nation, the ratios in 1970 being 25.8 percent for Japan, 28.6 percent for Italy, 30.5 percent for France,

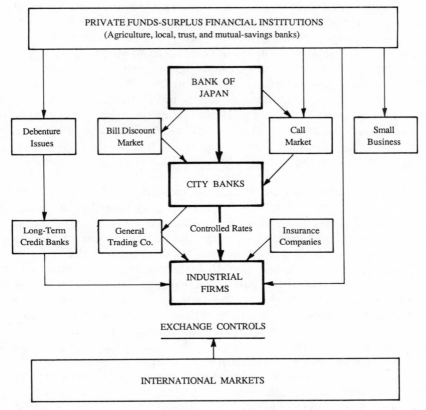

Figure 5-1.   The Bankers' Kingdom: Key Funding Relationships. Solid lines indicate flows of capital. For data on the magnitude of the financial flows in question, see Bank of Japan Research and Statistics Department, *Keizai Tōkei Nenpō* (Economic Statistics Annual) (Tokyo: Nihon Ginkō Chōsa Tōkei Kyoku, various issues).

39.2 percent for Sweden, 48.2 percent for West Germany, and 56.4 percent for the United States. The British ratio for 1975 was 44.1 percent.[7]

The Bankers' Kingdom structure of Japan afforded considerable leverage to private Japanese financial intermediaries in determining the direction and conditions of industrial credit flows, for at least four reasons. First, prospective borrowers had only limited alternative sources of funding to these intermediaries. Exchange controls inhibited cross-national borrowing, and authorization to borrow or issue internationally was difficult. Securities markets were not well developed and issuing conditions (sharply below market prices in almost all cases) were onerous.

A second reinforcement for the dominant position of private financial intermediaries in relation to prospective borrowers was the administered interest-rate system. From 1949 until the mid-1980s virtually all deposit rates in Japan were controlled; small-scale savings deposit rates were controlled right down to this writing. Through the Bond Arrangements Committee (Kisai Kondan Kai), headed by the Industrial Bank of Japan, interest rates on corporate bonds were controlled into the 1980s. Rates on government bonds, which were just beginning to be issued in significant amounts as the Bankers' Kingdom ended, were similarly determined through negotiations between the Ministry of Finance and the private-sector issuing syndicate at each underwriting.

Most important from the perspective of credit allocation, the Japanese financial authorities strove to keep long-term lending rates below market levels, thus creating an artificial shortage of industrial credit. This "low-interest-rate policy" (*tei kinri seisaku*) was particularly clear-cut under the Ikeda administration (1960–1964). From the end of 1960 to the spring of 1961 Ikeda consciously forced a comprehensive lowering of the entire interest-rate structure, including the rates on corporate debentures, time deposits, and long-term loans. He did this despite the sharp increase in the demand for credit being stimulated by announcement of the Income Doubling Plan,[8] to both decrease the cost of funds to heavy industry and to give the state more leverage in the allocation of credit.

The low-interest policy produced somewhat different results than Japan's developmental strategies intended. By creating manifest disequilibria in supply and demand for credit, it bred, as economic analysts would predict, a menagerie of private-sector evasive measures. Typical of these was "hidden lending," whereby loans were advanced only during the month and collected at month's end so as not to enter the formal statistics reported to the financial authorities.[9] The low-interest-rate policy also provoked covert demands, on the part of the private commercial banks in particular, for low-interest "compensating balances"—deposits for their borrowers at low interest, as a quid pro quo for receiving loans. The proliferating of informal compensating balances, negotiated between banks and their borrowers, under conditions of credit shortage giving banks substantial leverage, raised effective interest rates, even as the Ikeda interest-rate controls remained in place. Ultimately, the low-interest policy probably did lower both the cost of capital to heavy industry and the rate of return to savers, while significantly increasing the profitability of financial intermediaries. Compensating balances, to be sure, tended to impinge more heavily on the small businesses that were the customers of mutual savings banks, credit associations, and other small financial institutions than they did on Japan's largest industrial firms.[10] City banks themselves may well have demanded significantly greater compensating balances of smaller firms, thus cross-subsidizing lower-interest loans to the large industrial firms. But it does appear clear that the prevailing pattern of political and economic forces in the high-growth period did allow private banks, rather than the state, to serve as the primary arbiters of interest rates on private-sector loans to industry, allowing them to reap substantial profits despite the low-interest policy.

Throughout the high-growth period when the supply of capital was tight, private banks in Japan were substantially more profitable than industry. During 1953–1957, average annual banking profits after tax were nearly double those of industry as a whole, with a roughly 40 percent differential continuing until the late 1960s.[11] With rising financial liquidity during the 1970s, current banking profits after tax per capital account fell by half from 1968–1972 to 1973–1977, but it was not until the late 1970s, as the Bankers' Kingdom was coming to an end, that industry profits finally passed those of Japanese banking, as figure 5-2 suggests. The Bankers' Kingdom period was thus substantially more lucrative for banks than for industry, despite the low-interest-rate policy of the industrial strategists.

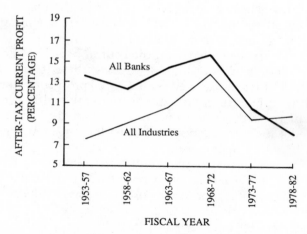

Figure 5-2. Banking and Industrial Profits in the Bankers' Kingdom. Profit rates are after-tax current profits per capita account.

Source: Akiyoshi Horiuchi, *Economic Growth and Financial Allocation in Postwar Japan* (Washington, D.C.: Brookings Institution, 1984), 23. Drawn from the following data: (1) Federation of Bankers *Associations of Japan, Analysis of Financial Statements of All Banks*; (2) Bank of Japan, *Financial Statements of Main Industrial Corporations* (excludes financial and insurance firms); and (3) Japan Development Bank, *Handbook of Financial Data of Industries*.

The importance of high banking profitability, based on administered interest rates, for the political and economic dynamics of the industrial finance during the Bankers' Kingdom period cannot be overstated. This situation made the private bankers credible guarantors for the industrial groups of which they were the linchpin. This set in motion a mutual insurance scheme that allowed the *keiretsu* member firms to invest with confidence, even under relatively volatile and uncertain economic conditions,[12] with limited reliance on the state. It also gave the bankers themselves powerful incentives both to combine in collusive defense of their profitable status quo, through cartelistic arrangements, and to resist the intrusion of bureaucrats into their affairs. Both the determined banking-sector opposition to MITI's Tokushin Hō proposals of the early 1960s and the subsequent appointment of the Bankers' Association president, Usami Makoto of the Mitsubishi Bank, as chairman of the Bank of Japan in 1964 must be seen against the backdrop of this lucrative status quo for the bankers, which gave them high stakes to protect from state interference.

A third aspect of the Bankers' Kingdom with important implications for the leverage of key private financial intermediaries—in this case vis-à-vis the bureaucracy—was its liquidity structure. To be sure, for most of the 1945–1955 decade Japanese private banks in general borrowed heavily (over 10 percent of loans outstanding) from the Bank of Japan; until 1963 the large city banks, cornerstones of the industrial groups, were in a similar position.[13]

Yet this private dependence on the central bank declined rapidly across the 1960s, and as chapter 3 suggests, there is little evidence that the Bank of Japan has used such limited prospective leverage as it has had with private intermediaries to forcibly alter their behavior, particularly with regard to the intersectoral disposition of loans. Its vaunted window guidance, in particular, appears to have been both routinized and incomplete in its application.

The striking and instructive comparative contrasts in liquidity structure are really between Japan, on the one hand, and continental Europe, particularly France, on the other. Private banks in both Germany and France continue to borrow heavily from the central bank—considerably more heavily than in Japan, relative to their total liabilities.[14]

Within the Japanese private financial sector, liquidity imbalances among institutions, which increase the state's leverage with these institutions, are far less severe than in France, as John Zysman's comparative data demonstrates.[15] In France, for example, there are a broad range of financial institutions, such as the Caisse des Dépôts, that are limited solely to deposit taking and others, such as the Crédit Hôtelier, that are limited to lending in specific narrow sectors of the economy. No such radical restrictions have been imposed by government on Japanese private financial institutions, either during the Bankers' Kingdom period or subsequently. The liquidity position of Japan's private financial intermediaries is thus more conducive to autonomy from the state than in continental Europe, especially as compared to France.

A final support for the autonomy of Japanese private financial intermediaries within the political economy as a whole, about which more will be said later, is their influential role in political life. The large Japanese banks have historically been central both in *zaikai*, the organized big-business world, and in business support for the ruling Liberal Democratic party. In return, the LDP has respected their autonomy and hesitated until the 1980s to systematically revise the favorable regulatory conditions conveyed on them during the transwar period, during and immediately after World War II.

In the importance of its banks as suppliers of industrial credit, and in the influence of its organized private sector within the national political economy as a whole, Japan bears striking similarities to Sweden and Germany. But unlike the Swedish and German private sectors, that of Japan also included powerful hybrid financial and commercial institutions, the general trading companies (*sōgō shōsha*). Their extensive international distribution operations, for products ranging from steel and semiconductors to crude oil and soybeans, stimulated in them an unusual sensitivity to market opportunities and a bias toward high-volume, low-cost production and aggressive marketing, since their income derived from trade flows rather than markups on products themselves. Through their direct investment and trade finance activities these versatile brokers, with a strong stake in rapid growth and industrial transformation, made it difficult after the mid-1950s for the Japanese government to pursue and enforce sharply restrictive industrial and trade credit policies, even though the state could still add its favorites to the private sector's preference list. These growth- and sales-volume-oriented trading firms came to dominate several of the large *keiretsu*, such as Mitsubishi and especially Mitsui, intensifying across many industries the private-sector competitive dynamic that Michael Porter has identified so clearly with global commercial success.[16] Their complex role in imparting a flexible, expansionary bias to Japanese corporate finance is discussed in greater detail later in this chapter.

To understand credit flows within the Japanese Bankers' Kingdom of the 1950s and 1960s, and particularly the unusual capacity of Japanese bankers and industrial groups to accommodate strategic vision to market discipline, it is necessary to understand both market forces and the policies of government. But to grasp the unusual flavor of organized private initiative that typifies postwar Japan one must understand not only the system in its aggregate, but also, even more importantly, the individual operation of many concrete private institutions—bankers' federations, industrial groups, industrial banks, and general trading companies. "Any study of the state," as Ezra Suleiman points out, "must also be a study of the society."[17] And it is the concrete institutions of Japan's unexampled society—in many ways more than those of its often decentralized and passive, if strategically oriented state—that have originated those features of Japanese public policy and economic performance that stand out most vividly in comparative perspective. They are the core of Japanese strategic capitalism and the central concern of this chapter.

THE CORE *KEIRETSU* FINANCIAL INSTITUTIONS

To a greater degree than any other industrialized nation save perhaps Sweden, the Japanese private sector of the 1950s and 1960s was segmented into clearly defined industrial groups, or *keiretsu*. These groups, like their prewar antecedents, the *zaibatsu* (literally "financial cliques"), aligned manufacturers with distributors and, most critically, with finance. Each industrial group typically contained four or five specialized financial institutions, which between them could spread the risk of such large-scale investment projects as the building of steel mills, shipyards, and petrochemical *combinats*.

The industrial groups have been a key element in Japan's rapid industrial development and transformation since the early 1950s. In sectors as diverse as petrochemicals, telematics, atomic power, real-estate development, and Middle East oil exploration, these private firms have taken the strategic initiative for Japan.[18] Their role in spearheading infant industry development—in these sectors and many others—has typically been greater than that of government. Their role in restructuring depressed sectors in flexible, market-conforming fashion has also been important, especially after the two Oil Shocks of the 1970s.

Financial power has been a key aspect of *keiretsu* strength in propelling Japanese economic transition. At the heart of the industrial groups' financing are the so-called "main banks"—Mitsubishi, Sumitomo, Fuji, Sanwa, and so on. These large city banks typically supplied 15 to 20 percent of total funding for each of their *keiretsu* members during the high-growth period, as suggested in table 5-1.

TABLE 5-1

Keiretsu as Autonomous Sources of Finance for Member Corporations, 1965–1990
(percentage of total finance)

Keiretsu	Number of Enterprises		Main Bank		Other Group Financial Affiliates		Total Group	
	1965	1990	1965	1990	1965	1990	1965	1990
Mitsubishi	85	217	20.17	10.23	14.18	9.2	34.89	19.43
Sumitomo	80	164	19.87	11.72	14.50	9.77	34.37	21.49
Mitsui	79	171	14.31	9.06	9.87	10.56	24.18	19.62
Fuji	78	223	18.81	9.31	7.47	8.11	26.28	17.42
Sanwa	53	247	21.88	10.81	7.05	7.38	28.93	18.19
Dai Ichi	41	190	18.03	10.07	2.60	2.45	20.63	12.52

Source: Takayanagi Hiroshi, ed., Kigyō Keiretsu Sōran (Almanac of Corporate Industrial Groups), 1992 ed. (Tokyo: Tōyō Keizai Shinpōsha, 1991), 37–49.

Note: "Sources of finance" aggregate figures for Mitsubishi, Sumitomo, Fuji, and Mitsui include totals for main banks and trust companies, as well as life insurance and ordinary insurance firms. Totals for Sanwa and Dai Ichi include only the first three categories, since these latter groups have no ordinary insurance affiliate. "Number of enterprises" refers to number of firms in which industrial-group members held over 10 percent of total corporate shares outstanding. Dai Ichi Bank totals for 1990 are for the Dai Ichi Kangyō Bank, formed through merger in 1971 of the Dai Ichi Bank and the Nippon Kangyō Bank.

Their role had declined somewhat by 1990, but the keiretsu main banks remained a stabilizing element in the financial environment of many large Japanese corporations.

Nearly as significant as the main banks, particularly in the case of the strongest groups, such as Mitsubishi and Sumitomo, have been the non-main-bank financial affiliates, including the trust banks, life insurance companies, and casualty insurance firms. These smaller private financial institutions, lying outside the long-coercive jurisdiction of the Bank of Japan, have no direct functional analogue in European industrial finance in their close integration with the lending of conventional banks. Indeed the tendency elsewhere has been for such nonbank financiers to be more clearly oriented toward arm's-length portfolio investment than toward direct industrial finance. The nonbanks have played a key role in enhancing the autonomy of the Japanese keiretsu from state industrial strategists, although they remain substantially closer to the regulatory-oriented bureaucrats at MOF than their counterparts in many industrialized nations. In facilitating a system of "dedicated" rather than "fluid" capital flows toward industry, these "nonbank" financial institutions play a critical role in the ability of the Japanese private sector to take a long-term approach to credit-allocation decisions.

The role of life insurance companies—including some that are not *keiretsu* members—as a source of "dedicated capital" for Japanese industry appears to be especially important, if underresearched.[19] These firms have, thanks to favorable regulatory policies of the MOF, enormous assets—¥127.3 trillion at the end of 1990[20]—and tremendous profitability. Yet they are strongly insulated from short-run market forces in their capital-investment decisions, both by the character of most of them as mutual rather than joint-stock companies, and by MOF's "convoy approach" regulatory policies, which inhibit competition.[21] The insurance firms generally follow rather than lead strategic private-sector allocators like the long-term credit banks in their lending decisions, but can provide huge amounts of "dedicated capital" and serve as stable shareholders.

At NEC, Japan's top semiconductor producer, Sumitomo Life Insurance served in 1991, for example, as NEC's largest shareholder, with 6.8 percent of total shares outstanding, while also providing ¥10.2 billion in long-term loans.[22] Insurance companies as a group held 16.3 percent of NEC's stock; together with the more than 17.8 percent held by other members of the Sumitomo group, these firms provided NEC with a much more stable basis for making farsighted strategic decisions on capital investment in integrated circuits, telecommunications, or computers—without the direct government direction or "guarantees" that the development-state model would stress—than was available to American rivals of NEC such as IBM or Digital Equipment.[23]

In addition to supplying manufacturers with a large enough proportion of their financing to give them considerable freedom in the money marketplace, *keiretsu* during the high-growth 1950s and 1960s also provided these firms with a marketing apparatus in the form of the general trading companies, and particularly for the 1950s, some degree of market power.[24] Even as their market power and profitability declined, the *keiretsu* remained important vehicles for protecting affiliated companies and their members from business adversity in the short run, while helping them to make long-run structural adjustments.[25] The *keiretsu* thus performed from within many of the functions undertaken in differently constructed economic systems by either government or markets. They were especially important in enhancing the market orientation of a political economy where the state, for historical reasons, loomed large at the onset of postwar growth. The existence of *keiretsu*, including the insurance companies and trust banks that supplemented the main banks, made borrower firms less reliant on strategic government credit than they otherwise would have been, given the absence of well-developed capital markets in Japan. Similarly, firms were able, through *keiretsu* membership, to distribute the risks otherwise likely to require government guarantees, given a tradition of reliance on the state, as well as the huge financial requirements of steel mills, petrochemical complexes, and other central elements of Japan's capital-intensive postwar heavy industrialization.[26]

While reducing the need for dependence on government financial supports, the existence of *keiretsu* also intensified, during the 1950s and 1960s, the corporations' need to resist onerous government restrictions, particularly those curbing *keiretsu* access to growth markets. As Miyazaki points out, the 1950s gave birth to fierce corporate rivalry, as the once monopoly-oriented groups furiously tried to acquire "one set" of the full portfolio of growth industries.[27] In such important industries as petrochemicals, this headlong drive of the *keiretsu* to compete in all sectors led them, as outlined in chapter 4, to defy MITI investment guidelines and engage in "excess competition," aggressively building capacity for production that could often be marketed only at prices likely to entail corporate losses, international trade tensions, or both. The *keiretsu*, in short, not only helped frustrate state-directed strategic credit allocation in Japan, but also played a major autonomous role in shaping Japanese industrial structure.

Amid the stock market volatility of 1990–1992, which wiped out more than 50 percent of the Tokyo Stock Exchange's $5 trillion-plus valuation of 1989, some analysts saw emerging signs of sales of shares cross-held among *keiretsu* partners, as well as other anecdotal evidence that the industrial groups were beginning to unwind.[28] Impending implementation of Bank for International Settlements (BIS) capital adequacy standards and movements toward liberalization of life insurance premiums were considered likely to intensify these tendencies further.[29] Clearly there has been a slow erosion in the cohesion of Japan's industrial groups. But in view of the broadly functional role that these groups play in corporate risk reduction, reducing corporate transaction costs, and providing important collective goods, Japan's *keiretsu* seem likely to persist in modified form far into the future, encouraging the bias toward "dedicated capital" in Japanese corporate finance.

KEIRETSU ENTREPRENEURS:
THE TRADING COMPANIES

General trading companies (*sōgō shōsha*), central elements in Japan's *keiretsu* that have no exact analogue in Western industrial society, provided a different contribution to Japan's remarkable private-sector process of capital allocation. Rather than "dedicated capital," they contributed market-oriented entrepreneurial initiative—often in directions different from those stressed by the state. Indeed, the *sōgō shōsha* seriously compromised the efficacy of state credit-allocation controls in Japan during the high-growth years, with their aggressive, market-oriented arbitrage activities.

Because the largest trading companies were broken up during the Occupation—the only major financial institutions to be so treated—trading firms were not a major factor in the Japanese system until the late 1950s. Mitsui Bussan was reconstituted only in 1958, from 170 firms into which it had been split by the Occupation, and Mitsubishi Shōji from its 139 components in 1954. But by the mid-1960s both firms were playing a major role in complicating government efforts to control the financial markets, and thereafter their capacity to do so increased steadily. Together with seven smaller *sōgō shōsha*, these firms handled close to half of Japan's international trade, and a substantial share of domestic distribution as well. They had a fateful impact on Japanese industrial structure not only by promoting the growth of high-volume commodity sectors such as steel, paper, and aluminum through their marketing, but also through entrepreneurial infant-industry and resources-investment transactions, both at home and abroad.[30]

TRADING COMPANY FINANCE: FINESSING
CONTROLS AND PROMOTING GROWTH

Trading companies channeled funds across the Japanese economy through three mechanisms—trade finance activities (lengthening, for example, the terms of promissory notes to processors or users during periods of tight credit), project loans, and direct investment in ventures. The trading companies' role in facilitating market-oriented allocation of credit can be seen in the intersectoral distribution of their loans. Since, unlike banks, they are not required to publish loan portfolio breakdowns, precise statistics are impossible to obtain. But it is clear that during the high-growth period trading companies loaned heavily to precisely those promising but consumer-oriented sectors that government felt to be of lowest priority, thereby intensifying overall capital investment and accelerating the pace of growth through their industrial arbitrage.

During the 1950s and 1960s, for example, trading companies were a major supplier of funds to the paper-pulp industry; this was, in terms of the early postwar BOJ loan guidelines outlined in table 3-1 a "Class C," or proscribed, investment area. Trading companies assumed an unusually broad financial role in the paper industry, financing capital investment as well as extending trade credits that improved the overall cash-flow position of paper producers. Mitsui and Company (commonly Mitsui Bussan in Japanese) was perhaps the most active of the traders in supplying such funds, although Marubeni also aggressively cultivated relations with smaller paper firms. Mitsui's interests in paper stemmed from the prewar period, when the Mitsui *zaibatsu* held close to a monopoly through its affiliate Oji Paper.

Trading companies, of course, made money whenever they lent at relatively high rates in capital-scarce sectors. They made even more when they could also generate a trade flow by financing a growing industry's need for raw materials, as in the exploitation of Indonesian forest resources to provide logs for Japanese sawmills. Thus, much of the trading companies' "market-facilitating" investment was concentrated in sectors disadvantaged by controls that were also trade oriented. For this reason, textiles and sundry goods, both labor-intensive, low-priority sectors that many within MITI were prepared to see atrophy, long maintained themselves with general trading company funds—without which these "sunset industries" would probably have declined much more steeply than they in fact did. As their ability to service high-interest, high-volume loans declined, the trading companies spearheaded migration of these sectors to Southeast Asia and China through their plant exports—often of the same used equipment whose installation within Japan they and their *keiretsu* partners had originally financed.

The market orientation of trading companies took their investment into high-return sectors thought by government to be superfluous, thus aiding "sunrise" sectors with major future growth potential that were temporarily neglected by government. The traders began moving into leasing in 1966, for example, long before government grasped its benefits for industry, outside of the JECC government-leasing program for computers.[31] Trading companies were also heavily, and increasingly, involved in financing leisure industries and real estate development during the late 1960s, anticipating trends much more broadly recognized during the following decade. Mitsubishi, for instance, energetically supported Kentucky Fried Chicken's Japan operations. Trading companies began financing leisure industries and real estate before most banks became active in such areas and while the financial authorities still remained ambivalent about their development.[32] Even where trading companies directed funds toward government-supported sectors, they sometimes disrupted the operation of government controls so as to intensify private-sector capital spending and to accelerate short-run economic growth. In this respect they imparted an expansionary bias to commodity-industrial sectors in Japan not present in other nations with bank-centered industrial groups, such as Germany. Even after five major producers had become established and capacity was running far ahead of demand at prices permitting stable profits in the aluminum-refining industry, for example, Mitsui Bussan in 1969 masterminded and financed the establishment of a new refiner, Mitsui Aluminum, to compete with the others. In doing so it thus assured an independent Mitsui Group presence in what figured to be an attractive new growth sector. Many within MITI looked upon this development critically, but nothing was done about it. Trading companies also helped spearhead the expansion—overexpansion from MITI's viewpoint—of petrochemicals and oil refining.

THE SOURCES OF TRADING COMPANY AUTONOMY

How did trading companies attain such remarkably broad independence of government administrative controls? Their leaders had little involvement in organized big-business activities, such as the top leadership of Keidanren. Trading companies, especially the largest ones, also employed relatively few former senior bureaucrats.[33] And these firms were not notable for their continuing involvement with the LDP as a whole, despite some highly visible ties publicized through scandals, such as the Lockheed affair, involving individual politicians.[34] As a group, they contributed far less financially to the ruling Liberal Democratic party than the bankers, who ranked among the most important backers of the ruling party.[35]

The main source of trading company autonomy was that postwar Japanese regulatory structure seriously complicated state efforts to control the trading companies, particularly after they were licensed in January 1966 to hold foreign exchange. With potential oversight authority scattered over a number of jealous, turf-conscious bureaucracies, a fragmented state thus yielded initiative to an organized and intensely motivated private sector, as concrete consideration of trading company relationships with major ministries suggests.

MITI

The formal government supervisor of trading company operations was the International Trade Bureau of MITI, which held responsibility for foreign-exchange budgeting during 1952–1966.[36] This power provided the strategic capacity both to restrain imports competing with domestic production and to encourage capital-equipment imports critical for the development of new sectors,[37] of which MITI was deprived by the dismantling of foreign-exchange control during the 1960s. The state's control powers were further eroded by the flow of a few senior Trade Bureau officials to influential posts in the smaller, more aggressive of the Kansai trading companies especially intent on expanding market share. For example, Marubeni's long-time chairman during the 1980s, Matsuo Taiichirō, was a former Trade Bureau chief. So Trade Bureau officials were little given to restraining the arbitrage activities of the general trading companies.

The Bank of Japan

The BOJ had little incentive to bother the traders either. It had a particularly strong organizational interest in a viable Japanese balance of payments. The traders facilitated exports, thus simplifying the BOJ's task during the 1950s and 1960s of reconciling Japan's rapid domestic growth with its precarious balance-of-payments situation. Since the bank had no jurisdiction over nonbank financial institutions, it probably would not have been able to curb the traders even had it desired to do so.

Ministry of Finance

Although MOF had substantial formal regulatory powers over banks, however limited its intervention may have been in practice, it had very little control of any sort over the traders. The major reason was MITI's jealous defense of its *nawabari*, or territorial prerogatives, despite the traders' growing role in the general Japanese financial system. The traders had no responsibility to divulge financial data to MOF, and MOF conversely lacked the power to inspect or investigate them. The ministry's only recourse was to obtain data through the banks—but the traders were extremely circumspect in what they revealed to the banks as well. Traders also dealt with multiple banks—including several outside their *keiretsu*—to preserve their leverage. The autonomy conferred by their secretiveness enabled them to resist very serious attempts by MOF to control them, as when MOF gave administrative guidance to banks in 1973 to curb loans to traders for speculative real estate investments.

In the final analysis, the ministry's best means of exercising some control over trading companies during the 1950s and 1960s was through foreign-exchange controls. But here again, working responsibility for the allocation of foreign exchange to specific firms, as opposed to the formulation of macrolevel policies, lay with MITI until the abolition of controls in the mid-1960s. Finance at no time could directly control the traders' foreign-exchange position, and relaxation of controls after 1966 allowed the traders to "lead and lag" against the dollar in 1971, with as much as $1 billion a day in speculative transactions finally forcing MOF to float the yen in late August, after the infamous Nixon Shocks. The Ministry of Finance could delay the complete freedom of trading companies to raise funds overseas for somewhat longer,[38] but even this power eroded rapidly in practice during the first half of the 1970s.

The trading companies enhanced their autonomy through transnational linkages with foreign multinationals, beginning in the late 1960s. Mitsubishi Corporation, for instance, cultivated such close relations with Chase Manhattan Bank that its chairman during the late 1970s, Fujino Chūjirō, joined the Chase board of directors. Mitsubishi also relied heavily on Morgan Stanley for expertise in floating Eurobonds and on Boston Consulting for advice on strategy in Southeast Asia.

After 1970 the trading companies began to play a more consistent role in the political system, as domestic criticism of their speculative commodity and real estate dealings rose and as international trade became increasingly politicized. In 1971, at the initiative of Mitsui Bussan, the traders founded the Japan Trading Association (Nihon Bōeki Kai) to serve as their vehicle for contributions and other political activities. The major objective in increasing their political role was continued freedom from government regulation.

After 1972 there was substantial mass political pressure, as well as pressure from the traders' old bureaucratic enemies at MOF and MITI, to curb trading company autonomy within the financial system.[39] In 1974, at the Japan Socialist party's (JSP) initiative, the Diet at last passed a Large Scale Loan Control Law (Ōguchi Yūshi Kisei Hō), effective in 1979, to restrict the funds banks might loan to traders. The JSP had been pressing for such legislation since the early 1950s, but it was vigorously resisted by the Federation of Bankers' Associations (Zenginkyō). In 1975–1976, following the bankruptcy of the Ataka Trading Company, MITI's Industrial Policy Bureau, a control-oriented rival of the International Trade Policy Bureau, proposed a trading company law subjecting the traders' financial operations to much tougher controls. The Banking Bureau of MOF, alarmed that liberalization of foreign-exchange controls would leave it without any instrument to countervail the traders, eagerly went along, as did the Socialist party, the Communist party, and the Kōmeitō in the Diet. Yet even this broad and unusual coalition of bureaucrats and politicians was unable to reassert state control over the trading companies, and the legislation failed. The freedom of the *sōgō shōsha* from government constraints grew even more during the 1980s, with the globalization of Japanese corporate activity and the further liberalization of the Japanese financial system.

PROMOTING COHESION IN THE PRIVATE FINANCIAL WORLD: BANKERS' ASSOCIATIONS

Rivalry, as noted in chapters 2 and 3, has been a persistent theme of postwar Japanese bureaucratic history, undermining the struggle of state strategists for a coherent, unified approach to industrial development and rendering the Japanese state much more reactive in its policymaking than the conventional wisdom generally suggests. Vigorous rivalry, as noted above, has also been a hallmark of the industrial groups and even of the long-term credit banks of the Japanese private sector, rendering them powerful engines of innovation. Stability in the financial world, by contrast, has been provided by the bankers' associations, whose unifying efforts, juxtaposed to public rivalries, helped make the high-growth period the era of the Bankers' Kingdom, and one of "dedicated capital" responding to long-term incentives.

Historically speaking, Japan has had a relatively large number of private banks, compared to most industrialized nations other than the United States. With investment and trade-financial demand rising rapidly for most of the past century in Japan, the market for financial services there has also been large and swift to grow. As Kōsai points out, economic pressures toward competition in the Japanese banking system have been strong.[40] These have had prospectively adverse implications for bank profitability and even solvency, in the absence of public or private intervention to restrain such competition. With self-regulation prima facie more congenial than regulation from the outside, Japan's private banks have thus had steady incentive to make their pricing decisions collectively, specifically through an industry association, and the need for cooperation in clearing operations has reinforced this propensity for collective action.

Japan's private banking system, as we saw in chapter 1, antedates the state regulatory structure supervising it,[41] creating institutional contexts and traditions of private assertiveness that help to constrain any state capacity for strategy independent of the private sector. In view of this longstanding institutional strength, coupled with MOF opposition, MITI industrial planners have never been able to order the banks around. Private bankers' associations also predate both the Ministry of Finance and the Bank of Japan, affording them leverage with financial "regulators" as well as industrial "strategists." Japan's first private bankers' association, the Takuzen Kai, was in fact established by the great Meiji industrialist Shibusawa Eiichi in 1878, five years before foundation of the Bank of Japan.[42] Formation of the Takuzen Kai also antedated by three years establishment of the MOF Banking Bureau, which thereafter was frequently subjected to complex reorganizations and consolidations with other bureaus. It did not decisively emerge as a coherent, independent entity within MOF until 1946.[43]

Private initiative is a venerable tradition in Japanese financial regulation; given the immense potential profits to be made through coordination, it has also, not surprisingly, been a persistent one. Long before public financial authorities began actively to regulate the financial system, early private bankers' associations tried to limit establishment of new, allegedly unsound banks, put ceilings on deposit interest rates, and regulate both call market and general lending rates. In 1892, for example, the Tokyo Bankers' Association petitioned the newly established MOF to place capital restrictions on the creation of small new banks through revision of the Banking Ordinance (Ginkō Jōrei). Rebuffed by MOF, the association took its case to the Diet in 1893, ultimately seeing its proposals become law.[44] Beginning in Kyoto, Kobe, and Ōsaka, local bankers' associations independently set deposit-rate ceilings as early as 1899.[45] Following World War I the large private banks also established a conventional minimum rate on general loans, as well as interest rates on call loans and overdrafts; for almost forty years they continued to determine Japan's interest-rate structure through collective private action.[46]

During World War II private-sector industry associations in steel, shipbuilding, and electric power, to name only the most conspicuous, grew rapidly in size and influence relative to both individual firms and often enough the state itself, since they acted as primary operational coordinators of the war effort. This was equally true in finance, where the government in April 1942 established "control associations" under the National General Mobilization Law (Kokka Sōdōin Hō) for nine industries, as part of the mobilization for total war. The new National Finance Control Association (Zenkoku

Kinyū Tōsei Kai) into which were merged all the preexisting private financial associations, private banks, and government institutions, coordinated lending authorizations and the concentration of savings for the war effort.[47]

Five days after war's end, the financial control association dissolved itself in anticipation of Allied retaliation should it remain constituted as the same body that had pursued the war. But in September 1945, the Federation of Bankers' Associations of Japan (Zenkoku Ginkō Kyōkai Rengō Kai) emerged as one major successor to the National Finance Control Association, with the Tokyo Bankers' Association, the Regional Bankers' Discussion Group (Chihō Ginkō Kondan Kai), and other groups with more specialized financial interests arising soon thereafter. The demobilization of the private bankers, and their high degree of unobtrusive but excellent organization as SCAP spread out across the land, seeking what it might reform, were critical to the survival of the still fledgling Bankers' Kingdom, which had begun taking shape during wartime.

As Miyazaki Yoshikazu points out, the city banks of Japan were treated much more favorably by the Allied Occupation than their counterparts in West Germany; indeed, the extensive evidence of public favoritism to private bankers in early postwar Japan goes far toward explaining why they were able to become the linchpin of the Japanese political economy during the succeeding two decades.[48] Banks in Japan were, for example, accorded more favorable treatment than manufacturers in the early postwar evaluation of corporate assets for tax purposes.[49]

Procedures for ending wartime subsidies to military industry showed the same systematic favoritism for private banks, contrasting sharply with the converse favoritism displayed in Germany toward manufacturers. Special losses of Japanese armaments firms resulting from the ending of wartime subsidies were not charged to the accounts of their former creditors, the banks, but instead for the most part assessed against the firms' shareholders—in many cases the *zaibatsu* holding company giants disbanded by the Occupation. The banks, which had found themselves in a favorable position under currency reform as debtors of their depositors, were also given preferential treatment as creditors of the armaments firms. In addition, the main banks of the former *zaibatsu* were not designated either as holding companies or as companies subject to deconcentration during 1946–1948. Indeed, these banks emerged from the *zaibatsu*-dissolution process essentially unscathed.[50] In Germany, by contrast, financial deconcentration proceeded considerably further, giving rise to the so-called *Landesbank*, although the largest German banks were able to regain a large measure of cohesion and much of their dominance over industry during the 1950s and 1960s.

From the late 1940s, private banks in Japan did face important legal constraints on their freedom to set lending rates. In mid-1947 the Fair Trade Commission ruled that Tokyo Bankers' Association maximum rates for loans and discounts, a tradition since the Taishō period (1913–1925), contravened the new Occupation-initiated Anti-Monopoly Law, thus displacing interest-rate determination into the public sector. On October 23, 1947, the Bankers' Association canceled the agreement among its members on maximum interest rates; a few weeks later, in December 1947, the Temporary Money Rates Adjustment Law (Rinji Kinri Chōsei Hō) was passed. This law, which applied to practically all banks except government financial institutions, empowered the Minister of Finance, through the Bank of Japan, to determine interest rates on all loans of less than one year and over ¥1 million, while also setting all private deposit interest rates. Together with parallel measures controlling long-term lending rates, this made it possible for the government, should it wish, to regulate credit strategically, without regard to the interests of the banking industry. But such a development did not materialize.

This systematic favoritism for banks stemmed partly from their ability to amass savings at a time when only increased savings could restrain inflation and advance productivity. Tristan Beplat, director of the SCAP Banking Section, emphasized this function at the 1947 annual meeting of the Federation of Bankers' Associations as the overriding responsibility and raison d'être of Japanese banks.[51] But savings could have been amassed through other types of financial intermediaries as well. Bankers' associations, both through their ability to exert pressure on policymakers and their ability to implement government objectives, were an important element helping to assure that banks, rather than securities firms or other entities, became the principal coordinating force in postwar Japanese economic life, and that they were left with a general discretion to allocate credit on their own terms.

Between 1945 and 1950 the private bankers' associations cooperated passively with government-led efforts at reconstruction, including the priority-production policy of credit allocation (*keisha seisan hōshiki*). They concentrated on preserving their position as preeminent private financial intermediaries and did not challenge government preeminence in the credit-allocation process. After the outbreak of the Korean War, however, the bankers' associations, particularly the national federation (Zenginkyō), took an increasing role in allocating credit.[52] During July 1951, for example, Zenginkyō established a Loan Self-regulation Committee (Yūshi Jishū Iinkai) to scrutinize its members' lending decisions both by sectoral composition and terms concluded. As the public financial authorities' own will and ability to allocate credit waned following the resignation of Governor Ichimada Naoto from the Bank of Japan in 1954, the role of private banking associations in the credit-allocation process became correspondingly stronger.

In October 1955 a parallel Investment and Finance Committee (Tōyūshi Iinkai) was established at the Federation of Bankers' Associations, the two being merged in December 1957 to become the Capital Adjustment Committee (Shikin Chōsei Iinkai).[53] This committee made regular judgments on the major lending decisions of its member banks—declaring in 1965, for example, that both steel and automobile industry capital investment needed to be stretched out, to avoid the emerging dangers of excess capacity.[54] With the coming of greater liquidity in the Japanese political economy and its transformation into a ceremonial body, the committee was abolished in 1968, although Zenginkyō as an institution continued periodically to speak out against speculative lending in such sectors as real estate investment.[55]

After 1958 the secretary general of Zenginkyō's Capital Adjustment Committee also served on the Industrial Capital Subcommittee (Sangyō Shikin Bukai) of MITI's major adviser on industrial structure, the Industrial Structure Rationalization Council. This latter body merged after 1964 with the Industrial Structure Research Council to become the Industrial Structure Deliberation Council (Sangyō Kōzō Shingikai). Through its membership on the Industrial Capital Subcommittee, Zenginkyō developed a formal, ongoing relationship with MITI, but without ever coming under MITI control; on the contrary, it played a decisive and successful role during 1962–1964 in defeating MITI's efforts to establish unified government control over credit allocation under the ministry's own auspices, as we saw in chapter 2.

Beyond the formalities of BOJ loan guidelines and window guidance, occasional general requests from MOF for lending restraint in the light of balance-of-payments problems and the mixed performance of the MITI-affiliated Industrial Capital Subcommittee, examined in chapter 4, the bankers' federation probably exercised more influence over the allocation of domestic credit than did any noncorporate collective authority. From the early postwar days, Zenginkyō administered the day-by-day details of MOF/BOJ loan guidelines, receiving detailed information on firm-level compliance from individual banks and passing on only a summary, indicating bank and industry totals, to the Ministry of Finance. The ministry had no direct way, other than periodic banking examinations (*ginkō kensa*) conducted every two to three years, of knowing on what terms individual banks made their lending decisions. Although somewhat more knowledgeable, the BOJ did not routinely share such information with the Ministry of Finance either. When MOF wanted specific adjustments in lending, it had to rely on Zenginkyō, which held the figures in proprietary form, to compel the compliance of individual banks. MITI had no significant working relationship with Zenginkyō.

Generally speaking, MOF review of banking-sector lending policies, like that of the BOJ after the 1950s, appears to have been relatively passive; MOF made active demands of Zenginkyō only in response to balance-of-payments crises (particularly during the 1950s), to threats of possible bank failure, or to demands from the Diet for a change in lending policies by the private banks. In late 1957, for example, Zenginkyō pressed individual member banks to cut back lending, at the specific request of MOF, due to a severe balance-of-payments crisis that had cut Japan's foreign currency reserves to only $455 million that September and ultimately forced Japan to borrow $137 million from the IMF.[56] Funds for the electric power industry were supported at this time, but those for new investments in the fledgling television industry, whose development was held not to be urgent, were suppressed.[57] Other lending discouraged during this period by Zenginkyō's Capital Adjustment Committee as being "useless or non-urgent capital" (*fuyō jukyū shikin*) included loans for: disaster relief (February 1957); *ryokans* (Japanese-style inns) and international tourist hotels (January 1958); parking lots and land development (November, 1959); and for installation of new telephones (August 1960).[58] Conversely, Zenginkyō was continually urging that scarce capital, made scarcer by the need for credit restraint to cool the economy and bring the balance of payments back into equilibrium, be directed toward the capital-intensive electric power, steel, and shipping industries, just as in the late 1940s.

Although the evidence is fragmentary, it appears that Zenginkyō's bias in its recommendations to member banks conformed closely to the concept of the *circle of compensation*, introduced earlier in this volume—that is, support for the existing configuration of the financial world,[59] continued or expanded credit for existing recipients, and limited funds for newcomers, no matter how much long-run growth potential the new sectors in question might have. This conservative calculus hardly anticipated the future. Both electronics and telecommunications, for example, were largely ignored throughout the 1950s. There is little evidence of a strategic approach to industrial transformation in the lending resolutions of the Federation of Bankers' Associations, just as one similarly finds little in the regulation-oriented policies at MOF.[60]

Zenginkyō's positions were also animated to some extent by pressure from the Diet, particularly regarding the terms of small-business finance. Since interest rates after 1947 were controlled in Japan by bureaucratic fiat, private banks had to rely heavily thereafter on the compensating balances (kōsoku yokin) typically demanded of borrowers. Since small-business-loan volume per firm was low and since small-business ties with the banks were often relatively weak, banks under profit pressure from the government's ceiling on interest rates often cross-subsidized their heavy-industrial loans with profits from the large compensating balances demanded of small business. The Diet stepped in—sporadically, but at times aggressively—to arrest this practice.

In 1954 Zenginkyō set up a reporting system on compensating balances, in response to pressure from the ruling Liberal party (Jiyūtō) in the Diet, for whom small business was a major constituency; a sense of the need for action was conveyed to Zenginkyō by the Ministry of Finance. Both in 1957 and 1962 compensating balances became an issue in the Diet. The Ministry of Finance demanded reform from the bankers without intervening directly, and Zenginkyō in response issued a "self-policing" code of ethics (jishū moshiawase). During the mid-1970s Zenginkyō once again agreed to monitor and restrain compensating balances in response to yet another Diet request, conveyed by MOF. In 1981 exactly the same procedures were applied to high-interest consumer loans (sarakin) and in July 1987 to real estate investments.

In addition to Zenginkyō's administrative functions and technical responsibilities, such as check clearance, personal credit information, and bank-employee training,[61] which for the two decades of the high-growth period defined the Bankers' Kingdom, it has also long been influential as a pressure group—primarily in defending the bank prerogatives. It broke MITI's major attempt to usurp control of industrial credit in 1962–1963 through its effective lobbying against the Special Measures Law for the Promotion of Designated Industries (Tokushin Hō). It also successfully resisted proposals spearheaded by the Japan Socialist party, with broader political backing, for limits on large-scale lending to individual borrowers (so-called Ōguchi Yūshi Kisei) in a long siege from 1953 to 1974; many bankers of the period regarded this as Zenginkyō's most important achievement.[62]

As one of the three largest financial supporters of the ruling Liberal Democratic party throughout the high-growth period—a member of the powerful Gosanke (literally "honorable three families") together with the steel and electric power federations—Zenginkyō generally wielded influence in the formation of policy that other industries and even officials could not match. The only less than complete successes for the federation during its thirty-five years of preeminence from the early 1950s to the mid-1980s were its partial failure to check the expansion of postal savings and to arrest the shift of corporate clients toward the securities industry. Together the postal savings program and the securities industry helped bring banking's preeminence in Japanese corporate finance to an end. But it was ultimately market and political pressures—rather than unilateral bureaucratic fiat—that enabled these challengers of banking preeminence some measure of success.

PRIVATE-SECTOR STRATEGIST OF HIGH GROWTH: THE INDUSTRIAL BANK OF JAPAN

Just as trading companies, and the *keiretsu* more generally, came to play a major informal role in actively spurring the birth of new consumer-oriented sectors, so the Industrial Bank of Japan and to a lesser degree its two smaller brethren—the Long-Term Credit Bank of Japan and the Nippon Fudōsan Bank—assumed a major, rarely recognized role in channeling the flow of Japanese heavy-industrial credit in innovative directions. Throughout most of the 1950s and 1960s the IBJ alone provided significantly more "dedicated capital"—responsive to long-run market logic rather than short-run concerns—to Japanese industry than did even the principal public purveyor of industrial credit, the Japan Development Bank. And IBJ allocated more flexibly than JDB, unencumbered by bureaucratic restrictions and reserve.[63] The IBJ's sense of initiative helped assure the rise of such important new sectors as petrochemicals and automobiles at a stage when state strategists were still ambivalent about their expansion. The IBJ was indeed a major private-sector coordinator with public functions, playing many of the credit-allocation roles that developmental state theory ascribes to MITI and its public-sector surrogates, as well as functions often ascribed to private sector main banks of the industrial groups, described above.

Patterned after the French Crédit Foncier, the IBJ opened its doors in 1902—forty-nine years before the government-owned Japan Development Bank, which has been often regarded as the central coordinator of national policy finance in the industrial sphere.[64] The IBJ raises funds through the sale of financial debentures (*kinyūsai*) and uses them to finance massive multiyear projects, which over the years have shown a special concentration in heavy industry. It also does feasibility studies on—and helps organize—large-scale capital-intensive international projects; in the late 1980s and early 1990s, for example, it served as technical agent for the Dover Channel Tunnel, prepared a regional development plan for the Dalian area of southern Manchuria, and studied alternatives in international maritime transport to the Panama Canal.[65] Although foreign to American tradition, similar institutions have played important roles in coordinating industrial finance for the major continental European nations, particularly West Germany and France.

Before World War II, the IBJ was a "special" public-private bank under government control, in which the Treasury held an important minority interest on behalf of the government.[66] It is emblematic of the IBJ's quasi-public status that its director was titled sōsai, or governor—a term otherwise applied solely to the head of the Bank of Japan. The IBJ was important as a financial arm of the Imperial government in underwriting certain critical undertakings in China, offering large concessionary loans to the right warlords, and almost single-handedly financing the industrial development of Manchukuo. In 1936, for example, 96.3 percent of all the capital raised by Japanese enterprises in Manchukuo through yen-denominated debt issues was underwritten by the Industrial Bank.[67]

After 1937 the IBJ assumed a central role in financing national military expansion in China and ultimately elsewhere in the Pacific. From 1938 to 1940 it served as the sole loan window for forced military loans and remained the main conduit for war-industry finance until 1942–1943. It expanded its loans outstanding from ¥779 million in 1937 to ¥2.7 billion in December 1941, and over ¥14.6 billion in August 1945.[68] This massive eighteen-fold expansion from 1937 to 1945 was more than twice as rapid as the expansion in loans by commercial banks, and six times the rate of wholesale price inflation, mainly due to the IBJ's unusually heavy involvement in funding the war effort. By war's end 35 percent of IBJ loans outstanding went directly to war industry and most of the rest to related sectors.[69]

The IBJ in 1945 was thus the very epitome of an instrument of war and an obstacle to the evolution of equilibrating financial markets. But for various political and economic reasons discussed above, SCAP could not abolish it. The most SCAP could do was cut down the IBJ's branch network, limit its debenture issues to ten times capitalization, and render it an unambiguously private institution, in a legal sense, through the Long-Term Credit Bank Act of 1952. Since then the government has held no shares in the IBJ.

Why the IBJ's Role Became Crucial

The Industrial Bank's activist role in Japan's strategic capitalism of the high-growth period emerged from the following realities:

1. Unlike Japanese commercial banks such as Mitsubishi, Mitsui, and Sumitomo, but like German universal banks, the IBJ was permitted to issue bonds and debentures. (No banks were allowed to issue certificates of deposit until this prohibition was modified for the commercial banks in 1979.) Since 1952 the IBJ has raised the bulk of its funding through five-year debentures and one-year discount bonds.[70] In fiscal 1990 industrial bank debentures made up 49.8 percent of total IBJ liabilities.[71]

2. Conversely, the IBJ's access to individual and corporate deposits was severely restricted. In accordance with the 1952 Long-Term Credit Bank Act, the three long-term credit banks were permitted to accept deposits only from the government, local authorities, corporate borrowers, companies that have entrusted the business of debenture issues to the IBJ, those for whom the banks provide safe custody of property, and exchange correspondents. The IBJ's endemic problem of a weak deposit base was exacerbated by stiff government restrictions on its branch network expansion; the IBJ had only twenty-six branches in 1978 and forty-four in 1992.[72]

3. Therefore, the IBJ's capability to loan money to others, and to play a central role in the national financial system, has traditionally depended on the cooperation of the other major financial power centers—MOF, the commercial banks, and the securities firms. The MOF set the interest rates on financial certificates (*kinyūsai*) and controlled the overall volume of *kinyūsai* issues outstanding through periodic changes in the IBJ's borrowing authority. The commercial banks bought a substantial, although decreasing, portion of *kinyūsai*, and the securities firms marketed the dominant proportion (nearly three-quarters across the 1970s and 1980s) of *kinyūsai* that were sold to individuals. The IBJ's breadth of transaction relationships became an important source of strength.

4. The IBJ is widely perceived as neutral in the feverish struggles among the great industrial groups in which Mitsubishi, Mitsui, Sumitomo, Sanwa, and other banks engage, and the IBJ's own "group" is less well defined than that of other major financial institutions, although it does perform some "main bank" functions. Although the IBJ has a stable of firms, such as Nippon Steel, Nissan Motors, and Hitachi, to whom it has been close since prewar days, it lends broadly to other firms, including many in the other groups. In 1976, the IBJ lent to 840,

or 53 percent, of all the listed firms on the Tokyo Stock Exc
cluding all ten major trading companies, and all nine elect
companies. It also lent to 96 percent of shipping firms, 91
those in shipbuilding, 81 percent of those in chemicals, and 7·
of steel firms listed on the Exchange.[73] In1985 it still lent to 7
and was top lender to 166 companies, a larger number than a₁
bank in Japan could claim.[74]

5. The IBJ had unsurpassed technical expertise, particularly in credit evaluation, macroeconomic analysis, and large-scale project organization at a critical formative period in the 1950s and 1960s, when the key public organizations, such as the Japan Development Bank, were new and the major private banks were still in a postwar state of disorganization and transition. The IBJ's expertise in these areas, much of it stemming from a central role in organizing the Japanese economy for World War II, even exceeds that of the trading companies, whose wartime experience was almost entirely commercial rather than organizational. The IBJ used its hard-learned organizational expertise to play the central role in organizing a number of massive *combinat* projects, domestically and overseas, both during the Bankers' Kingdom period and thereafter, and in training the analytical staffs of many other financial institutions. Indeed, it dispatched IBJ staffers to the government-owned Japan Development Bank, often in instructional roles, continuously from May 1951 right down to March 1970.[75]

6. The IBJ has sophisticated internal mechanisms for making industrial-credit decisions, including a highly esteemed Planning Office attached directly to the office of the chairman, a sophisticated credit department (*shinsa bu*) for evaluating long-term risk, and the largest industrial research department among Japan's major financial institutions. These research-oriented mechanisms within IBJ are powerfully situated institutionally, both because of their scale (nearly two hundred employees in 1992—roughly ten times the size of the internal research staff at Japan's largest commercial bank) and because of their venerability. The IBJ has had a credit department since 1929, and a large industrial research department in various incarnations since around 1955.[76] Top officials of the IBJ have served in both, giving these divisions of the bank special legitimacy.

7. The IBJ has been unusually active in neutralizing—indeed, even at times actively gaining the support of—its political environment. The IBJ was a consistent ally of growth-oriented Prime Minister Ikeda Hayato (1960–1964), and the bank's chairman, Nakayama Sōhei, was reportedly one of the central figures marshaling support for the expansionist Tanaka Kakuei when he ran for prime minister in 1972.

The IBJ's Human Network: A Crucial Strength
in Lending Decisions

The IBJ's neutrality, technical expertise, and paradoxically its vulnerability—its lack of a strong private-sector deposit base and its inability to invoke public sanctions like MITI and JDB—have long made it a useful, nonthreatening associate for a wide range of Japanese firms. As a consequence, the IBJ was able during the Bankers' Kingdom period to build up a formidable intelligence and human-relations network that generated the inside information on corporate performance and prospects to allow it to lend long-term with confidence. That smoothly integrated network, energized by the market forces operating uniquely on private firms, was as close to a central coordinating mechanism as has ever existed within the Japanese system of industrial finance, in sharp contrast to the decentralization and frequent rigidity of the public sector.

The IBJ's vaunted human network flows from a systematic and longstanding program of personnel transfers and industrial finance seminars that creates strong personal bonds between key IBJ analysts and executives elsewhere in Japanese (and recently global) industry. Most of the bank's Credit Appraisal Team (eighty officers in 1991) has experience on secondment with other firms—a rarity in Japanese business as a whole. Global networks are fostered through the extended Industrial Finance Seminars for foreigners, inaugurated in 1962.

In 1978, as the Bankers' Kingdom era was ending, there were also 93 IBJ alumni serving permanently in senior executive positions with other firms. Among this group were 22 executive officers, including Kawamata Katsuji of Nissan Motors (longtime vice-chairman of Keidanren), Watanabe Shōgō, chairman of Nikkō Securities, and Mitsuda Hirotaka of Daikyō Oil.[77] Kawamata, who went to Nissan in 1947 as IBJ's representative there, was without question the dominant figure in its rise to global prominence, serving as managing director (1949–1957), president (1957–1973), and chairman (1973–1985) for a total of thirty-six years of top-level service.[78]

Another 137 active-service IBJ employees were temporarily posted to other firms,[79] as well as 10 in government financial institutions, 17 in nonfinancial government corporations, and others in the Ministry of Finance, the Economic Planning Agency, the Ministry of Foreign Affairs, and the Ministry of Transportation. In all, 74 percent of IBJ employees who had been with the bank sixteen years or more had by the mid-1970s served in other organizations. Furthermore, 68 percent had served in the research division of the IBJ, which systematizes intelligence gained through IBJ sources concerning the many organizations with which the IBJ interacts.[80]

To foster international contacts as noted above, the IBJ has promoted its well-known International Finance Seminars for more than thirty years. By 1991 these seminars boasted more than fourteen hundred alumni in strategic executive positions throughout the world.[81] Over two hundred IBJ executives also have Western MBAs. Combined with the domestic personnel exchange described above, this remarkable two-way traffic between IBJ personnel and the world outside, fundamental to an efficiently functioning dedicated capital allocation system,[82] has sharply contrasted with the human isolation of Japanese public institutions more insulated by their official character, including preeminently the Bank of Japan.

The IBJ's human ties with industry even today center overwhelmingly on the basic industry sectors (especially steel, shipping, electric power, and shipbuilding) and on energy. This heritage from the past inevitably biases the bank's lending and coordinative approach, causing some adjustment difficulties as the Japanese economy becomes increasingly service oriented. The problem—that human networks establish a circle of compensation that constrains future allocative choice, without regard to institutional strategy—inhibits entry into newly emerging business fields. It is strikingly parallel to the difficulty often confronting Japan's public sector, although generally not so severe, due to the IBJ's private character and consequent greater ease in shedding unprofitable clientelistic associations.

The IBJ's sophisticated analytical network clearly works better in some economic environments than others. Apart from its uncanny prescience in the industrial sphere, about which more will be said later, it did identify some emerging consumer industries, such as fast foods and supermarkets, in the late 1970s and encouraged the IBJ to begin lending to them. But the IBJ made some spectacularly naive lending decisions during the speculative, easy-money era of the late 1980s, including unrecoverable loans of $1.8 billion to a Kansai restaurant owner, Onoue Nui, that forced the resignation of IBJ chairman Nakamura Kaneo in October 1991.[83] It seemed on far firmer ground using its industrial finance expertise and human network to aid new industrializers in China and other developing countries, an enterprise that its leadership stressed ever more strongly as the 1990s wore on.[84]

The only real analogue to the IBJ's powerful human network that can be found anywhere else in the world is probably in the powerful and entrepreneurial universal banks of Germany, such as the

Deutsche Bank and the Dresdner Bank. Like the IBJ, these German banks have also by tradition lent heavily to industry, while participating simultaneously in the management of their borrowers through a complex personal network of bank officials rotating on secondment through the borrower firms. In both cases these industrial-banking personnel networks appear to have played key roles in sensitizing the private industry of Japan to emerging business opportunities and aggressively supporting commercialization at the crucial transition from venture business to maturing industry where so many American manufacturing enterprises fail competitively.[85]

Dimensions of the IBJ's Allocative Role

The strong human connections, unsurpassed intelligence network, flexibility, and relatively low profile of the private-sector IBJ contrasted strikingly with the characteristic isolation of the public-sector BOJ, and the rigidity of the similarly public JDB during the Bankers' Kingdom period. The IBJ's attributes, plus its market-oriented receptivity and dynamism, gave it maximum opportunities during that period for leadership in industrial finance. Most of the other great institutional and personal mediators in Japan's recent political history, including the *zaikai* leadership of the early postwar years (mainly from small vulnerable firms) and such *kuromaku* (behind-the-scenes fixers) as Kobayashi Ataru and Sasakawa Ryōichi, have shared the IBJ's basic traits of vulnerability to public and private suggestion, neutrality, and broad personal connections. How fully did these traits allow the IBJ to become the arbiter and interest aggregator for the Japanese financial system as a whole during the epoch of high growth?

We must first reemphasize the IBJ's longtime strategic allocative role in chairing the Kisai Kondan Kai, or Bond Arrangement Committee.[86] This group met monthly throughout the high-growth period to determine the volume of new private-sector debt issues, the firms that issue, and the specific terms of each issue.[87] During the forced low-interest-rate period from about 1955 to 1970, the IBJ was in a most strategic position, given its status as the only permanent, nonrotating private-sector member of the Kisai Kai. But detailed discussions of what went on with former members who participated during the period of really tight controls (1958–1965) indicate that the IBJ's role was not the sort of "top-down" allocation posited under the developmental state model. To the contrary, the IBJ's role was more one of mediator. The convention of the council was to react to specific requests to issue rather than to formulate general guidelines, with the IBJ organizing a case-by-case consensus on these requests by private manufacturers.

Criteria for determining bond ratings (which implicitly allocate small firms out of the selection process without any explicit decision) were set by MOF administrative fiat, but adjusted with little nuanced sense for industrial strategy; our model of MOF's "regulatory" orientation, developed in chapter 3, would predict such an outcome. Collateral requirements had been fixed by legislation passed in 1933. These, rather than the Bond Committee's decisions, excluded trading companies and hotels from opportunities to issue bonds. Routine, rather than any explicit strategy, also constrained the Kisai Kai's discretion in formulating intersectoral allocation. Precedent assured, for example, that private railways and utilities should get priority because they had issued many bonds before the war; they were established members of the circle of compensation. Banking and securities industry pressure also forced the IBJ into a brokering as opposed to dictating role, since these two groups met separately before Kisai Kai meetings were convened to decide common strategies.

Ultimately the IBJ's role in the chair amounted to mediating among conflicts over a range of choices both restricted by authority and circumscribed by tradition. The Bond Arrangement Committee, through the IBJ's mediation, usually resolved conflicts by allowing the maximum possible number of applicants to issue and by reconciling supply and demand by cutting accepted requests pro rata. These patterns precisely conform to the routinized mandate of *baransu* (balance), noted by John Campbell in his study of general-account budgeting.[88] Thus, there appear to have been very few direct, decisive, discriminatory allocation decisions made in the Bond Committee—by the IBJ or anyone else. "Balance" and "precedent" have generally prevailed instead, with the IBJ doing little to disturb the pattern. In terms of Theodore Lowi's public policy typologies, Kisai Kai decision rules would be politically undemanding "constituent policies" or "regulative policies," with few politically delicate "redistributive" policies ever undertaken.[89] Bond decisions, in short, imposed little strain on the political system, but at the same time failed to provide the comprehensive review of strategic alternatives that one might expect in a "developmental state."

Until 1963, IBJ influence with industry and other banks was reinforced by MOF regulations making its financial debentures (*kinyūsai*) collateral for Bank of Japan loans, prized by the commercial banks due to their preferential interest rates.

The IBJ's coordinating role was enhanced from the mid-1960s on by rising influence over securities firms, which market its debentures. In 1965, for example, the IBJ and Finance Minister Tanaka Kakuei moved vigorously to prevent the bankruptcy of Japan's fourth largest securities firm, Yamaichi Securities, into whose presidency the IBJ then moved its own man, Hidaka Teru.[90] Faced during the late 1960s with a deteriorating market for debentures at the banks, which made the IBJ increasingly reliant on the securities companies, the Industrial Bank "captured" the presidency of the second largest firm, Nikkō Securities, and sent a senior director to third-ranking Daiwa. In 1970 it also created a new number-five firm, New Japan Securities, by engineering the merger of two smaller companies.

Apart from its role in bond issues and securities, the IBJ also harnessed government funds directly. In return for IBJ willingness to loan funds to strategic industrial sectors at preferential rates, and to provide consulting and organizational services as needed along with the loans, the Financial Bureau (Rizai Kyoku) of MOF took large positions in IBJ debentures, the Trust Fund Bureau itself not having been allowed since World War II to lend directly to private firms. This arrangement was, in a sense, a continuation of the government's prewar practice of loaning substantial funds to the IBJ for strategic investment; it was also available to the other two long-term credit banks. But the IBJ took most of the funds available, due to its particularly longstanding relations with government, and funneled them to sectors judged to have strong future potential. Under the terms of the program the IBJ provided, for example, loans to aluminum refining in May 1952, to steel and shipping in April 1953, to electric power in March 1962, to numerical-control machinery in 1965, to finance oil-refinery stockpiles in July 1975 and April–June 1976,[91] and to support software development after 1980. The lending decisions, it should be emphasized, were made by the private-sector IBJ, rather than within the government, although the general categories for lending were MITI-determined.

Until the Oil Shocks well over half of the IBJ's total loan portfolio was to manufacturing, as indicated in table 5-2, and the bank continues to be the backbone of key sectors in Japan's powerful industrial base. In 1991 the IBJ held 39.3 percent of plant and equipment loans outstanding to the electric power industry, together with 22.1 percent of steel, 18.3 percent of transportation machinery (mainly autos), and 16.6 percent of communications. These shares were several times the IBJ's 5.6 percent share of Japanese industrial equipment loans as a whole.[92]

TABLE 5-2

Transformation in Industrial Bank of Japan Lending Priorities (percentage of loans outstanding allocated to given sector)

Industry	1952	1955	1960	1965	1970	1975	1980	1985	1990	1991
Manufacturing total	64.5	52.4	55.6	60.9	62.8	53.7	43.0	29.3	15.2	17.0
Electric Power	8.7	16.6	16.8	13.6	8.5	8.8	13.0	13.4	8.1	7.4
Mining	1.5	9.3	5.8	4.1	1.3	1.3	1.0	0.9	0.4	0.3
Shipping	3.0	10.6	8.6	3.7	3.0	3.0	2.3	2.3	1.2	1.0
Steel	12.9	12.8	13.4	12.4	12.5	9.7	8.1	5.7	2.4	2.3
Nonferrous metals	2.5	1.1	1.4	1.6	4.0	4.0	4.1	2.7	1.2	1.2
Machinery	2.4	11.5	12.7	17.4	17.1	13.2	8.8	6.4	4.1	4.9
Electrical machinery				6.5	4.6	3.5	2.1	1.7	1.2	1.4
Transport machinery				8.2	9.6	6.9	5.0	3.5	1.7	2.4
Chemicals	10.2	8.2	9.8	12.4	11.9	10.1	7.7	5.3	2.2	2.7
Petroleum refining	3.4	1.2	1.6	1.7	3.2	3.1	3.5	2.0	1.1	1.5
Textiles	14.4	8.7	7.2	5.7	3.9	3.2	2.7	1.3	0.7	0.8
Commerce/distribution	4.0	3.8	2.8	3.2	6.6	8.0	10.0	8.0	10.5	11.1
Agriculture	1.6	1.5	2.3	1.8	1.2	0.7	0.6	0.3	0.2	0.2
Telecommunications				0.7	1.0	1.2	1.2	1.4	2.6	2.9

Source: Nihon Kōgyō Ginkō Nen Shi Henshū Iinkai, ed., *Nihon Kōgyō Ginkō Nana Jyū Go Nen Shi* (A Seventy-five-year History of the Industrial Bank of Japan) (Tokyo: Nihon Kōgyō Ginkō, 1982), appendix, 96–101; and IBJ internal unpublished data.

Note: Electrical machinery, transport machinery, and telecommunications were distinguished as separate categories only after 1964.

The IBJ's earliest and most consistent priority has been steel. Indeed, as chapter 4 pointed out, the IBJ was a far more substantial supporter and orchestrator of the first and second steel rationalization programs of the 1950s than the government-run Japan Development Bank. Even most of the JDB's own steel rationalization activities during this period were undertaken by IBJ executives on secondment to the JDB. Nakayama Sōhei, chairman of IBJ, personally orchestrated the 1970 merger giving birth to Nippon Steel, the largest steel producer in the world, and actively supported its subsequent growth. On the eve of the first Oil Shock in 1973, the IBJ had 11 percent of its loans out to the steel industry,[93] although this share has since declined to 2.3 percent.

The IBJ played an especially notable role in the rise of Japan's chemical and machinery industries, supporting them strongly from the early and mid-1950s. Petrochemicals, autos, and electronics were special beneficiaries. Following the Oil Shock the IBJ turned aggressively first to the electric power industry, spearheading Japan's diversification away from fossil-fuel power generation, and then to rationalization of the distribution sector and to mechatronics. Finally, from the early 1980s, it moved toward telecommunications and service, becoming a major backer, for example, of Tokyo Disneyland and Japan's fast-food industry.

The late 1970s and the 1980s were in some respects a dark period for the IBJ. The Oil Shocks severely damaged some of its best customers; the bank was forced to sharply expand its loans to petroleum refining between 1975 and 1980, for example, despite the depressed, unattractive state of that sector, to save its clients from bankruptcy. Good longstanding clients such as autos were so profitable during the 1980s that they did not need loans, forcing the IBJ toward smaller firms with often speculative operations. The number of IBJ clients spiralled from three thousand in 1970 to over seventy-five hundred in 1990, complicating credit assessment. It was this fluid environment, foreign and inhospitable to long-term credit banks, that provoked the bizarre Onoue lending scandal of 1991, involving $1.5 billion in IBJ loans to an Osaka restaurateur for stock speculation.

Collapse of the 1980s financial bubble during 1990–1991, however, coupled with a resurgent investment boom, showed promise of reviving, in some measure, the IBJ's traditional role of private-sector spearhead for industrial change. In 1991, as table 5-2 points out, the share of the IBJ's loans flowing to manufacturing began rising again, after years of steady decline stretching back to the first Oil Shock. Especially active were new loans to electrical and transport machinery, together with telecommunications—the cutting edge of Japan's mechatronics and information revolutions.[94] Once again the IBJ showed a prospect of becoming, albeit in a market-oriented era diminishing some of its traditional regulatory advantages, a primary catalyst of industrial change.

The IBJ's Innovative Lending in Comparative Perspective

To establish the creative catalytic role of the IBJ in Japanese industrial finance more clearly, it is instructive to compare the IBJ's new capital equipment lending to that of other major financial actors at various points in the product life cycle of key industries. As figures 5-3, 5-4, 5-5, and 5-6 suggest, the IBJ has consistently lent much more aggressively to emerging sectors than has the government's own Japan Development Bank. It has also consistently been far more supportive of manufacturing in general than either the JDB or Japanese banks in general, even though all Japanese financial institutions—public and private alike—shifted funds heavily toward services and infrastructure from the first Oil Shock until the end of the 1980s.[95]

As figure 5-3 indicates, in 1953 the government-run Japan Development Bank committed nearly 90 percent of its new loans to the four established priority sectors of the late 1940s—shipping, mining, steel, and power. Shipping and power, in particular, got very heavy funding. It was the IBJ, by contrast, that spearheaded movement into what were at that time emerging industrial sectors of the future. Machinery, where the IBJ placed 12 percent of its new loans in 1953 compared to less than 1 percent for the JDB, was a striking case in point. In chemicals (especially petrochemicals) and in steel, the IBJ was decidedly more aggressive than the JDB, in the context of a proportional commitment to manufacturing as a whole that was twice as intense as that of the JDB.

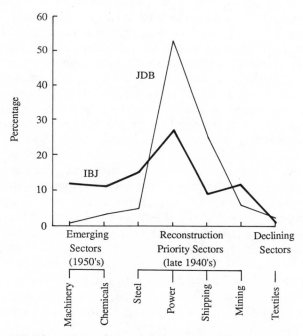

Figure 5-3. IBJ's Pioneering Role in Machinery and Chemicals, 1953

Autos provide an especially compelling illustration of the farsighted IBJ approach to emerging industrial sectors, contrasting to more reactive policies within the Japanese government itself. After five years of small-scale aid to autos during 1951–1956, spurred heavily by the need to expand Korean War procurement for U.S. forces, the JDB totally suspended new loans for Japan's auto industry during 1957–1966—hardly a gesture of even indicative, much less substantive, support.[96] By contrast, the IBJ did a number of insightful and very early studies of U.S., European, and Japanese auto-industry competitiveness; it concluded that Japan had a defensible niche in small cars and advocated aggressive financial support for the sector.[97] Based on this analysis, the IBJ spearheaded the industry's decisive expansion and modernization of the early 1960s. It did so long before MITI and the JDB came back in to attempt—with only limited success—a consolidation of the industry in the mid-1960s.

The details of IBJ lending to the auto sector, focusing on Nissan, reveal a degree of intimate involvement in sectoral development that the public sector, with its obsession with neutrality and risk aversion, could never match. The IBJ held a large, continuing equity stake, not only in Nissan, but in ten of its major affiliated companies across the metal, electronics, chemical, and auto component sectors, which helped insulate them from risk and allowed them all to think long-term.[98] The IBJ served as a catalyst for change by lending for such major initiatives as Nissan's development of diesel engine capacity after 1949,[99] and for expanding the company's distribution and parts production network.[100] The IBJ loaned the money to settle major disputes with workers (1950), and to assist parts suppliers and dealers during strikes.[101] The IBJ not only lent its own money, but it also guaranteed $14 million in U.S. Export-Import Bank loans (1959–1961) to finance the crucial modernization of Nissan's Oppama Works,[102] which became one of the most modern automobile plants in the world. The IBJ, in short, was omnipresent at Nissan.

The private Mitsui Bank also played an important early role at Toyota, particularly in supporting the expansion of its installment sales during the 1950s.[103] Indeed, Mitsui's longtime representative at Toyota, Nakagawa Fukio, was the only non-Toyota family member to serve as president of the preeminent auto maker, from 1961 to 1967.[104] Toyota also, beginning in 1959, received a succession of former presidents of the Mitsui Bank as its auditor,[105] thus establishing clear institutional ties that continued even as Toyota, over the course of the 1970s, became increasingly liquid and independent of bank finance.

Consumer electronics presents a similar pattern of private-sector initiative in a promising growth industry. During and after 1964, to be sure, the JDB and MITI reacted sharply and strategically to American inroads in the European computer industry, and to IBM's announcement of the 360 computer series at that time. But prior to that point the Japanese government had only a very limited support program for computers, as we saw in chapter 4. The IBJ's creative research department, with its broad, microlevel network of private industrial contacts, put together detailed and strongly bullish projections for the Japanese electronics industry as early as the spring of 1960, stressing the competitive success of Phillips in Europe against the powerful Americans, and emphasizing that the low raw-material content and high value added of the electronics industry made it an excellent one for Japan.[106] By the time MITI decisively committed to the electronics industry in 1965, the IBJ was already devoting over 6.5 percent of its loans to this sector. The longtime president of the IBJ, Nakayama Sōhei, thought so highly of the consumer electronics sector that he served for years as an outside director of Matsushita Electric, Japan's (and the world's) largest maker of color televisions and other household appliances.[107] The Ministry of International Trade and Industry, and industrial policy generally, by contrast, played only a minor role in the highly successful consumer electronics sector's development.

The clear pattern of private-sector IBJ leadership in industrial finance—and the converse rigidity and caution of government institutions—is clearly shown in figure 5-4. Even in 1965, over 60 percent of JDB loans remained committed to the priority sectors of two decades before, while the IBJ was far more diversified and oriented

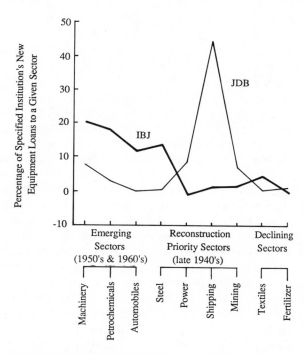

Figure 5-4. **IBJ as Innovator during the High-Growth Period, 1965**

toward new manufacturing sectors. It had begun moving beyond the autos and petrochemicals that it had so successfully developed during the late 1950s and the early 1960s toward a new generation of industries in the electronics area—well before MITI's vaunted pronouncements of the early 1970s about moving toward a "knowledge-intensive society."

By the mid-1970s, in the wake of the Oil Shock, a new generation of industries, many of them clearly postindustrial, was emerging in Japan. Their postindustrial character was clearly difficult for the IBJ, configured as it was toward heavy industry. Ongoing networks of human ties with older sectors likewise complicated the transition in priorities, as it had earlier for the JDB. As figure 5-5 suggests, however, the IBJ continued to remain aggressive in developing emerging sectors during the 1970s. The JDB, stimulated by the Oil Shock, foreign technological challenge, and political turbulence, was perhaps more innovative than during the 1960s, significantly expanding lending relating to the environment, urban renewal, information industries, and alternate energy. Its computer leasing progress, JECC, was particularly vigorous, and led to the high share of lending committed to the computer industry that is indicated in figure 5-5. But the IBJ clearly seems to have been more activist than the JDB in fostering new manufacturing sectors, such as mechatronics, which were at a critical stage in their struggles for global competitiveness.[108] It also played a more aggressive role than JDB in modernizing the Japanese distribution system.

The IBJ in the 1990s confronts a dramatically different world from that of the high-growth era. Japan is now among the most affluent nations on earth, with an increasingly globalized economy. The role of domestic industry within the economy as a whole is dramatically reduced. Yet within that transformed economy the IBJ remains innovative.

In several sectors pivotal to Japan's growth and prosperity over the coming decade, the IBJ remains central. It remains substantially more committed to entrepreneurship than do ordinary private banks. In computers and telecommunications, for example, the IBJ has twice or more the proportional commitment of banks across Japan in the aggregate.[109] In the modernization of the distribution and of the machinery industry, the IBJ is playing a more central role than either the JDB or the commercial banks, although recent legislative changes have given the JDB new scope in the electronics and telecommunications area. In 1990, for example, 10.5 percent of new IBJ lending went to distribution-sector modernization, compared to only 3.1 percent of new JDB loans and 8.5 percent of commercial banks as a group.[110]

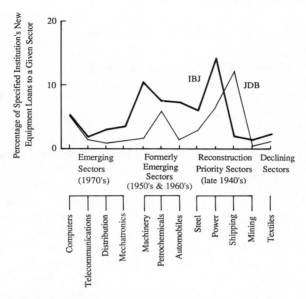

Figure 5-5.   Innovation in the Shadow of Oil Shock, 1974

Like MITI, MOF, the BOJ, and the government financial institutions, the IBJ has not had the leverage to consistently dominate the process of Japanese industrial-credit allocation alone. But it has nevertheless possessed information, personnel networks, and an aggressive, entrepreneurial spirit that allowed it to be a major player in directing resources toward potentially competitive Japanese industries of the future. It has, in this sense, been an effective purveyor of "dedicated capital." To a greater degree than most public institutions, which are often more constrained by the conservative requisites of law and administrative process, this private body has spearheaded the development of Japan's most internationally competitive industries. The IBJ thus illustrates clearly the powerful impact of private initiative in Japanese postwar economic development.

As we saw in chapters 2, 3, and 4, the Japanese state has been far less unified, far less strategic, and far more reactive in its credit-allocation behavior than generally appreciated: a disunity and at times even a conceptual paralysis giving long-term credit banks and other private institutions important opportunities to shape the profile of industrial finance. That private sector has been animated in its definition of Japan's industrial future not only by lenders, but also crucially by the individual firms that borrow. It is to their struggle for credit, and how it weaves into the overall tapestry of credit allocation in Japan, that we now turn.

CHAPTER 6

Private Borrowers
and Public Credit Controls

THE STORY of private-sector initiative in Japanese government-business relations is not solely that of the bankers and their lending compatriots. It is also at critical junctures a chronicle of the borrowers as well. For contrary to the assumptions of the state-centric developmental model of the Japanese political economy, or even the logic of the Bankers' Kingdom, the private-sector borrowers—no less than the private-sector lenders—have been highly dynamic in the credit-allocation process. Their internal capital allocation decisions have generally emphasized long-term growth, and they have aggressively sought the capital to make that possible.[1] Their incentives and forms of maneuver have often decisively shaped actual credit decision making, causing the actual allocation across firms of scarce industrial capital to be often highly dynamic, pluralistic bargaining process, rather than a matter of government fiat.

The questions of how borrower calculations have influenced industrial-credit outcomes—and the forms those calculations have taken relative to government industrial-credit policies—are the central concerns of this chapter. Since these questions are microeconomic and micropolitical—although crucially important to an understanding of the Japanese political economy as a whole—they are approached here through case studies, albeit case studies with transcendent empirical and theoretical relevance. At the end of this chapter the broader implications of these cases for business-government relations in Japan as a whole are considered.

Three patterns of borrower response to government credit controls are presented, each corresponding to one of the logical modes of reaction to the prospective compromise of corporate objectives that control implies. The analysis thus parallels Hirschman's classic typology of responses to decline in firms, organizations, and states: "exit," "voice," and "loyalty."[2] It draws conceptually upon Hirschman's formulation in elucidating both the pressures that cause Japanese private borrowers to respond as they do to state efforts to allocate credit and the external circumstances that shape the choice of borrowers among these three options.

The broad progression of Japanese government-business relations over the past fifty years has been from relatively passive corporate adherence to wartime mobilization dictates (loyalty) through a period of resistance to controls on the part of competitive industry as high growth began (exit), and on to a business-government interaction that is increasingly a matter of noncompetitive firms pursuing the state (voice). The three cases explored in depth here—auto parts in the transwar years, Kawasaki Steel in the 1950s, and Sasebo Heavy Industries in the post–Oil Shock period—represent this historical progression and can easily be presented within the Hirschman analytical framework. By exploring these cases in the loyalty-exit-voice sequence, we can thus simultaneously explore in microcosm the details of the private-sector borrowing behavior so decisive to the actual outcome of industrial-credit decisions, while also gaining a better sense of evolutionary patterns within the Japanese political economy as it has evolved over time. In grasping concretely the persistent activism—as well as the occasional passivity—of Japanese private-sector borrowers confronting an intrusive yet fragmented and often reactive state, we can understand better the dynamic, pluralistic interplay of state and society that has been central to Japan's dramatic postwar economic success.

Loyalty—the acquiescence of private corporate borrowers in state efforts at control—is the norm assumed by those viewing Japan as a strong, developmental state, as being typical generally of Japanese private-sector relations to the Japanese state. This characterization, it should be stressed, has at some very important junctures, particularly amid the reconstruction of the early postwar period—when demand for capital was high, the state was relatively cohesive, and the private sector had little capacity to challenge—conformed fairly closely to Japanese reality. Such instances of private-borrower cooperation with the state in its dirigiste allocative efforts conform fairly well to generalizations about Japan as a developmental state. The first case presented here—that of the Japanese auto parts industry from the 1930s through the 1960s—captures this pattern of strong state leadership, culminating in dominant international competitiveness. The case is of an entire industry rather than a specific firm, because the key analytical dynamics are collective—the firms are very small, and industry associations of several firms, together with MITI, are the principal actors.

Availability of the exit option—the ability to avoid controls altogether—is, as Hirschman points out, the classical assumption of normal competition and of the free enterprise system.[3] Yet recent mainstream thinking about the Japanese system of industrial policy, particularly for the two transwar decades of the most stringent economic controls, has implied that such an option was not practically available to Japanese firms or at least not exercised.[4] Many have argued that Japan, at least during this transwar control period, was not a free enterprise system.

Yet the second case in this chapter—that of Kawasaki Steel, where the exit option of evading controls was successfully pursued by a major borrower in a priority basic industry (*kikan sangyō*)—presents a challenge to this conventional viewpoint. We explore not only the details of the case, but also the broader circumstances under which Kawasaki was able to bob and weave with such success. In doing so, we illustrate circumstances—much more pervasive than the developmental state model implies—under which private-sector initiative becomes determining in the face of public passivity and institutional fragmentation.

Voice is the only way that dissatisfied would-be borrowers can actively redress the status quo when the exit option is unavailable or unattractive. In the acquisition of industrial credit, voice amounts to political activism—explicit use of the political process to influence state decisions on credit. The case presented here—Sasebo Heavy Industries' attempts in the late 1970s to avoid bankruptcy by directly appealing for political support of its borrowing efforts—shows one set of circumstances in which political appeals were successful, and the implications for other similar cases, which have become more numerous since the dual Oil Shocks of the 1970s. Taken jointly, the three cases show that a careful consideration of Japanese private-sector borrowers is clearly a prerequisite to understanding how fully the industrial-credit policies of the Japanese state are actually implemented.

THE LOYALTY OPTION: STATE STRATEGY AND THE AUTO-PARTS INDUSTRY, 1936–1967

Even in the credit-control period, borrowers seem to have acquiesced less often in the bureaucratically directed allocation of credit than conventional wisdom suggests. But there was considerable variation. Sometimes would-be borrowers did cooperate closely with government, as in the case of the Japanese auto-parts industry, at least until the mid-1960s, although the broader implications for industrial competitiveness remain controversial.[5]

Wartime Origins

Japan's indigenous auto-parts industry, now producing items from transmissions and engine parts to steering wheels and windshield wipers, was a creature of the industrial mobilization for war with China after 1937. Autos had, of course, been produced in Japan well before that. Japan's first auto company, Tokyo Jidōsha, was founded in 1904, only about a decade after the dawn of the automotive age in the West. But parts manufacture had been monopolized throughout the 1920s and early 1930s by the American multinationals Ford and General Motors.

The U.S. firms began to increase local subcontracting of parts in Japan after MCI raised the tariff on parts imports in 1931.[6] It was only after the military-dominated government effectively shut down the auto-assembly operations of foreign firms in the turbulent years after 1936 that an indigenous Japanese parts industry attained real significance. Indeed, the Japanese parts industry was able to grow at all during the 1930s only because government, for strategic reasons, suppressed the operations of foreign producers, while the Automobile Manufacturing Enterprise Law (Jidōsha Seizō Jigyō Hō) of 1936 required the domestication of parts production and authorized the minister of commerce and industry both to co-designate firms in need of modernization and to direct funds toward firms conforming to government plans. Ever since the 1930s the omnipresence of the foreign threat and the joint resolve of business and bureaucracy to combat it through government-led cooperation have been persistent themes in the industry's history.[7]

When Japan finally did begin to develop an automotive-parts industry (particularly oriented toward truck parts) under the exigencies of wartime, the sector was accorded high strategic priority. This fact contributed profoundly to the industry's clear early subservience to the state. Cut off from foreign supplies of pistons, bearings, engines, and carburetors while at war with first China and then the Western Allies as well, Japan simply had to develop an efficient automotive-parts industry to ensure that its tanks and trucks would run. Strategic imperatives dictated massive bureaucratic intervention in auto-parts industry development from its earliest days; the pronounced institutional conservatism of Japan then "froze" in place the prewar pattern of control for nearly three decades.

The Organized Private Sector: A Key Supporting Role

Even in auto parts, however, there was an important role for the private sector in working-level policy administration from the earliest days of the industry. In May 1938 the MCI masterminded the establishment of a Japan Auto Parts Industrial Association (JAPIA) composed of private firms in the industry, which it frequently used as an intermediary in reorganizing the auto-parts sector. In 1941 all the suppliers in the industry came under its jurisdiction. From 1942 to 1945 JAPIA undertook to supply raw materials and to apportion production responsibilities on the MCI's behalf through its operational arm, the Regional Automobile Maintenance and Distribution Corporation (JIHAI).[8] In 1946 a former MITI official became an executive officer of JAPIA and continued in that position for three decades. This strategic network connection between government and business helped make JAPIA, a private association with strong MITI ties, a key element in the transformation of the auto-parts industry across the postwar period, providing private-sector advice and cooperation with MITI's developmental plans.

Postwar Bureaucratic Backing

Following World War II, the auto-parts industry initially languished in the face of SCAP restrictions on militarily related industries and the pressing needs of reconstruction elsewhere in the economy. After 1948 it did get some stimulus from the U.S. military's program for rebuilding surplus military equipment, known as Operation Roll-Up. The Korean War, of course, was also helpful.[9] But systematic growth really began when auto parts began to attract MITI's attention in the mid-1950s. The Bank of Japan, under Governor Ichimada Naoto, opposed the development of an indigenous auto industry during the early 1950s, but MITI realized that autos showed considerable export potential and encouraged development of that sector. Auto parts were an area of particular concern for MITI because:

1. Their costs made up a large proportion of total auto-production costs and were hence a key element in determining the export competitiveness of the auto industry as a whole.

2. Their imports consumed a good deal of foreign exchange, so to manufacture domestically promised crucial import substitutions.

3. In the early 1950s the industry was highly fragmented, with 80 percent of parts firms in 1954 capitalized at under ¥50 million and

many of them producing a relatively broad and therefore inefficient range of automotive parts,[10] offering important gains in efficiency through specialization, consolidation, and modernization under MITI administrative guidance.

Auto parts, in sum, had kept their strategic significance for a poor industrial country, and hence for MITI.

Conversely, MITI had not lost its attraction for the auto-parts industry. Auto parts firms were growing rapidly, with a concomitant thirst for cash. Furthermore, few of them had strong connections with major banks or industrial groups, a pattern very different from those of the shipbuilding, computer, or petrochemical firms. The auto-parts makers, particularly in the 1950s, badly needed stable access to investment funds and had few institutional advocates in the financial system to provide it. The ministry and its strategic industrial priorities were the auto makers' strongest safeguards against the volatility in credit supply, interest rates, and compensating balances that typically beset small firms, until they began acquiring independent access to capital markets during the 1960s. Toyota's suppliers—larger, more efficient, and more profitable than those of Nissan or the other producers—were the first to do so.

The demand of the auto-parts firms for credit was large in relation to their size, but not relative to the funds demand of firms in heavy-industrial sectors such as steel or petrochemicals. This situation—relatively small absolute demand for funds accompanied by distance from the commercial banking sector—offered the greatest possible discretionary authority to MITI. It could supply auto-parts borrowers through funding sources largely under its control (the Japan Development Bank and the Small Business Finance Corporation) without having to coordinate positions with the often antagonistic Bank of Japan, armed with its great influence over the commercial banks. While MITI possessed the maximum freedom to maneuver, the auto-parts borrowers were constrained by the weakness of their commercial bank ties, their strong desire for investment funds, and their own poor political connections. This complementarity between bureaucratic strength and private-borrower weakness was at the heart of the unusually strong government influence in the allocation of credit that was long typical in auto parts, especially during the 1950s. A common interest in growth and international competitiveness cemented the government-business alliance.

In June 1952, shortly after the end of the Occupation swept away SCAP control over Japanese development of strategic industries, and while the exigencies of war in Korea still continued to make them profitable, MITI inaugurated subsidies for the auto-parts sector. In July 1953 a program of rationalization loans began, with roughly 10 percent of the firms in the industry being screened to receive funds. On May 19, 1954, the Japan Development Bank for the first time extended loans to three firms in the industry at 6.5 percent interest—at least 3 to 3.5 percent below commercial rates.[11]

Despite various sporadic attempts by MITI during the early 1950s to allocate credit among auto-parts firms, the systematic postwar development of the industry within a control framework was initiated somewhat later. In the summer of 1955 MITI proposed creation of a small but powerful Machinery Industry Promotion Corporation (Kikai Kōgyō Shinkō Jigyōdan), a public body under its direct control, which would selectively allocate government loans and subsidies among firms in eighteen priority sectors,[12] including communication and electrical equipment, as well as auto parts.[13] The efforts of MITI to expand its powers to allocate credit incurred fierce opposition from both commercial banks and the Bank of Japan. Nippon Telephone and Telegraph, the government telecommunications monopoly, also put up fierce resistance, fearing loss of organizational independence, and MITI's proposal was temporarily shelved. But in June 1956 the Diet passed a revised measure to grant MITI more limited allocative authority—a Special Measures Law for Promotion of the Machinery Industry (Kikai Kōgyō Shinkō Rinji Sochi Hō). This legislation, prepared by MITI bureaucrats, was pushed through the Diet by perhaps the most politically potent contingent of MITI alumni ever to serve there during the postwar period, headed by the LDP secretary general Kishi Nobusuke, soon to become prime minister.

The new law, known in abbreviated form as the Kishin Hō, provided that the MITI minister (in effect, the MITI section in charge of a particular industry) might designate sectors within the general sphere of machinery for promotion and also designate specific projects by individual firms to be "assured" of funds within the areas selected. The Kishin Hō also provided for the formation of plans to direct the evolution of the various industrial sectors falling within its scope, rather than allowing those industries' development to be determined by short-term market forces. Although MITI was denied the opportunity of allocating credit through a public corporation under its own exclusive control, it was empowered to "assure" credit to projects it deemed of priority concern. To this end it was empowered to issue lists of eligible firms, which served as a mandatory basis for lending by the Japan Development Bank and the Small Business Finance Corporation. The law also created an advisory committee (shingikai) to offer general policy suggestions to MITI, although this committee had no direct involvement in specific allocation decisions.

This sweeping statute, initially valid for five years, was twice renewed and hence provided the governing framework for government-business relations in the auto-parts industry from 1956 to 1971. When this pattern of strong government influence after the war is juxtaposed with the similar prewar pattern, it becomes clear that the Japanese state enjoyed unusually broad powers in relation to the auto-parts industry for the first twenty-five to thirty years of its existence.

What concrete evidence suggests this? First, the existence of the comprehensive legal framework for control and the asymmetry of power relations between MITI and its client companies both suggest a depth of bureaucratic power. In addition, the critical role of the auto-parts sector in the auto industry's overall development, and the threat of foreign competition, gave the bureaucracy the *incentive* to apply credit control with energy and purpose. Third, the control element shows up in the omnipresence of planning organizations[14] and of plans[15] in the industry's history.

Again, control shows up clearly in government's efforts to encourage sectoral concentrations in the various sectors of the parts industry. This was induced by administrative pressure for mergers, business tieups, and even enforced bankruptcies, rather than leaving events to the indirection of the market. Through the Auto Section of the Heavy Industry Bureau and the Subcontractor Section of the Small Business Agency (an affiliate organization under MITI's direct control), MITI decided what the organizational structure of the industry was to be and then proceeded to carry that policy out by manipulating loan and technological licensing agreements.

One policy guideline frequently resorted to was consolidation of parts sectors into three firms—one a Nissan and one a Toyota affiliate, and one an independent.[16] Under pressure from MITI, the concentration of production in auto parts rose steadily throughout the 1960s—three-firm production of clutches rose from 79 percent in 1963 to 96 percent in 1968, for example. By the late 1960s a full 100 percent of piston rings and spark plugs were produced by three firms, and those ratios were rising rapidly for speedometers, radiators, carburetors, and miscellaneous engine components as well.[17]

In auto-parts distribution, which until the 1960s was one of the key bottlenecks of Japanese auto competitiveness, rationalization occurred through a combination of public and private long-term credit-banking efforts. Tradition and complex ongoing business relationships with established distributors discouraged the manufacturers from dealing directly with parts producers, particularly for established labor-intensive items such as windshield wipers. The ministry felt that such institutional arrangements seriously raised automobile production costs, and it resolved to streamline distribution. To this end it enlisted the support of the Industrial Bank of Japan and set up an industry committee under IBJ auspices to study potential changes.[18] This Auto Parts Distribution Rationalization Committee, convened in November 1964, had by August 1965 approved comprehensive guidelines for practically all aspects of distribution, down to the allocation of appropriate margins among various wholesalers.[19] Using its leverage on financial and technological questions, MITI secured the plan's adoption by the parts industry, greatly enhancing auto-export competitiveness.

The success of MITI, in cooperation with the IBJ, in rationalizing the auto-parts distribution sector during the mid-1960s was in striking contrast to its failure during the 1970s to rationalize the consumer goods distribution system, over which it also holds administrative responsibility.[20] Unlike the small retailers who have long enjoyed strong links with the Communist, Socialist, and Kōmeitō parties, as well as the ruling LDP, the small auto-parts makers have had virtually no political connections except marginal ones with the conservative opposition Democratic Socialist party, a traditional friend of small manufacturing. This lack of political ties has greatly enhanced bureaucratic leverage vis-à-vis the parts industry.

The relatively substantial component of loans from government financial institutions in the total loan indebtedness of the parts companies, particularly during the 1956–1960 period, reinforces one's sense of a powerful state presence in the Japanese auto-parts industry at critical junctures in industry development.[21] As a proportion of total loans, government loans for the entire 1956–1971 period, when the auto-parts industry was under strong formal governmental direction, averaged over 15 percent, or double the overall average in manufacturing.[22] And for priority firms at critical junctures in their development, the figure frequently reached 50 percent and higher—their effectiveness being reinforced by especially favorable depreciation programs.[23]

These loans were typically tendered at concessionary rates at least 3 to 4 percent below market levels and were most decisive to industry development during 1956–1958, just after the Kishin Hō was introduced, and during 1963–1968, when large-scale rationalization was under way.[24] The largest loans flowed from the Japan Development Bank and the Small Business Finance Corporation, although U.S. Export-Import Bank loans were also tendered in 1961. Auto parts typically received about 30 percent of all the government loans disbursed to machinery industries during the 1960s.[25]

The Decline of MITI Dominance

To be sure, MITI did occasionally experience failures in auto parts, especially when its efforts conflicted with the interests of large private firms. During 1966–1971, for example, it tried to realign the parts firms into large "subassembly producer" groups cutting across *keiretsu* ties. A number of subcontractors merged into primary-parts manufacturers.[26] Two large Nissan affiliates in the lighting-equipment area merged. A three-way clutch venture, including Toyota and Nissan affiliates, was considered. But the projected cross-*keiretsu* functional reorganization went unimplemented as the makers affected borrowed from their *keiretsu* leader (Nissan, Toyota, and so on) rather than from the government.

This incident demonstrated that, at least by the late 1960s, MITI's capacity to control was uncertain at best when it came to overriding the desires of the major *keiretsu* leaders in matters of credit-allocation, particularly when those private auto manufacturers were sufficiently liquid to finance their subcontractors directly. As these major producers grew increasingly flush on burgeoning exports during the 1970s, MITI influence with the parts manufacturers by virtue of its credit-allocation capabilities eroded even further.[27] Bureaucratic influence with the auto-parts industry, incomplete even in its heyday, declined rapidly after 1967.

Despite lapses in the structure of control, the auto-parts industry case demonstrates, particularly for the 1936–1967 period, a pattern of relatively effective direction of credit allocation and overall industrial policy by the bureaucracy.[28] But it is important to remember that even in that sector the government-business relationship was a two-way street. Corporate needs for capital and freedom from the pronounced uncertainties of small business in high-growth Japan were served by a strategy of "loyalty" even as national industrial goals were also achieved. The dictates of MITI alone cannot explain the evolving patterns of credit allocation and sectoral development.

THE EXIT OPTION: AVOIDING CONTROLS AT KAWASAKI STEEL, 1950–1956

Along National Highway 16, just as one leaves the outskirts of Chiba City along Tokyo Bay, stands a slightly dilapidated, smoke-belching steel mill. By current Japanese standards, the Chiba plant of Kawasaki Steel, two generations old, is not very big. It has only 6.5 million tons of crude steel production capacity, as against 16 million for Nippon Kōkan's giant Fukuyama Works on the shores of the Inland Sea. Chiba is dwarfed by these modern giants, including also the huge Oita and Kimitsu plants of Nippon Steel, which cost ten to fifteen times its ¥27.3 billion.

But for what it symbolizes about the operation of controls in the heart of the Japanese financial system, and the dynamism of Japan's private sector, the very existence of the Chiba Works is a beacon. It represents the incapacities of bureaucratic controls in the face of determined corporate efforts to finesse them. This important case represents the *birth* of active competition in the postwar Japanese steel industry. It shows how this competition and the enormous boost to economic growth that it generated arose from private-sector decision rather than, as some have argued, state strategy.[29]

Ichimada Naoto, governor of the Bank of Japan from 1946 to 1954, violently opposed the building of the Chiba Works when it was proposed in mid-1950. "I will show you unruly wild grass growing on that spot," he is said to have raged.[30] Ichimada himself insists that the expression is apocryphal, the invention of a literary-minded journalist, but concedes that he strongly opposed the plan.[31]

Chiba, to Ichimada, represented a frontal threat to the ordered system of planning and stable growth that he saw as Japan's only course in the turbulent postwar years. Numerous high officials in both MITI and the Ministry of Finance, together with leaders of the Japan Iron and Steel Federation, opposed the plant's financing and construction during a period when the power of credit controls was at its height. Yet the necessary funds were raised, even though they amounted to fifty-four times Kawasaki's 1950 capitalization, and the Chiba plant was built.

Even had it not faced fierce government opposition, Kawasaki Steel in 1950 would hardly have seemed a firm likely to succeed in raising ¥27.3 billion for a new steel mill. When it made its initial loan application in 1950, "Kawatetsu," as it is abbreviated in Japanese, was a small, Ōsaka-based open-hearth steel producer capitalized at ¥500 million, or about 3 percent of the amount it first proposed to raise.[32] It had a production capacity of eight hundred thousand tons of crude steel, one-sixth of the ultimate capacity of the plant it was trying to build.

To make matters worse, Kawasaki had a history of troubled relations with banks, including unusually distant ties with its main bank, the Dai Ichi. And being a smaller firm from Kansai, or western Japan, without membership in a major industrial group such as Mitsui or Mitsubishi, Kawatetsu lacked many of the establishment connections that might have substituted for a strong main bank affiliation. The firm was, in short, the sort of maverick with high aspirations that frequently does not prosper in Japan's ordered, group-oriented society.

The basic strengths of Kawatetsu as borrower in its struggle to finance Chiba were its fierce desires for organizational autonomy and for expanded market share—concerns in some degree common to virtually all Japanese businesses. The main constraints on Kawatetsu's autonomy were banks, MITI, and preeminently the Big Three integrated steel producers—Yahata, Fuji, and Nippon Kōkan. In 1950 Kawasaki Steel was only an open-hearth producer specializing in rolled steel products such as strip and sheet. Unlike the Big Three, Kawasaki had no blast furnaces and was hence dependent on those larger firms for the crude steel to produce rolled products. Since those firms used their control over Kawatetsu's supply of pig iron to limit its expansion, Kawatetsu was, of course, eager to establish its independence by obtaining a blast furnace of its own.

Nishiyama Yataro, Kawatetsu's expansion-oriented engineer-president, had been dreaming of a massive, new, integrated Kawasaki steel mill since his days as section chief (kachō) in the steel division of Kawasaki Shipbuilding in 1935. Originally he wanted to build in the Chita Peninsula of Aichi prefecture in central Japan, but changed this after the war to Yamaguchi prefecture, the home area of numerous MITI bureaucrats. Even so, Nishiyama's plan was still not received favorably by MITI.

Finally, in the wake of intense lobbying by municipal and prefectural authorities in the Chiba area, Nishiyama decided to propose construction of a major steel mill on Tokyo Bay. This mill was to be the first major new steel mill built in Japan since World War II and the first integrated plant for Kawasaki Steel. It promised, in short, to revolutionize the structure of the Japanese steel industry if completed, by breaking the Big Three oligopoly and initiating an era of more competitive growth. Since Kawatetsu was such a small firm and since credit was tight so soon after the war, whether the plant could be built or not depended fundamentally on whether the credit could be raised.

Bank of Japan governor Ichimada first learned in the summer of 1950 that Kawatetsu seriously planned a major steel mill and was violently opposed. Influenced both by his encounters with the German hyperinflation of the 1920s and subsequent experiences within Japan, he saw Kawasaki's plan as both economically irrational and inflationary.[33] Throughout the second half of 1950, Ichimada considered the danger of inflation ominously real. In a September 27 address in Nagoya he stressed his fears that the Korean War would lead to inflation and balance-of-payments deficits for Japan, as world commodity prices spiraled ominously upward.[34]

The State Divided

Kawatetsu's initial strategy was political—to finesse Ichimada's opposition by lining up allies who could either pressure him to change his mind or at least inhibit active opposition. Its president, Nishiyama, went first to local government in Chiba prefecture, which was eager to see the Chiba Works built due to the substantial expansion of employment and tax base that the plant promised to provide. In informal negotiations spanning the summer and early fall of 1950, Nishiyama hammered out an arrangement calling for Kawasaki Steel to buy a 1.98-million-square-meter tract of land in Chiba, purchased originally by Hitachi Aircraft for a wartime aircraft factory that was never built. In return for Kawatetsu's decision to locate in Chiba, Nishiyama obtained from local authorities: (1) exemption from local taxes, extending until five years after completion of the *entire* mill; (2) a ¥15 million, fifteen-year loan (nearly tripled in 1952) from Chiba City at 5 percent below commercial rates,[35] and extended without provision for collateral; (3) gratis provision of port and water facilities, together with materials for landfill operations; (4) free improvement of electric power lines in the area of the steel mill; (5) Chiba city and prefectural aid in erecting dormitories and other social welfare facilities for workers and their families.[36]

In addition to the concrete material concessions, and perhaps more important from the perspective of realizing the Chiba project as a whole, Nishiyama got political support from local government and its allies in his confrontation with the Bank of Japan's Ichimada. On November 15, 1950, just after Kawatetsu had submitted to the BOJ its formal notice of intention to build, the Chiba City Council passed a resolution of support for the Chiba Steel plant project, endorsing the sweeping concessions granted to Kawatetsu in return for its locating in Chiba. Five days later the Chiba Prefectural Council passed a similar resolution.

Nishiyama's second move, after securing support from local government, was to approach MITI, where Kawatetsu had substantial, but not unanimous, support. Buoyed by the prospect of imminent endorsement from the local authorities, on November 7 he submitted to MITI minister Takahashi Kōtarō a moderate construction plan for a 500,000-ton crude steel capacity mill, together with a request for an ¥8 billion government loan, drawn from U.S. Agency for International Development (AID) counterpart funds under the control of MITI.[37] This loan request represented almost half the original ¥16.3

billion projected cost for the Chiba mill. Kawatetsu sanguinely assumed that despite Bank of Japan opposition, it would be able to fund its steel mill project with a heavy infusion of government money.

Officials in the Tokyo Bureau of MITI, clients in a sense of the Kantō area's local governments, supported Kawatetsu.[38] Low-level, technically oriented MITI officials such as a strategic section chief in the Iron and Steel Bureau, Tobata Shintarō, a pragmatic technician hostile to oligopolistic Big Three control of the steel industry, felt the Chiba plan was realistic and well conceived, and they supported the loan application. But the higher-level officials at MITI were inhibited by their prevailing interpersonal networks: close ties to retired seniors "descended from heaven" into the steel oligarchy, including the presence of a wartime MCI vice minister at Yahata Steel. Thus the Iron and Steel Bureau chief during 1950–1952, Nakamura Goro, and the Commercial Promotion chief, Hirai Tomisaburō, who coordinated administration of loan subsidies during 1949–1952,[39] were both cool toward Kawasaki's plans.[40]

Aside from the support of oligarchic prejudices, the opponents of the Chiba project within MITI and the Bank of Japan were also bolstered by the overall Japanese economic situation in 1950. The country, and particularly the steel industry, was suffering a severe shortage of raw materials due to disruption of trade with China and a general lack of foreign exchange. Coking coal and pig iron were being rationed by MITI, and this was expected to continue; one blast furnace in Kokura had only a ten-day ore supply by late December.[41] Only twenty-two of the thirty-seven blast furnaces in Japan were operating, and MITI saw attainment of the fiscal 1950 steel production target (3 million tons of blast furnace and 410,000 tons of open-hearth crude steel) as problematical. Under such circumstances, even to talk, as did Kawatetsu, of 500,000-ton additions to national steel capacity struck the conservatives within MITI as premature.

Given divisions within MITI on the Chiba project, the ministry's response was predictable: delay. Three months after Kawatetsu's initial loan application, MITI informed it that the prospects were "not promising at present"; three months after that, in May 1951, MITI asked Kawatetsu, together with other firms, to submit a "rationalization plan." Kawatetsu scaled its proposal down and, to defuse opposition, divided it into four segments that could be implemented separately, but still could not finalize a government loan.

In early 1952 Kusagawa Oji, more favorably disposed toward Kawatetsu than his predecessor, became Iron and Steel Bureau director general. Against the backdrop of a Korean War economic boom sharply intensifying domestic demand for steel, MITI became more actively supportive. In March 1952, under MITI pressure, the Bank of Japan Policy Board convened to deliberate on the long-pending question of a government loan for Kawatetsu. Kawatetsu president Nishiyama and MITI's Kusagawa testified forcefully of the need for the Chiba mill in light of overall national supply-and-demand relationships in steel. Even Mitō Takashi, president of the Japan Iron and Steel Institute and of Yahata Steel, a leading member of the oligarchic order Kawatetsu was trying to break, was persuaded to formally support Kawatetsu's loan application. But the old antagonisms at the BOJ toward the Chiba project had not died. The Policy Board voted to refer the loan application, now a year and a half old, to the BOJ's Loan Mediation Bureau (Yūshi Assen Bu) for "study." Five months later the Policy Board at last approved Kawatetsu's initial stage financial plan for Chiba.[42] But no money was immediately forthcoming, despite the growing national demand for steel.

Crucial Scope for Private Initiative

Had the Japan of the early 1950s been a truly centralized decision-making unit, with no centers of policy initiative to rival MITI and the Bank of Japan, the story of government financial support for the Chiba Steel Works might have ended right there—in clear rejection for the private borrowers. But Kawasaki Steel was able to evade an initial negative allocative judgment by the Bank of Japan through the support of a different government actor—in this case the Japan Development Bank.

The Japan Development Bank in the early 1950s was formally under the authority of both the Bank of Japan and MITI, in that its operating instructions were to come from MITI and major loans were formally to be cleared with the Bank of Japan Policy Board.[43] But its chairman and vice-chairman were men of considerable independent political standing, giving the JDB substantial independence of BOJ in its loan decisions. The JDB's chairman, Kobayashi Ataru, was a close political confidant of erstwhile finance minister Ikeda Hayato,[44] while Vice-Chairman Nakayama Sōhei was a top official and president-to-be of the powerful Industrial Bank of Japan. Both were prominent members of the "pro-growth" faction within conservative political ranks.

With MITI self-neutralized in the Chiba stalemate, Kobayashi decided to commission an independent assessment of Kawatetsu's plan. Using highly professional staff on loan from the Industrial Bank of Japan, and with Kawatetsu's enthusiastic cooperation, JDB's Research Division prepared a detailed memorandum on the prospective Chiba Works, which strongly supported Kawatetsu's case. The JDB research team noted that the sheet-oriented Chiba mill, capable of supplying the nascent motor vehicle and consumer electronics sectors of Japan, would help break a prospectively dangerous supply bottleneck created by the war-induced bias toward heavy plate in Japanese steel production capacity. Chiba would be an advanced facility technologically and would enhance the competitiveness of Japanese steel internationally; its construction also appeared justified in regard to long-term supply-and-demand factors, the report noted.[45]

The JDB's vice-chairman, Nakayama Sōhei, convinced of the project's desirability, went to Kawatetsu's main bank, Dai Ichi, and told its chairman, Nakayama (no relation), that the JDB would cooperate if Dai Ichi decided to put its weight behind the Chiba project.[46] The JDB also extended a short-term loan to Kawatetsu in fiscal 1952, further undercutting the position of Ichimada and the MITI conservatives, who had still not given formal approval to the project. In addition, Kobayashi and Nakayama exerted pressure for action on Kawatetsu's longstanding loan request.

Once the BOJ Policy Board had formally approved Chiba, the JDB went ahead on its own initiative. On October 9, 1952, it extended Kawatetsu a ¥1 billion loan. This sum was only one-eighth of the sum originally requested, two years after Kawatetsu had applied, and the terms were relatively unfavorable.[47] But considering the context of intense opposition from the Bank of Japan and certain quarters in MITI, any sort of loan was a tribute to Kawatetsu's footwork.

A Transnational Dimension

The decentralization of the allocation process and the determined advocacy of the Kawatetsu cause by the JDB's Kobayashi came out even more clearly in the pattern of World Bank funding for Japanese steel projects during the early 1950s. Japanese law at the time required no formal involvement of the Bank of Japan in evaluating any such loan, so BOJ governor Ichimada had no direct means of making his aversion to the Chiba project felt. The Japan Development Bank was fully empowered to guarantee World Bank loans on its own authority. And the World Bank, for its part, could, and did, evaluate loan applications primarily in terms of project feasibility, with little concern for the political implications of a project's realization. Thus the World Bank was a strong force aiding aspiring firms in finessing Japanese domestic credit controls.

In October 1952 the first World Bank survey mission came to Japan, six months after the end of the Allied Occupation, in search of attractive projects that would shore up the vulnerable Japanese economy. The Chiba Works particularly attracted the survey mission due to Chiba's concentration on thin-plate and sheet production, for which there appeared to be a strong and expanding market.

The JDB's Kobayashi had had trouble securing Japanese government loans for Kawatetsu due to Bank of Japan opposition. But he stepped wholeheartedly and successfully into the fight for World Bank loans, meeting personally with the steel representative in the second survey team, Chester Case. After MITI had formally approved stages two to four of the Chiba project, with a price tag of ¥22 billion ($61 million), Kobayashi, together with the IBJ's Nakayama Sōhei, jointly drafted the government's official request to the World Bank for Chiba-related funds. Ultimately 70 percent of the total funds requested from the World Bank for the entire Japanese steel industry at this time were proposed as loans for Chiba. The request was to provide nearly half of all the funds projected as necessary for the latter stages of the project.[48]

Not only was the proposed World Bank loan nearly ten times the magnitude of that obtained directly from the JDB, but the terms were better. The JDB vigorously lobbied with the World Bank on Kawatetsu's behalf throughout the subsequent period of evaluations in Japan and Washington until finally, on December 20, 1956, the full sum requested was approved.

As is clear from table 6-1, Kawasaki Steel's original plan to raise capital for Chiba contrasted sharply with conventional patterns of industrial finance in the Japan of 1950. Kawatetsu failed miserably in its efforts to secure government money, receiving only slightly over ¥1 billion of the ¥8 billion it sought. But even this amount represented a substantially larger percentage of total capital outlay for Chiba than did non-BOJ governmental loans as a share of total new industrial funds for Japan as a whole. In other words, government financial institutions (in this case, primarily the JDB) awarded Kawasaki Steel a disproportionate share of funds, despite substantial Bank of Japan and some MITI opposition to the project. This anomaly once again suggests the scope for private-sector evasion of initial government allocative dictates that was possible, particularly when the transnational dimension is considered.

Table 6-1 suggests the patterns of financing actually adopted by Kawasaki Steel in building the Chiba Works and contrasts those to its original expectations and to Japanese industrial norms: the most striking anomaly was the low contribution anticipated from com-

TABLE 6-1
Unorthodox Financing for the Chiba Steel Mill (percentage)

Source	A. Proposed Sources of Financing for Chiba, 1950		B. Net Supply of Industrial Funds (Entire Japanese Economy), 1950
	Proposed	Actual	
Government loans			
Non-BOJ	49.2	17.6	2.5
BOJ	0.0	0.0	10.2
Bonds (domestic issues)	19.0	8.1	8.5
Capital increase	15.3	20.3	6.2
Retained earnings	10.4	10.8	
Commercial banks	6.1	16.2	72.6
Foreign loans	0.0	27.0	
TOTAL	100.0	100.0	100.0

Sources: Kawasaki Steel Corporation, Kawasaki Seitetsu Ni Jyū Go Nen Shi (A Twenty-five-year History of Kawasaki Steel) (Tokyo: Kawasaki Seitetsu Kabushiki Kaisha, 1975), 77; Bank of Japan Research and Statistics Department, Keizai Tōkei Nenpō, 1976 ed.; and Kawasaki Steel Corporation, Kawasaki Seitetsu Yūka Shōken Hōkoku Sho (Kawasaki Steel Corporation Securities Reports), 1951–56.

Note: Loans from U.S. counterpart funds, the nearest analogue to "Government loans, Non-BOJ," under heading B, amounted to ¥28.9 billion in 1950, or 5.6 percent of total industrial funds supplied to the Japanese economy. This figure is larger than the total for "Government loans, Non-BOJ," because Reconstruction Finance Bank loan repayments in 1950 were much larger than new loans, thus diminishing the "Government loans, Non-BOJ" category.

The "Capital increase" and "Retained earnings" categories are combined under heading B. The minimal foreign loans tendered to Japanese industry in 1950 are not included under B.

mercial banks. Whereas these institutions provided three-quarters of total Japanese corporate finance at the time, Chiba was built with one-fifth of that ratio—and even that 15 percent was more than Kawatetsu's president Nishiyama had originally anticipated. This failure to resort more to the banks is particularly striking in that their loans were generally cheaper than most other sources of finance in 1950.

Commercial Banks Inhibited by BOJ Opposition

The low proportion of commercial bank loans in total financing for Chiba illustrates the one major effect that Bank of Japan governor Ichimada's opposition seemingly had on it: it inhibited commercial bank lending that might otherwise have materialized. The commer-

cial banks' heavy reliance on central bank "overloans" and on "loan
introductions" through the BOJ's Loan Mediation Bureau (Yūshi
Assen Bu) made them reluctant to risk BOJ disfavor. During fiscal
1952 and 1953, for example, Kawasaki Steel received only about
¥5.5 billion and ¥4.2 billion respectively in loans for Chiba.[49] And
roughly 40 percent of the loans it did receive, an extraordinarily high
proportion by conventional standards, came from either Kawatetsu's main bank, Dai Ichi, or from the two major expansion-oriented financial institutions—the Japan Development Bank and the
Industrial Bank of Japan.[50] Other banks, including all other commercial banks aside from Dai Ichi, steered largely clear of the Chiba project, despite rates of return over 11 percent, when compensating balances are figured in. The banks did not, in short, respond fully to
market incentives, apparently due to the threat of BOJ sanctions
against them. The Bank of Japan could, ironically, control the private banks much better than the public ones in the Chiba case.

Aside from co-opting local political authorities and various public
financial institutions, what did Kawasaki Steel do in the Chiba case
to establish the capacity to finance its venture in the face of such
eminent opposition? Its basic strategy was to develop close alliances
with the securities and regional banking communities, brokered by
political figures, and to rely heavily on equity finance and internally
generated earnings to finance its development. This approach is, of
course, in many ways more similar to the financial strategy employed in the United States than that commonly resorted to in Japan,
except for the politicization involved in the Chiba case.

A Key Role for the Securities Sector

As figure 6-1 indicates, the capital ratio of Kawasaki Steel Corporation rose from 19 to nearly 45 percent in the fall of 1950, as Kawatetsu doubled its capitalization from ¥500 million to ¥1 billion, to
pay for the initial phases of Chiba's construction—a ratio to be compared with a 1950 average of about 28 percent for the industry as a
whole and 20 percent for steel. Subsequent capital increases of ¥1
billion in July 1952 and ¥2 billion in July 1953 helped provide a significant part of the funds for the early stages of the Chiba plant's
development, albeit at a relatively high cost to Kawatetsu, and a correspondingly attractive return to its new shareholders.[51] For the
1950–1952 period in particular, Kawatetsu's reliance on equity finance was substantially above that of Japanese manufacturing in
general, as figure 6-1 indicates.

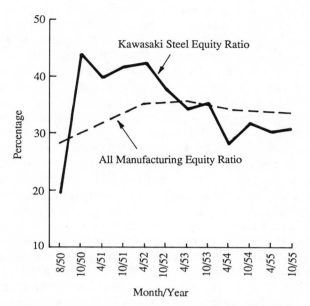

Figure 6-1. Kawasaki Steel Corporation: Trends in Shareholders' Equity Ratio, 1950–1955 (percentage). Numbers beneath the columns indicate month and year.

Sources: Kawasaki Steel Corporation, *Kawasaki Seitetsu Ni Jyū Go Nen Shi* (A Twenty-five-year History of Kawasaki Steel) (Tokyo: Kawasaki Seitetsu Kabushiki Kaisha, 1975), p. 78, Ministry of Finance Securities Bureau (Ōkurashō Shōken Kyoku), Hōjin Kigyō tōkei Nenpō (Yearbook of Corporate Statistics) (Tokyo: Ōkurashō Insatsu Kyoku, 1950–1955).

The BOJ's governor, Ichimada, opposed the Kawatetsu capital increases. But he had no regulatory authority over them.[52] That authority rested in the hands of his political rival, Ikeda Hayato, the minister of finance. And Ikeda was an ardent economic expansionist, as well as a close associate of the securities firms, his major source of political finance. Ikeda, it will be remembered, made the crucial introduction of Kawatetsu's Nishiyama to the JDB's Kobayashi. He had also authorized Kawatetsu's three major capital increases. These greatly benefited Nomura and Daiwa Securities, the Kansai-based firms that underwrote them and that were headed, unsurprisingly in a Japanese setting, by old classmates of Ikeda's at San Kō (the famous "third school" in Kyoto) and Kyoto Imperial University.

Although Ikeda stood in the critical role of broker, by virtue of the formal regulatory constraints on the Japanese financial system (such as those over securities issues), he did not create the relationship between Kawatetsu and the securities industry. That was an old one, dating from at least the prewar Depression days. During 1930–1931, for example, Fujimoto Bill Broker, the predecessor of Daiwa Securities and a firm with both banking and brokerage capabilities, had extended rescue loans to the distressed Kawasaki Zōsen, Kawatetsu's predecessor.[53] Kawatetsu had, for its part, long systematically cultivated the securities companies by regularly financing a significant part of its activities through bond issues, despite underwriting fees running from 3.0 to 3.5 percent. President Nishiyama, known affectionately as "Nishiyama Tennō," or "Emperor Nishiyama," because of his forceful personality, also intensely cultivated the securities industry leaders, whom he invited on frequent guided tours of his expanding Chiba plant. They in turn hosted receptions and dinners throughout regional Japan on his behalf to mobilize the nest-egg savings of local bankers, doctors, small businesspersons, and members of the Chamber of Commerce—on behalf of Kawatetsu.

Through securities issues, particularly capital increases, Kawatetsu was able to expand rapidly in the early stages and present MITI and the BOJ with a fait accompli. The ministry admitted as much in its rueful addendum to formal licensing of Chiba's first stage, which observed that Kawasaki had spent ¥3 billion on the project before approval was granted and that to deny approval would result in tremendous waste.[54] Japanese banks, by nature cautious when faced with BOJ opposition, would not have provided this preemptive "cutting edge" of early funds; that could be achieved only by the securities firms in league with local banks (as purchasers) and politician-brokers.

Kawatetsu's final major source of funding for Chiba was internal finance—inventory profits, funds from accelerated depreciation, and so on. The sections of MITI that aligned with Kawatetsu gave the firm a quick, early boost on April 1, 1951, by releasing price controls on scrap iron, manganese, steel, and coking coal.[55] Kawatetsu had been quietly stockpiling massive supplies of these commodities in anticipation. Its profits were enormous. Industrywide tax provisions also helped in financing Chiba, though in the latter stages rather than the critical early days.

Perhaps the largest single contribution to the retained earnings that went to fund Chiba was the ¥1.5 billion or so that accrued through Kawatetsu's failing to pay dividends from December 1954 to April 1956. During this period Kawatetsu made a profit, although only a small ¥140 million in fiscal 1954, down ¥500 million from the previous year. Many Japanese firms, including Kawasaki Steel after the Oil Shock of 1973, were forced by administrative and stockholder pressure to continue paying dividends despite substantial deficits. In light of the Ministry of Finance's bank-oriented policy since the early postwar period of forcing high levels of dividend payout through administrative guidance, Kawatetsu's "mid-1950s dividend holiday" is highly anomalous.

It is said that authorization for this "holiday," like that for the capital increases of the early 1950s, was obtained through the good offices of Ikeda Hayato, Kawatetsu's longtime growth-oriented ally, at the time secretary general of the Liberal party during the last Yoshida cabinet. The resumption of dividends, not surprisingly, appears to have been forced by former Bank of Japan governor Ichimada, Kawatetsu's old nemesis, who became finance minister after the initial dividend holiday had been approved.

One cannot help but see the Chiba case as a watershed in the history of Japanese credit allocation and economic growth. The Chiba mill was built—efforts of supposedly omnipotent bureaucratic organs to restrict credit could not prevent it—and rival producers in competition with Kawatetsu had to do the same. Thus opened a competitive round of investment in steel that broke the Big Three oligopoly and served as a major driving force behind the entire nation's economic growth for nearly a generation. Contrary to long-received opinion, this competitive investment did not originate in the strategic guidance of the Japanese state, but, rather, as we have seen, in the persistence of the private sector—against state opposition—in pursuing private goals.

THE VOICE OPTION: POLITICAL PRESSURE AND CORPORATE SURVIVAL AT SASEBO HEAVY INDUSTRIES, 1978

During the high-growth period of the 1950s, 1960s, and early 1970s, the key credit-allocation decisions in Japan were frequently the sort epitomized in the Kawasaki Chiba steel mill case of 1951 and in the Sumitomo Metals case of 1965.[56] They were, in other words, largely issues of how the private sector could amass sufficient credit to expand capacity to what it viewed as optimal levels, while the state reactively played a stabilizing role. As chapters 3 and 4 suggest, the Bank of Japan, MOF, and even at times MITI played this sort of routine, low-profile, and often futile veto role in the credit allocation process for over two decades.

With the slowing of growth in the mid-1970s and the onset of severe structural recession in industries such as petrochemicals, textiles, and shipbuilding, the equation changed profoundly. With growing liquidity and widening deregulation, competitive firms were less insistent on state support—policy interaction drew together primarily the state and the noncompetitive firms. The operative policy question became increasingly whether such noncompetitive firms could obtain "bailout" credit simply to survive, often in defiance of market forces.

In the four years after the 1973 Oil Shock a major auto manufacturer (Tōyō Kōgyō), trading company (Ataka Sangyō), construction firm (Eidai Sangyō), precision machinery maker (Tōyō Valve), and shipping company (Japan Line) all faced imminent bankruptcy, as did Sasebo Heavy Industries in the spring of 1978. For Sasebo, "exit" from credit relations with the state through market reliance, in accordance with the Kawatetsu pattern, was infeasible. "Loyalty" to prevailing state guidelines on industrial transformation would have meant bankruptcy or drastic reorganization for such an inefficient, declining firm. "Voice"—the active appeal for political aid on welfare and national security grounds in securing credit—was the only viable option.[57]

In fiscal 1977, as its crisis began, Sasebo Heavy Industries was Japan's eighth largest shipbuilding firm, with sales of ¥79.4 billion ($258 million).[58] The firm was heavily dependent on exports, which provided 78 percent of its total income in 1977, and had been badly hurt by the worldwide collapse in shipbuilding orders after the Oil Shock of 1973. This led to a declining ratio of production to capacity at SHI late in 1977, as the backlog of pre-oil-crisis orders gradually ran out. By the spring of 1978, SHI yards were operating at only around 50 percent of capacity, with the company anticipating a further 30 percent decline in sales for 1979. High fixed-labor and debt-service costs, due to lifetime employment and high corporate leverage, threatened a massive ¥10 billion loss (20 percent of sales) for fiscal 1979, according to company projections.[59] By the beginning of 1978 SHI's very ability to survive required a forceful and sustained rescue effort by its affiliated banks and stockholders, which nevertheless clearly found such an operation difficult and unattractive, due to the deep-seated and long-term nature of SHI's problems.

Financial Crisis and Management Isolation

Sasebo's liabilities in early 1978 were not overwhelmingly large from a Japanese government or banking-sector perspective—only ¥120 billion. Nippon Steel typically carried five to ten times that much debt.[60] But SHI was situated in an industry deep in structural recession, with 35 to 40 percent overcapacity,[61] and furthermore had terminally high production costs—20 percent higher than the ship-building industry norm. Sasebo's management was apathetic and isolated from day-to-day corporate operations—nine out of the twelve managing directors with direct line responsibility (tantō jōmu) lived in Tokyo or Kanagawa prefectures, with only three residing in Sasebo City itself.

Partly as a result of such management isolation, SHI was highly unresponsive to adverse changes in its competitive environment as the firm's situation steadily darkened. Unlike other shipbuilders, Sasebo failed to develop new technical expertise or to diversify aggressively into land-based operations after the Oil Shock. Only 15 percent of its total sales were land based by 1978, as opposed to 66 percent for Mitsubishi Heavy Industries and 73 percent for Ishikawajima Harima (IHI), Japan's two largest erstwhile shipbuilders.

In early 1978, as the management of SHI's major banks contemplated their course of action in the face of the firm's dismal prospects, those banks were not so deeply committed that they could not withdraw and allow SHI to go bankrupt. Although Sasebo had a debt-equity ratio of nearly twenty to one in March 1978, its debts were only a relatively small ¥120 billion. [62] Furthermore, this debt burden was distributed among a large number of banks. Even Dai Ichi Kangyō (DIKB), Sasebo's main bank, had only ¥3.074 billion out to the firm,[63] and owned only 0.8 percent of its stock.

In addition, Dai Ichi Kangyō had no extensive commercial relations with the Sasebo area that might be endangered by a bankruptcy. Out of its 320 branches throughout Japan, DIKB did not have even one in Sasebo, a substantial town of around 250,000 people, and undertook few commercial transactions there. The bank's traditional perquisite of nominating a retiring executive to Sasebo's board of directors was hardly attractive to the bank, given Sasebo's grim prospects.

The Sasebo crisis began in earnest late in January 1978. On January 23 the firm called for a thousand "voluntary" retirements, promising those who complied particularly favorable retirement benefits. Announcement of the retirement plan triggered widespread distrust of SHI in the local community by fostering a perception that the firm was unstable. Local suppliers began demanding payment in cash, and local banks began calling in their loans.[64] Such curtailment of credit intensified the emerging cash-flow problem at Sasebo, deepening the crisis of confidence.

By March SHI's principal trading company, Nissho Iwai, was demanding payment in cash, and employees of the firm, fearing bankruptcy, were withdrawing their money en masse from the company credit union. On March 2 SHI applied, through a managing director (jōmu) who had formerly been with DIKB, for ¥5 billion in new loans, but received an equivocal response. As the financial crisis fed on itself, SHI president Murata hastened to Tokyo on March 29 to reveal the full details of his firm's precarious financial state to the company's main bank, Dai Ichi Kangyō, arguing to DIKB president Kobayashi that without further credit SHI would go bankrupt.[65]

The questions of whether Murata would receive the desired credit and of who would bear the risks of extending it represent the core credit-allocation issues of this case study. The credit immediately at issue amounted to ¥37.3 billion—¥8.3 billion to cover severance payments to "voluntarily" retiring redundant workers and ¥29 billion in operating funds to carry SHI through to March 1978, when business was expected to improve. This sum represented a 30 percent increase on Sasebo's ¥120 billion in loans outstanding—an additional commitment that Sasebo's main banks were hesitant to provide.

To explain how a firm with prospects as dim as SHI's in 1978 received so substantial an extension we must delve into politics. The Dai Ichi Kangyō Bank's initial response to Murata's appeal was to temporize: it demanded that future loans be guaranteed by either the government or the four major SHI stockholders (Kurushima Dock, Nippon Kōkan, Nippon Steel, and Nissho Iwai Trading). With this in mind, President Kobayashi of the DIKB and his deputy went the next day to visit Tokuda Hiromi, director general of the Ministry of Finance Banking Bureau, and Shashiki Munato, director general of the Ministry of Transportation Shipping Bureau. The MOF Banking Bureau was sympathetic to the plight of the lender banks facing prospective losses, but was noncommittal about government guarantees.

Shashiki, chief of MOT's Shipping Bureau and the official most sympathetic to the plight of SHI, agreed to approach the stockholders concerning the possibility of a stockholder loan guarantee. But he had little success in convincing them. Nippon Kōkan vice-president Ueda Kiokatsu told Shashiki on March 30, "The stockholders have no involvement in Sasebo's management, and do not intend to assume any." After bureau chief Shashiki's failure in early April to move the stockholders, MOT escalated its efforts, with the vice-minister and finally the minister of transport himself brought into persuasion efforts.

Although relatively cool to the fate of SHI, Ministry of Finance officials were concerned about reducing the risks faced by the major banks. To this end, they preferred, at least in the short term, SHI survival to SHI bankruptcy, *provided* that the major banks, whose interests they stoutly defended, did not have to assume the new risk of extending further loans.

In the early stages of the crisis, MOF officials took two concrete steps: first, on April 2 Banking Bureau director general Tokuta encouraged Sasebo mayor Tsuji Ichizō to come to Tokyo and pressure central government officials for some special assistance. Second, from April 25 officials of the Kita Kyūshū regional bureau of MOF were working to organize a consortium of five local banks in the Sasebo area to extend 10 to 20 percent of the total funds necessary to keep SHI afloat. Once again, MOF's solicitude was for the money-center banks.

Two significant conclusions can be drawn from MOF's early involvement in the Sasebo Heavy Industries case. First, MOF's primary initial interaction was with actors in local areas—local banks and local politicians—rather than those in Tokyo itself. These local actors both sought central government support and offered their own assistance to complement it in a mutually supportive fashion typical of circles of compensation in operation. Such interaction between the central bureaucracy, on the one hand, and local business and political groups, on the other, laid the foundations for solution of the Sasebo case by reducing the risks of the central players aside from MOF. Second, MOF and the local actors were able rapidly to reach a mutually congenial resolution, in sharp contrast to the efforts of the Ministry of Transport to move the large stockholders, or even the efforts of MOF in many other cases to move large business or major city banks. Ever since MOF and the Bank of Japan relied heavily on local banks as a source of funds for the war effort during World War II, the close cooperation between MOF and the small, often inefficient local banks with a surplus of funds, enhanced by strong political ties of these smaller banks and their heavy recruitment of MOF alumni as senior executives, has been a central feature of the Japanese financial system.

The Entry of Politics

The conventional paradigm of Japanese policymaking stresses cooperation among establishment institutions in the event of crisis. It was striking throughout the Sasebo case how very reluctant—indeed, obdurately unwilling—so many such institutions were to aid SHI. The Bank of Japan, for example, assumed a hands-off attitude throughout the crisis, with Governor Morinaga Teiichirō going so far as to formally announce, on May 24, 1978, that the BOJ would not grant a special salvaging loan to SHI; the Bank is also said to have criticized earlier efforts by MOF to get banks to finance SHI's "retirement payments" as violating sound banking policies.[66] Likewise, on May 15 Industrial Bank of Japan president Ikeura refused a request by Japan Chamber of Commerce chairman Nagano Shigeo, chief mediator in the case and one of the legendary "Four Emperors of Zaikai," for the IBJ's financial participation in the rescue effort and for dispatch of an IBJ executive to SHI as the relief effort director. Sasebo Heavy Industries' main banks and major stockholders, including Japan's largest bank and the top two steel firms, also refused to aid Sasebo.

But suddenly, beginning in the last week of May, the parties to the dispute became much more conciliatory; the banks agreed to an unsecured loan, while the stockholders agreed to subscribe to a capital increase. On June 22 an agreement between stockholders and bankers was concluded, largely resolving the Sasebo case. Political pressure was crucial to this fateful transition.

The range of political actors involved in the Sasebo affair was extraordinary. Within the ruling LDP, members of the Fukuda, Ōhira, Tanaka, and Shiina factions, the first three being the largest in the party, all had compelling personal reasons for supporting SHI.[67] Opposition parties, particularly the DSP, also supported aid to SHI.[68] Local government officials, especially Nagasaki prefectural governor Kubo Kanichi and Sasebo City mayor Tsuji Ichizō, also played vigorous roles.

Mayor Tsuji was especially important. He lobbied far more intensively and persuasively for aid to SHI than did the company's president. Tsuji had ample political incentive to do so: SHI accounted for 52 percent of Sasebo City's industrial production and, together with its 250 subcontractors (several of the biggest owned by the mayor himself), at least one-third of the total employment in Sasebo.[69] Sasebo, in short, was a company town.

Mayor Tsuji had the political resources as well as the incentive to lobby persuasively. As the conservative mayor of Sasebo since 1953, he had built up a tremendous number of IOU's vis-à-vis the central government, particularly in the area of defense policy. Sasebo has long been one of Japan's premier naval ports, having served from shortly after the Sino-Japanese War of 1894–1895 as a major base for the Imperial Navy. In 1945 it became a base for the U.S. Seventh Fleet and still remains a U.S. oil and ammunition supply base, although combat forces have been withdrawn since 1976 and the Japanese Self-Defense Forces currently occupy the base. Sasebo under

Tsuji took many of the politically controversial but strategically important visits to Japan by U.S. nuclear-powered vessels that the main U.S. naval base at Yokosuka, with its proximity to Tokyo militants, could not. In 1963 Tsuji, despite strong protests from antinuclear demonstrators, welcomed the *Sea Dragon*, the first nuclear submarine to visit Japan; in the following four years he approved eleven further visits by nuclear subs. In January 1968 Tsuji took the even more controversial step of welcoming the nuclear carrier *Enterprise* at the height of the Vietnam War. For all of this he had received numerous calls of appreciation from Prime Ministers Ikeda and Satō, as well as, it is said, concrete benefits for his city.

In the Sasebo Heavy Industries case, Tsuji wanted a government guarantee of SHI's financial viability, for which he made six trips to Tokyo in the spring of 1978. His initial approach was to represent the SHI bankruptcy case as a nuclear power rather than a financial issue and to enlist government officials and business leaders strongly on the side of the development of nuclear power in Japan. He effected this linkage by pledging, together with Nagasaki governor Kubo Kanichi, that Sasebo port (and hence Sasebo Heavy Industries) would be available for repairing the controversial nuclear ship *Mutsu*, for almost three years without a home port, should the government arrange a way of assuring credit to Sasebo Heavy Industries.

Tsuji's first appeal to the nuclear power lobby was to Science and Technology Agency chief Kumagai Tasaburō, whom Tsuji met on April 2, even before going to the Transport and Finance ministries. A week later Tsuji conferred with Nakayama Sōhei and Imazato Kōki,[70] the two chief proponents of nuclear power, at Nakayama's country villa. Given the *Mutsu* promise, and their positions as chairman and vice-chairman of the Nagasaki Prefectural Development Association, Nakayama and Imazato mobilized a powerful mediator, Nagano Shigeo, to effect a solution to the case, although they did not intervene directly themselves in the crisis resolution.[71] Thus Nagano's entry into the Sasebo case on April 15 was, indirectly, the result of local political pressures and big-business concurrence, rather than a decision from the center of the Japanese political system. Prime Minister Fukuda, for example, is said to have played no major role in initiating this choice.[72]

Besides obtaining the intervention of a powerful mediator, local political forces in Sasebo exerted some direct influence toward a settlement. First, Sasebo City agreed to guarantee ¥1 billion of the ¥8.3 billion loan to be extended to SHI as retirement allowances for its sixteen hundred "voluntarily" retiring workers, helping to bridge the gap between Sasebo's stockholders and its bankers over who would aid SHI. Second, Mayor Tsuji helped apply grass-roots pressure on Tokyo at a critical moment, helping to move the Sasebo case toward resolution. In late May 1978, just as Prime Minister Fukuda was becoming involved in the case but before the banker-stockholder deadlock had been clearly broken, Tsuji organized a grass-roots People's Council for Aid to Sasebo Heavy Industries. The group planned demonstrations for early June in support of SHI that seemed likely to be well covered by the national media. Many of the demonstrators would be SHI workers who had been promised their retirement allowances but had not received them. Should aid to SHI not be a clear prospect by the initially scheduled date of around June 8, the demonstrations would inflict severe national political embarrassment on the Fukuda government, with the LDP presidential elections just six months away.

End Game: Key Role for the Prime Minister

The local pressure tactics catalyzed a commitment from the central government. On June 6 Nagano called Mayor Tsuji to pass on a demand from Prime Minister Fukuda that the demonstrations be canceled. The alternative, Nagano indicated, might be government withdrawal from the case. Tsuji complied. Two days later a partial solution to the crisis was announced, and a comprehensive solution emerged within the month, under intense pressure from Prime Minister Fukuda.[73]

Aside from Mayor Tsuji, the central political actor in the crucial *last* stage of decision making was Prime Minister Fukuda Takeo. Fukuda had been characteristically cautious in making public commitments to SHI until relatively late in the case. But just as typically, once he moved he was intensely active behind the scenes and applied the decisive political pressure that finally forced an agreement that even the renowned *zaikai* leader Nagano Shigeo could not achieve. He not only mediated a consensus; he imposed a solution after the fashion of American chief executives.

Fukuda's goals in the Sasebo case were straightforward. First, he wanted SHI rescued from bankruptcy at all costs.[74] As Fukuda told Sumitomo Real Estate president Ando Tarō during an evening reception at the elegant Shimbashi *ryōtei* (traditional restaurant) Kichō on June 1, "A major bankruptcy just now would damage business confidence at a critical state in the recovery."[75] It would also, Fukuda felt, tarnish his reputation as a consummate "steward of the economy," in which he took much personal pride.[76] Then there was the embarrassing political problem of the nuclear ship *Mutsu*: who would consent to repair it if SHI went bankrupt? The Science and Technology Agency had been seeking a refuge for it for three years to no avail. The consequences for the Sasebo regional economy (and how that might translate into votes for Ōhira and Kōmoto, two of his three opponents in the December LDP presidential election) must also have crossed Fukuda's mind. Finally, there was the strategic issue: SHI was experienced at repairing naval vessels, and both the U.S. Seventh Fleet and the Japanese Naval Self-Defense Forces found this capability attractive.[77]

Prime Minister Fukuda's second clear objective was to make Tsubouchi Hisao, a relatively obscure local businessman from Shikoku with whom he and his faction had personal political connections, president of a rejuvenated Sasebo Heavy Industries. Tsubouchi was one of the first political backers of Ochi Michio, Fukuda's son-in-law and chief of political operations, who like Tsubouchi came from Ehime prefecture in Shikoku. Tsubouchi is said to have periodically made substantial political contributions to the Fukuda faction through Ochi Michio and therefore had political claims on Fukuda.

Tsubouchi had been greatly interested in the prospects of Sasebo Heavy Industries since at least October 1975, when he purchased a 16.7 percent share of the company's stock.[78] He reportedly believed (prematurely, many experts felt) that the prospects for massive oil strikes in the East China Sea were extremely good and that Sasebo City would one day be the Aberdeen, Scotland, of East Asia.[79] Accordingly, he had been eager to assume leadership of SHI, despite its apparently dismal near-term prospects, and reportedly exerted political pressure to attain his goal.

Many of the main actors in the Sasebo case did not favor Tsubouchi as president. Leaders of Dai Ichi Kangyō Bank and Nippon Kōkan, and even mediator Nagano Shigeo to some extent, regarded Tsubouchi as a nouveau riche local businessman with insufficient establishment connections and experience to head a major corporation. They favored installing an executive from the powerful Industrial Bank of Japan, as had occurred at the Japan Line early in 1978, or a senior officer of a major steel firm. The prime minister's insistence on Tsubouchi, and Tsubouchi's ultimate selection on June 29, was such a major departure from standard Japanese practice as to demonstrate clearly the prime minister's own ability to shape policy when he chose to do so.

Fukuda was also successful in securing the loans necessary for Sasebo's survival. His initial moves were largely reactive and tactical, and his essentially minimalist approach made him hesitate to intervene until events threatened SHI with imminent bankruptcy. Thus he made a general statement of support for SHI when Mayor Tsuji came to see him on April 20 and twice talked Nagano out of resigning as mediator. When SHI faced short-term financial crises at the end of both April and May, Fukuda also directed MOF to ensure, by administrative guidance against the banks, that SHI did not fail out of inability to settle its end-of-month bills. But it was only four months into the crisis, when the possibility of a Sasebo bankruptcy became clear, that Fukuda stepped in energetically.

On May 24 Bank of Japan governor Morinaga Teiichirō formally refused to have the BOJ grant a special loan to SHI. The next day Prime Minister Fukuda summoned Transport Minister Fukunaga and Transport administrative vice-minister Nakamura to his residence and demanded that they prepare a plan to save SHI. Later in the day he sent his private secretary, Yasuda, to see Yoshize Shigea, MOF administrative vice-minister, demanding action. Yoshize conveyed Fukuda's strong request personally to Banking Bureau chief Tokuta. Then Fukuda intervened personally with Finance Minister Murayama Tatsuo to ensure that the upcoming supplementary budget would be altered to include necessary subsidies for SHI. And Fukuda had MITI minister Kōmoto brief president-to-be Tsubouchi on prospective oil-storage projects and depressed-areas legislation that could benefit SHI to stimulate Tsubouchi to commit more of his own money toward guaranteeing SHI's liabilities.

In addition to mobilizing various sectors of government, particularly MOF, and insuring SHI against cash-flow difficulties, Fukuda also interceded directly with the firm's principal antagonists, an especially unusual step for a prime minister. On June 1 he met Chairman Yokota of the Dai Ichi Kangyō Bank at the traditional restaurant Kichō, directly requesting Yokota's help in rescuing SHI. Fukuda gained this help within three weeks, after repeated contacts with DIKB through the Finance Ministry, offering various incentives for a settlement. The DIKB, together with the other fourteen banks of the SHI loan consortium, agreed to provide nearly ¥15 billion in unsecured loans, together with ¥8 billion in loans secured with only SHI's volatile shares as collateral.[80]

The prime minister had his way in this instance of credit allocation, despite opposition from leaders of the Bank of Japan, Keidanren, the Industrial Bank of Japan, Japan's largest steel firms and commercial banks, and the most influential segments of the national business press. Sasebo Heavy Industries survived, not by its commercial vitality, but by the skill with which its fate was woven into the tapestries of Japanese local and national politics.[81] Voice succeeded as corporate strategy where neither exit from the policy-finance system into the realm of markets nor abject loyalty to bureaucratic dictates could have done so.

CREDIT CONTROLS AND BORROWER RESPONSE: CROSS-CASE COMPARISONS

The preceding cases present three distinct private borrower reactions to state involvement in the allocation of credit. Kawasaki Steel chose exit from the elaborate system of controls centered on the Bank of Japan that prevailed in the early 1950s. A generation later Sasebo Heavy Industries elected for voice—active attempts to secure government financial support through the political process. The auto-parts industry, alone among the three, opted for loyalty—cooperation with the bureaucracy in a state-directed, and ultimately successful, modernization of the sector in which credit allocation played a central role. Yet even there the period of clear bureaucratic dominance was limited; by 1960 auto-parts firms were emerging from abject dependence on the state and raising at least some funds in private capital markets.

The most important general conclusion from these cases, taken together, is that a much more diverse spectrum of relationships existed between Japanese state and industrial society with respect to credit between the 1950s and the 1970s than the vision of postwar Japan as a strategic developmental state suggests.[82] Clearly this is not the full story. Private borrower preferences, together with those of private financial intermediaries, figure importantly in industrial-credit outcomes in the Japanese system of strategic capitalism.

The auto-parts case, with its transwar provenance, comes closest to sustaining generalizations about state leadership and dominance of industry. There centralized liaison channels with government, weak corporate ties to the political world, poor transnational linkages, high demand for credit, and limited alternatives to government lending forced the private sector into dependence on MITI and its developmental instincts, until alternatives began to emerge during the 1960s. But the Kawasaki and Sasebo cases show that even in the subdued and vulnerable environment of early postwar Japan, and as the shaken victim of the Oil Shock a quarter of a century later, initiative or necessity could lead a company to transcend the schematic deference toward government that the standard model ascribes to the private sector.

To move beyond generalizations about "control," "state strength," and "private initiative" toward a more refined understanding through case analysis of how government and business actually decide the financing of Japanese industry, one must pursue two major strands of inquiry.

First, what elements of the cases selected were critical to the outcome? In other words, what configuration of private- and public-sector circumstances led variously to loyalty, exit, and voice? Second, how representatively valid has each of the case-based patterns presented actually been? This chapter presents some observations on the first question, while the second is taken up thereafter.

HOW BORROWERS CAN FINESSE
STATE CREDIT CONTROLS

The Kawasaki story presents a case in which state efforts at controlling the allocation of credit clearly failed, due to aggressive evasion efforts by the private sector. It suggests that a private borrower can finesse state credit controls and raise funds independently—even counter to the desires of influential government officials—when the following facilitative conditions prevail:

1. Allocative controls are not administratively centralized. In the Kawasaki case MITI, MOF, the Japan Development Bank, and local governments, as well as the Bank of Japan, were all involved, without clear, routinized coordination or division of responsibility.

2. Important private-sector financial institutions do not support state financial-control guidelines. In the Kawasaki case the securities industry helped Kawasaki sell equity to offset the difficulties in obtaining commercial loans that the Bank of Japan's opposition to its proposed investment created.

3. Political forces intervene to frustrate allocation efforts. This occurs, of course, when the firm desiring to finesse controls has the support of political brokers capable of introducing alternative sources of finance and of preventing the bureaucracy from unifying in opposition to the proposed project. Japan Development Bank chairman Kobayashi Ataru served as such a broker for Kawasaki. Strong local political support for the Chiba Works from Chiba prefectural authorities also aided the project's development, both by increasing funding and by encouraging MITI's Tokyo regional bureau to be more sympathetic.

4. Transnational actors help in compromising the controls. In the Kawasaki/Chiba case, the World Bank ultimately agreed to provide an

unanticipated but absolutely crucial 27 percent of total funding. The bank agreed to provide funding due to a positive technical assessment of the project and pluralism within the Japanese government, which allowed the Japan Development Bank to guarantee World Bank loans, despite the BOJ's ambivalence.

HOW POLITICS CAN SKEW STATE INTERVENTION

The Sasebo case presents a situation in which public policy is skewed in a clientelistic, nonstrategic direction through political efforts instigated by a medium-scale local shipbuilder. This is, as chapter 7 points out, a pattern of increasing relevance to students of Japanese policymaking in the post-high-growth era. Despite financial liberalization, low interest rates, and excess liquidity in the Japanese financial system as a whole, many private borrowers were increasingly forced back on the state as a source or a guarantor of credit after the 1973 and 1979 Oil Shocks. This was particularly true of small businesses generally, and of shipbuilding, fertilizer, steel, and petrochemical producers in particular. These latter industries were hit suddenly by the sharp transformation in Japan's dual economic structure forced by rising energy prices and the transition to lower economic growth after 1973.

The Sasebo case helps refine our understanding of how party politics can skew state intervention in the distribution of credit in nonstrategic directions. (See figure I-1.) This case suggests that the "voice" option for borrowers, of securing state cooperation in the credit area through political activism that can alternatively be viewed as a quest for clientelist benefits, proves effective when the following facilitative conditions are met:

1. Strong, unified local backing exists for the loan project in question. In the case of Sasebo, local support for a rescue package was especially strong, since SHI represented the core of the local economy. Besides SHI, local banks, SHI subcontractors, unions, DSP, JSP, and Diet members all supported and lobbied their national contacts for a rescue package. Such broad local backing was crucial to a successful outcome because it helped impart a strong aura of legitimacy to the project.

2. Clear conduits link local demands to national decision-making centers; once again, interpersonal networks prove important to decision making. Sasebo mayor Tsuji Ichizō, whose unusual range of national contacts dated back to the early 1960s, played the principal role in merging Sasebo local concerns with national policymaking. He made

six trips to Tokyo in three months on behalf of the rescue package. But the increasingly important political party structure, linked to this case through local Diet members, and the national media, mobilized by Tsuji, also played an important role in transforming the SHI support issue from a local into a national policy question.

3. A national political broker has the ability and incentive to negotiate, with a suitably Japanese inconspicuousness to the general public, an appropriate policy package in the national political arena. Prime Minister Fukuda Takeo played a decisive role in this case, intervening directly with MOF and with Sasebo's main bank to force a solution. The national visibility of the issue, the proximity of impending LDP presidential elections, and longstanding ties to several concerned principals in the case provided Fukuda's incentives, while his standing as prime minister and a MOF alumnus, coupled with six previous years as MOF minister, gave him the leverage to achieve a solution.

4. Foreign policy considerations are involved. Sasebo had been, since Meiji times, a major naval base and had accepted the controversial port calls of numerous U.S. Navy vessels without complaint, even during the Vietnam War. Sasebo had likewise long been a major naval contractor for both the U.S. Navy and Japanese Maritime Self-Defense Forces. The United States had reportedly expressed some concern to the Fukuda government about how U.S. security concerns would be affected by an SHI bankruptcy.

The findings presented in this chapter flow, it should be reemphasized, from individual case studies. We will consider the general applicability of these propositions in summary form in chapter 8, after first probing the major changes currently under way in the broader political and economic context of Japanese industrial finance.

Taking the three cases together—each representative of a particular epoch in the evolution of Japanese decision making on credit-allocation issues—one can see both evolutionary patterns and important continuities that have major relevance to the overall arguments of this book. Broadly speaking, to use the language of figure I-1 in the Introduction, one can see the bifurcation of the classic developmental state pattern of state intervention and strategic resource allocation in two directions: first toward corporate-led capitalism (Kawasaki) in which private-sector strategy overrules a reactive state to promote competitive industries, and then later toward a clientelist approach (Sasebo) in which noncompetitive firms seek state support as a refuge from the market. Both patterns represent frustration for government industrial planners in their attempt to shape the allocation of credit in Japan.

Another surprising theme that emerges from the cases is the strength of many borrowers vis-à-vis both the state and the banks; this finding reverses the conventional wisdom in such matters. The borrower, in the cases presented here, was able to use the pluralism of the Japanese financial system—insufficiently appreciated in most previous accounts—to frustrate the efforts of bureaucrats to control and manipulate its behavior. Both Kawatetsu and Sasebo, through contrasting "exit" and "voice" strategies, were able to achieve their ends. They, rather than government officials, were the decisive arbiters of industrial credit allocation.

Distributed as these three cases are across the postwar period, they collectively present a richly textured history of private-borrower response to the changing Japanese financial system and to government's role in mediating and constraining those responses. Financial liquidity, for example, is rising across the period of these cases, undermining state allocative capacities with respect to all but the most desperate firms, whom private lenders would not consider. Decentralization of administrative and political power is also increasing, leading to more complex and pluralistic Japanese decision-making processes that make it simultaneously easier both for competitive firms to escape from government constraints and for noncompetitive enterprises to co-opt them. The contrasts between the auto-parts case, where borrowers had few options early on, and the other cases, where options were wider, in part reflect the structural evolution in Japan's financial system over time.

Two other long-term trends discernible across the cases cut in more complex fashion. Private-sector cohesion, like administrative centralization, seems by the time of the Sasebo case to be declining in Japan, making decisive private-sector leadership more difficult, even as administrative cohesion also declined. The result, the Sasebo case suggests, was by the 1970s a form of complex political gridlock, in which foreign pressure and prime ministerial intervention were increasingly important even on industrial-credit decisions, as the willingness of banks to aid affiliated firms declined. The economically competitive private sector was increasingly freed from the state's embrace, but where public support was necessary due to the borrower's commercial unattractiveness the process was increasingly more tortured.

Transnational interdependence across our cases is rising, increasing pressure on Japanese decision makers to be internationally responsive. But the relevant form of interdependence, as it applies to industrial-credit policymaking, is changing. With rising liquidity in Japan, foreign lenders became progressively less important from the

1950s as direct sources of capital, as the World Bank had been in the Kawasaki case. But due to broader economic and political interdependence, as well as rising pluralism in Japanese domestic politics, foreign political actors (such as U.S. ambassador Mike Mansfield in the Sasebo case) nevertheless gained new prominence in Japanese financial decision making and new ability to influence outcomes through even relatively passive symbolic steps.

Throughout the structural change in finance and politics across the period of our three cases, which range from the late 1930s to 1978, a pattern of initiative and entrepreneurship by private borrowers, and a pluralism and surprising passivity on the part of the state, stand out, albeit with an occasional important exception. Case-study analysis of actual credit decisions thus reaffirms and deepens the more general and more structural analysis of previous chapters. Yet even since the late 1970s, when the story of this chapter ends, the Japanese financial system and its credit practices have undergone major change, undermining the role of the state, and highlighting the importance of private actors, still further. That change, and its broader implications for Japan's strategic capitalism, are the subject of the next chapter.

CHAPTER 7

Changing Parameters

POLICYMAKING, it is increasingly clear, presents a great dialectic between established institutions for decision making and the broader social problems with which they seek to cope.[1] Institutions tend to be conservative and to pursue remarkably constant goals over time, even in the face of changing circumstances. As in the case of Japanese industrial institutions forged in World War II, or American social-policy structures forged in the Depression of the 1930s, they tend to mirror, often for decades, the preconceptions and priorities of the turbulent days in which they were founded or sweepingly transformed. The more powerful and the more complex an institution, the stronger this endemic conservatism tends to be.[2]

The ability of Japan's industrial-credit bureaucracy to respond sensitively to changing external circumstances inevitably confronts this natural conservatism of established state institutions, as the case studies of chapter 6 make clear. This handicap in a fluid, changing world has fortunately been modified somewhat in Japan by continuous communication with a well-organized and long-term-oriented private sector. Political inputs have also become more important, with mixed implications, as has been noted.

As the power of the ruling Liberal Democratic party becomes more institutionalized, and as changing economic circumstances force the bureaucracy to draft new legislation requiring Diet approval in areas from telecommunications to finance, party politics intrudes more into Japanese policymaking than was previously the case. With substantial internationalization and economic liberalization, especially since 1970, the parameters within which Japanese policy is made have also clearly shifted. Under the dual impact of both deregulation and politicization, Japan's policy process itself has changed character substantially over the past two decades.

This chapter details the shifting economic and political context of Japanese industrial-credit policies from the classic Bankers' Kingdom period of actively state-dominated credit allocation during the 1950s and 1960s to the less dirigiste but in important ways more politicized patterns that prevailed two decades later, around and after the time of the Sasebo case just recounted. The Bankers' Kingdom credit structure, as outlined in previous chapters, evolved a maze of formal controls: artificially low interest rates, a quasi-governmental committee to regulate bond issues, window guidance by the Bank of Japan, and in reserve another range of sanctions ready to be invoked in extremity. Private entrepreneurship did make strategic manipulation of these controls difficult, as has been seen. But the presence of the controls themselves, and the leverage that capital shortages gave to the state in an era of high-speed, capital-intensive industrialization, gave birth to a complex, brokerage-oriented, often clientelistic politics of industrial credit in which the industrial-policy bureaucracy had some major advantages. This chapter examines how those advantages were eroded over the course of the 1970s and 1980s and summarizes the very different problems with respect to credit and ultimately industrial transformation that Japan's long-strategic capitalism has come to confront.

FORCES FOR CHANGE IN FINANCIAL STRUCTURE

Many of the advantages of the Japanese state in directing industrial credit began slowly to unravel during the early 1970s. Among the first pillars of the edifice to weaken was corporate demand for externally generated funds. With capital deepening and increasingly favorable tax treatment for corporations, depreciation ratios at major Japanese firms rose steadily from 17.9 percent of total corporate funds during 1966–1970 to 28.0 percent during 1976–1980 and 34.5 percent during 1981–1982.[3] Rising international competitiveness—coupled with trade-policy developments such as voluntary export restraints on steel, color televisions, and automobiles—also intensified Japanese corporate profitability, and with it the availability of internal corporate funds for investment. At the same time, the slump in global economic growth after 1973, combined with rising foreign protectionism and a structural shift in the Japanese economy away from capital-intensive sectors such as steel and shipbuilding, reduced the overall corporate demand for funds. Total corporate liabilities in Japan fell astoundingly from ¥181.6 trillion in fiscal 1975 to ¥9.5 trillion in 1980, and to only ¥8.3 trillion by fiscal 1985.[4]

Many industrial firms not only reduced their borrowing and other means of raising capital, but even generated substantial surpluses, which they began lending to others, intensifying domestic excess liquidity. Across the manufacturing sector as a whole, financial assets in proportion to liabilities rose from 42.6 percent in 1975 to 66.3 percent in 1984.[5] Portfolio assets of Japanese firms rose from ¥7.8

trillion in 1975 to ¥23 trillion in 1985.[6] By the late 1970s Toyota Motors and Matsushita Electric had accumulated such great surpluses that they were known as "banks."[7] By 1984 they enjoyed annual financial earnings—unrelated to their manufacturing operations—of ¥48.9 billion ($211.7 million) and ¥57.7 billion ($249.8 million), respectively.[8]

By 1987 Toyota's financial profits had tripled from 1984 levels to ¥149.6 billion, with its total cash hoard swelling to ¥1.7 trillion ($13.4 billion), or enough to buy Honda.[9] Matsushita's financial profits, while less spectacular, were nothing to be ridiculed—in 1987 they totaled ¥109.2 billion or nearby double 1984 levels. By the mid-1980s financial manipulations known as *zaitech* ("financial technology") had become the major source of profitability for a broad range of Japan's major electronics, automotive, and precision-machinery producers. As table 7-1 indicates, for many of Japan's best-known manufacturers highly entrepreneurial financial operations became a major source of corporate profits, or a cushion against losses in more conventional operations. *Zaitech* played a major role in enabling these firms to withstand the steep upward movement of the yen during 1985–1987, which made manufacturing for export from Japan suddenly less and less profitable. It remained a major feature of the Japanese financial scene throughout the late 1980s, although its attractiveness for firms was diminished somewhat by the deflationary policies of BOJ governor Mieno Yasushi, which caused share prices to drop more than 60 percent from their peak by mid-1992.[10]

A second underpinning of the Bankers' Kingdom had long been a strong corporate reliance on indirect financing through commercial banks. As corporate demand for funds began to fall after the 1973 Oil Shock, firms gained greater freedom to diversify their modes of fi-

TABLE 7-1
Financial Profits at Major Japanese Manufacturing Firms, Fiscal 1987 (in ¥ billions)

Manufacturing Firm	Nonoperating Profits (Financial)	Financial Profits/ Pretax Profits
Toyota Motor	¥149.6	37.6%
Matsushita Electric	109.2	58.8
Nissan Motor	89.4	65.3
Sharp Electric	28.0	73.2
SONY	27.2	62.8
Honda Motor	22.7	26.1
Sanyo Electric	21.5	134.2
Isuzu Motors	16.4	1962.4

Source: Wako Economic Research Institute.

nancing, since they became less vulnerable to oligopolistic bank pressures. This tendency toward diversification was also facilitated by regulatory changes. Between 1970 and 1974 bank lending accounted for an average of 84 percent of cross-industry corporate financing in Japan. By 1980–1984 this share had fallen to an average of 60 percent, and in 1984 to 44 percent.[11]

Where government policies discouraged equity and bond finance, as was frequently the case during the early 1970s, changing flow-of-funds patterns emboldened firms to diversify into new modes of financing. The securities firms, in close alliance with key concentrations of political power, in turn used these changes in the corporate incentive structure to generate regulatory support for more market-oriented vehicles of corporate finance. The traditional system of equity issues at par value, long enforced by bank pressure and MOF administrative guidance, began to erode in favor of the market pricing of issues. This development greatly reduced the cost of equity capital, as did the steady rise in Japanese share prices. By 1985 straight equity issues alone accounted for 36.3 percent of the funds raised by Japanese corporations—double the share of the 1970s.[12] Convertible bond issues by Japanese firms also increased, reaching ¥2.5 trillion in 1985 and ¥9.4 trillion by 1989.[13]

The third pillar of the Bankers' Kingdom regulatory structure had been the banking sector's heavy reliance on the Ministry of Finance and the Bank of Japan, particularly true of the city banks at the core of major industrial groups. It had been a truism that "corporations are in debt to the banks, who are in debt to the Bank of Japan." But after 1970 the changes in the flow of funds dramatically altered the bargaining relationships between private banks and the bureaucracy. Excess liquidity, for example, decreased the attractiveness of the Bank of Japan's discount window to commercial banks; such borrowing fell steadily from 5.8 percent of total liabilities and net worth of the city banks in 1970 to only 2.3 percent by 1986 and 0.8 percent at the end of 1990.[14]

Even more important in this erosion was the explosion of government domestic debt after 1973. As indicated in table 7-2, the total value of all Japanese national government bonds outstanding increased over twenty times in nominal terms (more than five times in real terms) between 1973 and 1990s, even as foreign currency debt disappeared.[15] Between 1966 and 1975 the Bank of Japan had generally repurchased the bulk of all government bonds absorbed by the major banks a year after they were issued; but after 1975 it greatly reduced such repurchases, and its holdings of government debt outstanding fell from 37.5 percent of total debt in 1975 to 17.0 percent in 1980 and to only 10.9 percent in 1990.[16]

TABLE 7-2

The Explosion of Japanese National Government Debt, 1965–1990 (in ¥ billions)

	Total National Government Debt	National Government Bonds Outstanding (Domestic)	Refunding Bonds	Foreign Currency Bonds	Liabilities to Trust Fund Bureau
1950	554	240	—	100	2
1955	1,057	425	—	88	19
1960	1,340	446	—	81	41
1965	1,766	688	—	57	198
1970	6,226	3,597	—	54	504
1973	13,154	8,267	606	39	948
1975	22,795	15,776	1,677	33	2,677
1980	95,011	71,905	3,299	15	10,894
1985	163,571	136,610	24,295	0.7	16,188
1990	223,793	168,547	77,136	0.0	31,155

Source: Bank of Japan Research and Statistics Department, Keizai Tōkei Nenpō, 1990 ed., 233–34.

Note: All figures are as of the end of the Japanese fiscal year for the years indicated (i.e., March 31 of the following calendar year). Aside from the three major subcategories of government debt indicated, the Japanese national government also borrows in smaller amounts through short-term "food bills" and "silk bills" and through transfers from the general and special accounts as well as from postal life insurance and postal annuity funds. Treasury borrowing from postal savings is included under the figure for "Liabilities to Trust Fund Bureau." Refunding bonds are government bonds issued not to cover a specific expenditure, but to redeem government bonds previously issued.

The Ministry of Finance was forced to negotiate terms with the private banks for their purchase of this vast body of obligations. This task became increasingly difficult during the early 1980s, as ten-year government bonds issued in large quantities around the time of the 1973 Oil Shock and the subsequent slowdown in economic growth began to mature. National bond refunding issues rose sharply, as indicated in table 7-2, from around ¥3.3 trillion in 1980 to ¥24.3 trillion in 1985 and ¥77.1 trillion in 1990. This development, combined with pressure from the United States to liberalize the financial system, gave the larger city banks leverage in securing other market-oriented changes to increase their liquidity. Among these changes were relaxation of regulations on secondary-market bond sales and the introduction of certificates of deposit (1979) and money-market certificates (1985). These measures helped increase the fund-raising capabilities of such institutions as the city banks, whose deposit bases were smaller than their large lending portfolios.

A final pillar of the classical Bankers' Kingdom had been the network of exchange controls that insulated the domestic Japanese financial system, with all its finely calibrated defiance of market logic, from an international financial environment where market forces held sway. Only somewhat amended, the Foreign Exchange and Foreign Trade Control Law of 1948 and the Foreign Investment Law of 1950 prohibited in principle all foreign-exchange transactions unless specifically permitted by the government. These laws conferred on regulatory authorities great discretion in mediating between the domestic financial system and its global environment, and provided the basic legislative framework that governed foreign exchange transactions for more than a generation, until December 1980.

Justified as exchange controls once might have been by the chronic foreign-exchange shortages that plagued Japan until the late 1960s, rapidly rising Japanese trade and current account surpluses thereafter quickly erased the rationale for such barriers. Japan no longer needed exchange controls to conserve foreign exchange, since it was rapidly accumulating a chronic foreign-exchange surplus. The fiscal crisis within Japan also undermined MOF's ability to maintain a separation. In return for underwriting huge quantities of government bonds domestically, Japanese banks had to be given increasing opportunities to deal in securities, to expand overseas operations, to raise funds abroad by the most flexible means in ever more varied circumstances, and to repatriate those funds freely.[17] In 1972, for example, Japanese banks were given permission by MOF to float CDs on the New York and London financial markets. They also gained a rapidly increasing range of business opportunities in corporate finance outside Japan, albeit subject to the 1975 Three Bureaus Agreement that Japanese banks not serve as lead managers for offshore bond issues by Japanese corporations, or "act against the spirit of Article 65 of the Securities Exchange Act," which separated the business activities of Japanese banks and securities firms.[18]

The December 1980 revisions of the longstanding Foreign Exchange and Trade Control Law (FEFTCL), which had regulated Japanese foreign-exchange transactions since 1949, did not initiate or result in categorical relaxation of Japanese foreign exchange controls.[19] Other incremental steps had been taken previously. Furthermore, important provisions for exchange controls to be invoked in times of financial crisis remained even after the revised FEFTCL came into effect. But the removal of controls in principle in normal times helped ratify and accelerate the historical movement of Japanese corporate finance away from the reliance on domestic bank loans that had been the essence of the Bankers' Kingdom political economy of the 1950s and the 1960s. Most important, the erosion of exchange controls that began during the 1970s and was accelerated by revision of the FEFTCL led Japanese corporations en masse to issue straight and convertible bonds overseas, particularly in the Euromarkets. There the absence of collateral requirements and mandatory prospectus issues, together with the broad range of financial instruments, swaps, and exchange-rate hedging mechanisms not available in Japan, made raising funds cheaper and often quicker and more convenient than in Japan itself.

Starting in 1961 with Sumitomo Metals and Kawasaki Steel, Japanese corporations had periodically issued bonds abroad during the high-growth period. But the total was small: during the early 1970s the Euromarkets accounted for only 1.7 percent of Japanese corporate financing, a share of which had risen by the late 1970s to 19.6 percent, mainly to finance offshore operations. In the early 1980s reliance on offshore finance began to rise even more sharply, primarily through large-scale corporate bond issues in the Euromarkets, with the Japanese surge abroad driven by both expectations of a strong yen (in the case of foreign currency denominated issues) and the more flexible issuing conditions outside Japan. In 1979 the value of straight and convertible bonds of Japanese corporations issued within Japan totaled over ¥1.6 trillion, more than double that of offshore issues;[20] but by 1985 total Japanese corporate bond issues offshore had risen by ¥3.3 trillion, more than a quarter greater than the total for all Japanese corporate issues within Japan itself.[21] Total Euromarket financial issues, with terms dictated by markets rather than by bureaucratic fiat, supplied over half of all Japanese corporate bond financing and one-third of total corporate finance, despite the low cost of capital to domestic issuers within Japan.

The explosion of offshore financing by Japanese corporations during the early 1980s, particularly the rapid increase in unsecured corporate bond issues, further intensified the pressures building within Japan for financial liberalization. In addition to undermining any qualitative allocation powers remaining to the Bank of Japan and the Ministry of Finance, this flight offshore also rendered the activities of the Bond Committee (Kisai Kai) increasingly irrelevant. By the mid-1980s only 4 percent of all Japanese corporate funds was raised through the domestic bond market, whose issuing conditions the Kisai Kai had determined for fifty years. In 1985 the Ministry of Finance announced plans to consider a bond-rating system,[22] which would effectively circumscribe the Kisai Kai's ability to determine bond-issuing conditions.

Offshore financing by Japanese corporations also increased pressure to relax issuing restrictions, especially those on collateral requirements, which did not prevail in many of the Euromarkets where Japanese firms were ever more intensively seeking capital. The banks had long opposed any relaxation of collateral requirements within the domestic bond market, from whose stringency many reaped considerable fee income. But they began to reassess this position during the early 1980s, as the rush offshore cut back their share of corporate financial business.

Foreign governments and financial institutions also developed a rapidly growing interest in internationalization and liberalization of the Japanese financial system, particularly as Japan became a massive international creditor with huge international surpluses to be recycled. During the 1970s Japan's current-account surpluses had averaged only $1.9 billion a year; Japan's external assets at the end of 1981 totaled only $10.9 billion, compared to $140.7 billion for the United States.

Within five years this position had been more than reversed, with the United States becoming a net debtor and Japan emerging with over $200 billion in external assets needing sophisticated management. As major actors in global markets, with broad expertise in both underwriting and funds management, Western financiers saw major competitive opportunities for themselves as Japanese capital markets and pension funds began to grow, together with Japanese investments elsewhere in the world. Foreign manufacturers, eyeing a yen remarkably weak in trade terms, also pressed for regulatory changes, both to internationalize and to strengthen the currency. Foreign governments, particularly the Americans and the British, strongly backed their financiers and manufacturers in calling for regulatory change, as Japanese trade and financial surpluses soared upward.

SKEWED, UNEVEN LIBERALIZATION
OF PRIVATE-SECTOR FINANCE

The market forces building since the late 1960s beneath the Bankers' Kingdom institutions and patterns of credit allocation have detonated. Industrial borrowers, corporate investors, securities houses, city banks, foreign governments, and even the Bank of Japan have each had their reasons for seeking to liberalize beyond recognition the regulatory status quo of the last two generations. Market forces have aided all these institutions to some degree in attaining their objectives.

But the process of financial liberalization during the 1970s, 1980s, and early 1990s has not been a simple triumph of market forces. Although market forces have gained considerable salience in some areas, in other parts of the financial system bearing on the allocation of credit they have as yet failed to make much headway, as government structure and interest-group pressure alike have skewed the liberalization process.

Liberalization proceeded during the 1970s and 1980s on at least five axes, with crucial implications for the allocation of credit throughout the economy as a whole. Perhaps most important, Japan adopted fundamentally new mechanisms for allocating credit toward the financing of long-term Japanese public debt. Until the early 1980s virtually all of this debt was underwritten at rates bureaucratically set well below the market, either through syndicates of banks and securities firms or by the MOF-controlled Trust Fund Bureau. Secondary markets in government debt were virtually nonexistent, both due to the small scale of debt offerings and the huge prospective capital losses to investors in reselling debt whose unreal prices had originally been absorbed by the underwriting syndicates. But around 1978 serious conflict began to develop between MOF and the syndicates due to the huge prospective risks the syndicates were confronting as government bond issues hypertrophied.[23] In at least seven monthly offerings between July 1981 and July 1984, the banking syndicate refused to buy bonds at the price levels determined by MOF, forcing MOF to suspend the offerings and to reissue them later at prices more closely reflecting market realities.[24] In 1980 the Bank of Japan began marketing a portion of this debt through tender offers, with such offers rising to 25 percent of all new government debt issues by 1985.[25] And as the scale of refunding issues expanded so steadily after 1981 (from ¥890 billion in 1981 to ¥8.95 trillion during the succeeding four years alone), the government was forced to countenance the issuing of even syndicate-underwritten Treasury securities at close to market prices. By 1985 the syndicates were reselling over 70 percent of their total purchase amount of government bonds,[26] and had to choose between outright refusal and huge capital losses if MOF did not price its offerings in accordance with prevailing market rates.

To ease the plight of the banks that were underwriting its heavy debt issues, MOF took a number of important new liberalizing steps. In October 1985 a government bond futures market was introduced. In February 1986 it also began the issue of short-term government bonds (TBs), which by 1990 had become an important factor in the Tokyo money markets. The Ministry of Finance also compensated the banks by loosening restrictions on their performance of security-related business—permitting them in October 1988 to securitize mortgage loans, for example.

The ministry also took important steps toward market orientation in the regulation of corporate bond issues, which made the control-minded policies of the Bond Committee more difficult. As we saw earlier, collateral had in principle been required for all Japanese corporate bond issues between 1933 and the early 1980s, although the definition of collateral had been construed by MOF broadly enough to permit a few issues of unsecured convertible bonds by such firms as Mitsubishi and Marubeni, Kawasaki Steel, and Komatsu Limited during the early 1970s. Keidanren had called for relaxation of this requirement as early as 1971,[27] with MOF's Securities Exchange Council and MITI's Industrial Structure Deliberation Council later echoing this recommendation.

In March 1979 Sears Roebuck became Japan's first noncollateralized convertible bond issuer, followed the next month by Matsushita Corporation and twenty-one other firms during 1979–1984.[28] In January 1985 the large magnetic-tape manufacturer TDK undertook the first unsecured straight bond issue in the Japanese domestic market since 1932; by February 1987 more than 350 other firms had also been authorized to do so.[29] In 1985 MOF's Securities Exchange Council proposed the eventual abolition of the collateral rule, a change facilitating the flow of capital toward consumer- and service-oriented firms at the expense of by-now capital-rich heavy industry. And in 1986 the Bond Issue Arrangement Committee (Kisai Kai) itself, which had played such a key nonmarket role in determining allocation of credit through the corporate bond market since the early 1930s, was formally abolished.

As was suggested earlier, the relaxation of foreign-exchange restrictions and the resultant rapid expansion of offshore bond issues by Japanese firms during the early 1980s seem to have done much to bring about the dismantling of constraints at home. The fivefold increase in offshore Japanese straight and convertible bond issues in the course of a single decade (1975–1985) put enormous pressure on domestic regulators in Japan to match offshore issuing conditions.[30] Local securities firms could credibly threaten to take their domestic underwriting business offshore, as a matter of survival, thus threatening MOF's prerogatives still further. And MITI also joined this coalition for further liberalization, supporting the arguments of its borrower clients for a lower cost of capital, in a striking contrast to its traditional dirigiste approach to industrial credit.[31]

A third area of financial liberalization has been MOF's increasing acceptance of market as opposed to par-value securities issues.

Through issues at market, corporations have been able to lower their costs of equity capital. They have also gained further incentives to reduce reliance on debt, accelerating their move away from dependence on the commercial banks.

Foreign-exchange trading has undergone important deregulation since introduction of the 1980 Foreign Exchange and Foreign Trade Control Law. In April 1984 the Ministry of Finance abolished the so-called "real demand" rule, which had long prevented firms from effectively hedging or speculating in foreign-exchange markets by requiring banks to verify that all foreign-exchange trades were based on real commercial transactions. In February 1985 MOF also allowed banks to deal directly with one another in yen-dollar trades, instead of through the eight Tokyo foreign-exchange brokers.[32] In late 1986 MOF also inaugurated an offshore market formally analogous to New York's International Banking Facility (IBF). In May 1987 MOF gave further latitude to the banks in their transborder operations, permitting them, together with securities firms and insurance companies, to trade in overseas financial futures markets. In June 1989 it allowed the opening of an International Financial Futures Exchange in Tokyo.

Liberalization of deposit rates has been relatively slow due to the threat liberalization poses to the smaller, less-efficient financial institutions that are so numerous in Japan and so closely connected to the political process. But important, if gradual, liberalization has nevertheless occurred. In April 1979 certificates of deposit in a minimum amount of ¥500 million were introduced, with minimum deposit amounts being progressively reduced to ¥50 million over the ensuing decade.[33] By 1990 the CD market exceeded ¥2 trillion. In March 1985 money-market certificates were also introduced, in denominations reduced to ¥1 million by March 1990.[34]

Interest rates on time deposits with commercial banks have also gradually been liberalized, beginning with deposits of over ¥1 billion in October 1985, and continuing down to denominations of over ¥50 million in October 1987. By late 1990 deposit rates had been liberalized on roughly half of all bank deposits in Japan, according to BOJ estimates,[35] with full decontrol of time deposits in 1993, and demand deposits in 1994. This gradual decontrol meant higher costs of funds for funds-short financial institutions, particularly the city banks, which procure roughly one-third of their funds in various interbank markets. Such higher costs are gradually being passed on in the form of higher lending rates throughout the financial system, where banks have had the power to do so. But rising competition among various types of financial institutions is inhibiting their ability to make abrupt changes.

Since 1979–1980 Japan has become increasingly innovative in the introduction of new financial instruments, although it remains behind the American and the British financial systems in this regard. Aside from certificates of deposit (1979) and money-market certificates (1985), Japan has introduced yen bankers' acceptances (1985), short-term government bonds (1986), commercial paper (1987), securitized mortgage loans (1988), and a range of financial futures (from 1988).

In the wake of the new liberalization measures, and given the immense liquidity of a Japanese financial system generating huge and persistent current-account surpluses, Japanese money markets grew explosively across the course of the 1980s, expanding nearly sixfold in scale, as indicated in figure 7-1. They also changed significantly in composition, with new open-market instruments such as certificates of deposit, commercial paper, and Treasury bills increasing their overall share from 11.5 to 49.1 percent by the end of the decade.

By Anglo-American standards, liberalization of the Japanese financial system still had farther to go in the early 1990s. Despite the 1986 creation of a Tokyo offshore market, for example, various regulatory complexities, such as stamp duties and corporate taxes levied against its transactions, continued to impede effective operations. Domestically, consumer lending through credit-card overdrafts beyond thirty days remained proscribed. The quasi-controlled call and bill-discount "markets," in which Bank of Japan intervention was a persistent, central reality, remained a principal source of short-term funds, as noted in figure 7-1. The financial system as a whole remained strikingly more liberal at the long end of the maturity spectrum than at the short end.

Branching authorizations were still a centrally allocated prerogative of the Ministry of Finance, used to maintain the efficacy of MOF "moral suasion." Life insurance companies, major financial actors in their own right, also faced complex mazes of restrictions, such as fiduciary requirements limiting their overseas investments to 30 percent of assets. The net effect of these restrictions on capital flow is virtually impossible to calculate with precision. But it seemed to reinforce such prerogatives of the traditionally favored institutions of the Bankers' Kingdom (principally the smaller banks and the Bank of Japan) as still remain, together with the traditional flow of funds toward manufacturing rather than to services.[36]

Structurally, the Japanese private financial system in 1992–1993 was at a point of significant transition, with the passage in mid-1992 and the gradual implementation in 1993 of major financial reform legislation. The sixteen new reform laws enacted in June 1992, re-

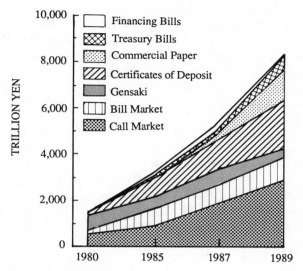

Figure 7-1. Tokyo's Expanding Money Markets

sponding to market forces in motion for many years, significantly compromised the longstanding segmentation of the financial system by allowing city banks, long-term credit banks, trust banks, and securities firms, among others, to enter each others' respective business areas through subsidiaries, and by permitting nonfinancial companies, potentially including major manufacturers or general trading companies, to establish brokerage subsidiaries. But in choosing this approach to reform, and in persuading the Diet to sustain it, as opposed to universal banking or other alternatives less constraining to the private sector, MOF preserved the prospect of some significant continuing supervision, inspection, and administration control over Japan's financial institutions. While MOF's role is clearly in the process of redefinition as reforms proceed, it appears likely to be surprisingly activist in the increasingly pluralistic private Japanese financial system of the foreseeable future and to remain a key element of Japan's strategic capitalism.

MARKET FORCES AND THE FUTURE OF GOVERNMENT FINANCE

Among the distinctive features of the postwar Japanese financial system, seen in comparative context, has been the unparalleled access of the Japanese public sector to a large captive pool of private funds.

As was noted in chapter 4, the Japanese postal-savings system in absolute magnitude represents by far the largest deposit base of any financial institution in the world. The postal-savings system also looms large relative to other financial intermediaries in Japan. Postal savings in Japan constitute over 30 percent of total savings deposits—over double the ratios in France, West Germany, and the Netherlands, for example. The United States and Canada have no postal savings systems at all.[37]

For many years, the existence through postal savings of a huge pool of private capital subject to state control was of immense strategic benefit to Japan's government finance programs. Cost of funds to the government through postal savings was substantially lower than what it would have been had the government raised funds through capital markets in Anglo-American fashion, although somewhat mitigated until 1987 by the tax revenue foregone on the tax-exempt postal-savings deposits. Low liquidity and related high levels of risk in the volatile Tokyo capital markets encouraged risk-averse individual Japanese investors to prefer postal-savings and bank deposits to securities, even at relatively low savings deposit rates of return. The cost of postal-savings funds to government financial institutions was also highly competitive with the cost of funds incurred by Japanese private banks, due to government subsidies for the operation of the postal-savings branch network. In nine of the twelve years from 1974–1985 the postal-savings special account was in deficit due to an excess of expenses over revenues,[38] with that deficit covered from the government general account. Between 1981 and 1984 this deficit averaged ¥105.3 billion annually.[39]

The existence in Japan of an unusual pool of captive private funds for public allocation allowed the Japanese bureaucracy to avoid heavy reliance on private banks and other financial institutions for the funds to strategically promote government programs. This was a degree of autonomy that the American, British, West German, and even to some degree the French government could not achieve. The huge assets of postal savings and postal life insurance also provided MOF with a useful pool of capital for covering fiscal deficits, independent of capital markets and underwriting syndicates. The finance ministry used this pool extensively during the late 1970s and the 1980s to ease the impact of rapidly expanding government bond issues on a financial system that still lacked well-developed capital markets. Between fiscal 1978 and fiscal 1985 Trust Fund Bureau purchases of government debt rose twenty-six times from ¥300 billion to ¥7.9 trillion, accounting in 1985 for 39.7 percent of all government bond issues.[40] By the end of fiscal 1985 the Trust Fund Bureau held 11.8 percent of all national government bonds outstanding, as indicated earlier.

Yet there were rigidities built into the Japanese postal-savings and government finance systems that threatened their viability in a market-oriented financial environment. During the politically turbulent early 1950s, when Japan was both rebuilding industrially and developing extensive subsidy programs for domestic agriculture and small business, there was severe competition between heavy industry and the conservative political world for budgetary resources. Since 1946–1947 the Ministry of Finance had been devoting much of the general account budget to industrial subsidies, especially to priority sectors such as steel, shipping, coal mining, and railways. With the fiscal stringency imposed after 1949 under the Dodge Line, political opposition to this support for basic industry rose steadily. Finally, in 1953 the Trust Fund Bureau Law (Shikin Unyōbu Hō) introduced at Diet insistence a floor of 6.05 percent on the lending rate for Trust Fund Bureau loans (*itaku kin*) to the government financial institutions, except in specially authorized circumstances.

Although originally introduced by the agricultural lobby to prevent heavy diversion of general-account funds toward interest-rate subsidies for industry, the floor on Trust Fund Bureau lending rates—the cost of funds for government banks—had very different implications in the highly liquid, increasingly market-oriented Japanese financial system of the 1980s. This mandatory floor made it increasingly difficult for the government financial institutions to preserve the cost advantages over private financial institutions that made government credit attractive to private borrowers, and that consequently allowed the Japanese state to use government credit to encourage private-sector support of government strategic goals.

As the surplus of savings over investment in Japan began to intensify during the early 1980s, long-term interest rates that had been gradually liberalized from the early 1970s on began to fall in response to market forces. Japan's long-term prime rate, for example, dipped from 9.5 percent in mid-1980 to 6.4 percent by early 1986. Government administrative policies were unable to determine the interest-rate structure, especially given the growing integration of international and Japanese domestic capital markets. By 1985 the decline in long-term market interest rates had erased the 2 percent differential between the long-term prime rate and the FILP cost of funds, below which the Japan Development Bank and other public institutions could not lend without subsidies. Private-sector loans thus rivaled the cost of unsubsidized government credit for the first time in Japanese history.

The crisis of government credit in the Japanese financial system of the mid-1980s can be seen more clearly when one examines closely the interest-rate structure of this system in the process of liberalization. By late 1985 the cost of funds encountered by government financial institutions when borrowing from the Trust Fund Bureau was around 0.7 percent higher than the cost of funds encountered by long-term credit banks, the Nōrin Chūkin Bank, and other issuers of corporate debentures. Government funds were also more than one full percentage point costlier than those paid by city and local banks on their time deposits. Yet prospective competition from both private banks and direct financial issues, including corporate bonds and even equities, made it difficult for government financial institutions to raise their rates and remain attractive to private borrowers. In a buyers' market for credit, Japan's government banks labored under substantial disadvantages due to their forced reliance on high-cost funds drawn from politically protected postal savers.[41]

By the mid-1980s these market developments forced the Japanese government financial system to confront a highly unpalatable dilemma. It had three options for action, each of them entailing significant prospective political and economic costs. One was to let market forces take their course, without changing the underlying structure of the system. This option seriously threatened the ability of the government banks to lend, due to competition from private-sector institutions in a market-oriented, highly liquid financial system in which the government banks had high costs. The second possibility was to subsidize government credit institutions—a course that necessitated specific budgetary outlays. The third option was to begin dismantling the government financial system itself and to begin deploying the huge resources at its command at higher, more market-oriented rates of return.

Throughout the first half of the 1980s the Japanese government pursued a cautious hybrid of the first and second options. As lending rates plunged at the private banks during 1984–1985, government financial institutions did not follow. Instead, they tried to expand lending volume at close to commercial rates by appealing to broader and broader constituencies. The Japan Development Bank, for example, started wooing small firms it had previously ignored—in stiff competition with the Hokkaidō-Tōhoku Development Corporation and other small-business institutions.[42] In mid-1982 the JDB also extended its first loans to a 100 percent foreign-owned firm, Fairchild Japan, for the construction of a ¥5.5 billion electronic components plant at Isahaya in Nagasaki prefecture.[43] Government loans to foreign firms, attractive to such firms as a mark of legitimacy in Japan more than for economic reasons, increased steadily in subsequent years, with even the small and highly political Peoples' Finance Corporation ultimately lending to small foreign businesses. But the government banks, aside from the Housing Loan Corporation, had an increasingly difficult time finding Japanese customers.

The market-induced crisis of Japanese government finance can be seen graphically in the evolution of government-financed leasing programs during the first half of the 1980s. During the 1960s and 1970s, institutions such as the Japan Electronic Computer Corporation played a key role in stimulating stable demand for domestically produced high-technology capital goods, even when the underlying market was volatile and the technology unproved. The value of lease contracts in Japan overall rose substantially during the 1982–1985 period. Yet the value of lease contracts concluded by government financial institutions dropped dramatically, from ¥6.3 billion in 1982 to *one-thirtieth* of that amount only three years later. This occurred despite the existence of extensive government leasing programs in such high-growth sectors as computers, robots, and medical equipment. The clear reason for this striking change was the declining price competitiveness of the government loans behind the public leasing program, as market interest rates available to competitors continued to decline.

The second prospective strategy for the government financial institutions was to subsidize their credit, so as to assure its competitiveness with the private sector and to enhance its effectiveness as a strategic and political tool. The lower the cost of government credit, relative to market rates, the more attractive it became to prospective recipients. Under political pressure from the ruling LDP, MOF also to some extent embraced credit subsidies during the early 1980s, particularly with respect to housing and agricultural credit. As noted in chapter 5, support for government corporations in the national general-account budget increased from ¥1.8 trillion to ¥2.56 trillion between fiscal 1978 and fiscal 1985. Of this share, the proportion going to interest-rate subsidies at government financial institutions rose from 11.7 percent to 21.8 percent of the total.[44] More than one-fifth of all general account subsidies to government corporations, ¥558.5 billion, was thus being devoted to interest-rate subsidies at the government financial institutions by 1985.[45]

Interest-rate subsidies were concentrated heavily in two areas: support for housing and support for agriculture. In 1985 housing alone consumed ¥341.3 billion in interest-rate subsidies, up 19.2 percent from the previous year, stirring fears that it was becoming a "second JNR," like the totally insolvent Japan National Railways.

The press was particularly critical of the large proportion of high-income people borrowing for housing loans, noting how such activity was subverting the redistributive purposes of the programs.[46] Agricultural loan subsidies were also increasing, faster than rice prices, which had been frozen in 1982 before beginning to decline five years later.

Despite rising subsidies and an aggressive, albeit often unsystematic, search for new customers, by the mid-1980s Japan's government financial institutions were having trouble overcoming the deepening dilemma into which market forces newly prominent within the Japanese financial system had forced them. The proportion of unused FILP funds rolled over into future budgets rose from only 0.8 percent of the total FILP budget in 1981 to 10.6 percent by 1984—the second highest level since the founding of the program.[47] Yet rigid legislative floors on the cost of funds to the FILP from the Trust Fund Bureau, reinforced by desires of the political world to preserve a high return on the postal savings that supplied the Trust Fund Bureau, made escape from the deepening dilemma impossible without rising subsidies to the government banks.

On December 5, 1986, in the face of escalating market and political pressures on both the government financial institutions and the postal savings program, the cabinet announced prospectively far-reaching changes in the treatment of postal savings. Postal-savings accounts were made taxable as the private financial institutions had been demanding, except in a restricted range of welfare cases, with the likely effect of slowing postal-savings growth. At the same time, the Ministry of Post and Telecommunications was accorded from July 1987 the right to deploy an increasing share of postal-savings assets through independent management (*jishū unyō*), which would involve direct MPT borrowing from the Trust Fund Bureau. Starting with management of ¥2 trillion in fiscal 1987, drawn from a projected increase in funds available to the Trust Fund Bureau, funds under independent MPT management rose to ¥15 trillion by March 1992, and were projected to rise to nearly ¥40 trillion, including ¥5 trillion in newly invested postal savings funds annually by March 1997, under a December 1991 agreement between MOF and MPT. At the 1997 level independently invested MPT postal savings funds would rival the portfolios of Japan's largest life insurance companies.

The 1990s thus found Japan's postal-savings program, its government financial institutions, and its private financial sector all in a state of momentous transition, under frontal challenge from emerging market forces. The tension between economic forces and preexisting institutional structure was far sharper than in the Anglo-

Saxon world, where the logic of markets had been earlier and more extensively accepted. Institutions in traditionally control-oriented economies such as France faced some analogous problems to those in Japan, but in attenuated form, because capital surpluses were not accumulating or market interest rates declining as rapidly as in Japan. Given differences in state structure and interest-group configurations between Japan and the major Western industrial nations, markets were assuming a different role in Japanese finance than in either the Anglo-Saxon systems or those of the late developers of the European continent. But clearly market forces in Japan were calling sharply and insistently into question the ability of the state to systematically channel flows of credit toward public purposes. Even more than during the high-growth period, markets were strengthening the hand of the Japanese private sector in defining and determining the fate of public projects.

THE POLITICAL DIMENSION

The conventional wisdom of Japanese economic policymaking has long been that "politicians reign but bureaucrats rule."[48] Evidence from the industrial-credit area suggests that this generalization needs significant qualification for the early postwar period as well as for the 1970s and 1980s. Chronic factionalism and a strong grassroots orientation, both stemming in large measure from Japan's unusual multimember district electoral system, have encouraged politicians to cultivate a small number of intense supporters, in competition with other candidates of their own party. These endemic traits of Japanese politics inhibit Japanese politicians from playing a systematic policymaking role, even when they have the technical expertise to do so, and have instead forced them to focus on grass-roots constituent support. But politics greatly compounds the efforts of industrial strategists within the bureaucracy to pursue strategic credit allocation, by inspiring the creation of politically oriented government financial institutions, by skewing the allocation of government credit toward noncompetitive sectors, and by obstructing discreet business-bureaucratic efforts to cross-subsidize heavy-industrial loans to large firms through the system of compensating balances.

Politics has also played a crucial veto function in Japanese policymaking, sustaining long-established and often obsolete regulatory patterns such as the differentiated structure of Japanese banking, controls on savings deposit rates, and the position of postal savings.

Since the 1950s at least, politics has also helped sustain the privileged and immensely profitable position of banks in the Japanese political economy as a whole, while simultaneously providing gradually expanded opportunities to the securities industry. Although the Diet has only intermittently been the scene of major substantive decision, it has, after all, continually served as the locus of ultimate formal authority in Japan; its general concerns have defined the overall legal parameters within which bureaucracy and business have made the detailed, microlevel decisions. The role of politics, thus, has been more than simply static approval of bureaucratic dictates. It became more systematically important during the 1970s and 1980s but had significant impact in complicating state industrial strategy long before that.

Patterns of the High-Growth Period: Politics as Welfare

The classic function of politics in the financial policy formation of the 1950s and 1960s, as it had also been in the prewar period, was to broaden access for small business and agriculture, which were hardly the priorities of MITI's industrial strategists.[49] Small-business pressure against politics thus fueled the growing complexity and decentralization of the government financial system that made it ever more unwieldy as a strategic tool. The Yoshida government, for example, created the People's Finance Corporation (Kokumin Kinyū Kōko) amid the depression of 1949, diluting deflationary pressures against a politically strategic constituency through off-budget financing. The Small Business Finance Corporation followed in 1953, for parallel political reasons in tension with industrial strategy, as a Diet-initiated measure intended to insulate small-business finance from competing big-business demands at the Japan Development Bank, through which many small firms had previously been funded.[50]

Similarly, the Environmental Sanitation Business Finance Corporation (Kankyō Eisei Kinyū Kōko) emerged in 1967 under the political auspices of Tanaka Kakuei, secretary general of the ruling LDP, to provide funds for *ryokans*, coffee shops, and bathhouses that lay well outside MITI's priorities. Tanaka reportedly hammered out arrangements for this new institution in a single night of hard bargaining with officials of the Japan Innkeepers' Association (Nihon Ryōkan Kumiai) not long before the 1967 general election. The new institution duplicated the functions of the two preexisting government corporations in the field and never even established independent credit-verification facilities. But it provided an assured, independent source of credit for small businesses at the political grass roots. Such firms are strategic gathering spots in urban communities and prospectively important locales for displaying posters and undertaking other sorts of subtle political activity—particularly because of Japan's stringent legal restrictions on television and other conventional Western forms of campaign activity.

The Agriculture, Forestry, and Fishery Finance Corporation also emerged, albeit less dramatically, in political response to interest-group pressure, reacting against MITI's efforts to channel scarce funds toward industry. When the Japan Development Bank was set up in 1951, agriculture was initially accorded only a special account within the JDB. But in 1953 the Diet initiated legislation to establish a separate agricultural finance institution, so that agriculture would not be forced to compete directly for scarce government funds with the basic industries that were the JDB's fundamental clientele: a process of differentiation that closely paralleled—indeed, set the precedent for—small-business finance.[51]

Just as the interest pressures of agriculture and various branches of small business assured their own specialized financial advocates, complicating the centralizing task of industrial strategists, so also did the medical profession get its own specialized support body, with a budget insulated from broader competition for funds at the initial, MOF-dominated stage of budgeting.[52] As the 1961 White Paper on Welfare (Kōsei Hakusho) pointed out, before 1960 doctors had received limited loans from the two major government small-business finance bodies. But there was no recognition of the special needs of medical organizations, particularly the small hospitals and clinics that are so numerous in Japan.[53] Doctors desired a more responsive funding organization and during a period of political turmoil in 1960 secured Diet-sponsored legislation providing them with a privileged source of government funds, the Medical Care Facilities Finance Corporation (Iryō Kinyū Kōko), which began operations in July 1962. Significantly, the doctors had broad support on the Left as well as on the Right for their demands—just as small business and agriculture had a decade earlier when they were successful in having captive government banks established on their behalf. At such points, party adherence was not yet set in stone.

Support for underdeveloped regions of Japan has been a traditional concern of the Japanese government since the Meiji period. Special credit facilities for Hokkaidō, and for Okinawa as well since its revision in 1972, can be explained on these grounds. But party politics has introduced important nuances into these programs. For example, about a year after the Hokkaidō Finance Corporation was founded in June 1956 to provide long-term development funds, seven Tōhoku prefectures (including Niigata, which had not been traditionally considered a part of Tōhoku) were added to its coverage, which became the Hokkaidō Tōhoku Finance Corporation. Not coincidentally, Niigata was the home prefecture of the highly entrepreneurial prime minister-to-be, Tanaka Kakuei, who actively promoted its interests during this period.

The Intensified Distributive Politics of the 1970s

During the early 1970s party politics acquired the ever more important function of inspiring major new programs at existing government financial institutions; spiraling administrative costs and rising political resistance to high retirement benefits for the senior ex-bureaucrats who directed these bodies reduced the chance of establishing new ones. But the pressure on inefficient sectors of the dual economy in the face of protracted low growth and the credit restraint required to slow post-Oil Shock inflation were severe. Small businesses did not enjoy the framework of assistance conferred on agriculture by rice price supports, import quotas, and the *nōkyō* cooperative system. Small business bankruptcies rose steadily after 1973, even under the relatively loose credit conditions that prevailed after the inflation of 1972–1974 had been subdued.

Reinforcing the motivation of conservative politicians to aid small business during the early 1970s in Tanaka Kakuei's Japan, as in George Pompidou's France, was the steadily rising political strength of the Left and the strategic position of small business as a swing constituency in a political economy undergoing wrenching transition. This was dramatically apparent in the 1972 Japanese Lower House elections. Communist strength in the Diet nearly tripled from fourteen to thirty-eight seats, much of it on the strength of small-business backing in Kyoto, Ōsaka, Tokyo, and Kanagawa prefecture. Membership in the Japanese Communist party (JCP)–affiliated Democratic Commercial Association (Minshū Shōkō Kai) small-business federation soared from 62,000 members in 1965 to 175,000 in 1971—with about one-sixth of all Japanese small businesses involved somehow in the organization.[54]

The LDP responded with a new program, the so-called no-collateral loan system (*mutanpo yūshi seido*). This system entitled small businesses to borrow up to ¥5 million (around $20,000) in low-interest loans, without mortgage or security. The only requirement was that small-business applications be scrutinized by management advisers (*keiei shidōin*) affiliated with local branches of the conservative-oriented Japan Chamber of Commerce and Industry. Loans could be made for any purpose, so no clear strategic criteria were applied.

To the contrary, the system's purpose was purely political—to draw small businesspersons away from the Left-oriented Minshō. Government funds allocated to the no-collateral loan program soared from ¥30 billion in 1973 to ¥510 billion in 1978.[55] By the early 1980s 2 million of the 4.5 million Japanese small businesspersons had ties to the no-collateral loan system and its conservatively oriented administration.[56] This lending program—whatever its deficiencies from the standpoint of industrial strategy—was effective in political terms. Minshō membership, even by that organization's own calculations, abruptly stagnated after the system was introduced in 1973 and never went appreciably beyond that high-water mark.[57]

Post–Oil Shock Consumer Activism

The classical Japanese financial system of the high-growth 1950s and 1960s (the Bankers' Kingdom) strongly subsidized large-scale business borrowers at the expense of the individual depositor. It allowed city banks to keep the effective interest rates on loans relatively low to preferred big-business customers by offering only meager returns on deposits. The owners of small financial institutions that supplied funds to industry also benefited at the expense of depositors, since they provided such funds to the call market at rates substantially above the rigidly controlled savings deposit rates. Patrick calculates the gross redistributive effect from depositors to stockholders during the mid-1960s at around 1.3 to 2.0 percent of personal disposal income, a substantial sum.[58] Yet there was remarkably little overt political opposition to this transfer, or to the relatively high profits of the banks, during the high-growth period.

Citizen activism on financial issues, however, abruptly exploded into prominence in Japan during 1974–1975, provoking a major shift in the political parameters of Japanese finance. Inflation, surging rapidly ahead of both wage increases and nominal increases in national savings following the Oil Shock, angered the general public. As the press prominently reported, the average Japanese household lost 12.7 percent of the value of its savings from the end of 1972 to the end of 1973 alone.[59] Yet the Japanese government, in sharp contrast to the policy responses of such other major industrialized nations as West Germany, made no upward adjustments in savings and other deposit rates to compensate.

The protest from the Opposition and from citizens' groups was unprecedented and highly diverse. The Zensen Dōmei textile workers' union sued the government for losses from postal-savings deposits whose value was badly eroded by inflation.[60] In November 1974 the Japan Consumers' Union began a campaign against the banks' practice, permitted by MOF since 1950, of not paying interest on deposits under ¥1000, even as banks themselves collected interest on housing loans down to ¥100 increments. These longstanding but contradictory practices, charged the Consumers' Union, generated an annual ¥5.8 billion in unfair banking profits during the early 1970s. Its leaders confronted chairmen of the twelve major city banks, demanding also to know how high deposit rates would be allowed to rise in compensation for inflation. Their claims were reinforced by a "one-yen deposit movement," which inundated many urban bank branches with minute, unprofitable protest accounts.

The Japan Socialist party, together with the Kōmeitō, spearheaded criticism of the LDP, proposing to create a class of "small-scale accounts" (koguchi yokin) of up to ¥500,000, on which the banks would be required to pay 10 percent interest.[61] A "welfare deposit" system was also proposed under which the elderly and single-mother families would be accorded preferential rates, to offset inflation.[62]

We saw how often agriculture and small business have succeeded against the strategic rationales of the developmental state in implementing their financial proposals, particularly during periods of broad national political turbulence such as the early 1970s. Consumer-oriented reforms have fared somewhat differently, as the disposition of the consumer demands noted above clearly shows, for while the banks relented over paying interest on small deposits— Chairman Sasaki of the Federation of Bankers' Associations agreed to credit them on all amounts greater than ¥100 from August 1975 on—no substantive adjustment of deposit rates to compensate for inflation was made, and the preferential "welfare accounts" and "small-deposit accounts" died by the wayside. The heaviest political resistance to these innovations came from the small, consumer-oriented financial institutions, such as the consistently marginal and highly politicized credit associations (shinyō kinko),[63] founded through Liberal and Socialist party intervention during 1950–1951. Established members of the LDP circle of compensation thus blocked the entry of new, consumer-oriented groups.

Compensating Balances as a Political Issue

Controls, as economic theory so insistently suggests, invariably create their own distortions. As we saw in chapter 4, a fundamental element of Japanese government industrial strategy for many years after the war was to depress long-term interest rates below market levels. Such low-interest policies have both reduced the costs of capital-intensive industry and provided some allocative power to the banks and bureaucrats responsible for low-cost capital, in the face of heavy demand for rationing it at below-market controlled prices. But interest-rate controls also intensified pressures on the lenders of low-interest funds to recoup income foregone due to the controls through collusively raising their noninterest income.

The most common means by which Japanese banks recouped profits lost to controls was through the system of compensating balances. When firms borrowed money from Japanese banks, they customarily redeposited a portion of it with the bank from which they originally borrowed, generally receiving only very low interest on these redeposits. Both large and small firms were subjected to this practice. Yet small firms, as a result of their lesser leverage with the financial world, were generally forced to maintain proportionately much higher compensating balances. Credit associations and mutual savings banks, which dealt primarily with small business, during the mid-1960s demanded compensating balances roughly four times those charged by the city banks, which primarily funded large firms. Even in 1980 this differential, albeit substantially narrowed, continued to exist.

Compensating balances bear relationships too complex and circumstantial in the vast world of borrowing and lending to be easily outlawed. And financial authorities, who must continually deal with the large banks, have had few incentives of their own to intervene. Policy response has thus been limited, sporadic, and discretionary—in short, distributive to those fortunate enough to be the beneficiaries of regulatory attempts to curb bankers' demands for such balances.

A continual bargaining process among business, bureaucracy, and the political world has produced few gestures at decisive control. So politicians—of the Democratic Socialist and Socialist parties as well as the LDP—have been given the chance deeply to affect the issue. Their leverage with big business and the state has been enhanced, especially during the late 1960s and early 1970s, by the Japan Communist party's persuasive counterappeals to small-business voters.[64]

The compensating-balance issue first arose as a major question during 1948–1949,[65] under the early Dodge Line stringencies. At first MOF was against the practice, which it declared illegal in March 1951.[66] But gradually MOF became more conciliatory to the banks, led particularly by its Banking Bureau, and geared down to routine calls for bank "self-policing," ten of which were issued between 1949 and 1964.[67]

Compensating balances became salient as a political issue following the adoption of explicit low-interest policies during 1960–1961.[68] Financial authorities, led by MITI minister and then prime minister Ikeda Hayato, author of the Income Doubling Plan, mandated below-equilibrium bond issuance and long-term lending rates that stimulated a capital-spending boom and acute capital shortage. This situation gave financial institutions considerable leverage to demand compensating balances, particularly from small business, and the only way such small firms could neutralize this pressure was through recourse to the political process.

During 1963–1964, when compensating balances came explicitly to the fore politically, Prime Minister Ikeda Hayato and BOJ governor Yamagiwa Masamichi promised to study the issue, while MOF minister Tanaka Kakuei appointed a special investigative commission. The Fair Trade Commission proposed that compensating balances be considered an antitrust question. The Finance Committee of the Diet demanded that compensating balances be phased out entirely by the banks within one year.[69] Under such complex multiple pressures, and confronting the stark prospect of losing jurisdiction over the issue to the FTC, MOF reactively issued an administrative order (tsūtatsu) on June 25, 1964, controlling compensating balances.[70]

The compensating-balances question reappeared with each period of tight credit; small business would mobilize politicians to put pressure on banks not to use the market power that credit shortages gave them to raise real interest rates. During 1974–1975 the issue re-emerged with the full force of 1948–1949 and 1963–1964. As in the other cases, major legislative initiative was taken by Opposition parties with strong small-business ties, particularly the JSP, DSP, and Kōmeitō,[71] tacitly supported by a Japan Communist party continuously and scathingly critical of bankers' pressure on small business.

The LDP, strongly connected to the banking world through Keidanren and deriving much financial support from the large banks, rarely made such moves. But given the electoral significance of small business and a strong populist streak among party members who had not once been bureaucrats, the ruling conservatives typically went along with the anti-elitist Diet rumblings against the commercial banks once they surfaced. Such political pressure may well have provided intermittent topical relief for small businesses.[72] But it did not generate structural changes in the Japanese financial system comparable to those that many of the policy innovations discussed above accomplished. The shifting political parameters of the 1970s effected no clear change in the political economy of the compensating-balance system, leaving it a complicating element in the futile attempts of government strategists to gain full control over industrial lending rates.

Politics and the Business Mainstream: Elite Interest-Group Structure and Its Transformation

Party politicians have periodically intervened in the distribution of industrial credit to *compensate* nonelite groups disadvantaged by underlying economic trends, as noted in the preceding pages. This pattern, which dates from before World War II, became more pronounced during the postwar high-growth period. It gained special force during the politically turbulent early 1970s, as the demands of the disadvantaged within a dual-structure economy convulsed by rapid transition gained particular resonance due to the precarious position of the ruling Liberal Democratic party in the Japanese political system as a whole.[73]

Beginning in the mid-1970s politics also became a vehicle for articulating some consumer interests in the financial sphere, although this process has been a hesitant and underdeveloped one by international standards. During the 1980s transnational politics also came to influence the configuration of Japanese credit flows and the structure of the domestic financial system, reflecting growing global economic interdependence. This new phenomenon of transnational politics and its relation to changing economic parameters will be considered at the end of this chapter.

Perhaps the most important impact of politics on the configuration of Japanese domestic industrial credit has been its most obscure: its role in shaping the position of banking, securities, and postal savings in the financial system as a whole. As noted earlier, the essential features of the Bankers' Kingdom system of industrial-credit allocation were virtually all in place by the end of the Allied Occupation in April 1952. Domestic politics within Japan had relatively little to do with creating the structure itself, which was more an outgrowth of wartime mobilization. But politics clearly played an important, if unobtrusive, role in sustaining a bank-centric financial and industrial system once that system was established. It was hence indirectly crucial to strategic capitalism.

Among the salient realities in the politics of Japanese finance has long been the strong support that the banks—particularly the large money-center banks—provide to the ruling Liberal Democratic party as an institution. The All Japan Bankers Federation (Zenginkyō), embracing both large banks and small, was a major driving force behind the creation in 1961 of the Kokumin Kyōkai (literally, the People's Association). This was Keidanren's mechanism for efficiently funding the LDP without provoking competition still operative within the business world for its favors. Together with steel and electric power, banking was one of the three traditional funding mainstays (Gosanke) of the LDP throughout the high-growth period. Its standard assessed share of Kokumin Kyōkai political contributions in early 1974, for example, was reportedly 16.7 percent of the total for the business world as a whole, compared to 8.3 percent for steel, 7.6 percent for electric power, and sharply less for other sectors.[74]

The large city banks provided by far the largest share of their industry's standard contributions to the Kokumin Kyōkai, with the sixteen members of the Tokyo Bankers' Association representing the largest financiers in Japan, providing 12 percent of all contributions to the LDP in early 1974, or roughly three quarters of the total for all banks.[75] The regional banks provided 2.4 percent of national business support, the trust banks 1.0 percent, and the mutual savings banks 1.3 percent.[76] From the late 1970s on, however, the relative share of the city banks fell and that of the local banks rose,[77] reflecting changes in both relative profitability and perceived interests, as the banking sector confronted financial liberalization.

The banks, particularly the large city banks, also lent and donated substantial sums to the LDP directly. In October 1974, for example, nine major city banks (Dai Ichi Kangyō, Fuji, Sumitomo, Mitsubishi, Sanwa, Mitsui, Tōkai, Taiyō Kobe, and Daiwa) had ¥9.9 billion in loans outstanding to the LDP without collateral, at interest rates between 9.0 and 9.5 percent, which was low in the context of the times. In 1972 city-bank lending to the LDP had been ¥6 billion.[78] Banking support appears to have played a crucial role in both the general election of December 1972 and the Upper House election of mid-1974, both presided over by former prime minister Tanaka Kakuei.

Despite their heavy political contributions, the large banks have received mixed treatment at the hands both of the ruling LDP and the financial bureaucracy. To be sure, MOF regulatory policies assured great profits for the city banks under the Bankers' Kingdom regime. But in many ways the smaller banks were treated even better, despite their significantly smaller political contributions. Despite heavy funds demand, for example, the access of the city banks to new funding sources was strictly limited; regional banks during the 1955–1973 period were allowed to expand their branching network three times as rapidly as were the city banks, despite their being less called upon for loans. The regulatory decisions of the MOF after 1973 also progressively intruded on behalf of industry on the lending prerogatives of private banks in such areas as compensating balances, while national policy also allowed progressive expansion of postal savings at the expense of large banks. Particularly since the early 1970s, commercial banks have been joined in political struggles related to selective credit policy by a range of other pressure groups, many of them from outside the financial sector entirely.

Throughout the postwar period large banks have been presented with a classic free-rider problem in their relationship to the Japanese political process. Together with the similarly risk-averse and heavily regulated steel and electric power industries, they have maintained a broad, pervasive interest in the stability of the prevailing political and economic arrangements, safeguarded by continuous, conservative one-party dominance. Other elements in the business world, including the securities and construction sectors, have shared this interest in continuous, conservative one-party dominance, but have lesser incentives to provide strong financial backing to the LDP as an institution—the Gosanke was fulfilling that function eminently well. Instead, they have concentrated on cultivating individual factions and politicians rather than the LDP as an amorphous whole, intervening pragmatically and strategically to secure distributive benefits for themselves. The large banks, meanwhile, sustained a more comprehensible but vaguer structure of conservative dominance, which yielded them progressively less direct benefit.

Seen in comparative context, Japan's securities industry over the course of the 1980s also exhibited unusual influence in financial policymaking—an influence that helps explain why Japanese financial structure has diverged from that of other strong bureaucratic states in the way it has. In France, for example, the *agents de change* who serve as brokers on the Bourse have traditionally been pawns of bureaucratic power, and during the late 1980s and early 1990s were gradually losing their role in the French financial system.[79] They have had very little relationship to politics, having failed to develop reciprocal ties that might otherwise help sustain them in the face of growing pressures for deregulation.

In sharp contrast to this situation, brokerage houses in Japan after 1980 steadily increased their role in both the Japanese national and the international financial systems. Indeed, by the late 1980s they were the most affluent and rapidly growing financial intermediaries in Japan. Controversial revelations during 1991 made clear that they had major influence on stock-price movements through complex covert compensation schemes for major customers and dealings that stretched as far as the underworld.

The meteoric rise in the profitability and the economic influence of the securities industry has been deeply rooted in the political system. The support that party politics has given to the Japanese securities industry is probably the single most important political influence on the Japanese financial system since World War II and stretches back to the early reconstruction period. Essentially the securities sector, as an outsider during the Bankers' Kingdom period, was forced to appeal to politics for redress of its mounting grievances concerning the orientation of a financial system that had been biased in favor of banking by the experiences of wartime mobilization, as explained in chapter 1. It faced sharp public criticism for its political involvement during the 1991 financial scandals, but there were strong indications by the following year, such as the defeat of efforts to establish an independent Securities Commission in Japan, that the securities industry had escaped with its power largely intact.

The bias of early SCAP regulatory policy, as noted in chapter 5, tended to favor banking, reinforced by the personal biases of General MacArthur himself against securities. Within the Ministry of Finance the supporters of banking held preeminence over those of the securities industry, influenced in part by the much greater age and size of MOF's Banking as against its Securities Bureau. The ministry's insistence on equity issues at par and on restraint in the issue of convertible bonds showed this pro-banking bias clearly.

Among the earliest political associates of the securities industry was former MOF vice-minister Ikeda Hayato, who reportedly obtained much of his faction's political funding from Nomura Securities, the largest of Japan's securities firms, headed for many years by his close friend Sejima Minoru. Another supporter was Tanaka Kakuei, MOF minister from 1962 to 1965, who pressured Bank of Japan officials into granting a special emergency loan to the near-bankrupt Yamaichi Securities in 1965—the only such special loan extended by the BOJ to a nonbanking institution in its entire history, before or since.[80] The number of politicians close to the securities industry increased particularly fast after 1975, when changes in the

Japanese campaign-financing law engineered by the Miki administration made stock manipulations increasingly important as a
source of campaign funds, due to constraints placed on direct dona-
tions by individual corporations. Some of the dynamics at work became publicly clear in the Recruit Scandal, involving the provision
of special shares to key politicians at below-market prices, which
forced the resignation of Prime Minister Takeshita Noboru in the
spring of 1989. They were also apparent in the string of scandals during 1991 involving efforts of the Big Four securities firms, headed by
Nomura, to manipulate share prices and compensate favored clients
for occasional losses.

Fiscal deficits and excess corporate liquidity were, to be sure, the
central factors driving the liberalization of Japanese finance during
the 1970s and the 1980s. But politics has profoundly influenced the
details of that transformation, particularly in defining the rights and
responsibilities of the massive postal-savings fund in the emerging,
market-oriented financial system. It was LDP politicians, for example, who obtained for the Ministry of Post and Telecommunications
the right, beginning in July 1987, to manage a ¥15 trillion share of
postal-savings funds independently of the Ministry of Finance by
1991,[81] with investment fees going to the major securities companies. Similarly, LDP politicians structured the terms for privatizing
huge public firms like Nippon Telephone and Telegraph during the
mid-1980s, generating underwriting fees that enriched the securities
firms even as huge sums in principal flowed into the public treasury.
The political world, whose strength has been slowly but steadily
growing by most estimates, has helped to produce, in short, a financial system in which the securities industry wields unusual influence. Its power was blunted and inhibited temporarily by the
scandals and financial retrenchment of the early 1990s, but hardly
broken. Politics in this sense played a major role in steering the
steady divergence of the Japanese from the French-model financial
system over the post-1975 decade, which even by the early 1980s
had called into serious question John Zysman's argument for their
similarity.[82]

The Emergence of Transnational Financial Politics

Closely related to the rising influence of both banking and securities
against the state in the Japanese political economy—indeed, a primary cause of both developments—has been the rapid intensifica-
tion of Japanese private-sector financial ties with the broader world.

In 1970 the Euromarket, for example, provided less than 2 percent of Japanese corporate financing; by 1984 this figure had risen to 36.2 percent, including nearly 52 percent of all corporate bond issues.[83] In 1970 Japanese capital outflows were virtually nil; the country had been in chronic balance-of-payments deficit throughout the postwar period. By 1988, however, these outflows had risen to over $130 billion annually, largely mediated by Japanese financial institutions.[84] In 1990 fresh capital outflows fell to under $40 billion a year,[85] but the $500 billion-plus stock of Japanese portfolio investment offshore, the heavy Japanese corporate financing undertaken in offshore capital markets, and the huge volume of short-term cross-border flows in increasingly integrated global capital markets testified to the heavy financial interdependence between Japan and the broader world that had arisen in one short generation. Accompanying this development, Japanese banks and securities firms had grown to become the largest in the world, although with very different strategic concerns than during the high-growth era of the 1950s and 1960s.[86]

Although the dominant Japanese financial institutions were huge in international terms, and increasingly mobile in their global operations by the mid-1980s, the Ministry of Finance continued to retain remarkably tight controls over their expansion into new business areas. The segmented character of the Japanese domestic financial system, purposely maintained by MOF, kept commercial banks out of trust banking at home, and out of most underwriting transactions both at home and also overseas. The conservative character of MOF regulation also inhibited the emergence of important new instruments in the Tokyo financial market, such as commercial paper and bankers' acceptances, while likewise suppressing the free flow of investment capital from Japanese insurance firms to all corners of the world.

In the globalized financial system that was rapidly emerging during the 1980s, actors in many nations had a stake in the evolution of the Japanese industrial-credit system—in the range of credit-allocation issues that had conventionally been questions for the Japanese alone. In the United States, for example, the Semiconductor Industry Association and the National Association of Manufacturers began, from the early 1980s on, to complain bitterly that government restrictions within Japan kept interest rates low for key industrial sectors and the yen chronically and artificially weak.[87] Foreign banks and securities companies, together with U.S., British, and German financial authorities, among others, made increasingly insistent demands for change in Japanese financial structure that were given ever greater credence by the rapid advances of Japanese firms into overseas financial markets.

Within Japan itself, major interests were divided on the propriety of financial liberalization, giving foreign pressure a potentially decisive role in propelling and structuring the process. Broadly speaking, those traditionally benefiting from the usual, administratively enforced segmentation within the Japanese domestic financial system, such as the trust and long-term credit-banking sectors, opposed liberalization. Their reservations were evident in the International Banking Facility (IBF), trust banking liberalization, and Euroyen underwriting liberalization controversies of 1982–1986.[88] On the other side, favoring liberalization, were manufacturers with multinational operations desiring more flexible, lower-cost access to credit, together with some commercial banks and securities firms. Japanese Diet members occasionally became involved, as when they pressed for a Tokyo International Banking Facility beneficial to the small regional banks with which many provincial Diet members were affiliated.[89]

Ultimately, however, it was transnational politics that inspired establishment of the Japan Offshore Market International Banking Facility (December 1986); the admission of foreign firms to the trust banking business (1984) and to the Tokyo Stock Exchange (June 1985); and the gradual liberalization of Euroyen underwriting and issuing (after 1984). Through mechanisms such as the U.S.-Japan Yen-Dollar Committee of 1983–1984, as well as more ad hoc threats and demands for reciprocity, foreign financial authorities decisively influenced the domestic Japanese liberalization debate then under way.

As the persistent segmentation of the Japanese financial system, controls over many savings deposit interest rates, and still underdeveloped retail financial services within Japan suggest, foreign pressure did not effect a total transformation of the Japanese financial system by any means. Domestic interest groups have continued to impede the liberalization process.[90] But where significant domestic support for change exists, transnational politics combining domestic interest-group representation and foreign pressure has recently become an important new ingredient in the Japanese financial policy equation. This transnational policy dynamic has significant long-term implications not only for Japan, but for a much broader world now critically reliant on the efficient flow of capital from Japan.

Gradually transnational politics, combined with market-driven arbitrage, is generating convergence in the cost of capital, especially debt capital, between Japan and the broader world.[91] During the first six months of 1991, for example, DRI/McGraw Hill calculations suggest that U.S. capital costs (a weighted average of debt and equity costs taking into consideration national tax policies, inflation levels, and accounting standards) had fallen to 5.92 percent, compared to 6.09 percent in Japan and 4.9 percent in Germany. During 1992 a weak Tokyo stock market pushed relative Japanese capital costs even higher. A more market-oriented system of Japanese industrial finance is thus clearly emerging, albeit with its own peculiarities—including abortive attempts to insulate key players from emerging market forces—such as the persistent financial scandals of the early 1990s suggested. Yet enduring public and especially private institutions—*keiretsu*, long-term credit banks, at-times entrepreneurial bureaucrats, and strongly interactive business-government communication—continue to give Japanese capitalism a distinctively strategic cast.

CHAPTER 8

Beyond Strategy?

INDUSTRIAL STRATEGY, we have argued throughout this volume, must be seen in a social context transcending the pronouncements of the bureaucracy about what that strategy will entail. Human beings all have dreams, but how those correspond to complex reality is a separate question from the content of the dreams themselves. In the case of Japanese credit allocation, political context, state structure, and private industrial organization have all constrained the industrial policy bureaucracy. They have likewise presented to the Japanese people contrasting social visions of their future, thus converting bureaucratic dreams of industrial transformation into the highly dynamic struggle for strategy detailed in the preceding pages.

As we have seen, industrial credit has not always fallen clearly within the regulatory purview of the Japanese state. Sector-specific industrial support policies clearly date at least back to the 1875 shipping subsidies to Mitsubishi; the Tokugawa shogun Yoshimune in fact singled out raw silk for special promotion in the early eighteenth century.[1] But these early interventions were few, usually no more than intermittent, and frequently ineffectual. Until 1925 Japan lacked a single distinct ministry whose primary concern was industrial development. Until the 1930s its private banking system lacked deep involvement in heavy industrial expansion. Until 1942 Japan even lacked a central bank with sufficient powers to exert real influence on the dispersal of long-term funds within the national economy. A comprehensive set of government financial institutions did not fully emerge until the 1950s.

Chalmers Johnson has argued that the modern Japanese state has assumed strong and distinctive developmental functions in contrast to the predominantly regulatory orientation of nations such as the United States.[2] The evidence of this volume suggests a more complex picture. A strong developmental orientation has often prevailed at MITI, but other ministries, such as MOF and the Bank of Japan, have often held a perspective closer to the American regulatory orientation than to MITI's developmental stance. Their preeminent orientation—and intermittently that of MITI bureaucrats as well—has been toward *stability rather than strategy*, thus confirming the generalizations of organization theory about the fundamental conservatism of bureaucrats.[3]

The institutional expression of Japanese industrial credit policy that has appeared most pervasively across these pages has been the emergence of "circles of compensation," combining public and private actors with common, established interests in a particular public policy endeavor. Typically such circles, established to meet a policy imperative at some particular historical juncture, have included the regulators supervising the sector in question and the dominant banks and industrial firms. Rather than picking winners and losers in flexible fashion across the political economy as a whole, the Japanese state has allocated benefits, including industrial credit, through these established circles, which have, in turn, provided diversified support to the bureaucracy. Internal allocation within the circles has often been routinized, with the systematic discrimination coming against outsiders. New members periodically enter the circles, but few leave, thus imparting a conservative, often clientelist bias to government industrial credit policy as a whole.

Intermittently, even MOF bureaucrats, who tend to be more "regulatory" than strategic on matters of industrial finance, have been entrepreneurial and sensitive to the strategic possibilities for themselves and for Japanese private-sector finance in their conservative policies toward banking. They exacted maximum leverage, for example, from the slow, deliberate process of financial liberalization during the 1980s and early 1990s. Yet this form of modest calculation, salvaging some limited tactical benefit from a transition fundamentally decreed by market forces, must be contrasted to the much more ambitious transformational industrial strategy ascribed to Japanese bureaucrats by developmental state theory.

Both the formulation and the implementation of developmental policies have taken place within political parameters that have forced industrial planners to struggle with mixed results to achieve their strategic goals, but have encouraged reactive support for the private sector. Due to biases inherent in the Japanese political system, especially the power of construction and real estate interests in the ruling Liberal Democratic party, the Japanese state has promoted the development of emerging sectors primarily by financing infrastructure to support these industries, rather than actually directing credit toward individual firms within them. Strategic credit policies of direct intervention have also often degenerated into clientelism, as the shipping, coal, and private-railway sectors so clearly show.

Apart from infrastructure-related policies, the Japanese state has also striven to transform some industrial sectors more directly, although it has made few aggressive cross-sectoral choices of winners and losers. It has had modest success in helping transform a small number of "public-interest" sectors with broader linkages, such as electric power, with whom it has maintained ongoing "circle of compensation" linkages over the years. The general picture, outside infrastructure, however, is of a more hesitant, reactive state, inhibited from rapid action, except in clear crisis, by many complex, controversial, and subjective strategic industrial issues, and heavily reliant on private-sector information and initiative. Government has been especially slow to get into emerging industries in Japan, and slow in getting out of declining sectors.

State structure clearly matters. In explaining patterns of Japanese industrial policymaking, structure crucially predetermines the ability of the Japanese state to be strategic and developmental. Where a strategically oriented ministry such as MITI has had clear administrative sanction to order a sector's development and hone its competitiveness, as in computers or auto parts during the 1960s, it can unilaterally impose controls to obtain strategic results, with little need to struggle against other players in achieving desired outcomes. The MOF, although less developmentally inclined, enjoyed somewhat analogous opportunities with respect to banking and securities reform during the 1980s and early 1990s. The results can be especially creative where ministries have the power within to encourage new industries at the interface of the old, as the cases of mechatronics, bioelectronics, and Japan's innovative electronics-intensive approaches to energy-conservation, environmental preservation, and "intelligent" construction over the past two decades suggest. Yet the Japanese state's ability to achieve planned sectoral development is often profoundly impaired by the boundaries of administrative jurisdiction. Where jurisdiction is shared, problems of arbitration and coordination occur, often drawing in rival ministries and the political world.

The existence of an extraordinarily complex and differentiated system of government credit institutions, mixed public-private dispensers of credit, and autonomous "promotion funds" under varied bureaucratic auspices in Japan have complicated targeting efforts addressed to specific sectors, as well as intersectoral allocation decisions. Complexities of state structure in the financial area—fragmentation that evokes Karel van Wolferen's image of the Japanese state as a pyramid with no one in control[4]—imparted a relatively pluralistic cast to allocation processes for Japanese government credit long before the financial liberalization of the 1970s and the 1980s began in earnest.

Such fragmentation and pluralism in allocation processes, it should be stressed, does leave *some* limited, second-best options for the state, as has been noted. Government can make the best of inevitable trends with a calculated strategy of gradualism, as the Minsitry of Finance did with respect to financial liberalization during the 1980s and early 1990s. It can attempt strategically to "upgrade" sectors where industrial support authorization and circles of compensation are already in place, as the Japan Development Bank has done since the 1950s with respect to electric power. And government can try to create and foster hybrid industries through technological "fusion," where administrative boundaries and legislative authorization permit, as they did in mechatronics during the 1970s for MITI.

Despite some limited possibilities, however, state fragmentation and complexity have gravely undermined the prospects for broad-gauge, cross-sectoral state targeting of the sort that the conventional wisdom has traditionally ascribed to the Japanese state, particularly that involving broad, cross-sectoral priorities. In this sense, the analogies current during the high-growth period between a government-directed "Japan, Inc." and a multidivisional company flexibly shifting resources across sectors in accordance with strategic priorities[5] were misplaced, even for the period with respect to which they were being made. Rather than produce total paralysis, as van Wolferen and some of his state-oriented revisionist colleagues suggest,[6] this fragmentation and decentralization of state structures has instead merely opened the way for more market-oriented actors, as shown in chapters 5 and 6. Precisely because state structure has mattered in Japanese credit allocation—in undermining the state's capacity to proactively promote industrial structure transformation, ironically enough—private-sector initiatives have had considerably more scope to fashion Japan's industrial future than often realized.

In successful industries as diverse as consumer electronics, textiles, and petrochemicals, it has been the private sector, in the main, that has defined strategic long-term goals, and market competition that has generated the structural transformations essential to competitive success. Even in some state-favored sectors such as steel, it has been private initiatives—often taken in defiance of the state—that have set really dynamic growth in motion, as the Kawasaki Steel case presented in chapter 6 makes clear. The Japanese state frequently generates elaborate macroeconomic and sector-specific plans, sometimes with detailed specifications regarding capital investment. But these appear to have had only marginal impact on actual economic outcomes, other than to foster euphoria and often aggressive overexpansion in favored sectors,[7] as the evidence presented in chapter 4 demonstrates.

One of the major findings of this volume has been the striking pluralism and vigor of the Japanese private sector—particularly its emerging industries, and the less-established firms within them. To be sure, there have been cartels and other attempts to restrain competition—not least in industrial finance. But these must be seen as feverish and often futile efforts to restrain the surging entrepreneurship and market-share rivalry that has been a more typical hallmark of Japanese corporate behavior, particularly during high-growth periods. Both the industrial-group structure, which became more and more clearly developed from the 1950s, with the recovery from wartime devastation and *zaibatsu* dissolution, and government support policies with respect to infrastructure, taxation, and credit intensified this uncoordinated rush into new sectors, which MITI typified as "excess competition."[8] The private sector dynamics at work and the relationship to Japan's fragmented, pluralistic public sector appeared clearly in the chapter 6 case study on construction of the Chiba Steel Works.

With very few exceptions, the initial demands for credit and the earliest actual working proposals for sectoral investment in Japan have come from private industry and banking rather than from the higher civil service or their alleged political masters. This has been true with respect to the scaling back of depressed industries, as well as with respect to decisions to enter new sectors.[9] During the past decade mixed public-private institutions such as the Key Technology Center, described in chapter 4, have become the most dynamic elements of the government financial system; during the early 1990s they continued to prosper despite the growing liberalization of the Japanese financial system as a whole. This private-sector activism on issues of national strategy, explored in detail over the past four chapters, must be seen as a never-ending and highly productive dialectic between public control and private enterprise. It is the heart of the "strategic capitalism" that has so fatefully contributed to Japanese global competitive success.

State credit controls and government financial institutions were surprisingly late emerging in Japan—much later, relative to the process of industrialization itself, than those of other late industrializers with stronger military and colonial incentives for state expansion in the 1870s, such as France and Germany. Japan ultimately plunged headlong into the economic development of colonies early in the twentieth century, but it did so, the case of Taiwan partially excepted, a generation behind the major continental European powers. Even before Japan had established large-scale public industrial-support institutions, a highly organized private sector, centering on the powerful *zaibatsu* industrial groups, had emerged. Thus, when the state rapidly expanded credit controls during the mobilization for World War II, it had to rely on the organized private sector to administer those controls. After a brief interlude of state dominance during the late 1940s, the well-organized private commercial and long-term credit banks—which, unlike the *zaibatsu* holding companies and trading companies, had not been dismantled in the aftermath of defeat—once again acquired great power in determining the flow of credit.

Bank of Japan overloans and Ministry of Finance branching restrictions no doubt implicitly constrained the working-level decisions of banks, especially in the early postwar years. But by the 1960s the Japanese state sorely lacked the administrative staff, the regulatory tools, and the informational base for activist credit allocation, outside narrow sectors where special circumstances prevailed. Officials in agencies such as MITI had to struggle to enforce their developmental vision amid bureaucratic complexity and diverse interest-group pressures.

In the face of these cross-pressures, important new opportunities emerged for cohesive private-sector organizations, less exposed to the demands and controversy inevitably confronting the state. Fortunately for Japanese economic evolution, this organized private sector, for a variety of historical reasons elaborated in chapters 1 and 3, was highly efficient and experienced at making long-term industrial-credit and marketing decisions, combining microeconomic expertise and a sensitivity to markets with a sense of strategy. It created a system of "dedicated capital," in Michael Porter's phrase, under which owner-investors provided substantial financial inputs for long periods of time, without regard to short-term returns.[10] Together the private-sector long-term credit banks and *keiretsu* institutions (especially banks and general trading companies) played a crucial role—arguably more important than the state—in encouraging the rise of postwar Japan's most dynamic market-driven industrial sectors, including automobiles, petrochemicals, telecommunications, and heavy electrical equipment.

The cases presented in this volume do *not* imply a pervasive and inevitable antagonism between state and private sector in matters of industrial credit, such as has been common in early industrializers such as the United States and Britain. Both sides in Japan generally agreed on broad policy objectives, including the encouragement of capital investment in heavy industry, as well as operational discretion for the private banks in handling individual loan decisions and other business matters; this pattern was particularly apparent in the early postwar period. But this general convergence of views in Japan did not inhibit the private sector there from dynamically leading the way into new sectors from consumer electronics and automobiles to services, where the "developmental state" played a supportive and reactive, rather than an initiatory role.

Japanese capitalism, in short, was "corporate-led strategic capitalism"—neither state dominated nor laissez-faire. The state, in the aggregate, was more stability than strategy oriented, despite the more ambitious impulses of certain MITI bureaucrats. Precisely because of the stability orientation, a symbiotic and lucrative relationship grew up between Japanese bankers and their state, as profitability figures for commercial banks during the 1950s and 1960s attest.

Richard Samuels has employed the concept of "reciprocal consent" to describe the symbiotic, often clientelistic relations between government and business in the Japanese energy sector.[11] The evidence presented in this volume suggests both the strengths and the limitations of this concept, as applied in the financial sphere. Reciprocal consent aptly characterizes the routinized, relatively static relationship between the Federation of Bankers' Associations (Zenginkyō) and financial authorities from World War II until roughly 1975, just as it may also characterize other industry-level relationships in steel, oil, and electric power during the high-growth period. But relations between the state and all but the most established individual banks and industrial firms were substantially less institutionalized and more fluid than the notion of reciprocal consent implies, particularly when concrete business transactions were under negotiation at the firm level. General trading companies, as we saw in chapter 5, purposely spurned routine ties with financial authorities so as to preserve more freedom in arbitrage. On important occasions many entrepreneurial industrial firms, such as Kawasaki Steel and Sumitomo Metals, ignored state injunctions to restrain borrowing and manipulated the manifest pluralism of the Japanese political economy to attain corporate objectives.

Reciprocal consent similarly cannot generate meaningful predictions about the actual conduct of concrete public or private institutions. Although a broadly useful notion, the concept is simply not specific enough to describe the private-sector incentive structure—particularly that of private industrial borrowers—that so fatefully influenced the Japanese credit-allocation process. Microeconomic and micropolitical notions more closely linked to private options for decision are required. This search for an understanding of the private-sector dimension returns us to the triad of exit, voice, and loyalty.

Even during the bureaucratic heyday of the 1950s only a few firms on a few occasions, such as Kawasaki Steel in the early 1950s, chose the option of exit from the control system, limited as it was until the late 1960s by credit shortages. But exit became increasingly popular after 1970, as growing excess liquidity in Japanese domestic finance eroded the credit controls and afforded borrowers a growing range of options. By the late 1970s, while the variety of fund-raising instruments in Japan was still substantially more limited than in the United States and Britain, virtually any firm that wanted to borrow funds could do so on the basis of market criteria without reference to state priorities. Until late 1987 Japan did not have a commercial paper market allowing corporations to borrow funds without using banks as financial intermediaries. But equity and convertible bond issues had essentially been liberalized, as pointed out in chapter 7.

Many corporate borrowers have favored voice—a resort to political activity—since at least the late 1940s, as the histories of the Shōwa Denkō (1948) and the shipbuilding (1954) government credit scandals make clear. The decisions in the early 1950s to create specialized credit institutions supportive of agriculture and small business also underline the importance of modulated and controlled dissent. The strength of well-organized industrial associations, such as the Japan Shipbuilding Industry Association (Nihon Zōsen Kōgyō Kai), heavily involved in the 1954 shipbuilding scandal, has been one factor contributing to the importance of political parties and interest groups in Japanese credit allocation. So has the strength of mass interest groups such as the Japan Small Business Political League (Nihon Chūshō Kigyō Seiji Renmei) and the All Japan Agricultural Cooperative Association (Zennō). But the reasons that voice resounded more clearly in Japanese credit allocation after the 1950s—and the clientelized cost to the Japanese state grew more painfully obvious—carry us deeper into the Japanese political system. Two aspects of that system have been especially crucial: the multimember constituency electoral system, highly sensitive to appeals from special-interest groups; and a pressure-sensitive ruling party, itself increasingly important in the Japanese national policy process.[12]

Prolonged LDP ascendancy in Japan meant rising political ability to control bureaucratic promotions, to recruit increasingly able bureaucrats as party political advisers, and increased familiarity on the part of politicians themselves with policy issues. The dominance of the LDP meant, in short, rising political influence over bureaucrats and rising political assertiveness in policymaking on nontechnical issues where the demands on politicians decreed policy intervention. All this tended to intensify the political bias of Japanese public policies, including those in the credit-policy area.

The growing ability of private-sector interest groups to use voice to attain preferential treatment from the Japanese state on credit matters coincided during the mid-1970s with the declining attractiveness for marginally competitive Japanese firms of market-oriented exit from the government's system of administered supports and controls. The transition to low growth following the Oil Shock of 1973 led to structural recession in shipbuilding, shipping, steel, and a range of energy-intensive industrial sectors that had long been given high credit priorities by the government. Low growth and high interest rates also released a cascade of small-business bankruptcies across the Japanese economy. Living and dying by the market did not look as attractive for the weaker contenders in Japan's dual-structure economy as it had before 1973. Under these circumstances, the pressures to deflect government credit toward the noncompetitive—the sort of dynamic epitomized in the Sasebo bankruptcy case discussed in chapter 6—became stronger and stronger.

To understand how state guidance interacts with private-sector industrial finance in Japan, one must thus go far beyond the dictates of bureaucracy, into both the incentive structure of private corporations and their relationship to broader political processes. Where loyalty predominates, one has a pattern close to reciprocal consent, analogous to that prevailing between government and private sector in the electric power, steel, and shipbuilding sectors. But government-business relations where exit and voice prevail are characterized by a different dynamic, in which incentives for the private sector to defect from routinized reciprocal consent arrangements are strong and government-business relationships are correspondingly more fluid. Across all three patterns government must "struggle" to enforce policy cohesion—without assuming it will come automatically. Producing and implementing "strategy" is neither automatic nor easy, since it occurs within political and organizational processes that state industrial strategists often cannot dominate.

THE "SUCCESS" OF CREDIT-ALLOCATION EFFORTS

The Japanese state's efforts to allocate credit have been variously cast as "success" and as "failure," without a great deal of concrete evidence regarding either the policies themselves or how they were put into practice. One of the major objectives of this research has been to investigate credit policy success across a broad range of cases. But first it is important to be clear about criteria for judging success and to distinguish the various distinctive roles that state intervention—including both the lending policies of government banks and public attempts to channel private credit—has had in the Japanese system of industrial finance.

Thurow suggests three basic functions for public investment banks: (1) socializing risk and speeding up market processes; (2) restructuring sick industries; and (3) providing public goods such as linkages and infrastructure.[13] These have also, broadly speaking, been the economic objectives of Japanese strategic credit programs, including both those operating through government financial institutions directly and those administered through private banks. Thurow's observation thus provides one useful benchmark for evaluating the success of those programs, although it remains at odds with the economic efficiency criteria that many of his colleagues in the economics profession might employ.

Reflecting the overall bias of Japanese public institutions toward stability rather than proactive strategy, the evidence of this volume suggests that Japanese government credit-allocation programs are best at providing broadly utilized public benefits such as linkages and infrastructure on a consistent, continuing basis. Roads, port facilities, and railroads have been a central concern of these programs—just as they have been of the national general account budget—since the late Meiji period; shipping has been the largest aggregate recipient of Japan Development Bank loans since the bank's establishment in 1951, continuing a pattern of state support that began in 1875. Private railroads have also been a major object of JDB support, and during the early 1990s the Japan Road Corporation (Nihon Dōro Kōdan) was the second largest nonbank intermediary involved in the distribution of government credit under the Fiscal Investment and Loan Program.[14]

Electric power provides a good concrete example of how government credit can help encourage the upgrading of a "public-interest" sector where a clear "circle of compensation" already exists. This sector has been a major client of the government-owned Japan Development Bank since the JDB's foundation in 1951, and in 1991 provided 26.7 percent of the total credit outstanding to the industry. This amounted to over ¥3.4 trillion, or more than $25 billion.[15] In reciprocation, every one of the nine Japanese power firms had at least one former official of either MITI, which administers the power industry, or one of the government financial institutions on its board of directors.[16] During the 1950s and 1960s the JDB, in its contribution to the "circle of compensation" with the power industry, engaged in general capital investment, expanding the capital stock of the industry. In the 1960s JDB supported coal to oil conversion. In the 1970s it backed the industry's experiment with nuclear power, as well as its efforts at pollution control, while in the 1990s the JDB financed the conversion to underground power lines and possible applications of high-temperature superconductivity in the electric-power sector.

It is worth reflecting on *why* government credit programs in the infrastructure area have been relatively successful, in the sense of consistently, predictably providing inputs of broad significance in the development process. Most important, the nature of the resource provided (infrastructure) has conformed to the functional need of the political system for distributive resources that politicians can help allocate. Second, no ad hoc strategic decisions have been required of government; the state can serve its purpose simply by routinely continuing to do what it has done for decades, associating with the same "circle of compensation" on a continuing basis. Third, the institutional context of decisions is simple: infrastructure can be financed through direct FILP loans to national or local public corporations, without any need for the state to compel private banks to support such development.

The role of government credit in restructuring inefficient industries has been somewhat more mixed, for reasons that also flow from congruence with political imperatives, the character of the strategic decisions in question, and the institutional framework for implementation. Where the prospective recipients have been small, with weak *keiretsu* ties or other alternate sources of credit, as in auto parts and machine tools during the 1950s and 1960s, the state has had considerable leverage for using credit to encourage mergers, specialization, or equipment modernization. This has been particularly true when the firms in question anticipated involvement in international trade and had strong independent incentives to rationalize, yet only a limited range of financial options. Auto parts at key junctures in the 1950s and early 1960s appears to represent this sort of case, and machine tools confronting the mechatronics revolution of the early 1970s may be another. This sort of microlevel, intrasectoral support for small firms, particularly component suppliers, is not the best-known form of government credit allocation in Japan, but it seems to have been among the most successful ways of rationalizing priority industries. Such cases deserve further study.

Restructuring an existing industry tends to require a proactive decision on the part of the state—in contrast to the mere provision of infrastructure, where routinized, reactive state decision making may suffice. Restructuring can also be much more politically controversial than infrastructural development—involving, as it does, the employment futures of individuals and the fates of communities. It is in the restructuring area that the weaknesses of the Japanese state, presented in detail throughout this volume, become critically important. When the restructuring decision has low political importance, involves few government agencies, and affords the afflicted groups broad options, however, as did the restructuring of the cotton-textile or sundry industries of the 1960s, government efforts may proceed smoothly and efficiently.

Fostering infant industries, like restructuring older sectors, presents the state with more complex issues for decision making than does providing infrastructure; not surprisingly, the record of the Japanese state in bringing up these infants is also mixed. As the analysis of chapter 4 pointed out, MITI appears to have seen the potential of machine tools early and was an important force in creating the hybrid mechatronics sector, linking machine tools and electronics. But it was slow to grasp the importance of computers—it acted only after the American challenge to the European computer industry became dramatically apparent in 1965. Likewise MITI shortsightedly rejected financial requests from autos (Toyota) and consumer electronics (SONY) at crucial early stages of their development. Even in steel, a self-declared priority sector for MITI, industrial-credit policy was remarkably rigid and hesitant in dealing with creative overtures from dynamic new firms. The ministry meekly accepted the bankruptcy of the creative early oxygen-furnace producer Amagasaki Steel in 1954 and only reactively backed Kawasaki Steel's Chiba Works (1950–1954) after it had become a fait accompli.

The government financial institutions have likewise generally been slow at developing infant sectors. Part of their problem has been their reliance on a legal mandate authorizing a policy-financial framework for the sector in question, which takes time and often does not emerge at the most opportune moment in product-life-cycle development. Inappropriate microlevel incentive structures, some of them unchanged relics of bygone eras when the government institutions in question were founded, are also often at work, together with endemic bureaucratic conservatism.

Japan's state industrial strategists, in short, have frequently failed to see the virtues of promising infant sectors and firms beyond their established circles of compensation. This static approach to industrial management shows up clearly not only in the case studies discussed above, but also in the aggregate analysis of both government lending and government decisions regarding private-sector credit. As chapter 4 suggests, the intersectoral distribution of Japan Development Bank credit in the late 1980s looked startlingly similar to that of thirty-five years before, despite large changes in both industrial structure and expressed government priorities. Shipping, agriculture, and mining were heavily dependent on JDB credit in both cases; the only new addition over thirty-five years was oil refining, a highly regulated—and deeply depressed—client of MITI. Similarly, aggregate cross-sectoral data presented in chapter 4 on operations of the Industrial Capital Subcommittee of the Industrial Structure Deliberation Council, MITI's principal advisory body on sectoral credit allocation, present a pattern of deep public-sector conservatism. The subcommittee's major concern was apparently to pare down private-sector investment plans; especially in unproven sectors, it persistently cut back the auto and consumer electronics industry expansion throughout the early 1960s, while leaving coal, a mature industry with low growth potential, virtually untouched.

In the face of fundamentally static government policies—galvanized to action only when a clear emergency such as Oil Shocks (1973 and 1979), environmental crisis (after 1970), or serious trade frictions (1970s and 1980s) materialized—Japan's powerful *keiretsu* and other large private firms were relentlessly expansionist and innovative across the high-growth period and beyond. State strategists often had trouble controlling them through credit allocation. Despite major JDB financial support of the Nissan-Prince merger in 1965, for example, MITI failed to achieve the broader consolidation it wanted in the automobile industry; Mitsubishi Motors even tied up with Chrysler, in one of MITI's greatest defeats in the history of Japanese industrial policy, because MITI tried forcing it into subordinate relationships with larger domestic firms.[17] Financial incentives also failed to restructure the computer industry in the early 1970s. Similarly, the threat of government financial sanctions proved useless in curbing new entrants into the steel industry during the early 1950s, the petrochemical industry in the early 1960s, and the consumer electronics industry in the mid-1960s, when MITI was trying to hold down the number of competitors in each of these areas.

When private firms had strong industrial group or other private banking ties, and strong microeconomic incentives for market entry, influencing their investment behavior through the terms and availability of government credit was futile. This reality, of course, was the source of the "excess competition" that plagued Japanese industry throughout the high-growth period. It led to rapid investment-led growth and the emergence of chronic excess capacity at prevailing world prices, as firms built aggressively ahead of their markets.

In growing industries, restructuring efforts supported by government credit generally led to industrial self-sufficiency and a withdrawal of government financing through mutual agreement of the state and the private sector. This was true in the steel and auto-parts industries, for example. But in declining industries government restructuring efforts often led instead to clientelistic, ongoing bailouts for inefficient firms, particularly when the declining industry in question was geographically concentrated, so that its demise would have catastrophic local effects. This was the pattern, for example, in both coal mining and shipping, where such inefficient firms as Sasebo Heavy Industries and Hokkaidō Colliery and Steamship were kept alive for years during the 1970s by subsidized government loans and state pressure on private bankers to continue their financial support. Government credit was a particularly attractive tool in such bailout ventures. The costs to the state were off-budget and did not present as direct a conflict with other policy interests as when funds came out of the general account. The benefits in political terms were palpable.

A third function of public investment banking in the view of some analysts is socializing risk and accelerating market processes. During the early postwar period, government credit programs socialized risk extensively. The Reconstruction Finance Bank, for example, was the very heart of the priority production scheme (*keisha seisan hōshiki*) that broke the vicious cycle of low coal and steel production in the late 1940s, paving the way to early postwar economic recovery. Japan Development Bank loans, together with heavy support from the long-term credit banks, also provided the catalyst for the huge first and second steel modernization programs (1951–1960). The huge cost of these programs ($1.8 billion in 1955 dollars) was sustained largely through bank borrowing and involved sizable risks that private banks could not afford to assume without strategic state support.

The early strategic leasing program for the computer industry, operating through the Japan Electronic Computer Corporation with the support of Japan Development Bank funds, also successfully accelerated the operation of market forces once the hesitant decision to forcefully support computer industry development was reached in 1965. The JECC did so by socializing the risk of owning large inventories of unsold domestic computers and thus ultimately accelerating demand for them through an extensive computer leasing program. Analogous leasing programs during the 1970s and 1980s also helped accelerate demand for Japanese-made medical equipment and robots, particularly among small domestic firms within Japan that otherwise could not afford to employ the equipment in question. Government credit also played a catalytic, risk-socialization role in supporting large, risky research-and-development undertakings such as the VLSI electronic circuitry and production-equipment project of the late 1970s.

As noted in chapter 4, the lack of compensation provided government bankers for their socialization of risk—denying them not only personal financial incentives, but even institutional rewards such as informally negotiated compensating balances that gave private bankers incentives to undertake long-term lending projects involving major uncertainty—discouraged these officials from pursuing risky undertakings from the very beginning, although the urge to rebuild Japan and assure it a respected place in the global order provided some stimulus to entrepreneurship in the early postwar days. During the 1970s and 1980s government financial institutions such as the Japan Development Bank gradually became even more conservative—more and more like private investment bankers—and less interested in risky, unproven sectors. Growing excess liquidity in the Japanese financial system, coupled ironically with high costs of funds to the public banks, due to political protection of savers under the postal savings program, handicapped public institutions in maintaining significantly lower lending rates. Excess liquidity also led Japanese government bankers to more and more comprehensively imitate commercial practices, thus further undermining their basic policy objective of risk socialization. Stability—almost always a primary objective of government bureaucrats—became increasingly preeminent as a goal of Japan's government banks, and innovation took place largely within established public-interest sectors like electric power.

Judging the efficacy of government efforts at influencing private-sector capital flows is more difficult than evaluating the lending policies of government financial institutions. But three basic points about government regulation of private bank lending can be made. First, the Japanese government's effort to engage in sectoral targeting should not be exaggerated. Comprehensive, formal Bank of Japan investment guidelines in relation to private-sector loans were only rigorously enforced from 1946–1949, with continuing high-level support for systematic qualitative allocation of private capital only through 1954. Occasional government intervention to encourage the flow of funds to specific industries continued at least through the Oil Shock of 1973, but this was generally limited to stabilizing cash flow on an ad hoc basis, as was true of support measures for electric power firms after they incurred huge, unexpected energy cost increases during 1973–1974. Government's control role with respect to private credit amounted to suppressing private efforts at what it viewed as overexpansion, both in industry and in real estate speculation. To this end the Bank of Japan reviewed private lending portfolios of banks, through window guidance, until the abolition of that venerable practice in mid-1991.[18] But many important private financial institutions, such as the rapidly growing Nōrin Chūkin Bank, which invested most agricultural savings and rose to become the seventh largest bank in the world by the late 1980s,[19] were only intermittently subject to its jurisdiction or not at all. Furthermore, BOJ window guidance involved little overt pressure regarding the details of specific loans.

The Industrial Capital Subcommittee of the Industrial Structural Deliberation Council, MITI's advisory body, monitored industrial capital flows on a fairly systematic basis throughout the 1960s, as was noted in chapter 4. But this involved active private-sector participation and never successfully constrained private-sector capital flows, as chapter 4 made clear. Both public and private groups ceased active efforts to influence the flow of funds into or out of specific industrial sectors around 1970.

Retaliation against deviations from public and private targets, such as it was, was also undertaken largely in the private sector, with deprivation of MOF branching authorizations, BOJ credit, and other similar benefits from government serving as ultimate sanctions. The private-sector Federation of Bankers' Associations (Zenginkyō) did its own independent monitoring and periodically discouraged overinvestment as noted in chapter 5. Even more important in shaping credit flows, both cross-sectorally and within individual industries, were the long-term credit banks and the *keiretsu* banks, whose activities chapter 5 considered.

This research uncovered a few instances of effective control allocation of private credit by the bureaucracy and corporate acquiescence to bureaucratic dictates. Among these were: Manchurian heavy industrial development under Japanese rule, 1936–1941; Bank of Japan direction of the lending practices of foreign banks operating in Japan from 1953 through the early 1980s (significantly, the BOJ did not appear to regulate domestic Japanese banks as stringently as it did foreign banks); MITI regulation of auto-parts industry loans, 1936–1967; and MITI encouragement of the mechatronics industry, 1971–1975. The ministry has developed loan programs for emergent businesses with poor banking connections in a number of strategic infant industries, such as medical equipment, biotechnology, solar energy, and software, but their efficacy has been more mixed. One persistent problem, as in the case of JDB lending, has been bureaucratic hesitancy and aversion to risk in emerging sectors where risk taking is often crucial to competitive success.

This research has, in short, found state allocation of credit in postwar Japan to have had much less importance in stimulating Japanese economic development—especially the promotion of emergent industries—than developmental state theorists such as Chalmers Johnson suggest. State intervention has helped provide high-cost, typically low-profit infrastructure crucial to the rapid development of basic industry, but through decision-making processes requiring few politically or institutionally difficult strategic choices. The sphere of effective, nonpoliticized control allocation of private credit by the bureaucracy toward specific industrial sectors has always been narrow, and is gradually narrowing still further, as state structure becomes more complex and clientelism proceeds. Indeed, the dual impact of political pressure for clientelistic allocation of government credit and of market forces has thrown the very possibilities and wisdom of strategic, bureaucratically dominated policy finance itself into question, as Japan looks to the future. These developments have created a pressing need for more eclectic approaches to the evolution of industry, even among strong believers in industrial policy.

JAPANESE CAPITALISM AND INDUSTRIAL CREDIT IN COMPARATIVE PERSPECTIVE

The picture of Japanese industrial decision making presented in this volume has, of course, major implications for broader comparative and international research. To clarify those implications, it is useful to return to the typology of relationships between state intervention and strategic resource allocation presented in the Introduction (figure I-1). That typology suggested two types of strategic resource allocation—the developmental state, involving state dominance of the process; and "corporate-led strategic capitalism," under which the government role was more limited. The typology also suggested the "clientelized state" as a conceptual alternative to the development state in cases where government control of resource allocation was extensive but nonstrategic.

Like most nations, Japan presents a range of empirical patterns depending on the sector, stages of the product life cycle, and administrative agency supervising the sector in question; the issue is one of central tendency. Japan has unquestionably possessed some important institutional trappings of a developmental state—particularly its strategically oriented Ministry of International Trade and Industry. In this respect, it is clearly more directed than many of the "soft states" of the developing world and such laissez-faire early developers as Britain and the United States. Although some aspects of Japanese government credit policy have indeed encouraged economic growth and structural transformation, the preceding pages have nevertheless suggested sharp divergences between the developmental state model and the overall realities of Japanese industrial finance across the postwar period. They suggest a different, bifurcated view of Japan—in terms of our typology—as being primarily, and increasingly, oriented toward "corporate-led strategic capitalism" on the one hand, and a "clientelized state" on the other.

These two central elements of Japanese capitalism, it is important to note, are interrelated. The distributive benefits conferred by a "clientelized state" have helped stabilize the one-party dominance that has continued since the mid-1950s. And this one-party dominance helped generate a predictable set of economic-policy parameters that encouraged the long-term strategic orientation of Japanese private investment behavior. But since the mid-1970s, as the cash flow position of Japanese firms has improved, as they have moved increasingly toward less capital-intensive investment, and as they have become more global in orientation, the importance of this stable domestic political base, rooted in clientelist distributive politics, has declined.

The preceding pages have presented some Japanese government institutions and practices, apart from the well-known MITI, with relevance and possible value elsewhere in the world. Japanese government credit policies have accorded high precedence to infrastructural development, providing roads, ports, railroads, power transmission facilities, and more recently, airports and optical-fiber telecommunications transmission networks that have no doubt stimulated private investment and economic growth. Within some individual sectors, most notably electric power, government has systematically encouraged an upgrading of private facilities, with positive broader implications for the economy as a whole. Government has also successfully encouraged the private sector to exploit possibilities of "technological fusion" at the interface of existing industries, as it did in mechatronics. All of these successes, which appear distinctive in comparative perspective, support the view of Japanese government as supportive of industrial transformation toward higher growth and higher value-added sectors. These programs may be of some relevance to the United States also, as it begins the process of "reinventing government" in an effort to enhance U.S. national competitiveness.[20]

Yet these modest successes do not add up to a picture of strategic, state-dominated industrial transformation. The Japanese political economy, as the foregoing pages have shown, has fundamental structural characteristics that complicate any characterization of it as a classical developmental state and suggest the bifurcated, corporate-clientelist pattern of Japanese capitalism outlined above. These traits include: (1) fragmented state administrative controls over industry and finance, with no strong central executive to integrate policy in these critical areas; (2) powerful and largely self-contained private industrial groups—more cohesive, market-oriented, and often more strategic than the public sector—which combine banks, general trading companies, and a host of specialized financial and industrial institutions; (3) private long-term credit banks, which likewise strategically fostered emerging industries such as automobiles and other precision manufacturing sectors; (4) a dominant conservative ruling party in power since 1955, providing stable political parameters for the private system of "dedicated capital," while actively seeking distributive benefits for constituents and generating powerful impulses toward clientelism in important sectors of government credit allocation; (5) a corporatist "Bankers' Kingdom," which has provided private banks, their political allies, and sympathetic regulators with powerful leverage in credit allocation, thus constraining government industrial strategists and blunting their impulses toward state-led, developmental transformation of the economy.

Japan's divergences from the developmental state pattern are best seen by comparison with two clearer cases of the developmental state in operation—France and South Korea. Both of these nations are strong chief executive presidential systems, in contrast to Japan's fragmented parliamentary democracy, creating some greater bias toward central authority in their cases. Views differ, of course, on the details of state capacity in these other nations—especially with respect to France. Zysman sees France, like Japan, as a quintessential strong state,[21] while Hayward and Loriaux see a political economy that is significantly and increasingly pluralist.[22] Feigenbaum, in a narrower look at France's state petroleum monopoly, sees a strong but "captured" state.[23] But whatever the variations in interpretation, there is little question that state structure in France is significantly more centralized than in Japan.

The French state has long had institutions centralizing formal control over industry and finance, such as the Trésor, which have no close analogue in Japan. Stimulated by the French example and the impending liberalism of its own economy, MITI tried in the early 1960s to seize powers analogous to those enjoyed by its counterparts in France, but failed, as noted in chapter 2. France's private financial system has also been far more sharply segmented between deposit and lending institutions than has that of Japan,[24] which has given further leverage to the French state that its Japanese counterpart has not shared.

Similarly, the South Korean state, like its French counterpart, also has enjoyed more centralized, integrated formal power over industry and finance than has the Japanese policy bureaucracy. In Korea's case, the Economic Planning Board, headed by the deputy prime minister, and the Economic Secretariat at the Presidential Palace have wielded more extensive power over private banks than MITI has ever been able to achieve in Tokyo,[25] not to mention Japan's Economic Planning Agency, which is of minimal political significance compared to its counterparts. The centralization of state power over economic matters seems to have been intensified in Korea, especially during the 1970s, by the role of the Bank of Korea (BOK) in the political economy, providing much larger and more differentiated policy loans as a share of corporate finance than the Bank of Japan ever did, and encouraging a dynamic of private overloans covered by the central bank that was much more pronounced than was true in Japan even at the high point of such practice under the Income Doubling Plan of the early 1960s.[26] The BOK's very lack of automony in relation to Korea's Ministry of Finance—parallel to the situation in France[27]—has further supported a centralization of economic decision making in Korea that the Japanese never achieved to the same degree.

The role of private banks in the Japanese system of industrial credit has also contrasted sharply to the patterns in France and South Korea. From the 1950s until the late 1970s the Japanese political economy was, as shown in chapter 3, effectively a Bankers' Kingdom; private banks strongly influenced effective interest rates and the sectoral allocation of credit, in the process becoming—not coincidentally—very profitable and autonomous of the state in day-to-day operations. This enormous influence and autonomy of the private banks was based on favorable regulatory decisions during the Allied Occupation, the position of the banks at the heart of the postwar industrial groups, their influence as preeminent political contributors to the ruling Liberal Democratic party, and the fragmentation of the Japanese state structure that regulated industrial finance, which contrasted so starkly to the cohesiveness of their own private industrial groups.

France and South Korea were different from Japan in virtually all these respects. Commercial and industrial banks there, first of all, were often owned by the state—South Korean banks were in public hands throughout most of the postwar period, while French banks were nationalized in 1982. Deposit and lending functions within the banking world were segmented in France, as noted above, eroding the autonomy of French banks. The deposit base of South Korean banks was always chronically poor due to deposit rate policies generally adverse to savings,[28] thus forcing these Korean banks into heavy dependence on the state for funds. Japanese banks were much freer of central bank control than their counterparts in France and Korea, given their substantial deposit bases and more integrated deposit and lending functions. Unlike their Korean counterparts, Japanese banks were also free to tie up with trading companies,[29] allowing the emergence of bank-led industrial groups, which the state firmly prohibited in Korea.

Japanese private banks were thus much freer than their counterparts in France and South Korea to pursue "corporate-led strategic capitalism," centering on private industrial groups combining banking, trading, and industrial functions. These private industrial groups proved a flexible, powerful form of capitalism that, as argued in chapters 4, 5, and 6, has been a central source of Japanese competitive success. They have been especially important over the past two decades of unusually pronounced international economic volatility, being able to both defuse risk and provide access to capital in uncertain times much more flexibly and dynamically than government institutions.

The vitality amid economic turbulence of Japan's variant of "corporate-led strategic capitalism" contrasts to the adjustment difficulties of the more dirigiste developmental state systems prevailing in France and South Korea. These have had particular trouble in market-driven industrial sectors like automobiles and sophisticated electronics, despite their earlier competitive success in commodity products such as steel, where state insensitivity to market signals was less of a drawback. As Loriaux and Woo point out, during the 1980s both France and South Korea moved to liberalize their state-led strategic capitalist path that the Japanese had earlier pursued, albeit with distinctive national nuances.[30]

Japan has, as we pointed out at the beginning of this section, diverged from the developmental state model not only in the assertiveness of its private sector, but also in the pervasiveness of clientelism across important sectors of government credit. This has taken two forms: (1) the co-optation of state developmental goals by business groups already within an established government-business "circle of compensation," and (2) new, politically motivated concessions to mass interests of particular concern to the ruling party. The first appears common to other "developmental states" such as France and South Korea, a manifestation of the widely observed tendency toward regulatory capture of the state, where it intrudes itself heavily into economic life, by the very interest groups that it ostensibly seeks to control.[31] The second pattern, however, appears to be unusual elsewhere, and needs to be explained in terms of the peculiar dynamics of Japanese party politics in a high-growth economy.

Clientelism has been especially noticeable in Japan's case in the continued flow of government credit in substantial amounts to sectors such as shipping, agriculture, and coal mining, which have patently lost any prospect of international competitiveness, or any rationale for high priority in terms of Japanese industrial strategy. The sectors in question are invariably industries that developed intimate ties with the state in earlier periods when they were clear strategic priorities, which succeeded in institutionalizing their access to credit through new specialized banks and credit programs, and which used continuing human networks and political influence to perpetuate their preferential access. There are clear, albeit even more extreme, clientelist parallels in the favored access of the Korean chaebols to government credit during the 1970s and 1980s, when they used it for dysfunctional purposes such as land speculation,[32] and in the backing that the French government has given its petroleum industry.[33]

The "clientelized state" aspect of Japanese capitalism diverges from that of France and South Korea, however, in the greater priority that it gives to small business and other nonlabor mass interest groups. As was noted in chapter 2, the two government financial institutions originally seen by industrial planners as the heart of government financial operations (the Japan Development Bank and the Export-Import Bank) by 1990 were only the fifth and sixth largest recipients of government funds. The Housing Loan Corporation dispersed over five times the loans of the Japan Development Bank, which was also outranked by two specialized small-business financial institutions and another for funding local public enterprises—and indirectly small businesses—in the public works area. This pattern of favoritism for small firms in Japan contrasts sharply to the difficulties that small Korean businesses, heavily dependent on the high-interest curb market, have had, and is far more extensive than anything offered by the French government to small French firms.[34]

Government credit to small business has been unusually high in Japan because small business has long been a crucial swing constitu-

BEYOND STRATEGY? · 267

ency for the ruling Liberal Democratic party. The LDP in turn has exercised unusual influence for a political party on government credit issues in Japan, particularly during periods when the party's nearly forty-year preeminence as Japan's ruling party has been threatened.[35] The big-business community's heavy reliance on debt financing and generalized aversion to abrupt political change has encouraged it to acquiesce in populist distributive politics designed to sustain LDP dominance. This has been true even when, as in the case of the no-collateral loan program, such policies have been patently inefficient in economic terms. A broad political coalition has thus sustained small-business clientelism in Japan—stabilizing the political scene for other private-sector actors more directly central to strategic capitalism. Japanese strategic capitalism is by no means unique on the global scene. But the coherence of the Japanese industrial groups, and the precedence of the banks within them, suggests that the most appropriate comparisons with respect to industrial credit allocation are between Japan and the banking-dominated systems of northern Europe, particularly Germany and Sweden, rather than to state-dominated systems such as France and South Korea, where the private sector has traditionally been more divided and anemic. In northern Europe, as in Japan, a heavy preponderance of financial transactions are in the "corporate-led strategic capitalism" quadrant of the typology presented here. The powerful universal banks of Germany, such as the Deutsche and Dresdner Banks, with their deep industrial linkages, and the private Swedish conglomerates such as the Wallenberg Group, combine financial resources and a concrete microlevel understanding of industrial markets in much the same way that the Mitsubishi, Mitsui, and Sumitomo Groups do in Japan. Not surprisingly, given Germany's structural parallels with Japan in the area of industrial finance, the two nations have achieved global competitiveness in many of the same sectors.[36] But important differences in private-sector commercial organization—particularly the salience of volume-oriented general trading companies in the Japanese case—have made Japanese industry somewhat more growth-oriented and aggressive in international competition than its German and Swedish counterparts.

Michael Porter argues that there are drawbacks in the system of "dedicated capital" provided by long-term credit banks closely linked to industry, which is characteristic of Japan and Germany.[37] The weaknesses of this central element of "corporate-led strategic capitalism" have also been evident in the research undertaken here. As chapter 4 suggested, Japanese industrial groups invested very aggressively in heavy industrial energy-intensive sectors such as petrochemicals, aluminum, shipbuilding, and oil refining during the

1960s, for example—indeed, far beyond MITI's guidelines—and then had to scrap much of this capacity a decade later, following the Oil Shocks. Because of Japan's poorly developed venture-capital markets and its often reactive state, Japanese firms have also been more hesitant to enter emerging fields such as software and biotechnology than counterparts in the United States, although the Japanese private sector has generally been more creative and aggressive in infant sectors than the state itself.

In the final analysis, the formidable strengths of "corporate-led strategic capitalism" at identifying long-term growth opportunities in the assembly and processing sectors, and then systematically commercializing them, are what stand out most clearly about Japanese industrial finance in comparative perspective. Automobiles, precision machinery, and heavy electrical equipment—in which both Japan and Germany have succeeded competitively to a far greater degree than the United States[38]—are graphic cases in point. This distinct form of capitalism, clearly not just a Japanese or East Asian phenomenon, needs much more systematic study, both at the macro and the microlevel, as the following section suggests in more detail.

ISSUES FOR FUTURE RESEARCH

Starting with the paradigm of the developmental state, this research has suggested considerable departure from that pattern in actual Japanese industrial practice, as suggested above. Clientelism has become more pronounced in government credit policy than the developmental-state paradigm, with its implication of technocratic preeminence, suggests; this has been especially true since the 1973 Oil Shock. "Corporate-led strategic capitalism" is also considerably more pervasive in Japan than the developmental-state model allows.

One aspect of this private-sector-dominated capitalism that is emphasized here—the industrial group, or *keiretsu*—is already receiving rapidly escalating research attention—both from the U.S. government in the context of the Structural Impediments Initiative (SII) and followup negotiations and from the American research community.[39] The focus so far of this ongoing work has been applied and policy oriented, considering principally the potential for trade diversion by such industrial groups, and recently their investment behavior. But the broader phenomenon of corporate-led strategic capitalism—of which the *keiretsu* are a central element—is arguably the most important reality of the Japanese political economy in the late twentieth century. Erosion in the power of the state due to the glo-

balization of industry and finance, combined with escalating research costs, risk factors, and market-scale economies that encourage interfirm cooperation, create a continuing rationale for systematic partnerships among Japanese enterprises, often with some
peripheral government collaboration. The logic of the *keiretsu* is becoming increasingly well recognized in major work in microeconomic and institutional theory.[40] This sort of private-sector-dominated strategic capitalism—especially important in Japan since the
sharp 1985–1987 doubling in the value of the yen led to an accelerated globalization of Japanese economic activity—needs even more
comprehensive study at both the macro and especially at the micro-
social level. So do its competitive implications, which appear to be
substantial.[41]

At the microlevel, detailed institutional studies of hybrid Japanese public-private partnerships such as NEDO, Japan's alternate-
energy promotion body, and the Key Technology Center, briefly
discussed in chapter 4, are in order. These could show how the increasing importance of rapidly changing, market-driven, non-capi-
tal-intensive sectors in Japan's industrial portfolio, such as software,
is driving a shift toward state tolerance of private-sector initiative in
government-business partnerships. It could also show how such
partnerships are carried out.

Also of importance is a more extended institutional study of the
Industrial Bank of Japan, identified in this analysis as one of the most
crucial architects of industrial change in the political Japanese economy over the past forty years. Particularly useful would be a detailed
organizational study of the internal capital allocation and investment monitering processes and evaluation standards used within
the IBJ that led it to identify and support such promising sectors as
automobiles and consumer electronics at a remarkably early juncture in their product-life cycle.[42] Such a study could usefully probe
the unusual integration of the long-range analytical and lending decision-making functions at the IBJ research and credit evaluation departments as they relate to broader interpersonal networks with government and industry. Parallel analysis could compare internal IBJ
credit allocation processes to those of other long-term credit banks,
to the commercial banks, and to government institutions such as
the Japan Development Bank, interpreting the variations in relationship to classic microlevel decision-making models.[43]

It would also be useful to know more about internal bureaucratic
decision-making processes on industrial credit issues, and how they
relate to broader dynamics of industrial policy. Chalmers Johnson,
in his masterful 1982 history of MITI, unfortunately did not consider
internal organizational dynamics as they have influenced external

policy in much detail, but we can by no means assume that MITI operates as a unified rational sector or that internal divisions and power relationships do not systematically influence external behavior.[44] Komiya Ryūtarō noted, for example, in the mid-1980s that the horizontal bureaus of MITI, dealing with cross-sectoral concerns such as environment, industrial location, and trade policy, had gained influence over the previous two decades at the expense of the sector-specific vertical bureaus.[45] But no research has yet considered the implications of such internal organizational power shifts for industrial policy. One could also consider how the changing external environment of economic deregulation and rising international frictions surrounding Japan has influenced MITI's behavior.

At the macro level, the nature of government-business collaboration under the newly emerging patterns of globally oriented strategic capitalism, and the broader implications for distribution and social equity, as well as competitiveness, clearly require further analysis. The salience of private-sector initiative in Japanese economic policymaking puts pressure on the clientelistic, compensation-oriented, economically irrational but welfare-providing support policies that emerged during the political turbulence of the 1970s. The administrative reform and privatization programs of the 1980s showed this corporate-dominated rationalization process at work. Big-business pressure has also aided the loosening of constraints on agricultural imports and the reduction of agricultural subsidies occurring in the early 1990s.

But it remains undemonstrated that the recent changes will lead to a purely market-oriented system in the Anglo-American sense of the term. Could not the initiative of globalized private industry also lead to new linkages between foreign aid and the industrial interests of Japanese firms, to new hybrid research-and-development programs (such as the research cartels of the 1970s and 1980s) of interest to them, and to new commercialization guarantees and investment incentives in high-technology industry? The strong influence of private interests in the Japanese political economy no doubt means important rationalization and some new responsiveness to market forces.[46] But could it also mean enhanced private leverage for government support and procurement programs of interest to industry as well, including some in the financial area, which is of central concern here?

Traditional views of the Japanese industrial-policy process have stressed bureaucratic dominance or routinized reciprocal consent. This analysis emphasizes a more pluralistic process of struggle, and frequent private initiative. In such a pluralistic world, interorganizational networks and their functioning are clearly of central importance. We have alluded to their centrality in passing in chapter 2 and presented frequent evidence of their decisive importance in case studies, ranging from the Industrial Bank of Japan's formidable research network to Sasebo mayor Tsuji Ichizō and Prime Minister Fukuda Takeo's broad personal political networks. Yet we have not had the chance to consider networks explicitly due to the central concern with institutions and policy outputs in this volume.

Government-business networks in Japan deserve extended study in their own right, particularly at the micropolitical and microeconomic level.[47] Our case studies, such as the analysis of the Sasebo Heavy Industries rescue effort and the critical roles of Prime Minister Fukuda, Sasebo mayor Tsuji, and SHI president Tsubouchi in it, clearly show the importance of networks as a variable. These networks play a crucial role in determining both policy and private-sector outcomes and information flows in a political economy that is far more fragmented and pluralistic than most conventional views concede.[48] Which firms and which political interests do bureaucratic "descent from heaven" (amakudari) and other forms of cross-organizational transfer actually link up? How are they supplemented by marriage cliques (keibatsu) and other social ties? What functional significance do various kinds of networks have in determining how government-business relations are actually conducted in Japan? When and how do they impart cohesion and strategic orientation to the fragmented Japanese state, or to the combination of that state and Japan's dynamic private sector to produce strategic capitalism?

In the analysis of the Japanese state itself, the traditional focus has been on MITI. This research has suggested clearly that MITI's views and approaches to policymaking are not necessarily typical of those prevailing across the Japanese government as a whole. This insight needs to be broadened and deepened, with detailed institutional studies of other ministries and agencies, for understanding why other ministries behave differently from MITI is profoundly rooted in their historical experience, which there was little opportunity to consider here. Detailed institutional studies of such bodies as the Ministry of Finance, the Ministry of Transportation, the Bank of Japan, the Japan Development Bank, and the smaller, more politicized government financial organizations could lend considerable force and nuance to the themes of pluralism and public-sector hesitancy that have been developed here. They could shed light on the rather different concepts of strategy and institutional interest that other ministries appear to have, such as MOF's strong bias toward equilibrium and "balance."

The picture of Japanese industrial decision making presented in this volume has major implications for broader comparative and international research. Although it confirms the general structuralist contention that institutions matter, it casts further doubt on the notion of state dominance in economic affairs, and as suggested in the previous section, on the general applicability of the "developmental state" concept. Even a "strong state" such as Japan, in a sector such as industrial finance, where the state might be expected to wield considerable leverage, appears incapable of systematically formulating and implementing a state-dominated transformation-oriented industrial strategy, contrary to the conventional wisdom.

Although the Japanese state may have trouble succeeding at strategy, it appears heavily and increasingly engaged, this research suggests, in providing welfare—for small business, agriculture, home dwellers, and a range of depressed industries from shipping to coal mining. The previous section suggested some parallel clientelist pressures in France and South Korea, albeit largely on behalf of large-scale industry. How pervasive across the rest of the industrialized world is this clientelist tendency? How do the forces propelling it elsewhere in the world compare to those operating in Japan? Is it too much to say that, in a post–cold war era of globalized industry, of deepening economic interdependence, and of fragmented, politically vulnerable governments everywhere, that the central function of states is becoming that of ward to the noncompetitive firm, cushioning the impact of industrial change and reactively offsetting its inequities, rather than filling more proactive functions? If so, what does this development imply for social cohesion, democracy, and economic efficiency?

There are clearly links between the international system and Japanese domestic credit allocation processes that need to be better understood.[49] The intrusiveness of the state in French economic life—and the French state's preoccupation with industrial strategy—seems, for example, to have been intensified by the perceived threat to national economic sovereignty posed by American international economic hegemony during the 1960s.[50] This research has suggested a parallel dynamic in the Japanese case, where the impending challenge of confronting international capital following Japan's accession to the OECD in 1964 seems to have lent greater urgency to MITI's dirigiste efforts at industrial consolidation. But the issue needs to be explored more fully.

Similarly, international capital flows, which were important in eroding state preeminence in the continental European political economies during the 1960s, also need to be explored more fully in their relationship to Japanese industrial finance. Foreign investment provided important support to a few Japanese industries, such as steel, during the 1950s and 1960s; World Bank loans were crucial to the construction of Japan's famed Shinkansen bullet train line, completed in 1964. In the Kawasaki Steel case presented in chapter 6, World Bank loans were decisive in allowing a project frowned upon by the chairman of the Bank of Japan to go ahead on its economic merits. But this occurred only because the Japanese government was split on the matter, and the growth-oriented Japan Development Bank stepped forward to guarantee the Kawasaki loan. It would be instructive to know how common such patterns of trans-Pacific coalition building have been, and what their cumulative impact has been on the evolution of Japanese industrial finance.

Perhaps the most fertile subject for comparative and international research raised by this volume concerns the broader relevance of the corporate-led strategic capitalism paradigm of government-business relations beyond Japan. Even the dirigiste French bureaucrats and their political supporters, long the most stalwart adherents of the developmental state, recognized the potency of this paradigm after 1984.[51] Under the Chirac privatization plan of 1989, France's Trésor strove to place roughly 20 percent of the shares of key banks and industrial firms then being privatized in the hands of "stable stockholders" (noyaux durs), in a clear imitation of Japanese practice.

But there are also suggestions that the Japanese system of "dedicated capital," by reducing risk, provokes a tendency to overinvest and to be overly slow in the redeployment of capital out of unattractive businesses.[52] The experience of Japanese heavy industry in the 1960s and 1970s, when sectors such as petrochemicals, aluminum, and shipbuilding first exploded in scale, and then hesitated in downsizing following the 1973 Oil Shock, would superficially seem to support such an argument. But such charges need much more serious empirical investigation.

There is growing evidence, as noted above, that the Japanese pattern of corporate-led strategic capitalism, and the "dedicated capital" that lies at its heart, is also prominent in Germany—with equally positive implications there for industrial development.[53] The supervisory boards (Aufsichtsrat) of financial institutions such as the Deutsche Bank seem to integrate financial and industrial considerations in ways similar to the planning offices of the Japanese long-term credit banks or the groupwide coordination meetings of top-level executives (Mitsubishi's Kinyōkai, for example) within the keiretsu industrial groups. What are the similarities and differences in how these Japanese and German private strategic bodies aggregate demands and make strategic choices internally? How do their specific corporate concerns interrelate with public policy and external capital markets?

Corporate-led strategic capitalism also has broader implications for both theory and policy in international affairs, suggested graphically by the 1990 announcement of strategic partnership between the Mitsubishi and Daimler-Benz industrial groups with respect to high-technology industrial development and East-West trade. Some of the rationale behind that particular partnership disappeared with the collapse of the Soviet Union, but the more general underlying logic of such private-sector group-to-group collaboration remains. Do these cross-industrial groupings—either singly or in strategic partnership—have the potential for organizing major elements of the global economy independent of governments themselves? If not now, may they not gain such capacity in the foreseeable future, given their apparent competitive strengths in a volatile yet increasingly integrated world economy? How will the actions of such private-sector groups relate to the public policies of nations in delicate areas such as high-technology, energy, and trade with pariah nations? Will they be seriously affected by financial turbulence, such as the Japanese stock market decline of 1991–1992? Do the groups provide an alternate means for integrating the world economy as superpower hegemony begins to fade?[54] Or do they only intensify the tensions of an emerging "cold peace" among rival regions, some practicing strategic capitalism and others not?[55] The implications for future analysis are virtually endless.

THE FUTURE OF STRATEGIC CREDIT

In the increasingly market-oriented Japanese financial system of the 1980s and 1990s, government has been faced with serious questions about the rationality and feasibility of trying to shape private investment decisions through the strategic provision of credit. The bureaucracy has lost virtually all control over the lending decisions of major private banks and retains only tenuous leverage over the powerful securities companies and other nonbank financial institutions, as demonstrated by the financial scandals of 1991–1992. The state's major remaining role in the provision of credit is through the government financial institutions. These in turn have been beset with a range of serious technical maladies of their own, not to mention the growing political co-optation engendered by interest-group pressures.

Japan's government financial institutions since the 1950s have been largely funded, as was pointed out in chapter 4, through the massive national postal-savings system. Their cost of funds—the deposit rate on postal savings themselves—has been kept high by grass-roots political pressure. As market-oriented lending rates dropped precipitously in Japan during the 1980s due to domestically and internationally generated excess liquidity, the Japanese government financial system faced a painful cost squeeze just as the state's willingness to finance fiscal deficits was eroded by the administrative reform campaign. Government lending rates, kept high by grass-roots political pressure for high returns on postal-savings deposits, threatened to become unattractive to all but those near-insolvent borrowers incapable of turning elsewhere, or to foreigners with similarly marginal ability to borrow in Japan. To make government loans attractive—a strong political and industrial-policy imperative for the Japanese state—subsidies for government credit from the general-account budget began to spiral during the early 1980s, as was noted in chapter 4.

From a single-minded focus on strategy during the 1950s, Japanese policy finance two generations later had seemingly moved to a primary commitment to welfare, of the past rather than the future; it was growing irrelevant to the mainstream of the business world, except in a few narrow public-interest sectors such as electric power. Government finance was, as one senior MOF official candidly put it, like a respected, beribboned, but slightly senile old general, whom no one quite knew how to discreetly retire.

This seeming irrelevance of the government financial system to industrial strategy was in part, ironically enough, a result of its success. Policy finance in the 1950s and 1960s had helped foster a complex of industries—steel, shipbuilding, shipping, and indirectly even machine tools and autos—that had succeeded massively in international competition. Competitive success had generated trade surpluses and resulting excess liquidity within Japan. This in turn intensified growing market pressure on the longstanding framework of domestic credit controls during the early 1970s.

The politicized turn toward welfare in Japanese government credit policies—toward a clientelized rather than a developmental state—was also facilitated by the broad prosperity that export-led growth produced in Japan. Throughout the two decades prior to the 1973 Oil Shock, the Japanese government was perennially in surplus, generating funds to meet a broad range of interest-group demands. The political fragility of LDP dominance during the early 1970s gave the ruling conservatives incentive to meet them. But the slowdown in economic growth after 1973, followed by the consolidation of LDP dominance, inspired a different policy dynamic.

The coming of markets, internationalization, and even clientelism, in some measure, to the Japanese financial system did not, however, self-evidently mean that some reconfigured version of policy finance could not serve important national needs. Japan in the 1990s remained a nation lacking substantial domestic energy resources, without assurance of either stable exchange rates or a stable, open international trading system. Despite short-run excess liquidity, long-run demand for capital appeared likely to be high in Japan—to provide telecommunications infrastructure, research support, and alternate-energy facilities, to name a few obvious priorities. As both the French Socialists and the British Labour party were pointing out even before 1985, and advisers to U.S. President Bill Clinton in the 1990s, the modern industrial state could productively employ loan-guarantee programs in these and other areas to reduce the cost of capital to favored industries and firms even under a financial system dominated by capital markets.[56]

The more resourceful and flexible of the government financial institutions in Japan were already developing new means of survival in the increasingly liberalized financial system. By 1990 29 percent of the Japan Development Bank's total operating capital was procured outside the Fiscal Investment and Loan Program—much of it through foreign bond issues accompanied by currency swaps. At the Japan Export-Import Bank this ratio reached 20 percent.[57]

Mixed public-private institutions with policy financial functions were another major innovation giving greater vitality to the government financial system. One typical example was the Japan Key Technology Center, founded in 1985. These new hybrid public-private institutions induced greater market orientation into policy finance, while still trying to preserve a risk-socialization aspect.

As Japanese capital exports began to surge in the mid-1980s, from virtually nothing in 1980 to over $130 billion in 1986, it became increasingly clear that the Japanese financial sector had an auspicious future on the global financial stage. Japanese banks and securities companies held privileged access to the massive pooled savings of Japan and appeared to be their natural intermediary to global markets. But foreign competitors, particularly Anglo-American financiers, were more experienced in international transactions such as underwriting, trust banking, and brokerage than their novice counterparts in Japan. International finance was for Japanese firms still an infant industry, despite the huge resources at their command.

Japan's emerging strategic approach to international financial services took several forms. Low domestic deposit rates within Japan, coupled with the access problems faced by foreign banks in securing yen funds,[58] gave Japanese banks decisive cost-of-funds advantages as they ventured forth into international competition, which was perpetuated into the 1990s by the glacial slowness of deposit-rate liberalization. Institutional vehicles such as the Japan Center for International Finance and the Nassau-based semigovernmental Japanese factoring corporation for Third World debt helped reduce informational and repayment uncertainties confronting Japanese banks as they began lending to foreign borrowers about whom they knew relatively little. Extensive Japanese Export-Import Bank loans also fostered the development of a Japanese international leasing industry that by 1985 handled a dominant share of the aircraft leasing business in the Pacific Basin.[59]

Developments of the early 1990s blunted the Japanese international financial offensive. The collapse of speculative bubbles in the securities and real estate market put severe pressure on the banks, already under the deepening imperative of meeting international capital adequacy standards. Both important banks and major securities firms were rocked by scandals that inhibited their ability to deal flexibly and aggressively with either clients or financial authorities. But their fundamental strength, based on unassailable roles as intermediaries for the savings and investment of the world's most affluent major nation, remained, and was magnified by the Tokyo stock market recovery of 1993.

This analysis of Japan's distinctive strategic capitalism has presented a Japanese state that finds stability congenial and entrepreneurial strategy difficult—however gifted and imaginative many of its industrial strategists may be as individuals. But whatever the weaknesses of the Japanese state in the aggregate, they are complemented by a creative, organized private sector, with a powerful sense of long-term objectives. They are also offset by an unusual sense of shared national destiny, which helps in the joint public-private struggle to offset clientelism, bureaucratic fragmentation, and international pressures—in pursuit of a coherent strategy for facing what most Japanese still regard as a volatile and threatening world beyond their ordered shores.

Appendix I

The Fiscal Investment and Loan Program:
Its Role in Japanese Government Finance,
Fiscal 1992

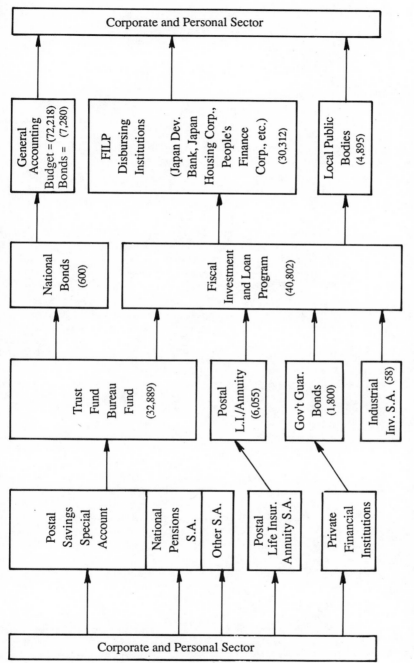

Source: Yamaguchi Kimio, ed., *Nihon no Zaisei* (Japan's Public Finance), 1992 ed. (Tokyo: Tōyō Keizai Shinpōsha, 1992), 390–95.
Note: Parenthetical figures are in ¥ billions. For a detailed breakdown of FILP disbursements by institution, see appendix II.

The Fiscal Investment and Loan Program, Internal Allocation

The Fiscal Investment and Loan Program: Internal Allocation, Fiscal 1991–1992 (in ¥ billions)

Name of Institution		Industrial Investment Special Account	Trust Fund Bureau Funds	Postal Insurance Funds	Government Guaranteed Borrowing	Total	REFERENCE	
							Own Capital	Grand Total
SPECIAL ACCOUNTS								
Urban Development Fund	1992	—	77.9	—	—	77.9	15.7	93.6
	1991	—	63.5	—	—	63.5	11.3	74.8
Special National Assets Adjustment	1992	—	46.6	—	—	46.6	184.7	231.3
	1991	—	3.0	—	—	3.0	219.5	222.5
National Hospitals	1992	—	50.8	—	—	50.8	4.2	55.0
	1991	—	47.0	—	—	47.0	3.1	50.1
National Schools	1992	—	75.9	—	—	75.9	93.6	169.5
	1991	—	55.9	—	—	55.9	97.0	152.9
Government Land Development Activities	1992	—	105.0	—	—	105.0	379.8	484.8
	1991	—	112.0	—	—	112.0	367.8	479.8
National Forest Activities	1992	—	260.7	—	—	260.7	92.9	353.6
	1991	—	258.0	—	—	258.0	93.0	351.0
Postal Activities	1992	—	—	78.9	—	78.9	250.5	329.4
	1991	—	—	65.7	—	65.7	196.6	262.3
Harbor/Airport Construction	1992	—	149.5	—	—	149.5	9.8	159.3
	1991	—	123.5	—	—	123.5	17.4	140.9
Postal Savings	1992	—	4750.0	—	—	4750.0	—	4750.0
	1991	—	4000.0	—	—	4000.0	—	4000.0

Name of Institution		Industrial Investment Special Account	Trust Fund Bureau Funds	Postal Insurance Funds	Government Guaranteed Borrowing	Total	REFERENCE Own Capital	Grand Total
GOVERNMENT FINANCIAL INSTITUTIONS								
Housing Finance Corporation	1992	—	6384.4	94.1	—	6478.5	-38.0	6440.5
	1991	—	6267.4	135.6	—	6403.0	302.0	6705.0
People's Finance Corporation	1992	—	2175.1	278.9	—	2454.0	1129.0	3583.0
	1991	—	1914.0	321.0	—	2235.0	1300.0	3535.0
Small and Medium Enterprise Finance Corporation	1992	4.0	1546.0	495.5	—	2065.5	392.8	2458.3
	1991	4.5	1385.1	557.4	—	1967.0	467.0	2434.0
Small and Medium Enterprise Credit Insurance Corporation	1992	—	—	—	—	—	—	—
	1991	2.0	—	—	—	2.0	401.6	403.6
Environmental Facilities Finance Corporation	1992	—	283.3	—	—	283.3	-48.3	235.0
	1991	—	236.6	—	—	236.6	-11.6	225.0
Agricultural and Fisheries Finance Corporation	1992	—	419.0	48.0	—	467.0	43.0	510.0
	1991	—	388.5	56.5	—	445.0	53.9	498.9
Public Corporations Finance Corporation	1992	—	—	—	1133.5	1133.5	84.0	1217.5
	1991	—	—	—	1133.5	1133.5	-26.3	1108.7
Hokkaidō-Tōhoku Development Corporation	1992	2.0	118.8	64.0	—	184.8	34.1	218.9
	1991	2.2	97.8	53.0	—	153.0	35.9	188.9

Organization	Year							
Okinawa Development Promotion Finance Corporation	1992	0.3	143.5	30.0	—	173.8	-10.0	163.8
	1991	0.3	109.0	35.7	—	145.0	-3.3	141.7
Japan Development Bank	1992	—	1456.7	80.3	—	1537.0	342.0	1879.0
	1991	—	1196.1	64.4	—	1260.5	366.5	1627.0
Japan Export-Import Bank	1992	—	1295.7	59.8	—	1355.5	247.5	1603.0
	1991	—	1111.2	59.8	—	1171.0	180.0	1351.0
PUBLIC CORPORATIONS								
Housing and Urban Facilities Corporation	1992	—	764.5	171.0	110.0	1045.5	1784.2	2829.7
	1991	—	519.3	151.0	220.0	890.3	1669.9	2560.2
Pensions and Welfare Corporation	1992	—	4624.6	—	—	4624.6	171.8	4796.4
	1991	—	4183.0	—	—	4183.0	199.8	4382.8
Employment Promotion Corporation	1992	—	26.5	7.7	—	34.2	210.1	244.3
	1991	—	12.7	1.9	—	14.6	180.4	195.0
Pollution Prevention Corporation	1992	—	78.3	—	—	78.3	9.8	88.1
	1991	—	68.3	—	—	68.3	4.4	72.7
Shipping Facilities Corporation	1992	0.3	50.8	2.5	—	53.6	23.0	76.6
	1991	0.3	42.0	2.5	—	44.8	19.2	64.0
Teitō High-Speed Transit Corporation	1992	—	28.4	21.1	—	49.5	73.1	122.6
	1991	—	21.1	21.1	—	42.2	59.2	101.4
Regional Promotion Facilities Corporation	1992	2.4	68.8	8.0	—	79.2	94.8	174.0
	1991	1.8	67.4	11.0	—	80.2	86.4	166.6
Japan Sewage Corporation	1992	—	12.9	2.0	—	14.9	15.5	30.4
	1991	—	12.3	—	—	12.3	12.9	25.2
New Energy and Industrial Technology Development Organization	1992	0.7	—	—	—	0.7	0.1	0.8
	1991	2.4	—	—	—	2.4	0.1	2.5

Name of Institution		Industrial Investment Special Account	Trust Fund Bureau Funds	Postal Insurance Funds	Government Guaranteed Borrowing	Total	REFERENCE Own Capital	REFERENCE Grand Total
Postal Insurance	1992	—	—	1400.1	—	1400.1	0.2	1400.3
	1991	—	—	1650.0	—	1650.0	—	1650.0
Railroad Facilities Fund	1992	—	242.8	11.4	63.6	317.8	862.8	1180.6
	1991	—	238.8	35.4	68.5	342.7	1132.1	1474.8
PUBLIC UNIT (KŌDAN) AND JIGYŌDAN								
Medical and Social Welfare Public Corporation	1992	—	224.1	—	—	224.1	-10.3	213.8
	1991	—	220.7	—	—	220.7	-10.7	210.0
Labor Welfare Public Corporation	1992	—	18.2	—	—	18.2	—	18.2
	1991	—	17.3	—	—	17.3	—	17.3
Fund for the Promotion of Research on and Assistance regarding Harmful Pharmaceutical After-Effects	1992	2.3	—	—	—	2.3	0.5	2.8
	1991	2.3	—	—	—	2.3	0.5	2.8
Foundation for the Promotion of Private Education	1992	—	12.3	12.4	—	24.7	42.3	67.0
	1991	—	11.6	11.6	—	23.2	38.8	62.0
Japan Scholarship Society	1992	—	37.6	—	—	37.6	3.8	41.4
	1991	—	36.1	—	—	36.1	3.3	39.4
Small Business Public Corporation	1992	—	32.0	5.5	—	37.5	230.0	267.5
	1991	—	14.2	5.5	—	19.7	242.9	262.6

Entity	Year							
Agricultural Land Development Corporation	1992	—	11.5	—	—	11.5	43.7	55.2
	1991	—	10.2	—	—	10.2	42.9	53.1
Forest Development Corporation	1992	—	19.2	—	—	19.2	75.3	94.5
	1991	—	18.7	—	—	18.7	70.1	88.8
Institution for Promotion of Research and Development in Designated Biotechnological Industries	1992	3.3	—	—	—	3.3	1.3	4.6
	1991	3.3	—	—	—	3.3	0.7	4.0
Japan Road Corporation	1992	—	1102.7	1075.0	120.5	2298.2	2044.3	4342.5
	1991	—	837.9	1075.0	144.8	2057.7	2061.7	4119.4
Capital Area Superhighway Corporation	1992	—	132.6	276.0	—	408.6	352.4	761.0
	1991	—	99.7	256.0	—	355.7	352.8	708.5
Hanshin Area Superhighway Corporation	1992	—	125.7	247.0	—	372.7	211.2	583.9
	1991	—	87.1	227.0	—	314.1	230.4	544.5
Honshu-Shikoku Bridge Corporation	1992	—	66.6	145.0	—	211.6	366.6	578.2
	1991	—	52.4	136.2	—	188.6	338.7	527.3
Japan Railway Construction Corporation	1992	—	55.2	20.0	55.0	130.2	524.0	654.2
	1991	—	54.9	20.0	55.0	129.9	435.5	565.4
New Tokyo Airport Corporation	1992	—	15.9	47.5	—	63.4	90.6	154.0
	1991	—	15.2	55.0	—	70.2	133.3	203.5
Japan National Railways Liquidation Corporation	1992	—	1042.0	55.0	200.0	1297.0	1571.4	2868.4
	1991	—	263.5	52.4	100.0	415.9	2967.1	3383.0
Water and Natural Resources Development Corporation	1992	—	50.6	40.5	—	91.1	251.6	342.7
	1991	—	75.5	56.9	—	132.4	208.5	340.9

Name of Institution	Year	Industrial Investment Special Account	Trust Fund Bureau Funds	Postal Insurance Funds	Government Guaranteed Borrowing	Total	REFERENCE Own Capital	REFERENCE Grand Total
Amami Islands Development Promotion Fund	1992	0.3	—	—	—	0.3	3.5	3.8
	1991	0.3	—	—	—	0.3	3.5	3.8
Metal Mining Public Corporation	1992	—	14.5	—	—	14.5	27.4	41.9
	1991	—	2.0	—	—	2.0	32.9	34.9
Japan National Oil Corporation	1992	—	149.5	11.7	—	161.2	813.6	974.8
	1991	—	34.7	15.0	—	49.7	1105.9	1155.6
Japan Scientific Technology Information Center	1992	3.8	—	—	—	3.8	11.8	15.6
	1991	3.8	—	—	—	3.8	11.0	14.8
Information Processing Promotion Association	1992	4.7	—	—	—	4.7	0.9	5.6
	1991	5.0	—	—	—	5.0	1.4	6.4
Basic Technologies Research Promotion Center	1992	26.0	—	—	—	26.0	5.6	31.6
	1991	28.6	—	—	—	28.6	4.7	33.3
Overseas Economic Cooperation Fund	1992	—	711.9	37.1	—	749.0	181.0	930.0
	1991	—	689.9	37.1	—	727.0	183.0	910.0
Postal Life Insurance and Pensions Welfare Corporation	1992	—	—	350.0	—	350.0	—	350.0
	1991	—	—	—	—	—	—	—
Telecommunications Broadcast Satellite Organization	1992	2.3	—	—	—	2.3	—	2.3
	1991	2.4	—	—	—	2.4	—	2.4
LOCAL PUBLIC BODIES	1992	—	[671.5] 3685.0	1210.0	—	[671.5] 4895.0	3819.0	8714.0
	1991	—	[603.0] 3285.0	1080.0	—	[603.0] 4365.0	3632.9	7997.9

MIXED PUBLIC-PRIVATE ENTERPRISES

Enterprise	Year							
Shōkō Chūkin Bank	1992	5.7	60.1	—	—	65.8	779.3	730.0
	1991	6.5	77.2	—	—	83.7	718.5	730.0
Tokyo Bay Highway Corporation	1992	—	—	—	56.7	56.7	70.1	126.8
	1991	—	—	—	42.6	42.6	52.9	95.5
Japan Airlines	1992	—	—	—	—	—	—	—
	1991	—	—	—	5.0	5.0	11.8	16.8
Kansai Airport Corporation	1992	—	—	—	37.1	37.1	254.9	292.0
	1991	—	—	—	63.6	63.6	226.8	290.4
East Japan Tourist Railroad Corporation	1992	—	—	—	—	—	—	—
	1991	—	3.7	11.3	46.9	61.9	340.6	402.5
Tōkai Tourist Railroad Corporation	1992	—	—	—	—	—	—	—
	1991	—	4.6	13.7	—	18.3	282.9	301.2
West Japan Tourist Railroad Corporation	1992	—	—	—	—	—	—	—
	1991	—	3.7	11.3	—	15.0	135.2	150.2
Japan Cargo Railroad Corporation	1992	—	—	—	—	—	—	—
	1991	—	11.6	—	—	11.6	32.7	44.3
Institution for the Promotion of Private City Development	1992	—	—	—	3.6	3.6	6.6	10.2
	1991	—	—	—	3.6	3.6	6.3	9.9
Electric Power Development Corporation	1992	—	85.4	19.0	—	104.4	33.9	138.3
	1991	—	74.0	19.0	—	93.0	27.5	120.5
TOTALS	1992	58.1	32,889.1	6055.0	1800.0	40,802.2		
	1991	65.7	28,534.9	6305.0	1900.0	36,805.6		

Source: Yamaguchi Kimio, ed., *Nihon no Zaisei* (Japan's Public Finance), 1992 ed. (Tokyo: Tōyō Keizai Shinpōsha, 1992), 390–94.

Note: Figures in parentheses indicate the contribution of postal pension and national pension funds. These totaled ¥5510.2 billion in 1992 and ¥4988.2 billion in 1991. In addition to the foregoing, the Trust Fund Bureau is scheduled to underwrite ¥6000 billion in national government bonds for fiscal 1992.

Notes

Introduction

1. See Chalmers Johnson, *MITI and the Japanese Miracle* (Stanford, Calif.: Stanford University Press, 1982); Sumiya Mikio and Taira Koji, eds., *An Outline of Japanese Economic History, 1603–1940: Major Works and Research Findings* (Tokyo: University of Tokyo Press, 1979); John Zysman, *Government, Markets, and Growth: Financial Systems and the Politics of Industrial Change* (Ithaca, N.Y.: Cornell University Press, 1983); Eugene Kaplan, *Japan: The Government-Business Relationship* (Washington, D.C.: U.S. Department of Commerce, 1972); Andrew Cox, ed., *State, Finance, and Industry: A Comparative Analysis of Postwar Trends in Six Advanced Industrial Economies* (Brighton, Eng.: Wheatsheaf Books, 1986); Marie Anchordoguy, *Computers, Inc: Japan's Challenge to IBM* (Cambridge, Mass.: Harvard University Council on East Asian Studies, 1990); Robert Wade, *Governing the Market: Economic Theory and the Role of Government in East Asian Industrialization* (Princeton, N.J.: Princeton University Press, 1990); and William R. Nester, *Japanese Industrial Targeting: The Neomercantilist Path to Economic Superpower* (London: Macmillan, 1991).

2. See, for example, David Friedman, *The Misunderstood Miracle: Industrial Development and Political Change in Japan* (Ithaca, N.Y.: Cornell University Press, 1988); and at a popular level Karel van Wolferen, *The Enigma of Japanese Power* (New York: Alfred Knopf, 1989).

3. "Strategic" in this analysis means "interactive with other decision-making entities, in accordance with a preconceived, if not necessarily formalized plan." Strategy, consequently, is the overall plan or artifice in accordance with which interactive decisions are made. On the general concept of strategy, see Avinash Dixit and Barry Nalebuff, *Thinking Strategically: The Competitive Edge in Business Politics, and Everyday Life* (New York: W. W. Norton, 1991), esp. 1–4.

4. For a succinct statement of this policy argument see, for example, Robert Kuttner, "Facing Up to Industrial Policy," *New York Times Magazine*, 19 April 1992, 11–26, 42.

5. The reference to theory here, of course, is to theory in the discipline of politics relating particularly to the issue of state capacity. As Robert Wade points out, it is methodologically difficult to test the efficacy of industrial policies, including selective credit policies, in terms of economic criteria such as reallocation of real resources. See Wade, *Governing the Market*, 29–33.

6. The most influential, of course, is Johnson, *MITI and the Japanese Miracle*.

7. Mechatronics, the fusing of the mechanical and electronics industries in the form of such products as industrial robots and numerical-control machinery, was stimulated, for example, by the merging in 1971 of legislation

governing the two industries. See Fumio Kodama, *Analyzing Japanese High Technologies: The Techno-Paradigm Shift* (London: Pinter Publishers, 1991), 44–45; and Tsūshō Sangyō Shō, *Nana Jyū Nendai no Denshi Kikai Sangyō* (The Electronics and Machinery Industries of the 1970s) (Tokyo: Tsūshō Sangyō Chōsa Kai, 1971).

8. For the most complete formulation of this approach, see Johnson, *MITI and the Japanese Miracle*, 3–14, and esp. 17–34.

9. On the rationale for the critical case, see Harry Eckstein, "Case Study and Theory in Political Science," in Fred I. Greenstein and Nelson W. Polsby, eds., *Handbook of Political Science: Strategies of Inquiry* (Reading, Mass.: Addison-Wesley, 1975), 7:79–138.

10. Zysman, *Government, Markets, and Growth*, 308.

11. On methods for assessing the efficacy of industrial policy, Wade, *Governing the Market*, 32–33.

12. On the importance of microanalysis to the understanding of major contemporary economic problems, see Martin Weitzman, *The Share Economy* (Cambridge: Harvard University Press, 1984); and Masahiko Aoki, *Information, Incentives, and Bargaining in the Japanese Economy* (Cambridge: Cambridge University Press, 1988), 151.

13. For a useful summary of these views, see Peter Hall, *Governing the Economy: The Politics of State Intervention in Britain and France* (New York: Oxford University Press, 1986), 5–15.

14. See ibid., 15–20.

15. Ibid., 15.

16. Stephen D. Krasner. *Defending the National Interest: Raw Materials Investments and U.S. Foreign Policy*: (Princeton, N.J.: Princeton University Press, 1978).

17. Eric E. Nordlinger, *On the Autonomy of the Democratic State* (Cambridge, Mass.: Harvard University Press, 1981), p. 203.

18. Johnson, *MITI and the Japanese Miracle.*

19. Zysman, *Governments, Markets, and Growth*, 234–51.

20. Ibid., 236.

21. Pempel in 1978 described the Japanese banking system as "among the most centralized and controllable in the world," noting that "at the top of the hierarchy stands the Bank of Japan, the single tap through which virtually the entire Japanese monetary and credit supply must flow . . . an organization which controls almost the entire credit supply." See T. J. Pempel, "Japanese Foreign Economic Policy: The Domestic Bases for International Behavior," in Peter J. Katzenstein, ed., *Between Power and Plenty: Foreign Economic Policies of Advanced Industrial States* (Madison: University of Wisconsin Press, 1978), esp. p. 736. It should be noted that by 1987 he had modified these views, while still perceiving a relatively powerful Japanese state. See T. J. Pempel, "The Unbundling of Japan, Inc.: The Changing Dynamics of Japanese Policy Formation," *Journal of Japanese Studies* 13, no. 2 (Summer 1987): 271–306.

22. See Pempel, "Japanese Foreign Economic Policy," 139–40; James Abegglen, ed., *Business Strategies for Japan* (Tokyo: Sophia University Press, 1970); and Kaplan, *Japan: The Government-Business Relationship.*

23. See, for example, Graham Allison, *Essence of Decision: Explaining the Cuban Missile Crisis* (Boston: Little, Brown, 1971), on the "bureaucratic politics model" of policymaking, which emphasizes these intrastatal conflicts.

24. See Inoguchi Takashi, *Nihon Seiji Keizai no Kōzu* (Contemporary Japanese Political Economy) (Tokyo: Tōyō Keizai Shinpōsha, 1983); and Michio Muramatsu and Elliss Krauss, "The Conservative Policy Line and the Development of Patterned Pluralism," in Yamamura Kozo and Yasuba Yasukichi, eds., *The Political Economy of Japan: The Domestic Transformation* (Stanford, Calif.: Stanford University Press, 1987), 516–54; and Ōtake Hideo, *Gendai Nihon no Seiji Kenryoku Keizai Kenryoku* (Political Power and Economic Power in Modern Japan) (Tokyo: Sanichi Shobō, 1979).

25. van Wolferen, *The Enigma of Japanese Power*.

26. Johnson, *MITI and the Japanese Miracle*.

27. See, for example, Bank of Japan Centennial History Editorial Department, *Nihon Ginkō Hyaku Nen Shi* (A Centennial Year History of the Bank of Japan), vols. 1–5 (Tokyo: Nihon Ginkō, 1982–85); Ministry of Finance Financial History Office, *Shōwa Zaisei Shi* (The Financial History of Shōwa), vols. 11–12 (Tokyo: Tōyō Keizai Shinpō Sho, 1967, 1976).

28. See, for example, Komiya Ryūtarō, Okuno Masahiro, and Suzumura Kōtarō, eds., *The Industrial Policy of Japan* (New York: Harcourt, Brace, and Jovanovich, 1988); Takenaka Heizō, *Kenkyū Kaihatsu to Setsubi Toshi* (Research, Development, and Capital Investment) (Tokyo: Tōyō Keizai Shinpōsha, 1984); and the ongoing Kyōikusha series of discrete volumes on each of the Japanese ministries and major administrative agencies (Gyōsei Kikō series, 1974–present).

29. In 1990 MITI proper had 9,231 employees, and three attached agencies (Natural Resources, the Patent Office, and the Small and Medium Enterprise Agency) had 3,162, for a total of 12,393. See Institute of Administrative Management, *Organization of the Government of Japan*, 1990 ed. (Tokyo: Gyōsei Kenkyū Center, 1991), 20–21.

30. For the figures, see Hanano Akira, Totsune Haruhito, and Morita Yoshinori, *Zusetsu: Zaisei Tōyūshi* (The Fiscal Investment and Loan Program in Graphics), 1991 ed. (Tokyo: Tōyō Keizai Shinpōsha, 1991), 238–41.

31. See Johnson, *MITI and the Japanese Miracle*, particularly chapter 2. It should be noted that Johnson specifically restricts the scope of his analysis to the 1925–1975 period, although he does not note any major transition away from this pattern.

32. Daniel I. Okimoto, *Between MITI and the Market* (Stanford, Calif.: Stanford University Press, 1989), pp. 196–202.

33. Ibid., pp. 177–228, esp. 225.

34. Richard J. Samuels, *The Business of the Japanese State: Energy Markets in Comparative and Historical Perspective.* (Ithaca, N.Y.: Cornell University Press, 1987).

35. Frances McCall Rosenbluth, *Financial Politics in Contemporary Japan* (Ithaca, N.Y.: Cornell University Press, 1989).

36. Harold D. Lasswell, *Politics: Who Gets What, When, How?* (New York: Meridian Press, 1958).

37. Samuels, *The Business of the Japanese State*, 8–9.

38. See, for example, Ezra N. Suleiman, *Private Power and Centralization in France: The Notaires and the State* (Princeton, N.J.: Princeton University Press, 1987).

39. Johnson, *MITI and the Japanese Miracle.*

40. See, for example, Abegglen, *Business Strategies for Japan;* and Pempel, "Japanese Foreign Economic Policy," 139–90.

41. Rosenbluth, *Financial Politics in Contemporary Japan.*

42. Joel D. Aberbach, Robert D. Putnam, and Bert A. Rockman. *Bureaucrats and Politicians in Western Democracies* (Cambridge, Mass.: Harvard University Press, 1981).

43. For a pioneering effort, see the work of Ellis Krauss and Michio Muramatsu, "Bureaucrats and Politicians in Policymaking: The Case of Japan," *American Political Science Review* 78 (1984). For a broad, creative, synthetic overview of literature, see Stephen Wilks and Maurice Wright, eds., *The Promotion and Regulation of Industry in Japan* (London: Macmillan, 1991).

44. See, for example, Ezra Suleiman and John Waterbury, eds., *The Political Economy of Public Sector Reform and Privatization* (Boulder, Colo.: Westview Press, 1990).

45. Peter J. Katzenstein, *Policy and Politics in West Germany: The Growth of a Semisovereign State* (Philadelphia: Temple University Press, 1987).

46. See, for example, Robert Keohane and Joseph Nye, *Power and Interdependence* (Boston: Little, Brown, 1977); Robert Keohane, *After Hegemony* (Princeton, N.J.: Princeton University Press, 1984); Peter Gourevitch, "The Second Image Reversed," *International Organization* 32, no. 4 (Autumn 1978): 881–912; and Stephen D. Krasner, *Structural Conflict: The Third World against Global Liberalism* (Berkeley: University of California Press, 1985).

47. On the logic and limitations of historical analysis in comparative politics, see Michael Loriaux, "Comparative Politics as Comparative History," *Comparative Politics* 21, no. 3 (April 1989): 357–79.

48. On Ishibashi in the context of the times, see Sharon H. Nolte, *Liberalism in Modern Japan: Ishibashi Tanzan and His Teachers, 1905–1960* (Berkeley: University of California Press, 1987).

49. For more details on the emergence of the indirect finance system, centered on the commercial banks, see Miyazaki Yoshikazu, "Rapid Economic Growth in Postwar Japan," *Developing Economies* 5 (June 1967): 332–36.

50. See, in particular, Stephen Skowronek, *Building a New American State: The Expansion of National Administrative Capacities, 1877–1920* (Cambridge, Eng.: Cambridge University Press, 1982).

51. Michael E. Porter, *The Competitive Advantage of Nations* (New York: Free Press, 1990), p. 393. In transportation equipment, for example, Japan in 1985 held nearly 23 percent of global exports, 28 percent in office equipment, and 28 percent in telecommunications equipment, far exceeding all other global producers in these categories.

Chapter 1
The Weight of the Past

1. Skowronek, *Building a New American State*, ix.

2. Niccolò Machiavelli, *The Prince and the Discourses* (New York: Modern Library, 1950).

3. On parallel Western developments during the 1870s, see Peter Gourevitch, *Politics in Hard Times: Comparative Responses to International Economic Crises* (Ithaca, N.Y.: Cornell University Press, 1986), 71–123.

4. See Peter Katzenstein, *Small States in World Markets: Industrial Policy in Europe* (Ithaca, N.Y.: Cornell University Press, 1985).

5. Nakamura Takafusa, *Economic Growth in Prewar Japan* (New Haven, Conn.: Yale University Press, 1983), 59. Originally published in Japanese as *Gendai Nihon Keizai Seichō no Bunseki* (An Analysis of Economic Growth in Prewar Japan) (Tokyo: Iwanami Shoten, 1971).

6. See Kobayashi Masaaki, *Nihon no Kōgyōka to Kangyō Haraisage* (Japan's Industrialization and the Sale of Government Enterprises), 1977; and Thomas C. Smith, *Political Change and Industrial Development in Japan: Government Enterprise, 1868–1890* (Stanford, Calif.: Stanford University Press, 1955).

7. On early shipping-sector subsidy programs, see William D. Wray, *Mitsubishi and the NYK, 1870–1914: Business Strategy in the Japanese Shipping Industry* (Cambridge, Mass.: Harvard University Council on East Asian Studies, 1984), 235–44, 416–20, and esp. 491–504.

8. In 1885 the yen was worth roughly 85 U.S. cents, making ¥51 million in shipping subsidies equivalent to about $60 million. See Bank of Japan Statistics Department, *Meiji Ikō Hondo Shuyō Keizai* (Hundred-year Statistics of the Japanese Economy since Meiji) (Tokyo: Nihon Ginkō Tokei Kyoku, 1966), 318.

9. Yukisawa Kenzō, "Ishin Seifu to Shihon Chikuseki" (The Restoration Government and Capital Accumulation), in Matsui Kiyoshi, ed., *Kindai Nihon Bōeki Shi* (A History of Modern Japanese Trade) (Tokyo: Yūhikaku, 1959), 272–74, cited in Nakamura, *Economic Growth in Prewar Japan*, 60. A typical example was the annual ¥250,000 shipping promotional subsidy to Mitsubishi begun in 1875.

10. Nakamura, *Economic Growth in Prewar Japan*, 60.

11. Wray calculates that Japanese shipping subsidies in 1901 were ¥15.28 per ton, compared to ¥1.22 per ton in Britain and ¥36 per ton in France. See Wray, *Mitsubishi and the NYK*, 497–98.

12. Nakamura Takafusa and Kumon Shumpei, "Nihon to Roshia no Keizai Hatten no Ruikei" (Types of Economic Development in Japan and Russia), *Keizai Hyōron*, no. 2 (1967).

13. For details on Edo period financial structure, see, for example, Phra Sarasas, *Money and Banking in Japan* (London: Heath Cranston, 1940), pp. 81–83.

14. On the concept of crisis and its relationship to public policy and institutional evolution, see Skowronek, *Building a New American State*, esp. 10–14; Gourevitch, *Politics in Hard Times*, 9–10; and in specific relation to

Japan, Kent E. Calder, *Crisis and Compensation: Public Policy and Political Stability in Japan, 1949–1986* (Princeton, N.J.: Princeton University Press, 1988), chaps. 1 and 2.

15. Chō Yukio, "Exposing the Incompetence of the Bourgeoisie: The Financial Panic of 1927," *Japan Interpreter*, 8, no. 4 (Winter 1974): 498.

16. Ibid., 498–99.

17. Arisawa Hiromi, ed., *Shōwa Keizai Shi* (An Economic History of Showa) (Tokyo: Nihon Keizai Shimbun Sha, 1976), 62.

18. Bank of Japan Research and Statistics Department, *Keizai Tōkei Nenpō* (Economic Statistics Annual), 1986 ed., 41–42. Mutual savings banks and *shinkin* banks are not included in this calculation.

19. Gotō Shinichi, *Nihon no Kinyū Tōkei* (Financial Statistics of Japan), 90–92, 108.

20. Between 1979 and the end of 1990, for example, the number of foreign banks operating in Japan grew from 63 to 85, and the number of offices of such banks from 85 to 130. See BOJ Research and Statistics Department, *Keizai Tōkei Nenpō*, 1990 ed., 79.

21. Abe Yasuji, *Ginkō Shōken Kakine Ronsō Oboegaki* (Memories of the Banking-Securities Border Dispute) (Tokyo: Nihon Keizai Shimbun, 1980).

22. In 1938, for example, only 0.8 percent of all Japanese corporate funding was raised through bond issues, compared to 29.9 percent in 1931. See Nagatomi Yūichirō, *Antei Seichō Jidai no Kōshasai Shijō* (The Public and Private Bond Markets in a Stable Growth Period) (Tokyo: Ōkura Zaimu Kyōkai, 1978), 16.

23. Ibid.

24. Abe, *Ginkō Kakine Ronsō Oboegaki*, 52.

25. T.F.M. Adams and Iwao Hoshii, *A Financial History of the New Japan* (Tokyo: Kodansha, 1972), 17; and Economic Stabilization Board, *Taiheiyō Sensō ni yoru Waga Kuni no Higai Sōgō Hōkokusho* (Comprehensive Report on Damage to Japan from the Pacific War) (Tokyo: Keizai Antei Honbu, 1949).

26. See Laura Hein, *Fueling Growth: The Energy Revolution and Economic Policy in Postwar Japan* (Cambridge: Harvard University Council on East Asian Studies, 1990), 65–70, 177–87.

27. Miyazaki Yoshikazu, *Sengo Nihon no Keizai Kikō* (The Economic Structure of Postwar Japan) (Tokyo: Shin Hyōron Sha, 1966).

28. See Kazushi Ohkawa and Henry Rosovsky, *Japanese Economic Growth: Trend Acceleration in the Twentieth Century* (Stanford, Calif.: Stanford University Press, 1973).

29. On this process of innovation, see Leonard H. Lynn, *How Japan Innovates: A Comparison with the U.S. in the Case of Oxygen Steelmaking* (Boulder, Colo.: Westview Press, 1982).

30. Tsuru Shigeto, *The Mainsprings of Japanese Growth: A Turning Point?* (Paris: Atlantic Institute for International Affairs, 1977), 14.

31. Sakakibara Eisuke and Noguchi Yukio, "Ōkurashō Nichigin Ōchō no Bunseki" (An Analysis of the Ministry of Finance and Bank of Japan Dynasty), *Bungei Shunjū* (August 1977): 96–115.

32. Japan's balance of payments situation at the time, together with immediate future prospects, made controls imperative. For a year and a half foreign exchange banks, particularly New York's National City Bank and the Yokohama Specie Bank, had been selling yen for dollars, gambling that Japan could not stay on the gold standard. Yokohama alone sold ¥740 million. The Bank of Japan's gold reserve plummeted from ¥1 billion in 1929 to ¥470 million in December 1931. See Nakamura Takafusa, *Shōwa Kyōko to Keizai Seisaku* (The Showa Depression and Economic Policy) (Tokyo: Nihon Keizai Shimbun Sha, 1978), 159–84; and John G. Roberts, *Mitsui: Three Centuries of Japanese Business* (Tokyo: Weatherhill, 1974), 272.

33. E. B. Schumpeter, ed., *The Industrialization of Japan and Manchukuo, 1930–1940.* (New York: Macmillan, 1940), 838–39.

34. Adams and Hoshii. *A Financial History of the New Japan*, 493.

35. On the oil foreign-exchange allocation question, see MITI (Tsūsanshō), *Tsūsanshō Ni Jyū Nen Shi* (A Twenty-year History of MITI) (Tokyo: Tsūshō Sangyō Shō, 1970), 129; and Chalmers Johnson, *Japan's Public Policy Companies* (Washington, D.C.: American Enterprise Institute, 1978), 125–27.

36. Adams and Iwao, *A Financial History of the New Japan*, 495.

37. See Ministry of Finance Financial History Office, *Shōwa Zaisei Shi* (The Financial History of Shōwa) (Tokyo: Tōyō Keizai Shinpō Sha, 1967), 11:67–68, for a detailed description of the origins of the Temporary Funds Adjustment Law.

38. Jerome B. Cohen, *Japan's Economy in War and Reconstruction*, (New York: Columbia University Press, 1950).

39. The driving force behind the measure was Hoshino Naoto, chief of the General Affairs Board of Manchukuo and chief economic adviser to General Tōjō Hideki. One of its chief supporters in the bureaucracy was Kishi Nobusuke, ultimately to become minister of munitions in the Tōjō cabinet and a postwar prime minister. Among its major opponents was Ikeda Seihin, then Governor, ironically, of the Bank of Japan, which was to receive substantially expanded powers. Ikeda was more significantly a former head of the Mitsui Bank and *ōbantō* (head administrator) of Mitsui Gomei, both of which appeared likely to be greatly constrained by the measure's provision for sweeping bureaucratic supremacy over business activities. He forthrightly took the private banking side, securing some concessions from the control forces (no forced loans by private banks; corporate freedom to issue dividends up to 10 percent). But these concessions proved to be merely tactical. The control forces nullified them by administrative decree within six months after the Mobilization Law's passage. See Roberts, *Mitsui*, 315–16; and Cohen, *Japan's Economy in War and Reconstruction*, 18.

40. See Michael K. Young, "Judicial Review of Administrative Guidance: Governmentally Encouraged Consensual Dispute Resolution in Japan," *Columbia Law Journal* 84 (1984); and Johnson, *MITI and the Japanese Miracle*, esp. 265–74, 296–302.

41. See MOF Financial History Office, ed., *Shōwa Zaisei Shi* (Tokyo: Tōyō Keizai Shinpō Sha, 1976), 12:4–5, for a useful explanation of the provisions

and implications of the Bank Funds Utilization Order (Ginkō nado Shikin Unyō Rei).

42. Ibid.

43. See Hugh Patrick, "Japan's Interest Rates and the 'Grey Financial Market,'" *Pacific Affairs* (Fall-Winter 1965–66).

44. See Shimura Kaiichi, *Gendai Nihon no Kō Shasai Ron* (A Theory of Public and Private Securities Finance in Modern Japan) (Tokyo: Tokyo Daigaku Shuppan, 1978), 6.

45. See Cohen, *Japan's Economy in War and Reconstruction*, 93–96; and MOF Financial History Office, *Shōwa Zaisei Shi*, 11:6–9, for details on the operation of these institutions.

46. Hugh T. Patrick, *Monetary Policy and Central Banking in Contemporary Japan* (Bombay: Bombay University Press, 1962), 33–34.

47. See Cohen, *Japan's Economy in War and Reconstruction*, 92.

48. Patrick, *Monetary Policy and Central Banking in Contemporary Japan*, 38.

49. For details concerning the operations in 1946 of one such council (known as a Rinji Shikin Shinsa Iinkai), see Fuji Ginkō, *Fuji Ginkō Hachi Jyū Nen Shi* (An Eighty-year History of the Fuji Bank) (Tokyo: Fuji Ginkō, 1960), 296.

50. Takehara Norio, *Sengo Nihon no Zaisei Tōyūshi* (Postwar Japan's Fiscal Investment and Loan Program), 106–7.

51. See Arisawa, ed., *Shōwa Keizai Shi*, 305–8, 314–17; Adams and Hoshii, *A Financial History of the New Japan*, 30–63; and Arisawa Hiromi, ed., *Shōken Hyaku Nen Shi* (A Hundred-year History of the Securities Industry) (Tokyo: Nihon Keizai Shimbun Sha, 1978), pp. 207–19, for useful elaboration of the Occupation's goals with respect to financial reform.

52. Nihon Kōgyō Ginkō Nen Shi Henshū Iinkai, ed., *Nihon Kōgyō Ginkō Nana Jyū Go Nen Shi* (A Seventy-five-year History of the Industrial Bank of Japan) (Tokyo: Nihon Kōgyō Ginkō, 1982), 119–25.

53. Yoshino Toshihiko. *Sengo Kinyū Shi no Omoide* (Reminiscences of Postwar Financial History) (Tokyo: Nihon Keizai Shimbun Sha, 1963), 195–99.

54. On the details, see Kil Soong Hoom, "The Dodge Line and the Japanese Conservative Party," Ph.D. dissertation, Department of Political Science, University of Michigan, 1977.

55. See Adams and Hoshii, *A Financial History of the New Japan*, 51–52. T.F.M. Adams, the official who achieved passage of this revision, which was of enormous financial significance to the securities companies, has been one of their *onjin* or "honored benefactors" ever since. In 1950 he became the only honorary chairman the Tokyo Stock Exchange ever designated.

56. Originally this Policy Board was to be independent of the central bank, like the U.S. Federal Reserve Board. But Ichimada succeeded in extracting a compromise from SCAP, providing that the board come into existence but be an auxiliary body of the Bank of Japan.

57. For a detailed analysis of SCAP attempts at financial reform, reaching broadly parallel conclusions, see William M. Tsutsui, *Banking Policy in*

Japan: American Efforts at Reform during the Occupation (London: Routledge, 1988).

58. Of the nine MOF purgees most were relatively junior people attached to the Gaishi Kinyū Kinkō (Foreign Capital Financial Treasury), which had handled expropriated foreign assets. The only major figure lost to the ministry was the Budget Bureau director general, who was about to leave office anyway. At BOJ no one was purged until June 1946, when Governor Araki Eikichi stepped down to make way for his deputy, Ichimada Naoto, without seriously disrupting operations.

Chapter 2
The Strategists and Their Tribulations

1. See, for example, Johnson, *MITI and the Japanese Miracle.*
2. Zysman, *Governments, Markets, and Growth,* 308.
3. John Creighton Campbell, *Contemporary Japanese Budget Politics* (Berkeley: University of California Press, 1977), 44.
4. See, for example, Warner Schilling, "The Politics of National Defense: Fiscal 1950," in W. Schilling, P. Hammond, and G. Snyder, *Strategy, Politics, and Defense Budgets* (New York: Columbia University Press, 1962); Roger Hilsman, *To Move a Nation* (New York: Doubleday, 1967); and Morton Halperin, *Bureaucratic Politics and Foreign Policy* (Washington, D.C.: Brookings Institution, 1974).
5. Allison, *Essence of Decision,* 85.
6. Cohen, *Japan's Economy in War and Reconstruction,* 73. On coordination problems in the Japanese military more generally, see Tobe Ryōichi, Teramoto Yoshiya, Kamata Shinichi, Suginō Yoshio, Murai Tomohide, and Nonaka Ikujirō, *Shippai no Honshitsu: Nihongun no Soshikirironteki Kenkyū* (The Essence of Failure: Organizational Research on the Japanese Military) (Tokyo: Diamondo Sha, 1984).
7. It is said, for example, that when MOF special envoy Kashiwagi Yusuke went to France shortly after the Nixon Shock in 1971 to plan common strategy with Pompidou and Giscard d'Estaing, his arrangements in Paris were made by the Bank of Tokyo, which met him with a private car at Orly Airport, rather than by the Japanese embassy. Not surprisingly, upon retirement from MOF Kashiwagi became chairman of the Bank of Tokyo, to be succeeded by another top MOF international financial negotiator, Gyohten Toyoo, in mid-1992.
8. See Johnson, *MITI and the Japanese Miracle,* chaps. 1–3. The pre-1945 predecessors of MITI were the Ministry of Commerce and Industry and the Ministry of Munitions.
9. For an early explicit statement, see Organization for Economic Cooperation and Development, *The Industrial Policy of Japan* (Paris: OECD, 1972).
10. Shiina Etsusaburō, "Nihon Sangyō no Dai Jikkenjō, Manshū" (Manchuria: the Great Proving Ground for Japanese Industry), *Bungei Shunjū,* February 1976, 126–34.

11. See Arisawa, ed., *Shōwa Keizai Shi*, 143–46, for a concise description of the course of economic planning in Manchuria during the 1930s.

12. This group, the largest of the so-called "new *zaibatsu*," which grew up in association with the military during the 1930s, produced trucks, chemicals, electronics, and military equipment, accounting for 7.1 percent of Japanese corporate paid-in capital, including overseas assets, in 1941. It was dissolved after World War II. For more details, see Michael A. Cusumano, *The Japanese Automobile Industry: Technology and Management at Nissan and Toyota* (Cambridge: Harvard University Council on East Asian Studies, 1985).

13. Johnson, *MITI and the Japanese Miracle*, 220–21.

14. Ibid., p. 209.

15. Ibid., 210. For example, the last MCI vice-minister, Matsuda Tarō, served on the JDB board from August 1952 to June 1957.

16. Ministry of Finance, ed., *Zaisei Kinyū Tōkei Geppo* (Financial Statistics Monthly: Loan and Investment Program Special Edition), April 1986, 98–125.

17. Ibid., 125.

18. For details on the foundation and early operation of the Industrial Investment Special Account, see Yamaguchi Hideyuki and Ishikawa Itaru, eds., *Zaisei Tōyūshi* (The Financial Investment and Loan Program) (Tokyo: Ōkura Zaimu Kyōkai, 1973), 216–34.

19. Ibid., 226.

20. Ibid.

21. For a discussion of the authorization of foreign bond issues, see ibid., 225.

22. Ibid., 226.

23. Satō Ken, Fujimura Hideki, and Kawamata Shinichirō, *Zusetsu: Zaisei Tōyūshi* (The Fiscal Investment and Loan Program Illustrated), 1990 ed. (Tokyo: Tōyō Keizai Shinpōsha, 1990), 237.

24. General Affairs Agency, *Tokushū Hōjin Sōran* (Almanac of Special Legal Entities), 1990 ed. (Tokyo: Gyōsei Kanri Kenkyū Center, 1990), 261–62; and 1978 ed., 270.

25. Ibid., 1990 ed., 262.

26. Ibid.

27. Johnson, *MITI and the Japanese Miracle*, 123.

28. Ibid.

29. On the broader role of the Economic Stabilization Board alumni network in the postwar Japanese political economy, see Calder, *Crisis and Compensation*, 195–97.

30. This is a major part of the unusually strong differentiation in the Japanese financial system as a whole, which has emerged since World War II. On this historical evolution in comparative perspective, see Raymond W. Goldsmith, *Financial Structure and Development* (New Haven, Conn.: Yale University Press, 1969), esp. 345.

31. Indeed, the Crédit Nationale is in form a private company, quoted on the Paris Bourse. For details, see Zysman, *Government, Markets, and Growth*, 117–19.

32. See MOF Financial History Office, *Shōwa Zaisei Shi*, vol. 12; and Cohen, *Japan's Economy in War and Reconstruction*, esp. 93–96.

33. For details, see Loriaux, "Comparative Political Economy."

34. See Johnson, *Japan's Public Policy Companies*, 87–92.

35. See Takehara Norio, *Sengo Nihon no Zaisei Tōyūshi*, 107–8.

36. Satō, Fujimura, and Kawamata, *Zaisei Tōyūshi*, 1990 ed., 224–26.

37. On the details, see Calder, *Crisis and Compensation*, chap. 2.

38. Matsuda Osamu, "Kōteki Kinyū no Mondaiten" (Problems Relating to Government Finance), *Senshū Daigaku Shakai Kagaku Nenpō*, no. 20 (30 March 1986).

39. See Satō, Fujimura, and Kawamata, *Zaisei Tōyūshi*, 1990 ed., 234–37.

40. Ibid. This figure represents the JDB/Exim share of total FILP allocations, including both the government financial institutions and the other recipients of FILP funds presented in table 2-2 and the Appendices.

41. On relevant aspects of these other political systems, see Ezra N. Suleiman, *Elites in French Society: The Politics of Survival* (Princeton, N.J.: Princeton University Press, 1978); Fred Deyo, ed., *The Political Economy of the New Asian Industrialism* (Ithaca, N.Y.: Cornell University Press, 1987); Alice H. Amsden, *Asia's Next Giant* (New York: Oxford University Press, 1989); and Jung-En Woo, *Race to the Swift: State and Finance in Korean Industrialization* (New York: Columbia University Press, 1991).

42. The parallelism is with respect to ceilings on bank lending. Certain types of loans, however, were not counted toward that ceiling, and certain loans could be discounted at the Banque de France with prior approval, as under the Bank of Japan bill-rediscount system. There were thus indirect as well as direct controls in France.

43. See Ojimi Yoshimasa and Uchida Tadao, "Nihon no Kanryō Gyōsei to Kanmin Kyōchō Taisei" (Japan's Bureaucratic Administration and the Public Private Cooperative System), *Gendai Keizai*, September, 1972, 30. Quoted in Johnson, *MITI and the Japanese Miracle*, 257.

44. See "Sengo Sangyō Shi e no Shōgen" (Witness to Postwar Industrial History), *Ekonomisuto*, no. 19 (11 May 1976): 82–89, and n. 20 (18 May 1976): 78–85.

45. For a graphic sense of the turbulence of MITI's struggle for strategy against the banks during the Tokushin Hō controversy, see the fictional but historically situated novel of Shiroyama Saburō, *Kanryōtachi no Natsu* (The Summer of the Bureaucrats) (Tokyo: Shinchōsha, 1980).

46. For Usami's views on the "Tokushin Hō" controversy, see Usami Makoto, "Kinyū Kai o Arau Atarashii Nami" (The New Wave Washing the Financial World), *Ekonomisuto*, 23 April 1963, 12–15.

47. Given MOF's anti-competitive reputation (in its regulation of the banks, for example), the preeminence of MOF people at the FTC has always seemed paradoxical to MITI observers. Sahashi claims that MOF often tries to use the FTC as a tool to break the power of its rival MITI, citing the particularly vigorous resistance to industrial coordination by the amazing number of MOF alumni turned FTC commissioners. See Shimura Kaiichi, ed., *Sengo Sangyō Shi e no Shōgen* (Witnesses to Postwar Industrial History) (Tokyo: Mainichi Shimbun Sha, 1978).

48. These included gestures constraining MITI's power to exclude banks from emerging sectors such as petrochemicals and automobiles, where MITI feared overcapacity, and expanding Japan Development Bank co-financing to reduce private-sector risk. See Sahashi interview in Shimura, ed., *Sengo Sangyō Shi e no Shōgen*.

49. Johnson, *MITI and the Japanese Miracle*, 260.

50. Tsurumi points out that in the case of oil this motive began to disappear after 1970, as the need for preserving the financial viability of Japanese independents grew more apparent. But the motivation to enforce artificially low industrial power rates persisted. See Yoshi Tsurumi, "Japan," in Raymond Vernon, *The Oil Crisis* (New York: W. W. Norton, 1976), 119–20.

51. For a case study of the political processes surrounding adoption of the Recession Industries Bill, see Kent E. Calder, "Politics and the Market: The Politics of Japanese Credit Allocation, 1946–1978," Ph.D. diss., Department of Government, Harvard University, 1979, 218–22.

52. See, for example, Chalmers Johnson, "The Reemployment of Retired Government Bureaucrats in Japanese Big Business," *Asian Survey* 14, no. 11 (November 1974): 953–65.

53. See, for example, Kent E. Calder, "Elites in an Equalizing Role? Ex-Bureaucrats as Coordinators and Intermediaries in the Japanese Government-Business Relationship," *Comparative Politics*, July 1989, 379–403; and Tuvia Blumenthal, "The Practice of Amakudari within the Japanese Employment System," *Asian Survey* 25, no. 3 (March 1985): 310–21.

54. Calder, "Elites in an Equalizing Role?" 383–91.

55. Calder, *Crisis and Compensation*, esp. chap. 4; and Gerald Curtis, *The Japanese Way of Politics* (New York: Columbia University Press, 1988). The multimember system prevails, it should be noted, not only in Japan's Lower House, but also for 152 of 252 seats in its Upper House. The remaining 100 have since the early 1980s been chosen under a d'Hondt-style list system similar to several prevailing in continental Europe.

56. Calder, *Crisis and Compensation*, 64–69.

57. See Nobutaka Ike, *A Theory of Japanese Democracy* (Boulder, Colo.: Westview Press, 1980); and on Italy, Joseph LaPalombara, *Democracy Italian Style* (New Haven, Conn.: Yale University Press, 1987).

58. Adams and Hoshii, *A Financial History of the New Japan*, 17.

59. Ibid.

Chapter 3
The Regulators and Industrial Credit

1. On the organic character of the Japanese conception of political economy, and contrasts to Western concepts of the organic state, see Okimoto, *Between MITI and the Market*, 211–15.

2. Aichi Kiichi, *Kore kara no Kinyū* (Finance in the Future) (Tokyo: Gakuyō Shobō, 1950).

3. See Ichimada Naoto Denki Suitoroku Kankōkai, ed., *Ichimada Naoto: Denki Suitōroku* (Ichimada Naoto: A Biography and a Memorial Record) (Tokyo: Tokuma Shobō, 1986).

4. See Arisawa, ed., *Shōwa Keizai Shi*, 335–38. Quantitative forms of allocation involve specification of *amounts* of credit to be received by particular borrowers. Allocation via pricing, in contrast, involves specifying only differential prices for various types of credit and allowing the market to do the rest.

5. See Johnson, *MITI and the Japanese Miracle*, 207–8, 229–30; 250–52, and so on.

6. See, for example, Johnson, *Japan's Public Policy Companies*, 92–95.

7. See Ikeda Hayato, *Kinkō Zaisei* (The Affairs of Government Financial Institutions) (Tokyo: Jitsugyō no Nihon Sha, 1952), esp. 30–48, 154–61.

8. Johnson, *MITI and the Japanese Miracle*, 18–19.

9. Even where Ikeda did, as MITI minister, on occasion adopt expansionist industrial-policy perspectives, his former colleagues at the Ministry of Finance often opposed him. For example, MOF strongly opposed the Income Doubling Plan in its early stages as inflationary and likely to impede a tax reduction, refusing to provide the necessary public finance data to fully formulate it. See Walter Arnold, "The Politics of Economic Planning in Postwar Japan: A Study in Political Economy," Ph.D. diss., Department of Political Science, University of California, Berkeley, 1984, 211–14.

10. Johnson, *MITI and the Japanese Miracle*, 19.

11. This does not, as was emphasized at the outset of this chapter, imply that when transformation appears inevitable, due to the operation of external market or political forces, MOF or BOJ may not try to use it strategically to perpetuate their institutional influence, as MOF in fact appears to have done during the financial liberalization of the 1980s and early 1990s. The point is that the financial "regulators" tend not to purposely provoke the process of transformation itself.

12. See Pempel, "Japanese Foreign Economic Policy," 736. Pempel has subsequently modified his general position on centralization in the Japanese political economy and briefly conceded liberalization of the confines of administrative oversight at MOF and BOJ, without going into detail. See Pempel, "The Unbundling of Japan, Inc.," 288.

13. See Patrick, *Monetary Policy and Central Banking in Contemporary Japan*.

14. The work of Suzuki Yoshio, longtime director of the Bank of Japan's Institute of Monetary Policy, is particularly important in this regard. See, in particular, Suzuki Yoshio, *Gendai Nihon Kinyū Ron* (Money and Banking in Contemporary Japan: The Theoretical Setting and Its Application) (Tokyo: Tōyō Keizai Shinpōsha, 1974, translated as Yoshio Suzuki, *Money and Banking in Contemporary Japan* (New Haven, Conn.: Yale University Press, 1980); and Suzuki Yoshio, *Nihon Kinyū Keizairon* (The Economics of Japanese Finance) (Tokyo: Tōyō Keizai Shinpōsha, 1983), translated as Yoshio Suzuki, *Money, Finance, and Macroeconomic Performance in Japan* (New Haven, Conn.: Yale University Press, 1986). See also Hamada Kōichi and Iwata Kazumasa, *Kinyū Seisaku to Ginkō Kōdō* (Monetary Policy and Bank Behavior) (Tokyo: Tōyō Keizai Shinpōsha, 1980); and Rōyama Shōichi, *Nihon no Kinyū Shisutemu* (The Japanese Financial System) (Tokyo: Tōyō Keizai Shinpōsha, 1982).

15. Among the relatively few works dwelling on the empirical details of monetary policy administration are Horiuchi Akira, *Nihon no Kinyū Seisaku: Kinyū Mekanizumu no Shishō Bunseki* (Monetary Policy in Japan: Empirical Analysis of the Monetary Mechanism) (Tokyo: Tōyō Keizai Shinpōsha, 1980); and Teranishi Jūrō, *Nihon no Keizai Hatten to Kinyū* (Finance and the Economic Development of Japan) (Tokyo: Iwanami Shoten, 1982).

16. Nihon Ginkō Hyaku Nen Shi Henshū Iinkai, ed., *Nihon Ginkō Hyaku Nen Shi* (Hundred-year History of the Bank of Japan), 5 vols. (Tokyo: Nihon Ginkō, 1982–85).

17. Federation of Bankers' Associations of Japan, *The Banking System in Japan*, 1989 edition (Tokyo: Zenginkyō, 1989), 20.

18. Patrick, *Monetary Policy and Central Banking in Contemporary Japan*, 35.

19. Ibid., 36–37.

20. On Ichimada and his accomplishments, see Arisawa, ed., *Shōwa Keizai Shi*, 335–38.

21. Yoshino Toshihiko, *Nihon Ginkō* (The Bank of Japan) (Tokyo: Iwanami Shinsho, 1963), 114–15.

22. Abe Yasuji, *Ichimada Naoto Den* (A Biography of Ichimada Naoto) (Tokyo: Tōkō Shokan, 1955).

23. Demand for commercial loans from long-term clients was strong, while deposit inflow was weak, due to the hyperinflationary conditions. Furthermore, the commercial banks had a large volume of loans outstanding to former munitions companies, which could not be collected because those firms' assets had been frozen.

24. Ōkurashō Zaisei Shi Shitsu, *Shōwa Zaisei Shi* (A Financial History of Shōwa), 12:114.

25. Fuji Ginkō, *Fuji Ginkō Hachi Jyū Nen Shi*, 295.

26. Interview with Tristan Beplat, former director of SCAP's Finance Division, Princeton, N.J., June 1988.

27. For a concrete technical overview of the mechanics involved in BOJ credit controls, drawn from the important period of monetary restraint right after the Korean War, see "Credit Curbs: How Done?" *Oriental Economist*, June 1954, 281–84.

28. Teijin in early 1991 was Japan's third largest textile manufacturer, after Asahi Chemical and Toray Industries. Teijin's sales in fiscal 1991 came to ¥610 billion. See the Oriental Economist, *Japan Company Handbook* (Tokyo: Tōyō Keizai Shinpōsha, 1991), 223.

29. Interview with Tristan Beplat, former director of SCAP's Finance Division, June 1988. The Commodity Credit Corporation began offering preferential credit for Japanese purchases of U.S. cotton in 1946, partially to help move U.S. surpluses of raw cotton; by mid-1948 surplus cotton stockpiles had concentrated in U.S. ports in sufficient volume to be a conscious concern of SCAP policymakers in Japan.

30. Preferred bills that did fall within those categories were discounted without penalty regardless of the overall level of borrowing of the bank in

question. They did not, in other words, count toward its "ceiling" at the Bank of Japan.

31. For a concrete example of one such guideline, issued November 15, 1946, see MOF Financial History Office, *Shōwa Zaisei Shi*, 12:177–78.

32. For parallels to European patterns, see John B. Goodman, "The Politics of Central Bank Independence," *Comparative Politics*, April 1991, 329–49.

33. Yoshino, *Nihon Ginkō*, 114–15.

34. Bank of Japan sources date the origins of window guidance to 1950, but Patrick argues that the system was really inaugurated in 1954. See Patrick, *Monetary Policy and Central Banking in Contemporary Japan*, 141.

35. *Nihon Keizai Shimbun*, 26 June 1991.

36. On the diffident, relatively passive character of BOJ regulatory policies during the 1970s, see "Case Study: Nihon Ginkō" (Case Study: The Bank of Japan), *Nikkei Business*, 10 May 1976, 28–40.

37. See Fuji Ginkō, *Fuji Ginkō Hachi Jyū Nen Shi*, 295.

38. For details, see Kusano Atsushi, *Shōwa Yon Jyū Nen Go Gatsu Ni Jyū Hachi Nichi* (May 28, 1965) (Tokyo: Nihon Keizai Shimbun Sha, 1986).

39. For details, see Uchino Tatsurō, *Japan's Postwar Economy: An Insider's View of Its History* (Tokyo: Kōdansha International, 1978), 99–100.

40. See OECD, *Monetary Policy in Japan* (Paris: OECD, 1972), 74–78.

41. These are balances yielding little or no interest that are held by corporate borrowers in response to bank demand. The effect of the compensating balances system has been to allow Japanese banks to vary their de facto lending rates even in the face of government interest-rate ceilings.

42. Arnold, "The Politics of Economic Planning in Postwar Japan."

43. See Robert C. Angel, *Explaining Economic Policy Failure: Japan in the 1969–1971 International Monetary Crisis* (New York: Columbia University Press, 1991).

44. See Asahi Shimbun Keizai Bu, *Keizai Seisaku no Butai Ura* (The Backstage of Economic Policy) (Tokyo: Asahi Shimbun Sha, 1974).

45. The Japanese general account expanded by 28.3 percent in fiscal 1972 and 31.0 percent in 1973—the two largest budgetary increases since 1949. See MOF Budget Bureau Research Section, *Zaisei Tōkei* (Financial Statistics), 1986 ed. (Tokyo: Ōkurashō Insatsu Kyoku, 1986), 201–2.

46. For historical details on the "regulatory' MOF approach to industrial finance, emphasizing such objectives as the "normalization" of bank lending by the curtailment of overloans, see Ministry of Finance Financial History Office (Ōkurashō Zaisei Shi Shitsu), *Shōwa Zaisei Shi*, 10:168–96.

47. On the broad and highly strategic functions of the Trésor in the French financial system, see Zysman, *Governments, Markets, and Growth*, 114–17.

48. See Nigel Adam, "L'Etat c'est nous," *Euromoney*, October 1980, 110.

49. On the relatively strict and effective MOF and BOJ regulation of foreign banks in Japan during the high-growth period, see Calder, *Politics and the Market*, 193–98; and Louis W. Pauly, *Opening Financial Markets: Banking*

Politics on the Pacific Rim (Ithaca, N.Y.: Cornell University Press, 1988), 12–18, 66–78.

50. For details, see Calder, "Elites in an Equalizing Role?" 379–403.

51. Yasuhara Kazuo, *Ōkurashō* (Ministry of Finance) (Tokyo: Kyōiku Sha Shinsho, 1974), 40–41.

52. See Jack Hayward, *The State and the Market Economy: Industrial Patriotism and Economic Intervention in France* (New York: New York University Press, 1986); and Calder, *Crisis and Compensation*, 231–410.

53. See BOJ Research and Statistics Department, ed., *Keizai Tōkei Nenpō*, 1991 ed., 44.

54. Data from the Oriental Economist, *Japan Company Handbook*, Spring 1992, 1046–56.

55. Administrative Management Agency, *Gyōsei Kikō Zu* (Diagrams of Administrative Structure), 1964 and 1978 eds. (Tokyo: Gyōsei Kanri Kenkyū Center, 1964 and 1978).

Chapter 4
Profiles of Public Action

1. See, for example, Anthony Downs, *Inside Bureaucracy* (Boston: Little, Brown, 1966); and Allison, *Essence of Decision.*

2. On the "compensatory" character of much FILP financing, see Phillip Trezise, "Politics, Government, and Economic Growth," in Hugh Patrick and Henry Rosovsky, eds., *Asia's New Giant: How the Japanese Economy Works* (Washington, D.C.: Brookings Institution, 1976; and Calder, "Politics and the Market," 314–26, 479–501.

3. In 1950 48.3 percent of Japanese workers were employed in agriculture, compared to 21.9 percent in manufacturing and 29.8 in services. By 1990 those ratios had shifted to 7.2, 33.6, and 59.2 percent, respectively. See Keizai Kōhō Center, *Japan 1992: An International Comparison*, 20.

4. See, for example, *Kigyō Keiretsu Sōran* (Almanac of Corporate Groupings), 1987 ed., 190–92.

5. On the history of the government support program for shipping and shipbuilding, see Maritime Industries Research Association, *Nihon Kaiun Sengo Josei Shi* (A History of Postwar Japanese Shipping Promotion), ed. Kaiji Sangyō Kenkyū Kai (Tokyo: Unyūshō, 1967).

6. Japan Development Bank, *Nihon Kaihatsu Ginkō Ni Jyū Go Nen Shi* (A Twenty-five-year History of the Japan Development Bank) (Tokyo: Nihon Kaihatsu Ginkō, 1976), appendix, 61–62.

7. On policy toward the oil-refining industry, including government lending, see Samuels, *The Business of the Japanese State*, 168–227.

8. This reactive character of strategic industrial finance not surprisingly parallels that of foreign economic policy, for parallel structural reasons centering on the complex organizational structure of the Japanese state. See Kent E. Calder, "Japan Foreign Economic Policy Formation: Explaining the Reactive State," *World Politics* 40, no. 4 (July 1988): 517–41.

9. For a detailed study of government-business relations in the development of the Japanese auto industry, see Phyllis Genther, *A History of*

Japan's Government-Business Relationship: The Passenger Car Industry (Ann Arbor: Michigan Papers in Japanese Studies, no. 20, 1990).

10. *Nihon Keizai Shimbun*, 12 April 1950.

11. Genther, *A History of Japan's Government-Business Relationship*, 58–59.

12. Ibid., pp. 87–88.

13. Ibid., p. 179.

14. The work of Michael Porter, for example, clearly shows the strong competitive potential of sectors fostered through private initiative, but with organized provision of infrastructure and some government regulatory support; the Japanese automobile industry is one such excellent case. See Porter, *The Competitive Advantage of Nations*, esp. 131–75, on the general theory.

15. See George Stigler, "The Theory of Regulation," *Bell Journal of Economics and Management Science* 3 (1971): 3–21.

16. For details on both government loans and related flow of government retirees, see Tōyō Keizai Shinpōsha, *Kigyō Keiretsu Sōran* (Almanac of Corporate Groupings), annual.

17. Tōyō Keizai Shinpōsha, *Kigyō Keiretsu Sōran*, 1990 ed., 534–39.

18. European steel, for example, appears to have retained generally higher continuing reliance on government credit, perhaps due to a greater salience of labor-union pressures and regionalism in Europe than in Japan. Heavy, persistent subsidies to the Belgian steel industry are a case in point.

19. Nihon Chōki Shinyō Ginkō Sangyō Kenkyū Kai, *Shuyō Sangyō Sengo Ni Jyū Go Nen Shi* (A Twenty-five-year Postwar History of Principal Industries) (Tokyo: Sangyō to Keizai Kabushiki Kaisha, 1972), 328–30.

20. Ibid., 330.

21. Thirty-eight percent also went to coal and 27 percent to electric power. See Nihon Kōgyō Ginkō, *Nihon Kōgyō Ginkō Go Jyū Nen Shi* (A Fifty-year History of the Industrial Bank of Japan) (Tokyo: Nihon Kōgyō Ginkō, 1953), 709.

22. U.S. Secretary of the Treasury, *Final Report on the Reconstruction Finance Corporation* (Washington, D.C.: Government Printing Office, 1959), 83. On the Reconstruction Finance Corporation's World War II efforts in building the U.S. steel industry, see Jesse H. Jones with Edward Angly, *Fifty Billion Dollars: My Thirteen Years with the RFC* (New York: Macmillan, 1951), 313–86.

23. On this concept and its application across the Japanese political economy, see Calder, *Crisis and Compensation*, 160.

24. See Ezra Vogel, *Comeback* (New York: Simon and Schuster, 1985), pp. 58–95; and Houdaille Industries, "Petition to the President of the United States through the Office of the United States Special Trade Representative for the Exercise of Presidential Discretion," unpublished.

25. For details, see Friedman, *The Misunderstood Miracle*.

26. On early government financial support to the Japanese machinery industry under the Kishin Hō, see Japan Development Bank, ed., *Nihon Kaihatsu Ginkō Ni Jyū Go Nen Shi*, 451–61.

27. During 1956–1960 the machine-tool industry received a total of ¥2.63 billion in JDB loans under the Kishin Hō. See ibid., 454; and Vogel, *Comeback*, 72.

28. The law authorizing these low-interest JDB loans formally is known as the Law on Temporary Measures for the Development of Specified Machinery and Electronics Industries. On its significance, see Kodama, *Analyzing Japanese High Technologies*, 44–46.

29. Friedman argues that politics, not planning, determined how government finance authorized under legislation such as the Special Law for the Promotion of the Machinery Industry was distributed and generally rejects strategic interpretations of government lending policies toward machine tools. But he fails to explore in detail the relationship between government financial support and efficiency-inducing changes in product specialization or possible lags in the efficacy of indicative lending. See Friedman, *The Misunderstood Miracle*, 86–91.

30. On the early history of government support for the Japanese computer industry, see Nihon Chōki Shinyō Ginkō, *Shuyō Sangyō Sengo Ni Jyū Go Nen Shi*, 492–94; and Kaplan, *Japan*, 77–101.

31. Kaplan, *Japan*, 82.

32. Johnson, *MITI and the Japanese Miracle*, 246–47.

33. Kaplan, *Japan*, 86.

34. Until 1963 JDB funds constituted around 50 percent of the capital available to JECC, with the balance provided by a consortium of major private banks. This share declined to around 25 percent of JECC financing in 1965, at which level it remained constant for several years. See Nihon Chōki Shinyō Ginkō, *Shuyō Sangyō Sengo Ni Jyū Go Nen Shi*, 493.

35. *Nihon Kaihatsu Ginkō Ni Jyū Go Nen Shi*, 488.

36. These funds totaled ¥5.7 billion during 1970–1974. See ibid., 491.

37. Kaplan, *Japan*, 97.

38. On the overall profile of government lending to the Japanese computer industry, see Nihon Kaihatsu Ginkō, ed., *Nihon Kaihatsu Ginkō Ni Jyū Go Nen Shi*, 482–91.

39. Ibid.; and Thomas M. Hout and Ira C. Magaziner, *Japanese Industrial Policy* (Berkeley: University of California, Institute of International Studies, 1980), 105.

40. Kaplan, *Japan*; and Hout and Magaziner, *Japanese Industrial Policy*, 102–7.

41. Kent E. Calder and Roy Hofheinz, Jr., *The Eastasia Edge* (New York: Basic Books, 1982), 154–57.

42. See Tōyō Keizai Shinpōsha, *Kigyō Keiretsu Sōran*, 1991 ed., 224, 383.

43. Gary R. Saxonhouse, "Industrial Policy and Factor Markets: Biotechnology in Japan and the United States," in Patrick, ed., *Japan's High Technology Industries*, 117.

44. For a more extended discussion of this concept, see Calder, *Crisis and Compensation*, 160. On related sociological distinctions, see Ishida Takeshi, "Conflict and Its Accommodation," in Ellis S. Krauss, Thomas P. Rohlen, and Patricia G. Steinhoff, eds., *Conflict in Japan*, (Honolulu: University of Hawaii Press, 1984), 18–20.

45. For details, see Chalmers Johnson, *Japan's Public Policy Companies* (Washington, D.C.: American Enterprise Institute, 1978).

46. Japan Development Bank Law, article 18, paragraph 2 (official English text).

47. Japan Development Bank Law, article 18, paragraph 1.

48. On the procedural complexities of the Japanese legislative process, see Calder, *Crisis and Compensation*, 202–5. It should be emphasized that although the passage of industrial-policy legislation was routine in general, it could occasionally become embroiled in politics, as in the case of the Tokushin Hō of the 1960s, and some telecommunications and software legislation during the 1980s, introducing additional uncertainty into the industrial-policy process.

49. See Downs, *Inside Bureaucracy*, 266–68.

50. See Hirose Michisada, *Hojokin to Seiken Tō* (Subsidies and the Party in Power) (Tokyo: Asahi Shimbun Sha, 1981), 49.

51. Rodney Clark, *Venture Capital in Britain, America, and Japan* (London: Croom Helm, 1987), 36–42.

52. Ibid., 37.

53. Ibid., 41. The default rate was only 6 percent of the total of 251 guaranteed projects.

54. Japan Development Bank, *Annual Report*, 1985 ed., 7.

55. Ibid., 11.

56. H. J. Welke, *Data Processing in Japan*, (New York: North-Holland Publishing Company, 1982), 15.

57. Saitō, Shiraishi, and Morita, eds., *Zusetsu: Zaisei Tōyūshi* (The Fiscal Investment and Loan Program in Graphics) (Tokyo: Tōyō Keizai Shinpōsha, 1992), 141.

58. See Samuels, *The Business of the Japanese State*, 231–34.

59. *Wall Street Journal*, 6 February 1989.

60. *Wall Street Journal*, 8 August 1986, 18.

61. Ibid.

62. Japan Development Bank, *Facts and Figures about the Japan Development Bank* (Tokyo: Japan Development Bank, 1981), 18.

63. Thomas Pepper, Merit E. Janow, and Jimmy W. Wheeler, *The Competition: Dealing with Japan* (New York: Praeger Publishers, 1985), 120.

64. "What Tokyo Can Do for You," *Business Tokyo* (June 1989): 23–24.

65. *ACCJ Journal* (April 1992): 13.

66. *Asahi Shimbun*, 10 March 1987.

67. On the details of the recycling proposals and their specific relationship to government finance, see Kinoshita Toshihiko, "Japan's Current Recycling Measures: Their Background, Performance, and Prospects" (Tokyo: Export-Import Bank of Japan, June 1988), mimeographed.

68. Hanano, Totsune, and Morita, *Zusetsu: Zaisei Tōyūshi*, 1991 ed., 143.

69. See Charles Tait Ratcliffe, "Tax Policy and Investment Behavior in Postwar Japan," Ph.D. diss., Department of Economics, University of California, Berkeley, 1969.

70. See Samuels, *The Business of the Japanese State*.

71. The largest *keiretsu* continue to this day, for example, to accept few former bureaucrats as senior executives; few foreign firms employed such people until the late 1970s. For details, see Calder, "Elites in an Equalizing Role?"; and *Kigyō Keiretsu Sōran* and *Kaisha Shokuin Roku* (Record of Corporate Employees), assorted issues.

72. This pattern strikingly parallels the preoccupation with *baransu*, described by John Campbell in his work on Japanese general-account budgeting for the same period. See Campbell, *Contemporary Japanese Budget Politics*.

Chapter 5
Private Financiers and Public Functions

1. On the important role of organized private actors in German policymaking, see, for example, Katzenstein, *Policy and Politics in West Germany*, esp. 3–106.

2. On the concept of "dedicated" capital, as opposed to the "fluid" capital that characterizes most American corporate finance, see Porter, *Capital Choices*, 11–19.

3. For analogies of Japanese patterns in the Western industrialized world, see Pierre Grou, *The Financial Structure of Multinational Capitalism* (Dover, N.H.: Berg Publishers, 1985), esp. 128–51.

4. On government-business relations in the Japanese electric power industry, which illustrates this point, see Samuels, *The Business of the Japanese State*, 135–67.

5. Suzuki, Money and Banking in Contemporary Japan, 14.

6. C. Tait Ratcliffe, *Japanese Corporate Finance, 1977–1980* (London: Financial Times, 1987).

7. Grou, *The Financial Structure of Multinational Capitalism*, 83–85.

8. Yutaka Kōsai, *The Era of High-Speed Growth* (Tokyo: University of Tokyo Press, 1986), 137–38.

9. On the details, see Patrick, "Japan's Interest Rates and the 'Grey Financial Market.'"

10. On this point, see the Fair Trade Commission data presented in Akiyoshi Horiuchi, *Economic Growth and Financial Allocation in Postwar Japan* (Washington, D.C.: Brookings Discussion Papers in International Economics, No. 18, August 1984), 21.

11. Ibid., 23.

12. On the mutual insurance dimensions of the *keiretsu* system, see Iwao Nakatani, "The Economic Role of Financial Corporate Groupings," in Masahiko Aoki, ed., *The Economic Analysis of the Japanese Firm* (Amsterdam: North-Holland, 1984), 227–58.

13. Bank of Japan, *Keizai Tōkei Nenpō*, various issues.

14. Organization for Economic Cooperation and Development, *Banking and Monetary Policy* (Paris: OECD, 1985), 110–11, 135–36.

15. See, for example, Zysman, *Government, Markets, and Growth*, 99–169, esp. 125–27.

16. Porter, *The Competitive Advantage of Nations.*

17. Suleiman, *Private Power and Centralization in France,* 299.

18. On the "waves" of industrial-group projects in many of these areas from the late 1950s through the 1980s, and their pioneering role in industrial transformation, see Michael L. Gerlach, *Alliance Capitalism: The Social Transformation of Japanese Business* (Berkeley: University of California Press, 1992).

19. For an introduction to the Japanese life-insurance company as a business enterprise, see Komiya Ryūtarō, *The Japanese Economy: Trade, Industry, and Government* (Tokyo: University of Tokyo Press, 1990), 233–64.

20. Bank of Japan, *Keizai Tōkei Nenpō,* 1990 ed., 91.

21. Komiya, *The Japanese Economy,* 233–36, 238.

22. The Oriental Economist, *Kigyō Keiretsu Sōran,* 1992 ed., 361.

23. Ibid.

24. Richard Caves and Masu Uekusa, *Industrial Organization in Japan* (Washington, D.C.: Brookings Institution, 1976).

25. Masahiko Aoki, *Information, Incentives, and Bargaining in the Japanese Economy* (Cambridge, Eng.: Cambridge University Press, 1988), 206.

26. On the role of *keiretsu* in promoting both economic growth and structural transformation, see Tōyō Keizai Shinpōsha, *Kigyō Keiretsu Sōran,* 1991 ed., 17–27.

27. See Miyazaki, "Rapid Economic Growth in Postwar Japan," 337–43.

28. See, for example, "Japan: Will It Lose its Competitive Edge?" *Business Week,* 27 April 1992, 50–58; *Nikkei Kinyū Shimbun,* 12 March 1992; and Richard C. Koo, "High-Quality Products but Low Profitability: Why Japanese Investors Are Increasingly Rejecting This Time-honored Formula" (February 1992), mimeographed.

29. *Nihon Keizai Shimbun,* 10 March 1992.

30. For a more detailed overview of *sōgō shōsha* activities in the global and Japanese economies, see M. Y. Yoshino and Thomas B. Lifson, *The Invisible Link: Japan's Sōgō Shōsha and the Organization of Trade* (Cambridge, Mass.: MIT Press, 1986); Nikkei Business, *Shōsha: Fuyu no Jidai* (The Age of Winter of the Sōgō Shōsha) (Tokyo: Nihon Keizai Shimbun Sha, 1983); Kunio Yoshihara, *Sōgō Shōsha: The Vanguard of the Japanese Economy* (Oxford, Eng.: Oxford University Press, 1981); and Yoshi Tsurumi, *Sōgō Shōsha: Engines of Export-based Growth* (Montreal: Institute for Research on Public Policy, 1980).

31. Mitsubishi Corporation began lease operations in 1966, followed by Sumitomo (1968) and Mitsui (1971). See Ashikaga Shigeo, *Lease Sangyō Kai* (The World of the Leasing Industry) (Tokyo: Kyōiku Sha, 1985), 70–71.

32. On trading company investment in emerging sectors as the Bankers' Kingdom system of controls began to erode, see Asahi Shimbun Keizai Bu. *Sōgō Shōsha* (General Trading Companies) (Tokyo: Asahi Shimbun Sha, 1977), 154–63.

33. Calder, "Elites in an Equalizing Role?" 379–403.

34. On the details of the Lockheed scandal, which linked former Prime Minister Tanaka Kakuei with Marubeni, one of the largest traders, see Larry

Warren Fisher, "The Lockheed Affair: A Phenomenon of Japanese Politics," Ph.D. diss., Department of Political Science, University of Colorado, 1980.

35. Asahi Shimbun Keizai Bu, *Ginkō* (Banking) (Tokyo: Asahi Shimbun Sha, 1976), 152–53; and Curtis, *The Japanese Way of Politics*, 183–84.

36. See Johnson, *MITI and the Japanese Miracle*, 194–95.

37. Ibid., 217.

38. The MOF's International Finance Bureau was required, for example, to approve all impact loans, all foreign straight and convertible bond issues, and all offshore transactions between Japanese banks and trading companies. Japanese banks provided two-thirds of the traders' offshore funds.

39. On the *sōgō shōsha's* financial role of this period, see Sasago Katsuya, *Shōsha Kinyū* (Trading Company Finance) (Tokyo: Kyōiku Sha, 1979).

40. See Kōsai, *The Modern Japanese Economy*, 93–105.

41. For a comprehensive view of the early modern Japanese financial system that illustrates this point, see Asakura Kōkichi, *Meiji Zenki Nihon Kinyū Kōzō Shi* (A History of Japanese Financial Structure in the Early Meiji Period) (Tokyo: Iwanami Shoten, 1961).

42. On the early history of the Takuzen Kai, see Ginkō Kyōkai Ni Jyū Nen Shi Henshū Shitsu, ed., *Ginkō Kyōkai Ni Jyū Nen Shi* (A Twenty-year History of the Bankers' Association) (Tokyo: Zenkoku Ginkō Kyōkai Rengō Kai, 1965), 3–5.

43. The Banking Bureau, although established in 1881, was absorbed into the Ministerial Secretariat in 1894, reestablished under another name in 1898, absorbed into the Financial Bureau in 1899, returned to the secretariat in 1915, reestablished as an independent bureau in 1918, merged with insurance operations in 1943 and the Finance Bureau in 1945 to create a large Finance Bureau, and finally rendered independent once again in 1946. See Ōkura Mondo. *Ōkurashō Ginkō Kyoku* (The Ministry of Finance Banking Bureau) (Tokyo: Paru Shuppan, 1985), 242.

44. Ginkō Kyōkai Ni Jyū Nen Shi Henshū Shitsu, ed., *Ginkō Kyōkai Ni Jyū Nen Shi*, 7.

45. Ibid., 14.

46. Adams and Hoshii, *A Financial History of the New Japan*, 131.

47. Ginkō Kyōkai Ni Jyū Nen Shi Henshū Shitsu, ed., *Ginkō Kyōkai Ni Jyū Nen Shi*, 16–17.

48. Miyazaki, "Rapid Economic Growth in Postwar Japan," 329–50.

49. Ibid., 332–33.

50. Ibid., p. 333.

51. Ginkō Kyōkai Ni Jyū Nen Shi Henshū Shitsu, ed., *Ginkō Kyōkai Ni Jyū Nen Shi*, 27–28.

52. Zenkoku Ginkō Kyōkai, ed., *Ginkō Kyōkai San Jyū Nen Shi* (A Thirty-year History of the Bankers' Association) (Tokyo: Zenkoku Ginkō Kyōkai, 1979), 133.

53. Ibid.

54. Ibid., 162.

55. See, for example, All Japan Banker's Federation Real Estate Finance Research Group (Zenkoku Ginkō Kyōkai Rengo Kai Fudōsan Kenkyū Kai),

Fudōsan Kinyū Kenkyū Kai Hōkoku (Report of the Real Estate Finance Research Group) (Tokyo: Zenginkyō, March 1992). Zenginkyō also spoke out strongly against real estate speculation in 1974–1975.

56. Uchino, *Japan's Postwar Economy*, 98.

57. Ginkō Kyōkai Ni Jyū Nen Shi Henshū Shitsu, ed., *Ginkō Kyōkai Ni Jyū Nen Shi*, 340.

58. Ibid.

59. See Tsutsui Yoshirō, *Kinyū Shijō to Ginkōgyō* (The Financial Market and the Banking Industry) (Tokyo: Tōyō Keizai Shinpōsha, 1988), esp. 106–31, on the regulatory dynamics of the banking industry.

60. For more details, see ibid., 331–66.

61. See Federation of Bankers' Associations of Japan, *The Banking System in Japan*, 1989 ed., 134–39.

62. Interviews with Zenginkyō member bank executives and Zenginkyō officials from 1955–1975 period, July–August 1987.

63. In 1961, for example, the IBJ provided ¥50 billion in new industrial equipment credit, compared to the JDB's ¥26.3 million. See MITI Enterprise Bureau, ed., *Shuyō Sangyō no Setsubi Toshi Dōkō*, 1963 ed., 6.

64. Due to turmoil in Japanese financial circles related to the Panic of 1900–1901, the IBJ postponed opening its doors until 1902, although its establishment was formally authorized two years earlier. For details, see Nihon Kōgyō Ginkō Nen Shi Henshū Iinkai, ed., *Nihon Kōgyō Ginkō Nana Jyū Go Nen Shi*, 1–7.

65. *IBJ Annual Report*, 1991, 35.

66. In 1903, the Treasury's share of total stock outstanding was 21.2 percent, which fell to 14 percent in 1919 before rising to 23.7 percent in 1930. By 1939 the government share had fallen to only 2.3 percent, with much of its former stake having gone to local banks, presumably to encourage their participation in funding the war effort. See Nihon Kōgyō Ginkō, *Nihon Kōgyō Ginkō Go Jyū Nen Shi* (A Fifty-year History of the Industrial Bank of Japan) (Tokyo: Nihon Kōgyō Ginkō, 1953).

67. Nihon Kōgyō Ginkō Nen Shi Henshū Iinkai, ed., *Nihon Kōgyō Ginkō Nana Jyū Go Nen Shi*, appendix, 128–29.

68. Ibid., 86–89.

69. Ibid., 88–89.

70. Ibid., 22–31.

71. *IBJ Annual Report*, 1991, 39.

72. Tōyō Keizai Shinpōsha, *Japan Company Handbook*, spring 1992 ed., 1043; Autumn 1978 ed., 930.

73. "Nihon Kōgyō Ginkō: Setsubi Shikin Ginkō no Ginkō Banare Jidai no Senryaku" (The Industrial Bank of Japan: A Capital Investment Bank's Strategy in an Era of Alienation from Banks), *Nikkei Business*, 11 April 1977, 43.

74. Takayanagi Hiroshi, ed., *Kigyō Keiretsu Sōran* (Almanac of Corporate Industrial Groups) 1987 ed. (Tokyo: Tōyō Keizai Shinpōsha, 1987), 46.

75. IBJ internal data.

76. From around 1955 to 1969 this was known as the Enterprise Research Section (Jigyō Chōsa Ka); it was renamed the Industrial Research Section in 1969.

77. Kawamata, it should also be noted, was longtime head of the Capital Subcommittee (Shikin Bukai) of the Industrial Structure Deliberation Council, in which capacity he worked closely with his old associates at the IBJ in coordinating loans to industry with the requisites of industrial structure transformation, insofar as this function was effectively performed anywhere in the Japanese economy. On the IBJ alumni, see Yamamoto Yūjiro, *Nihon Kōgyō Ginkō no Himitsu* (The Secrets of the Industrial Bank of Japan) (Tokyo: Nisshin Hōdō, 1978), 110–14.

78. On Kawamata's career at Nissan, and the relationship to the IBJ, see Cusumano, *The Japanese Automobile Industry*, 152–53, 172–73, 224–26.

79. In 1990 the equivalent figure was 149 IBJ employees dispatched to other firms of whom 51 held "representative powers" (*daihyōken*) in the firms receiving them—that is, the right to represent the firm legally in external transactions, normally granted to senior executives of managing director rank and above. This latter figure was among the highest for any bank in Japan. See Takayanagi, ed., *Kigyo Keiretsu Sōran*, 1992 ed., 91.

80. See *Nikkei Business*, 11 April 1977, 46.

81. *IBJ Annual Report*, 1991, 37.

82. Porter, *Capital Choices*, 66–67.

83. *New York Times*, 23 October 1991.

84. The IBJ, for example, took the initiative during 1990 in establishing the Japan-China Investment Promotion Organization and was the lead manager in the World Bank's first Euroyen bond issues. See *IBJ Annual Report*, 1991, 10.

85. See Porter, *Capital Choices*, 66–67.

86. On IBJ activities in relation to this committee, see, for example, Nihon Kōgyō Ginkō Nen Shi Henshū Iinkai, ed., *Nihon Kōgyō Ginkō Nana Jyū Go Nen Shi*, 358–64.

87. See Shimura, *Gendai Nihon Kō Shasai Ron*, 111–16.

88. See Campbell, *Contemporary Japanese Budget Politics*.

89. See Theodore Lowi, "Four Systems of Policy, Politics, and Choice," *Public Administration Review* (July–August 1972): 300.

90. Nihon Kōgyō Ginkō Nen Shi Henshū Iinkai, ed., *Nihon Kōgyō Ginkō Nana Jyū Go Nen Shi*, 779–93.

91. For details, see Nihon Kōgyō Ginkō Nen Shi Henshū Iinkai, ed., *Nihon Kōgyō Ginkō Nana Jyū Go Nen Shi*, esp. 522–24.

92. *IBJ Annual Report*, 1991, 27.

93. Nihon Kōgyō Ginkō Nen Shi Henshu Iinkai, ed., *Nihon Kōgyō Ginkō Nana Jyū Go Nen Shi*, appendix, 94.

94. On IBJ's aspirations for the 1990s, see Hayashi Nobumichi, "Kankyō Jōhō nado Kitai" (High Expectations for Environment and Information), *Nihon Keizai Shimbun*, 15 July 1992.

95. On the lending patterns of private banks in general, see Bank of Japan Research and Statistics Department, *Keizai Tōkei Nenpō* (Economic Statistics Annual).

96. Japan Development Bank, *Nihon Kaihatsu Ginkō Ni Jyū Go Nen Shi*, 60–63.

97. See, for example, "Sengo Jidōsha Kōgyō no Hatten Katei to Jidōsha Jūyō Bunseki" (The Process of Postwar Automobile Industry Development and an Assessment of Automobile Demand), *Nihon Kōgyō Ginkō Chōsa Geppō* (August 1957): 30–87.

98. Cusumano, *The Japanese Automobile Industry*, 56.

99. Ibid., 253.

100. Ibid., 261.

101. Ibid., 79–80.

102. Ibid., 223.

103. Ibid., 127.

104. Ibid., 77.

105. Ibid., 76.

106. See "Waga Kuni Denshi Kōgyō no Tenkai to Sono Kadai" (The Transition in Our Country's Electronics Industry and Related Topics), *Nihon Kōgyō Ginkō Chōsa Geppō* (April 1960): 45–93.

107. Yamamoto, *Nihon Kōgyō Ginkō no Himitsu*, 113.

108. On the mechatronics revolution, which reached a crucial commercialization phase around 1975, and the response of Japanese firms and public policy to it, see Kodama, *Analyzing Japanese High Technologies*, 3–4, 41–42, 44–45.

109. Bank of Japan Research and Statistics Department, *Keizai Tōkei Nenpō*, 1990 ed., 148.

110. Ibid., together with IBJ and JBD internal data.

Chapter 6
Private Borrowers and Public Credit Controls

1. On internal Japanese (and German) corporate capital allocation decision making and contrasts to the U.S. pattern, see Porter, *Capital Choices*, 50–67.

2. See Albert O. Hirschman, *Exit, Voice, and Loyalty: Responses to Decline in Firms, Organizations, and States* (Cambridge, Mass.: Harvard University Press, 1970).

3. Ibid.

4. See, for example, Pempel, "Japanese Foreign Economic Policy," 139–90.

5. Some suggest that government aid played a critical role in establishing parts-industry international competitiveness, but Campbell is more skeptical, viewing government loans as helpful but not determining, since they went primarily to the same firms that private banks would have assisted (the larger ones), and didn't succeed in their attempts at consolidating industry structure through mergers. See John Campbell in Cole and Yakushiji, eds., *The American and Japanese Auto Industries in Transition*, 86–88.

6. Cusumano, *The Japanese Automobile Industry*, 243.

7. For a succinct but comprehensive view of government-business relations in the Japanese auto-parts industry, see Genther, *A History*, 108–21.

8. Nihon Jidōsha Buhin Kōgyō Kai, *Jidōsha Buhin Kōgyō Hatten Shō Shi* (A Short History of the Development of the Auto-Parts Industry) (Tokyo: Nihon Jidōsha Buhin Kōgyō Kai, 1969), 152.

9. Genther, *A History*, 111–12.

10. Nihon Jidōsha Buhin Kōgyō Kai, *Jidōsha Buhin Kōgyō Hatten Shō Shi*; and Genther, *A History*, 109.

11. For details on major developments, financial as well as technological, in the Japanese auto-parts industry, see Nihon Jidōsha Buhin Kōgyō Kai, *Jidōsha Buhin Kōgyō Hatten Shō Shi*, esp. 154–60.

12. Funds for loans came from the *zaisei tōyūshi*, or fiscal investment and loan program, while those for subsidies came from the general account budget (*ippan kaikei*) or special account budgets (*tokubetsu kaikei*).

13. For details on the Jigyōdan proposal, see Japan Development Bank (Nihon Kaihatsu Ginkō), *Nihon Kaihatsu Ginkō Jyū Nen Shi* (Ten-year History of the Japan Development Bank) (Tokyo: Nihon Kaihatsu Ginkō, 1962), 294–95.

14. Among the planning organizations were the Industrial Structure Deliberation Council Subcommittee on Automotive Parts, the Auto-Parts Distribution Rationalization Committee (founded 1964), the Auto Subcommittee of the Heavy Industry Export Committee (founded 1956), the Auto-Parts Capital Investment Committee (with no banking members, interestingly enough).

15. Such plans include the general auto-parts industry rationalization plans of 1956, 1961, and 1966, and special plans such as those aimed at preparing for capital liberalization (1961–1968) and at rationalization of the parts-distribution sector (1965).

16. This policy seems to have been induced partly by pressure from the Big Two, suggesting that even though MITI may have had considerable power over the parts makers, it was circumscribed by the major auto producers in its overall formulation of policy.

17. Nihon Jidōsha Buhin Kōgyō Kai, *Nihon no Jidōsha Buhin Kōgyō* (Japan's Auto-Parts Industry) (Tokyo: Nihon no Jidōsha Buhin Kōgyō Kai, 1971), 200.

18. The chairman was a *sanyo*, or councillor, of the IBJ. Other members were drawn from auto producers, parts wholesalers, and parts-manufacturing firms. For a list of the committee's membership and details of its activities, see Nihon Jidōsha Buhin Kōgyō Kai, *Jidōsha Buhin Kōgyō Hatten Shō Shi*, 59–60.

19. See ibid.

20. See Calder, *Crisis and Compensation*, chap. 7.

21. Smitka identifies the 1956–1960 period as one during which government loans were especially important; international lending was all going to the auto assemblers, parts makers had major capital investment costs, and few could borrow commercially until after 1960. See Michael J. Smitka, *Competitive Ties: Subcontracting in the Japanese Automotive Industry* (New York: Columbia University Press, 1991), 72.

22. See Nihon Jidōsha Buhin Kōgyō Kai, *Nihon no Jidōsha Buhin Kōgyō*, 32.

23. See ibid., 31.

24. See Nihon Jidōsha Buhin Kōgyō Kai, *Jidōsha Buhin Kōgyō Hatten Shō Shi*, 40–41.

25. Nihon Jidōsha Buhin Kōgyō Kai, *Nihon no Jidōsha Buhin Kōgyō*, 31.

26. See Kaplan, *Japan: The Government-Business Relationship*, 119–20.

27. Toyota became known as Toyota Ginkō (Toyota Bank) because of this phenomenon. It reduced its own debts practically to zero and lent out vast amounts of cash to other firms, mainly auto-parts subcontractors with whom it had close relations. In 1977 Toyota had financial assets of ¥870 billion (around $4 billion), an amount that spiraled to $24 billion by the early 1990s. See Kondo Hiroshi, *Toyota Shōhō—Matsushita Shōhō* (Toyota's and Matsushita's Way of Doing Business) (Tokyo: Nihon Jitsugyō Shuppan Sha, 1977), esp. 65–73.

28. See Shimokawa Kōichi, "The Structure of the Japanese Auto-Parts Industry and Its Contribution to Automotive Process Innovation," paper presented at the International Policy Forum, Hakone, Japan, May 1982, 22–23. See also John Creighton Campbell, *The Automobile Industry and Public Policy*, Joint U.S.-Japan Automotive Study Working Paper, series 16 (Ann Arbor: University of Michigan Center for Japanese Studies, 1982), 12, where Campbell notes that government loans were helpful, although not determinative.

29. Zysman, *Governments, Markets, and Growth*, 341.

30. Literally, "Pen pengusa o hayashite miseru," which can only be approximately rendered into English.

31. See Asahi Shimbun Keizai Bu, *Shōwa Keizai Go Jyū Nen Shi*, (A Fifty-year Economic History of the Shōwa Era) (Tokyo: Asahi Shimbun Sha, 1976), 152–58.

32. The initial proposal was to raise ¥16.3 billion. This was revised upward in January 1952 to ¥27.3 billion, due to Korean War–related inflation of construction costs. Kawasaki Steel Corporation, *Kawasaki Seitetsu Ni Jyū Go Nen Shi* (A Twenty-five-year History of Kawasaki Steel) (Tokyo: Kawasaki Seitetsu Kabushiki Kaisha, 1975), 73–78.

33. See Yoshino Toshihiko, *Nihon Ginkō Sōsai Shi* (History of the Governors of the Bank of Japan) (Tokyo: Nihon Keizai Shimbun Sha, 1973), chap. 17.

34. *Nihon Keizai Shimbun*, 28 September 1950.

35. According to Kawasaki Steel's 1952 annual report, banks other than Kawatetsu's main banks extended credit at the rate of 11.3 percent in 1952 (3.1 rin per day per yen in the parlance of the period) and demanded collateral, whereas Chiba City asked 6.5 percent interest and demanded no collateral. See Kawasaki Steel Corporation, *Kawasaki Seitetsu Yūka Shōken Hōkoku Sho* (Kawasaki Steel Securities Report), 1952, 25.

36. For full itemization of the concessions Nishiyama obtained from Chiba local authorities, see Kawasaki Steel Corporation, *Kawasaki Seitetsu Ni Jyū Go Nen Shi*, 73.

37. These funds, accumulated by the Japanese government from the sale of U.S. foreign aid commodities, formed the basic financial resources allocated by the Japan Development Bank after its foundation in April 1951. The

Ministry of International Trade and Industry controlled them more or less independently of the Bank of Japan.

38. Ibid., 72–73.

39. See Ministry of International Trade and Industry, ed., *Tsūshō Sangyō Gyōsei: Shihan Seiki no Ayumi* (The Administration of Commerce and Industry: The Course of a Quarter Century) (Tokyo: Tsūshō Sangyō Shō, 1975), 96–103.

40. Hirai, after subsequently serving as vice-minister (1953–1955), moved via *amakudari*, or "descent from heaven," to Yahata Steel, of which he ultimately became president.

41. *Nihon Keizai Shimbun*, 27 December 1950.

42. This plan called for the raising of ¥14.6 billion in construction funds, including ¥1.2 billion in domestic bonds and ¥2 billion in foreign currency loans. See Kawasaki Steel Corporation, *Kawasaki Seitetsu Ni Jyū Go Nen Shi*, 79.

43. The MOF Banking Bureau was then, as today, responsible for the funds accounting of the JDB and for preparation of its initial overall annual budget.

44. Kobayashi was, in fact, recruited into the Chiba case by Ikeda, whom Kawatetsu's Nishiyama knew and prevailed upon for an introduction to Kobayashi. See Kawasaki Steel Corporation, *Kawasaki Seitetsu Ni Jyū Go Nen Shi*, 75.

45. On the details, see Japan Development Bank (Nihon Kaihatsu Ginkō), *Ashita e no Senryaku* (Strategies for Tomorrow) (Tokyo: Nihon Kaihatsu Ginkō, 1976).

46. See the reminiscences of Nakayama Sōhei on this point in Japan Development Bank, ed., *Ashita e no Senryaku* (Strategies for Tomorrow) (Tokyo: Nihon Kaihatsu Ginkō, 1976), 15–16. This book is a set of reminiscences and tributes to the Japan Development Bank, delivered on the twenty-fifth anniversary of its founding.

47. The terms on the ten-year loan were 10 percent annually, with the existing facilities as collateral. This rate was one-sixth percent over what Kawatetsu was paying its main bank and nearly half again what it was paying the city of Chiba. See Kawasaki Steel Corporation, *Kawasaki Seitetsu Yūka Shōken Hōkoku Sho*, 1953.

48. Kawasaki Steel Corporation, *Kawasaki Seitetsu Ni Jyū Go Nen Shi*, 94–95.

49. See Kawasaki Steel Corporation, *Kawasaki Seitetsu Yūka Shōken Hōkoku Sho*, 1952–1953 eds. These figures equal the sum of long-term loans outstanding and short-term loans for capital investment outstanding. The Chiba mill was the only capital project being undertaken by Kawatetsu at this time.

50. Ibid.

51. It is customary in Japan to issue new shares at a par value of ¥50 per share and to pay 10 percent dividends on the par value, thus resulting in an after-tax cost of capital to the firm of at least 15 percent. Kawasaki Steel followed this custom through 1954.

52. Until 1933 there had been a direct regulatory link between the securities companies and the Bank of Japan, since it was legally possible for a single

institution to engage in both banking and brokerage, as it still is in West Germany. But the separation of banking and brokerage functions cost the Bank of Japan its regulatory powers vis-à-vis the securities companies. Its only leverage, relatively slight in normal periods, is through its discretionary provision of funds for the Tokyo and Osaka Securities Finance Corporation.

53. The relationship, although a vital one for Kawasaki, was not totally altruistic on Fujimoto's part. Fujimoto took over much of Kawasaki's substantial art and antique collection, including what was purported to be one of Louis XVI's favorite chairs, as I learned from former Fujimoto executive Matsuura Shigenobu.

54. See Kawasaki Steel Corporation, *Kawasaki Seitetsu Ni Jyū Go Nen Shi*, 76.

55. *Nihon Keizai Shimbun*, 2 April 1951.

56. In the Sumitomo Metals case, MITI pressured Sumitomo strongly to refrain from expanding crude-steel production capacity amid the 1965 recession, but Sumitomo, with support from its banks, went ahead with expansion plans nevertheless.

57. On the concept of voice and its relation to politics, see Hirschman, *Exit, Voice, and Loyalty*, 30–43.

58. Figures are for Japanese fiscal 1977 ending 31 March 1978. See Tōyō Keizai Shinpōsha, *Japan Company Handbook*, 1978, 624.

59. Ibid. The projections were for conditions at the end of March 1979.

60. Nippon Steel's current liabilities in September 1990 totaled ¥1.307 trillion, slightly over ten times SHI's 1978 liabilities. See Tōyō Keizai Shinpōsha, *Japan Company Handbook* (Spring 1991): 457.

61. See Mesato Yasunobu, "Sasebo Jūkō o Tsubusenai Riyū" (The Reasons Sasebo Heavy Industries Cannot Be Crushed), *Bungei Shunjū*, August 1978.

62. Mitsubishi Heavy Industries, by contrast, had debts of ¥768 billion—over six times those of Sasebo's. But Mitsubishi's debt-equity ratio was only 3.6 to 1, versus Sasebo's 13.8 to 1. See Tōyō Keizai Shinpōsha, *Japan Company Handbook*, Second Half, 1978, 624, 626. See also *Asahi Evening News*, 24 May 1978.

63. Nihon Keizai Shimbun Sha, *Documento: Sasebo Jūkō* (Document: Sasebo Heavy Industries) (Tokyo: Nihon Keizai Shimbun Sha, 1978), 21.

64. Ibid., 15.

65. Ibid., 7.

66. See ibid., 160.

67. The Shiina faction's Nakamura Kōkai was a Diet member for the Nagasaki Second District, where Sasebo is located, as were Kaneko Iwazō (Ōhira faction) and Shirahama Nikichi (Fukuda faction). Ōhira Masayoshi himself was a close friend of the new SHI president, Tsubouchi Hisao, and both hailed from Shikoku. Tsubouchi was also close personally to Prime Minister Fukuda and even closer to his "pipeline" for political funds, Fukuda's son-in-law Ochi Michio. Ochi came from Ehime prefecture in Shikoku, the home territory of Tsubouchi, and originally planned to run for the Diet from there. Tsubouchi was one of his earliest local backers. Ochi subsequently decided to run from Tokyo instead, but his relationship with

322 · NOTES TO CHAPTER 6

Tsubouchi continued. See *Kokkai Yōran*, 1977, 366; and Nihon Keizai Shimbun Sha, *Documento*, 90.

68. Kasuga Ikko and Tsukamoto Saburō, DSP leaders close to the shipbuilding industry, appealed to Prime Minister Fukuda to save SHI, as did leaders of the conservative Dōmei labor union, affiliated with the DSP. Even the Japan Socialist party, normally highly vocal in its criticism of government "coddling" of industry, could not strenuously oppose a relief effort, because such an effort would prevent major unemployment and, perhaps more important, because Sasebo was in the electoral district of former JSP general secretary Ishibashi Masashi.

69. Mesato, "Sasebo Jūkō Tsubusenai Riyū," 133.

70. Nakayama was the former chairman of the Industrial Bank of Japan and Imazato the president of Nihon Seikō, Japan's largest ball-bearing manufacturer. Both were among the most influential leaders of the *zaikai*, or organized business world, and simultaneously natives of Nagasaki prefecture, where Sasebo is located.

71. Throughout the Sasebo crisis, Nakayama operated largely through Nagano rather than independently. On 20 May, for example, Nakayama, together with Imazato, Matsune Saichi (president of Alaska Petroleum Development), and Morita Akio (chairman of SONY), met with Nagano at the Hakone Country Club and later at Yakult president Matsuzono Naomi's villa in Hakone to plan strategy to cope with the intransigence of the banks and stockholders. But this group only made suggestions to Nagano, and did not operate independently.

72. See, for example, Mainichi Shimbun Sha, *Naze?* (Tokyo: Mainichi Shimbun Sha, 1978), chap. 2.

73. See Nihon Keizai Shimbun Sha, *Documento*, 131, for the full details of this episode.

74. It must be stressed that Fukuda's views differed sharply from those of many government and business leaders on this point. Keidanren chairman Doko Toshio and Japan Iron and Steel Foundation chairman Inayama Yoshihiko, for example, opposed aid to SHI, as did the BOJ governor Morinaga Teiichirō and the various other notables already mentioned.

75. *Nihon Keizai Shimbun*, 10 June 1978.

76. Fukuda has long been billing himself "Keizai no Fukuda," or "Economic Fukuda"—in other words, as a true economic specialist.

77. Fukuda is reported to have discussed the Sasebo case with U.S. Defense Secretary Harold Brown during his Washington visit in early May, with Brown appreciative of Fukuda's commitment to save SHI. Soon after the Sasebo issue was formally resolved in Japanese politics, the U.S. Navy announced the award of a number of ship-repair contracts to the still-beleaguered SHI. In early July, within ten days of the installation of Tsubouchi Hisao as the new SHI president, U.S. Ambassador Mansfield visited Sasebo. Clearly the United States welcomed the SHI rescue operation, although the extent of U.S. participation in the political process leading up to it is not clear.

78. Nihon Keizai Shimbun Sha, *Documento*, 16.

79. See Mainichi Shimbun Sha, *Naze?* for an interesting discussion on this point.

80. Other aspects of the financing for SHI included ¥9 billion raised through a new issue of equity, ¥5 billion generated by delaying payment on notes and purchases such as steel from Nippon Kōkan and Nippon Steel, and ¥3 billion from a delay in money due the governmental Export-Import Bank. See *Asahi Evening News*, 14 June 1978, 5.

81. Sasebo did, to be sure, return to intermittent profitability, although this prospect was decidedly unclear in 1978. By 1982 it was generating a current profit of ¥16.9 billion. Rising Korean competition and yen revaluation forced it into the red again in the late 1980s, but SHI generated a ¥4.5 billion profit in fiscal 1991, based on strong orders in power-station equipment, container shipping, and ship repair for U.S. forces—a substantial diversification from the 1970s. See *Japan Company Handbook*, Spring 1992, 775.

82. See Zysman, *Governments, Markets, and Growth*, 71–75. See also Johnson, *MITI and the Japanese Miracle*, chap. 1.

Chapter 7
Changing Parameters

1. See Jeffrey Pfeffer and Gerald Salancik, *The External Control of Organizations: A Resource Dependence Perspective* (New York: Harper and Row, 1978).

2. Downs, *Inside Bureaucracy*.

3. Sakakibara Eisuke and Nagao Yoriyuki, eds., *Study on the Tokyo Capital Markets* (Tokyo: JCIF Policy Study Series, no. 1, March 1985), 60.

4. Bank of Japan Research and Statistics Department, *Keizai Tōkei Nenpō*, flow-of-funds data from selected issues.

5. Bank of Japan, *Shuyō Kigyō no Keiei Bunseki*, 1984 ed.

6. Bank of Japan Research and Statistics Department, *Keizai Tōkei Nenpō*, 1976 and 1986 eds., flow-of-funds data.

7. See Kondo, *Toyota Shōhō—Matsushita Shōhō*.

8. C. T. Ratcliffe, ed., *Zaitech* (Financial Technology) (Tokyo: Kinyū Zaisei Jijō Kenkyū Kai, 1986), 7–9.

9. "Japan Inc.'s Most Profitable Factory," *Economist*, 25 June 1988, 75. By March 1992 Toyota's liquid assets had risen to ¥2.37 trillion ($18.1 trillion). See Toyota Motors fiscal 1991 financial report (Yūka shōken hōkokusho sōran) 58–59.

10. On Mieno's retrenchment policies, see *Economist*, 25 January 1992, 19–21.

11. *Far Eastern Economic Review*, 9 April 1987, 54.

12. Ibid.

13. Foundation for Advanced Information and Research (FAIR, Japan, *Japan's Financial Markets* (Toyko: FAIR, 1991), 13.

14. Bank of Japan Research and Statistics Department, *Keizai Tōkei Nenpō*, 1986 ed., 43–44.

15. Japan paid back its last foreign currency debt during fiscal 1988, amid its steady rise to financial superpower status. See ibid., 224.

16. Figures are for domestic Japanese holdings of short- and long-term government securities combined for the Japanese fiscal years in question. See BOJ Research and Statistics Department, *Keizai Tōkei Nenpō*, 1991 ed., 191–92.

17. See James Horne, *Japan's Financial Markets: Conflict and Consensus in Policymaking* (Sydney: George Allen and Unwin, 1985), 77.

18. This agreement was reached by the MOF Banking, Securities, and International Finance bureaus during August 1975, in response to the underwriting activities in the Euromarkets of the IBJ's merchant-banking subsidiary, IBJ International.

19. See Horne, *Japan's Financial Markets*, 164–72.

20. Ministry of Finance, *Ōkurashō Kokusai Kinyū Kyoku Nenpō* (International Finance Bureau Yearbook), 1982 ed. (Tokyo: Ōkurā Zaimu Kyōkai, 1982), 116.

21. Ministry of Finance, *Kokusai Kinyū Kyoku Nenpō*, 1986 ed., 148.

22. *Japan Economic Journal*, 22 January 1985.

23. Horne, *Japan's Financial Markets*, 65–70.

24. Edward J. Lincoln, *Japan: Facing Economic Maturity* (Washington, D.C.: Brookings Institution, 1988), 144–45.

25. Bank of Japan Research and Statistics Department, *Keizai Tōkei Nenpō*, 1986 ed., 205.

26. In 1985 12.3 percent of the total amount of government bonds initially purchased by the underwriting syndicate was ultimately resold, up from 20.3 percent of a much smaller amount in 1981. See ibid.

27. Nagatomi, *Antei Seichō Jidai no Kōshasai Shijō*, 206–7.

28. *Japan Economic Journal*, 13 November 1984.

29. Lincoln, *Japan*, 203.

30. FAIR, Japan, *Japan's Financial Markets*, 13.

31. See Ministry of International Trade and Industry Industrial Policy Bureau (Tsūshō Sangyō Shō Sangyō Seisaku Kyoku), ed., *Atarashi Sangyō Kinyū* (New Corporate Finance). Tokyo: Tsūshō Sangyō Chōsa Kai, 1988.

32. *Far Eastern Economic Review*, 9 April 1987, 73–74.

33. FAIR, Japan, *Japan's Financial Markets*, 322.

34. For a useful chronology of the liberalization, see ibid., 539.

35. Around 60 percent of city bank deposits in 1990 held liberalized interest rates, and over 45 percent at regional banks, with these ratios having doubled in the previous two years. See ibid., 604.

36. In this regard, for example, it was instructive that in 1990 around 60 percent of deposits held at the large city banks had liberalized interest rates, but less than 35 percent of deposits at the small *shinkin* banks. See FAIR, Japan, *Japan's Financial Markets*, 604.

37. For a more extensive cross-national comparison of Japan's postal-savings system with these of other major nations, see Kent E. Calder, "Linking Welfare and the Developmental State: Postal Savings in Japan," *Journal of Japanese Studies* 16, no. 1 (Winter 1990): 31–59, esp. 35–37.

38. Tanaka Shin, "Itaku Kinri Hikisage Mondai to Jiyū Unyōron o Kaibō Suru" (Analyzing Arguments about Self-management and the Problem of Reducing Interest Rates on Lending to the Trust Fund Bureau), *Kinyū Zaisei Jijō*, 28 October 1985, 19.

39. Ministry of Post and Telecommunications Savings Bureau (Yūseishō Chōkin Kyoku), "Tokubetsu Kōwa Shiryō," unpublished special lecture data, 4 June 1987, 121.

40. Bank of Japan Research and Statistics Department, *Keizai Tōkei Nenpō*, 1986 ed., 205; 1979 ed., 197.

41. On the relative cost of funds incurred by banks and the postal-savings program during the first half of the 1980s, see *Nihon Kōgyō Shimbun*, 7 October 1986, 13; and *Nihon Kōgyō Shimbun*, 11 November 1986, 17.

42. *Nihon Keizai Shimbun*, 21 August 1984, 12.

43. *Shūkan Tōyō Keizai*, 8 May 1982, 15.

44. Matsuda, "Kōteki Kinyū no Mondaiten," 132.

45. Ibid.

46. *Nihon Keizai Shimbun* (evening edition), 17 February 1984.

47. Unused funds were slightly higher in highly liquid 1978. See Ministry of Finance, *Zaisei Kinyū Tōkei Geppō*, assorted issues.

48. See Johnson, *MITI and the Japanese Miracle*, chap. 1.

49. Political initiative helped to create, for example, the Central Cooperative Bank for Agriculture and Forestry (Nōrin Chūō Kinkō) five years after the Rice Riots of 1918 and the Bank for Commercial and Industrial Cooperatives (Shōkō Kumiai Chūō Kinkō) in 1936.

50. Both the MOF and the Japan Bankers' Association were initially opposed to the idea of an independent Small Business Financial Corporation, while MITI advocated creation of a small-business special account (*tokubetsu kaikei*), under its own control. The major support for the idea that prevailed in the Diet when MITI and MOF could not agree came from the small-business-dominated Tokyo Chamber of Commerce and from the Japan Small Business Industrial Cooperative Association (Zenchūkyō), a major small-business pressure group. On the politics of the Small Business Finance Corporation's establishment, see Small Business Finance Corporation, *Chūshō Kigyō Kinyū Kōko Ni Jyū Nen Shi* (A Twenty-year History of the Small Business Finance Corporation) (Tokyo: Chūshō Kigyō Kinyū Kōko, 1974), 65–81.

51. See ibid., 75.

52. Establishing a relatively secure source of funding through the existence of an independent government finance body is tactically important for nonelite pressure groups because it strengthens them in the face of MOF pressures in the pre-MOF budget (Ōkura Genan) stage. That stage is, as Campbell points out, traditionally dominated by bureaucrats, in contrast to the highly political revival negotiations that follow. See Campbell, *Contemporary Japanese Budget Politics*.

53. Ministry of Health and Welfare (Kōseishō), *Kōsei Hakusho* (White Paper on Welfare), 1961 ed. (Tokyo: Ōkurashō Insatsu Kyoku, 1961), 328.

54. Hirose, *Hojokin to Seiken Tō*, 42. On the broader political context, see Calder, *Crisis and Compensation*, chap. 2.

55. Hirose, *Hojokin to Seiken Tō*, 44–45.

56. Ibid., 49.

57. According to Minshō unpublished figures supplied to the author, Minshō membership was around 300,000 in 1973 and around 365,000 in 1983.

58. Patrick, "Japan's Interest Rates and the 'Grey Financial Market,'" 326–44.

59. See Furukawa Kazu, "Yokin Meberi ni taisuru Shomin no Ronri" (The Average Person's Reasoning about the Erosion of Savings by Inflation), *Ekonomisuto*, 5 November 1974, 43.

60. Ibid., 42. See also Tsuruta Toshimasa, "Yokin Meberi Soshō to Seifu no Sekinin" (The Savings Erosion Suit and the Government's Responsibility), *Ekonomisuto*, 4 March 1975.

61. *Yomiuri Shimbun*, 23 February 1975.

62. Ibid.

63. Ibid.

64. See Calder, *Crisis and Compensation*, chap. 7; and Ellis S. Krauss, "The Urban Strategy and Policy of the Japanese Communist Party: Kyoto," *Studies in Comparative Communism* 12, no. 4 (Winter 1979): 322–50.

65. "Buzumi Ryōdate Taiji ni Kirifuda" (The Trump Card for Destroying Compensating Balances), *Ekonomisuto*, 23 June 1964, 22.

66. Zenkoku Ginkō Kyōkai, *Ginkō Kyōkai Ni Jyū Nen Shi* (Twenty-year History of the Bankers' Association) (Tokyo: Zenkoku Ginkō Kyōkai, 1965), 492.

67. "Buzumi Ryodate Taiji ni Kirifuda," 22.

68. In late March 1960, for example, both bank-deposit and bond-issue rates, public as well as private, were systematically lowered, independent of market forces, in an effort to reduce the cost of capital to basic industry. See Takamoto Mitsuo, ed., *Aitsuroku: Sengo Kinyū Gyōsei Shi* (The Real Story of Postwar Financial Administration) (Tokyo: Kinyū Zaisei Jijō Kenkyū Kai, 1985), 574–77.

69. Ibid., 23. On the political issue of compensating balances during 1963–1964 more generally, see Inoue Kaoru, "Buzumi Ryōdate ni Torikumu" (Wrestling with Compensating Balances), *Ekonomisuto*, 3 December 1963, 52–55; and Oizumi Tsuneo, "Buzumi Ryōdate no Jittai to Kinō" (The Reality and Function of Compensating Balances), *Ekonomisuto*, 14 January 1964, 40–43.

70. Zenkoku Ginkō Kyōkai, *Ginkō Kyōkai Ni Jyū Nen Shi*, 445.

71. On 4 April 1974, for example, Suzuki Yasuo of the Komeitō demanded that MOF use administrative guidance to prevent small businesses from being the principal victims of the restrictions on credit that followed the Oil Shock. See *Asahi Shimbun*, 5 April 1974.

72. Minister Ōhira Masayoshi of MOF announced on 21 February 1975, in the Lower House Budget Committee, following Opposition pressure, that the MOF Banking Bureau director general would issue a directive to all finan-

cial institutions to refrain from demands for compensating balances. See *Asahi Shimbun*, 22 February 1975.

73. For a broader treatment of linkages to the political process, see Calder, *Crisis and Compensation*, chap. 2.

74. The electronics industry, for example, was assessed 4.9 percent of total business contributions, construction and automobiles 4.5 percent each, private railways 4.3 percent, and securities 3.6 percent, according to *Asahi Shimbun* calculations reportedly leaked from confidential Kokumin Kyōkai sources. See Asahi Shimbun Keizai Bu, ed., *Ginkō* (Banks), 152–53.

75. Ibid., 152.

76. Ibid.

77. Curtis, *The Japanese Way of Politics*, 183–84.

78. Asahi Shimbun Keizai Bu, *Ginkō*, 150–51.

79. Financial reform plans of the mid-1980s were for the monopoly of *agents de change* on brokerage transactions on the Bourse to disappear within six or seven years. See Philip G. Cerny, "The 'Little Big Bang' in Paris: Financial Market Deregulation in a Dirigiste System," *European Journal of Political Research* 2, no. 17 (1989): 169–92.

80. On the details, see Kusano, *Shōwa Yon Jyū Nen Go Gatsu Ni Jyū Hachi Nichi*; and Ekonomisuto Henshū Bu, ed., *Sengo Sangyō Shi e no Shōgen* (Testimony to the Industrial History of Shōwa), 4:157–68.

81. *Tokyo Shimbun*, 1 July 1987.

82. On the argument for similarity in the Japanese and the French financial systems, see Zysman, *Governments, Markets, and Growth*, 99–169, 234–51.

83. Nobuyuki Ichikawa, "Kigyō Kinyū no Kōzō Henka wa Doko made Susunde iru no ka?" (How Far Is the Structural Change in Corporate Finance Proceeding?), *Kinyū Zaisei Jijō*, 8 December 1986, 34–39.

84. *Nomura Investment Review*, April 1991.

85. Ibid.

86. In 1990, for example, the five largest banks in the world in terms of total assets were all Japanese. See *Fortune*, 26 August 1991.

87. See, for example, Semiconductor Industry Association, *The Effect of Government Targeting on World Semiconductor Competition* (Cupertino, Calif.: Semiconductor Industry Association, 1980); and Chase Financial Policy, *The U.S. and Japanese Semiconductor Industries: A Financial Comparison* (New York: Chase Manhattan Bank, 1980).

88. On the politics of these liberalization controversies, see Rosenbluth, *Financial Politics in Contemporary Japan*, 50–95.

89. On 29 December 1984, for example, fifty-three LDP politicians formed the Dietmen's League for the Promotion of an International Market (Kokusai Shijō Ikusei Giin Renmei), which pressed for creation of an off-shore banking facility in Tokyo that would afford smaller banks new access to international finance. The group was apparently significant in promoting realization of the Japan offshore market, finally established in December 1986. See ibid., 84–88.

90. Ibid., 94–95.

91. See Paul Sweeney, "When the Cost of Money Evens Out," *Global Finance*, August 1991, 34–37.

Chapter 8
Beyond Strategy?

1. Wray, *Mitsubishi and the NYK*, 505.
2. Johnson, *MITI and the Japanese Miracle*, 19.
3. See, for example, Downs, *Inside Bureaucracy*; and Allison, *Essence of Decision*.
4. van Wolferen, *The Enigma of Japanese Power*.
5. See, for example, James C. Abegglen, "The Sources of Japanese Economic Growth," *Scientific American*, March 1970; and T. J. Pempel "Japanese Foreign Economic Policy: The Domestic Bases for International Behavior," *International Organization*, Autumn 1977.
6. In this respect, see especially ibid.; and James Fallows, "Containing Japan," *Atlantic*, May 1990. Revisionist authors Chalmers Johnson and Clyde V. Prestowitz, Jr., author of *Trading Places* (New York: Basic Books, 1988), have a more strategic view of the Japanese state, as has been noted.
7. On the correspondence of government plans and the reality of postwar Japanese economic development, see Arnold, "The Politics of Economic Planning in Postwar Japan;" and Haruhiro Fukui, "Economic Planning in Postwar Japan: A Case Study in Policy Making," *Asian Survey* 12, no. 4 (April 1972): 327–48.
8. On the pluralistic, competitive general character of corporate behavior within Japan, see, for example, Miyazaki Yoshikazu, *Sengo Nihon no Keizai Kikō* (The Economic Structure of Postwar Japan) (Tokyo: Shin Hyōron Sha, 1966); and James C. Abegglen and George Stalk, Jr., *Kaisha: The Japanese Corporation* (New York: Basic Books, 1985).
9. See, for example, Paul Sheard, "The Role of Firm Organization in the Adjustment of a Declining Industry in Japan: The Case of Aluminum," *Journal of the Japanese and International Economies* 5 (1991): 14–40.
10. Porter, *Capital Choices*, 9.
11. Samuels, *The Business of the Japanese State*, 8–9.
12. For further details on the relationship between interest-group pressure and policy change in Japan, see Calder, *Crisis and Compensation*, esp. chaps. 2 and 4.
13. Thurow, *The Zero Sum Solution* (New York: Simon and Schuster, 1985), 278–79. Socialization of risk is, of course, a controversial notion among economists due to the arguably inefficient overconsumption of risk it often induces.
14. Hanano, Totsune, and Morita, *Zusetsu: Zaisei Tōyūshi*, 1991 ed., 238–39. The largest was the Pension Welfare Service Public Corporation (Nenkin Fukushi Jigyōdan).
15. Oriental Economist, *Kigyō Keiretsu Sōran* (Almanac of Industrial Groups), 1992 ed., 559–61.
16. Ibid.

17. According to Chalmers Johnson, Mitsubishi's decision was the greatest shock MITI ever received in its entire history, hitting the director of MITI's Heavy Industry Bureau like "water poured into his ear while he was sleeping" (*nemimi ni mizu da*). See Johnson, *MITI and the Japanese Miracle*, 287.

18. *Nihon Keizai Shimbun*, 26 June 1991, 1.

19. According to *Fortune*'s 1990 annual survey, the Nōrin Chūkin Bank's $244.9 billion in total assets placed it seventh in the world in 1989, just ahead of France's Crédit Agricole, with $242.6 billion. Citicorp had $230.6 billion in total assets. See JETRO, *Nippon: Business Facts and* Figures, 1991 ed. (Tokyo: JETRO, 1991), 94.

20. See David Osborne and Ted Gaebler, *Reinventing Government* (Reading, Mass.: Addison-Wesley, 1992).

21. Zysman, *Governments, Markets, and Growth*.

22. Jack Hayward, *The State and the Market Economy: Industrial Patriotism and Economic Intervention in France* (New York: New York University Press, 1986); and Michael Loriaux, *France after Hegemony: International Change and Financial Reform* (Ithaca: Cornell University Press, 1991).

23. Harvey B. Feigenbaum, *The Politics of Public Enterprise: Oil and the French State* (Princeton: Princeton University Press, 1985), esp. 173–74.

24. Zysman, *Governments, Markets, and Growth*, 127; and Cox, *State, Finance, and Industry*, 85–108.

25. See Jung-en Woo, *Race to the Swift: State and Finance in Korean Industrialization* (New York: Columbia University Press, 1991), 129, 159.

26. Ibid., 162.

27. John B. Goodman, *Monetary Sovereignty: The Politics of Central Banking in Western Europe* (Ithaca: Cornell University Press, 1992), 103–41.

28. Jung-en Woo, *Race to the Swift*, 160.

29. Ibid., 164.

30. See Loriaux, *France after Hegemony*, 220–27; and Jung-en Woo, *Race to the Swift* 176–204.

31. On this dynamic see, for example, George Stigler, "The Theory of Regulation," *Bell Journal of Economics and Management Science* 3 (1971).

32. Jung-en Woo, *Race to the Swift*, 163.

33. Feigenbaum, *The Politics of Public Enterprise*.

34. For details on how political pressures have encouraged the expansion of small-business government credit programs in Japan, see Calder, *Crisis and Compensation*, 318–22.

35. Ibid., 156–230.

36. Porter, *The Competitive Advantage of Nations*, 366, 393.

37. See Porter, *Capital Choices*, 66.

38. Porter, *The Competitive Advantage of Nations*, 366, 393.

39. See, for example, the output of the Council on Competitiveness/Harvard Business School Project on Time Horizons of American Management, particularly Michael E. Porter, *Capital Choices: Changing the Way America Invests in Industry* (Washington, D. C.: Council on Competitiveness, 1992).

40. See, for example, Oliver E. Williamson, *Markets and Hierarchies: Analysis and Antitrust Implications* (New York: Free Press, 1975); and Aoki, *Information, Incentives, and Bargaining in the Japanese Economy.*

41. Porter, *The Competitive Advantage of Nations*, 393; and Porter, *Capital Choices*, 20.

42. On some of the relevant conceptual issues, see Porter, *Capital Choices*, 50–60.

43. See, for example, Herbert Simon, *Models of Man* (New York, 1957); James March and Herbert Simon, *Organizations* (New York: John Wiley and Sons, 1958); and Richard Cyert and James March, *A Behavioral Theory of the Firm* (Englewood Cliffs, N. J.: Prentice-Hall, 1963); and Jeffrey Pfeffer and Gerald R. Salancik, *The External Control of Organizations* (New York: Harper & Row, 1978). With respect to Japanese microeconomic decision making, see Aoki, *Information, Incentives, and Bargaining in the Japanese Economy*; and Masahiko Aoki, ed., *The Economic Analysis of the Japanese Firm.*

44. On the concept of bureaupluralism at the micro-level, and a creative approach to analysis, see Masahiko Aoki. *Information, Incentives, and Bargaining in the Japanese Economy*, 258–97.

45. Komiya Ryūtarō, Okuno Masahiro, and Suzumura Kōtaro, eds. *The Industrial Policy of Japan* (New York: Harcourt, Brace, Jovanovich, 1988), 19.

46. On this point, see, for example, Kent E. Calder, "Japan's Public and Private Sectors: Beyond the Revisionism Debate," *JAMA Forum 9*, no. 1 (August 1990): 3–7.

47. An insightful agenda of research issues in the analysis of Japanese government-business networks is presented in Wilks and Wright, eds., *The Promotion and Regulation of Industry in Japan*, esp. 311–43.

48. In this respect, the insights of Hayward regarding the French political economy, stressing both "limited pluralist power" and also networks, in the sense of an "economic policy community," are also relevant to research on Japan. See Hayward, *The State and the Market Economy*, 15–18.

49. See, for example, Sylvia Maxfield, *Governing Capital: International Finance and Mexican Politics* (Ithaca: Cornell University Press, 1990); Jung-en Woo, *Race to the Swift*; and Loriaux, *France after Hegemony.*

50. Loriaux, *France after Hegemony*, 288.

51. Ibid., 214–40.

52. Porter, *Capital Choices*, 66.

53. See Rolf Zeigler, Donald Bender, and Hermann Biehler, "Industry and Banking in the German Corporate Network," in Fruns N. Stokeman, Rolf Zeigler, and John Scott, eds., *Networks of Corporate Power: A Comparative Analysis of Ten Countries* (Cambridge, Mass.: Polity Press, 1985), 110. See also Porter, *Capital Choices*, 13.

54. See Keohane, *After Hegemony.*

55. Jeffrey Garten, *Cold Peace* (New York: Twentieth Century Fund, 1992).

56. Cerny, "The 'Little Big Bang' in Paris," 47–48.

57. Satō, Fujimura, and Kawamata, *Zusetsu: Zaisei Tōyūshi*, 1990 ed., 234.

58. Foreign banks could not, for example, readily raise yen funds wholesale due to the imperfections of the domestic CD market, nor could they create a substantial yen deposit base through Japanese bank acquisitions, as Citibank's attempted 1986 acquisition of the Heiwa Mutual Savings Bank demonstrated.

59. See, for example, "The Yen for American Clients," *Euromoney*, January 1986, 107–8; and Sharon E. Ruwart, "Leasing Update," *China Business Review*, January 1989, 17–19.

Bibliography

Abe Yasuji. *Ginkō Shōken Kakine Ronsō Oboegaki* (Memories of the Banking-Securities Border Dispute). Tokyo: Nihon Keizai Shimbun, 1980.
———. *Ichimada Naoto Den* (A Biography of Ichimada Naoto). Tokyo: Tōyō Shokan, 1955.
Abegglen, James C. "The Sources of Japanese Economic Growth." *Scientific American.* March 1970.
———. ed. *Business Strategies for Japan.* Tokyo: Sophia University Press, 1970.
Abegglen, James C., and William V. Rapp. "Japanese Managerial Behavior and 'Excessive Competition.'" *Developing Economies* 8 (December 1979): 427–44.
Abegglen, James C., and George Stalk, Jr. *Kaisha: The Japanese Corporation.* New York: Basic Books, 1985.
Aberbach, Joel D., Robert D. Putnam, and Bert A. Rockman. *Bureaucrats and Politicians in Western Democracies.* Cambridge, Mass.: Harvard University Press, 1981.
Adam, Nigel. "L'Etat c'est nous." *Euromoney,* October 1980.
Adams, T.F.M., and Iwao Hoshii. *A Financial History of the New Japan.* Tokyo: Kodansha, 1972.
Administrative Management Agency (Gyōsei Kanri Chō). *Gyōsei Kikō Zu* (Diagrams of Administrative Structure). 1964–88 eds. Tokyo: Gyōsei Kanri Kenkyū Center, 1968–88.
———. *Shingikai Sōran* (General Overview of Deliberation Committees). 1975–1988 ed. Tokyo: Ōkurashō Insatsu Kyoku, 1975–88.
———. *Tokushū Hōjin Sōran* (Almanac of Special Corporate Entities). 1976–88 eds. Tokyo: Ōkurashō Insatsu Kyoku, 1976–88.
Aggarwal, Vinod K., Robert O. Keohane, and David B. Yoffie. "The Dynamics of Negotiated Protectionism." *American Political Science Review* 81, no. 2 (June 1987): 345–66.
Aichi Kiichi. *Kore Kara no Kinyū* (Finance in the Future). Tokyo: Gakuyō Shobō, 1950.
Allison, Graham T. *Essence of Decision: Explaining the Cuban Missile Crisis.* Boston: Little, Brown, 1971.
All Japan Bankers Federation Real Estate Finance Research Group (Zenkoku Ginkō Kyōkai Rengo Kai Fudōsan Kenkyū Kai). *Fudōsan Kinyū Kenkyū Kai Hōkoku* (Report of the Real Estate Finance Research Group). Tokyo: Zenginkyō, March 1992.
Amsden, Alice. *Asia's Next Giant.* New York: Oxford University Press, 1989.
Anastassopoulos, Jean-Pierre C. "The Strategic Autonomy of Government-Controlled Enterprises Operating in a Competitive Economy." Ph.D. diss., Columbia University, 1973.

Anchordoguy, Marie. *Computers, Inc.: Japan's Challenge to IBM*. Cambridge, Mass.: Harvard University Council on East Asian Studies, 1990.

Andō Yoshio, ed. *Shōwa Seiji Keizai Shi e no Shōgen*. Vol. 3. Tokyo: Mainichi Shimbun Sha, 1972.

Angel, Robert C. *Explaining Economic Policy Failure: Japan in the 1969–1971 International Monetary Crisis*. New York: Columbia University Press, 1991.

Anthony, Robert N. *Planning and Control Systems: A Framework for Analysis*. Boston: Division of Research, Graduate School of Business Administration, Harvard University, 1965.

Aoki, Masahiko. *Information, Incentives, and Bargaining in the Japanese Economy*. Cambridge, Eng.: Cambridge University Press, 1988.

———, ed. *The Economic Analysis of the Japanese Firm*. Amsterdam: North-Holland, 1984.

Arakawa Shigeru and Saitō Nobuhiro. *Kinyū Kai* (The Financial World). Tokyo: Kyōiku Sha, 1975.

Arisawa Hiromi. *Nihon Kōgyō Tōseiron* (A Theory of Japanese Industrial Control). Tokyo: Yūhikaku, 1937.

———, *Nihon Sangyō Hyaku Nen Shi* (A Hundred-year History of Japanese Industry). 2 vols. Tokyo: Nihon Keizai Shimbun Sha, 1967.

———, ed. *Shōken Hyaku Nen Shi* (A Hundred-year History of the Securities Industry). Tokyo: Nihon Keizai Shimbun Sha, 1978.

———, ed. *Shōwa Keizai Shi* (An Economic History of Shōwa). Tokyo: Nihon Keizai Shimbun Sha, 1976.

Arndt, Hans Joachim. *West Germany: The Politics of Non-Planning*. Syracuse, N.Y.: Syracuse University Press, 1969.

Arnold, Walter. "The Politics of Economic Planning in Postwar Japan: A Study in Political Economy." Ph.D. diss., Department of Political Science, University of California, Berkeley, 1984.

Asahi Shimbun Keizai Bu. *Ginkō* (Banking). Tokyo: Asahi Shimbun Sha, 1976.

———. *Keizai Seisaku no Butai Ura* (The Backstage of Economic Policy). Tokyo: Asahi Shimbun Sha, 1974.

———. *Shōwa Keizai Go Jyū Nen Shi* (A Fifty-year Economic History of the Shōwa Era). Tokyo: Asahi Shimbun Sha, 1976.

———. *Sōgō Shōsha* (General Trading Companies). Tokyo: Asahi Shimbun Sha, 1977.

Asahi Shimbun Senkyo Honbu, ed. *Asahi Senkyo Taikan* (Asahi Electoral Almanac). 1986 ed. Tokyo: Asahi Shimbun Sha, 1986.

Asahi Shimbun Sha. *Asahi Nenkan* (Asahi Yearbook), 1977–91 eds. Tokyo: Asahi Shimbun Sha, 1977–91.

———. *Shōwa Keizai Go Jyū Nen* (Fifty Years of the Shōwa Era Economy). Tokyo: Asahi Shimbun Sha, 1976.

Asakura Kōkichi. *Meiji Zenki Nihon Kinyū Kōzō Shi* (A History of Japanese Financial Structure in the Early Meiji Period). Tokyo: Iwanami Shoten, 1961.

Ashikaga Shigeo. *Lease Sangyō Kai* (The World of the Leasing Industry). Tokyo: Kyōiku Sha, 1985.

Atsukawa Masao. *Ginkō Jidai no Owari* (The End of the Banking Age). Tokyo: Nihon Jitsugyō Shūppan Sha, 1973.

Audretsch, David B. *The Market and the State: Government Policy toward Business in Europe, Japan, and the United States.* New York: Harvester Wheatsheaf, 1989.

Bank of Japan Centennial History Editorial Department (Nihon Ginkō Hyaku Nen Shi Henshū Iinkai). *Nihon Ginkō Hyaku Nen Shi* (A Centennial History of the Bank of Japan). Vols. 1–5. Tokyo: Nihon Ginkō, 1982–85.

Bank of Japan Economic Research Department. *The Japanese Financial System*, 1978–90 eds. Tokyo: The Bank of Japan, biannual.

Bank of Japan Research and Statistics Department (Nihon Ginkō Chōsa Tōkei Kyoku). *Keizai Tōkei Nenpō* (Economic Statistics Annual). (Tokyo: Nihon Ginkō Chōsa Tōkei Kyoku, various issues.

Bank of Japan Research Department (Nihon Ginkō Chōsa Bu). *Nihon Ginkō Hachi Jyū Nen Shi* (An Eighty-year History of the Bank of Japan). Tokyo: Nihon Ginkō, 1963.

Bank of Japan Statistics Department (Nihon Ginkō Tōkei Kyoku). *Meiji Ikō Hondo Shuyō Keizai* (Hundred-year Statistics of the Japanese Economy Since Meiji). Tokyo: Nihon Ginkō Tōkei Kyoku, 1966.

Bardach, Eugene. *The Implementation Game: What Happens After a Bill Becomes a Law.* Cambridge, Mass.: MIT Press, 1978.

Baum, Warren C. *The French Economy and the State.* Princeton, N.J.: Princeton University Press, 1958.

Birnbaum, Pierre. *The Heights of Power: An Essay on the Power Elite in France.* Chicago: University of Chicago Press, 1982.

Bisson, T. A. *Zaibatsu Dissolution in Japan.* Berkeley: University of California Press, 1954.

Blumenthal, Tuvia. "The Practice of Amakudari within the Japanese Employment System." *Asian Survey* 25, no. 3 (March 1985): 310–21.

———. *Savings in Postwar Japan.* Cambridge, Mass.: Harvard East Asian Research Center, 1970.

Bower, Joseph L. *Managing the Resource Allocation Process.* Homewood, Ill.: Richard D. Irwin, 1972.

———. *When Markets Quake: The Management Challenge of Restructuring Industry.* Boston: Harvard Business School Press, 1986.

Bronfenbrenner, Martin. "Theories Concerning the Japanese Inflation of the SCAP Period." *Journal of Political Economy*, Fall 1973.

Bronte, Stephen. *Japanese Finance: Markets and Institutions.* London: Euromoney Publications, 1982.

Bryant, William E. *Japanese Private Economic Diplomacy.* New York: Praeger Publishers, 1975.

Burkhead, Jesse. *Government Budgeting.* New York: John Wiley and Sons, 1956.

"Buzumi Ryōdate Taiji ni Kirifuda" (The Trump Card for Destroying Compensating Balances). *Ekonomisuto*, 23 June 1964.

Calder, Kent E. *Crisis and Compensation: Public Policy and Political Stability in Japan, 1949–1986.* Princeton, N.J.: Princeton University Press, 1988.

———. "Elites in an Equalizing Role? Ex-Bureaucrats as Coordinators and Intermediaries in the Japanese Government-Business Relationship," *Comparative Politics,* July 1989, 379–403.

———. "Japanese Capital Outflows: Origins and Implications for the Global Political Economy." Testimony before the Joint Economic Committee of the U.S. Congress, 11 December 1986.

———. "Japanese Foreign Economic Policy Formation: Explaining the Reactive State." *World Politics* 40, no. 4 (July 1988): 517–41.

———. "Japan's Public and Private Sectors: Beyond the Revisionism Debate." *JAMA Forum* 9, no. 1 (August 1990): 3–7.

———. "Linking Welfare and the Developmental State: Postal Savings in Japan." *Journal of Japanese Studies* 16, no. 1 (Winter 1990): 31–59.

———. "Politics and the Market: The Dynamics of Japanese Credit Allocation, 1946–1978." Ph.D. diss., Department of Government, Harvard University, 1979.

Calder, Kent E., and Roy Hofheinz, Jr. *The Eastasia Edge.* New York: Basic Books, 1982.

Cameron, Rondo, ed. *Banking and Economic Development.* New York: Oxford University Press, 1972.

———. *Essays in French Economic History.* Homewood, Ill.: Richard D. Irwin, 1970.

Campbell, John Creighton. *Contemporary Japanese Budget Politics.* Berkeley: University of California Press, 1977.

———. *The Automobile Industry and Public Policy.* Joint U.S.-Japan Automotive Study Working Paper, series 16. Ann Arbor: University of Michigan Center for Japanese Studies, 1982.

"Case Study: Nihon Ginkō" (Case Study: The Bank of Japan). *Nikkei Business,* 10 May 1976, 28–40.

Caves, Richard E., and Masu Uekusa. *Industrial Organization in Japan.* Washington, D.C.: Brookings Institution, 1976.

Cerny, Philip G. "The 'Little Bang' in Paris: Financial Market Deregulation in a Dirigiste System." *European Journal of Political Research* 2, no. 17 (1989): 169–92.

Chandler, Alfred E., Jr. *The Visible Hand: The Managerial Revolution in American Business.* Cambridge, Mass.: Harvard University Press, 1977.

Chase Financial Policy. *The U.S. and Japanese Semiconductor Industries: A Financial Comparison.* New York: Chase Manhattan Bank, 1980.

Chō Yukio. "Exposing the Incompetence of the Bourgeoisie: The Financial Panic of 1927." *Japan Interpreter* 8, no. 4 (Winter 1974).

Clark, Rodney. *Venture Capital in Britain, America, and Japan.* London: Croom Helm, 1987.

Cohen, Jerome B. *Japan's Economy in War and Reconstruction.* New York: Columbia University Press, 1950.

Cohen, Stephen S. *Modern Capitalist Planning: The French Model.* Berkeley: University of California Press, 1977.

Commerce and Industry Research Association Toranomon Detached Office (Tsūshō Sangyō Chōsa Kai Toranomon Bun Shitsu). *Shōkōshō/Tsūshō Sangyō Shō Gyōsei Kikō oyobi Kanbu Shokuin no Henkan, 1925–1973* (Administrative Structure and Personnel Transfers of the Ministry of International Trade and Industry, 1925–1973). Tokyo: Sangyō Seisaku Shi Kenkyū Jo, 1977.

Cox, Andrew, ed. *State, Finance, and Industry: A Comparative Analysis of Postwar Trends in Six Advanced Industrial Economies*. Brighton, Eng.: Wheatsheaf Books, 1986.

"Credit Curbs: How Done?" *Oriental Economist*, June 1954, 281–84.

Crozier, Michel. *The Bureaucratic Phenomenon*. Chicago: University of Chicago Press, 1964.

Cullinan, Gerald. *The United States Postal Service*. New York: Praeger Publishers, 1968.

Curtis, Gerald L. *The Japanese Way of Politics*. New York: Columbia University Press, 1988.

Cusumano, Michael A. *The Japanese Automobile Industry: Technology and Management at Nissan and Toyota*. Cambridge: Harvard University Council on East Asian Studies, 1985.

Cyert, Richard, and James March. *A Behavioral Theory of the Firm*. Englewood Cliffs, N.J.: Prentice-Hall, 1963.

Dahl, Robert A., and Charles E. Lindblom. *Politics, Economics, and Welfare*. Chicago: University of Chicago Press, 1976.

Dai Ichi Ginkō, ed. *Dai Ichi Ginkō Shi* (A History of the Dai Ichi Bank). Vols. 1 and 2. Tokyo: Dai Ichi Ginkō Hachi Jyū Nen Shi Hensan Shitsu, 1957.

Dai Kasumi Kai. *Naimushō Shi* (A History of the Home Ministry). Vol. 3. Tokyo: Chihō Zaimu Kyōkai, 1971.

de Carmoy, Hervé. *Global Banking Strategy: Financial Markets and Industrial Decay*. Oxford, Eng.: Basil Blackwell, 1990.

Deyo, Fred, ed. *The Political Economy of the New Asian Industrialism*. Ithaca, N.Y.: Cornell University Press, 1987.

Dixit, Avinash, and Barry Nalebuff. *Thinking Strategically: The Competitive Edge in Business, Politics, and Everyday Life*. New York: W. W. Norton, 1991.

Downs, Anthony. *Inside Bureaucracy*. Boston: Little, Brown, 1966.

Duverger, Maurice. *The French Political System*. Chicago: University of Chicago Press, 1962.

Economic Planning Agency. *Economic Survey of Japan*. 1968–69 ed. Washington, D.C.: Government Printing Office, 1969.

Economic Planning Agency (Keizai Kikaku Chō). *Keizai Hakusho* (Economic White Paper). 1968–78 eds. Tokyo: Ōkurashō Insatsu Kyoku, 1968–78.

Economic Planning Agency General Planning Bureau (Keizai Kikaku Chō Sōgō Keikaku Kyoku), ed. *Kinyū no Kokusaika/Jiyūka* (The Internationalization and Liberalization of Finance). Tokyo: Ōkurashō Insatsu Kyoku, 1987.

Economic Stabilization Board (Keizai Antei Honbu). *Taiheiyō Sensō ni yoru Waga Kuni no Higai Sōgō Hōkokusho* (Comprehensive Report on Damage to Japan from the Pacific War). Tokyo: Keizai Antei Honbu, 1949.

Ekonomisuto Henshū Bu. *Asu no Sangyō Shin Chizu* (Tomorrow's New Industrial Map). Tokyo: Mainichi Shimbun Sha, 1978.

Ekonomisuto Sō Tokushū: Ginkō Sengoku Jidai (General Special Edition: The Banks' "Age of the Warring States"). 10 June 1978.

Eli, Max. *Japan, Inc.: Global Strategies of Japanese Trading Corporations.* New York: McGraw Hill, 1990.

Endō Shōkichi. *Zaisei Tōyūshi* (The Fiscal Investment and Loan Program). Tokyo: Iwanami Shinsho, 1966.

Evan, William M., ed. *Inter-Organizational Relations.* Philadelphia: University of Pennsylvania Press, 1978.

Evans, Peter B., Dietrich Rueschemeyer, and Theda Skocpol, eds. *Bringing the State Back In.* Cambridge, Eng.: Cambridge University Press, 1985.

Fair Trade Commission (Kōsei Torihiki Iinkai), ed. *Shuyō Sangyō ni okeru Seisan Shūchūdo* (Concentration of Production in Principal Industries). Tokyo: Kōsei Torihiki Iinkai, 1960.

Fallows, James. "Containing Japan." *Atlantic,* May 1990, 40–54.

Federation of Bankers' Associations of Japan. *The Banking System in Japan.* Tokyo: Zenginkyō, 1989.

Feigenbaum, Harvey B. *The Politics of Public Enterprise: Oil and the French State.* Princeton, N.J.: Princeton University Press, 1985.

Feldman, Robert Alan. "Financial Upheaval and Funds Rechanneling: The Case of Japan from the Panic of 1927 to the End of the Takahashi Era, 1936." B.A. thesis, Department of Economics, Yale University, 1976.

————. *Japanese Financial Markets: Deficits, Dilemmas, and Deregulation.* Cambridge, Mass.: MIT Press, 1986.

Feldstein, Martin, ed. *The American Economy in Transition.* Chicago: University of Chicago Press, 1981.

Fisher, Larry Warren. "The Lockheed Affair: A Phenomenon of Japanese Politics." Ph.D. diss., Department of Political Science, University of Colorado, 1980.

Foundation for Advanced Information and Research (FAIR), Japan. *Japanese Financial Markets.* Tokyo: FAIR, 1991.

Fousek, Peter G. *Foreign Central Banking: The Instruments of Monetary Policy.* New York: Federal Reserve Bank of New York, 1957.

Friedman, David. *The Misunderstood Miracle: Industrial Development and Political Change in Japan.* Ithaca, N.Y.: Cornell University Press, 1988.

Friedman, Milton, and Anna Jacobson Schwartz. *A Monetary History of the United States, 1867–1960.* Princeton, N.J.: Princeton University Press, 1963.

Fuji Ginkō. *Fuji Ginkō Hachi Jyū Nen Shi* (An Eighty-year History of the Fuji Bank). Tokyo: Fuji Ginkō, 1969.

Fuji Seikei Shimbun Sha. *Kokkai Yōran* (Diet Almanac). Tokyo: Fuji Seikei Shimbun Sha, various issues.

Fujita Sei, ed. *Zaisei Seisaku* (Financial Policy). Tokyo: Nihon Keizai Shimbun Sha, 1973.

Fujiwara Akira, Imai Seiichi, and Ōe Shinobu, eds. *Kindai Nihon Shi no Kisō*

Chishiki (Basic Knowledge about Modern Japanese History). Tokyo: Yūhikaku, 1972.

Fukui, Haruhiro. "Economic Planning in Postwar Japan: A Case Study in Policy Making." *Asian Survey* 12, no. 4 (April 1972): 327–48.

Fukukawa, Shinji. *Japanese Industrial Policy and Trade Policy in the High-Growth Era*. Tokyo: MITI Overseas Public Affairs Office, 1990.

———. *Recent Development of Industrial Policy and Business Strategy in Japan*. Tokyo: MITI Overseas Public Affairs Office, 1990.

Furukawa Kazu. "Yokin Meberi ni taisuru Shomin no Ronri" (The Average Person's Reasoning about the Erosion of Savings by Inflation). *Ekonomisuto*, 5 November 1974.

Garten, Jeffrey E. *Cold Peace*. New York: Twentieth Century Fund, 1992.

———. *Restructuring Financial Services in the United States and Japan*. New York: Japan Society, 1991.

Gendai Seiji Mondai Kenkyū Kai. *Jimintō Gigoku Shi* (A History of Liberal Democratic Party Scandals). Tokyo: Gendai Hyōron Sha, 1973.

General Affairs Agency (Sōmuchō). *Tokushū Hōjin Sōran* (Almanac of Special Legal Entities). 1990 ed. Tokyo: Gyōsei Kanri Kenkyū Center, 1990.

Genther, Phyllis. *A History of Japan's Government-Business Relationship: The Passenger Car Industry*. Ann Arbor: Michigan Papers in Japanese Studies, no. 20, 1990.

Gerlach, Michael L. *Alliance Capitalism: The Social Transformation of Japanese Business*. Berkeley: University of California Press, 1992.

Gerschenkron, Alexander. *Economic Backwardness in Historical Perspective*. Cambridge, Mass.: Harvard University Press, 1962.

Ginkō Kyōkai Ni Jyū Nen Shi Henshū Shitsu, ed. *Ginkō Kyōkai Ni Jyū Nen Shi* (A Twenty-year History of the Banking Association). Tokyo: Zenkoku Ginkō Kyōkai Rengō Kai, 1965.

Goldsmith, Raymond W. *Financial Structure and Development*. New Haven, Conn.: Yale University Press, 1969.

Goodman, John B. *Monetary Sovereignty: The Politics of Central Banking in Western Europe*. Ithaca, N.Y.: Cornell University Press, 1992.

———. "The Politics of Central Bank Independence." *Comparative Politics*, April 1991, 329–49.

Gotō Shinichi. *Nihon no Kinyū Tōkei* (Financial Statistics of Japan).

———. *Toshi Ginkō* (City Banks). Tokyo: Kyōiku Sha, 1978.

Gourevitch, Peter. *Politics in Hard Times: Comparative Responses to International Economic Crises*. Ithaca, N.Y.: Cornell University Press, 1986.

———. "The Second Image Reversed." *International Organization* 32, no. 4 (Autumn 1978): 881–912.

Greenstein, Fred I., and Nelson W. Polsby, eds. *Handbook of Political Science: Strategies of Inquiry*. Vol. 7. Reading, Mass.: Addison-Wesley, 1975.

Grinder, Walter E., and Alan Fairgate. "The Reconstruction Finance Corporation Rides Again." *Reason*, July 1975, 23–29.

Groth, Alexander J., and Larry L. Wade, eds. *Comparative Resource Allocation: Politics, Performance, and Policy Priorities*. Beverly Hills, Calif.: Sage Publications, 1984.

Grou, Pierre. *The Financial Structure of Multinational Capitalism.* Dover, N.H.: Berg Publishers, 1985.

Hadley, Eleanor M. *Antitrust in Japan.* Princeton, N.J.: Princeton University Press, 1970.

Hagen, Everett, ed. *Planning Economic Development.* Homewood, Ill.: Richard D. Irwin, 1963.

Hall, Peter. *Governing the Economy: The Politics of State Intervention in Britain and France.* New York: Oxford University Press, 1986.

Halperin, Morton. *Bureaucratic Politics and Foreign Policy.* Washington, D.C.: Brookings Institution, 1974.

Hamada Kōichi and Iwata Kazumasa. *Kinyū Seisaku to Ginkō Kōdō* (Monetary Policy and Bank Behavior). Tokyo: Tōyō Keizai Shinpōsha, 1980.

Hamburger, Michael J., and Burton Zwick. *Installment Credit Controls, Consumer Expenditures, and the Allocation of Real Resources.* New York: Federal Reserve Bank of New York Research Paper, no. 7607, January 1976.

Hanano Akira, Totsune Haruhito, and Morita Yoshinori. *Zusetsu: Zaisei Tōyūshi* (The Fiscal Investment and Loan Program in Graphics). 1991 and 1992 eds. Tokyo: Tōyō Keizai Shinpōsha, 1991–92.

Harari, Ehud. "Japanese Politics of Advice in Comparative Perspective: A Framework for Analysis and a Case Study." *Public Policy* 22, no. 4 (Fall 1974): 537–77.

Hartz, Louis. *Economic Policy and Democratic Thought: Pennsylvania, 1776–1869.* Cambridge, Mass.: Harvard University Press, 1948.

Hayes, Douglas A. *Bank Lending Policies: Domestic and International.* 2d ed. Ann Arbor: Graduate School of Business Administration, University of Michigan, 1977.

Hayward, Jack. *Governing France: The One and Indivisible Republic.* London: Weidenfeld and Nicholson, 1983.

———. *The State and the Market Economy: Industrial Patriotism and Economic Intervention in France.* New York: New York University Press, 1986.

Heclo, Hugh. *Modern Social Politics in Britain and Sweden.* New Haven, Conn.: Yale University Press, 1974.

Hein, Laura. *Fueling Growth: The Energy Revolution and Economic Policy in Postwar Japan.* Cambridge, Mass.: Harvard University Council on East Asian Studies, 1990.

Hiraiwa Takeo. *Tōsan Hasan* (Bankruptcy). Tokyo: Aiki Shobō, 1977.

Hirasawa Masao. *Nihon Kanryō Chizu* (An Atlas of Japan's Bureaucrats). 2 vols. Tokyo: Kokusai Shōgyō Shuppansha, 1976.

Hirose Michisada. *Hojokin to Seiken Tō* (Subsidies and the Party in Power). Tokyo: Asahi Shimbun Sha, 1981.

Hirschman, Albert O. *Exit, Voice, and Loyalty: Responses to Decline in Firms, Organizations, and States.* Cambridge, Mass.: Harvard University Press, 1970.

Honda Suzuki. *Nihon Neo Kanryō Ron* (A Theory concerning Japan's Neo-Bureaucrats). Tokyo: Kodansha, 1974.

Horiuchi Akira. *Nihon no Kinyū Seisaku: Kinyū Mekanizumu no Shishō Bunseki* (Monetary Policy in Japan: Empirical Analysis of the Monetary Mechanism). Tokyo: Tōyō Keizai Shinpōsha, 1980.

———. *Economic Growth and Financial Allocation in Postwar Japan.* Washington, D.C.: Brookings Institution, 1984.

———. "Sizing up the Bank of Japan's Policy Record." *Shūkan Tōyō Keizai,* 29 September 1982.

Horne, James. *Japan's Financial Markets: Conflict and Consensus in Policymaking.* Sydney: George Allen and Unwin, 1985.

Houdaille Industries, "Petition to the President of the United States through the Office of the United States Special Trade Representative for the Exercise of Presidential Discretion." Unpublished.

Hout, Thomas M., and Ira Magaziner. *Japanese Industrial Policy.* Berkeley: University of California Press, 1980.

Howell, Thomas R., Brent L. Bartlett, and Warren Davis. *Creating Advantage: Semiconductors and Government Industrial Policy in the 1990s.* Cupertino, Calif.: Semiconductor Industry Association, 1992.

Hughes, Jonathan R. T. *The Government Habit Redux: Economic Controls from Colonial Times to the Present.* Princeton, N.J.: Princeton University Press, 1991.

Hunt, Reed O. *The Report of the President's Commission on Financial Structure and Regulation.* Washington, D.C.: Government Printing Office, 1971.

Huntington, Samuel P. *Political Order in Changing Societies.* New Haven, Conn.: Yale University Press, 1968.

Ichimada Naoto Denki Suitōroku Kankōkai, ed. *Ichimada Naoto: Denki Suitōroku* (Ichimada Naoto: A Biography and a Memorial Record). Tokyo: Tokuma Shobō, 1986.

Ichinose Tomōji, Kikuchi Shōichirō, Terado Kyōhei, and Naoe Shigehiko. *Kōsha Kōdan Jigyōdan* (Public Corporations). Tokyo: Kyōiku Sha, 1978.

Ike, Nobutaka. *A Theory of Japanese Democracy.* Boulder, Colo.: Westview Press, 1980.

Ikeda Hayato. *Kinkō Zaisei* (The Affairs of Government Financial Institutions). Tokyo: Jitsugyō no Nihon Sha, 1952.

Industrial Bank of Japan (Nihon Kōgyō Ginkō). *Nihon Kōgyō Ginkō Chōsa Geppō* (Industrial Bank of Japan Research Monthly), 1957–64.

———. *Nihon Kōgyō Ginkō Go Jyū Nen Shi* (A Fifty-year History of the Industrial Bank of Japan). Tokyo: Nihon Kōgyō Ginkō, 1953.

———. *Shōken Binran* (Securities Handbook). 1977–78 ed. Tokyo: Nihon Kōgyō Ginkō Shōken Bu, 1977.

Industrial Bank of Japan Historical Editing Committee (Nihon Kōgyō Ginkō Nen Shi Henshū Iinkai), ed. *Nihon Kōgyō Ginkō Nana Jyū Go Nen Shi* (A Seventy-five-year History of the Industrial Bank of Japan). Tokyo: Nihon Kōgyō Ginkō, 1982.

Inoguchi Takashi. *Nihon Seiji Keizai no Kōzu* (Contemporary Japanese Political Economy). Tokyo: Tōyō Keizai Shinpōsha, 1983.

Inoguchi Takashi and Iwai Tomoaki. *Zoku Giin* (Tribal Dietmen). Tokyo: Nihon Keizai Shimbun Sha, 1987.

Inoue Kaoru. "Buzumi Ryōdate ni Torikumu" (Wrestling with Compensating Balances). *Ekonomisuto*, 3 December 1963, 52–55.

Inoue Takashi. *Gurin Cado* (Green Card). Tokyo: Keiei Jitsumu Shuppan, 1980.

Ishida Hirohide. *Watakushi no Seikai Shōwa Shi* (My History of the Shōwa Political World). Tokyo: Tōyō Keizai Shinpōsha, 1986.

Ishikawa Itaru and Gyhoten Toyoo, eds. *Zaisei Tōyūshi* (The Financial Investment and Loan Program). Tokyo: Kinyū Zaisei Jijō Kenkyū Kai, 1977.

Jaffe, Dwight M. *Credit Rationing and the Commercial Loan Market*. New York: John Wiley and Sons, 1971.

Japan Automobile Parts Industrial Association (Nihon Jidōsha Buhin Kōgyō Kai). *Jidōsha Buhin Kōgyō Hatten Shō Shi* (A Short History of the Development of the Auto-Parts Industry). Tokyo: Nihon Jidōsha Buhin Kōgyō Kai, 1969.

Japan Business History Institute, ed. *The Mitsui Bank: A History of the First 100 Years*. Tokyo: Mitsui Bank, 1976.

Japan Computer Usage Development Institute. *Computer White Paper*. 1983 ed. Tokyo: Japan Computer Usage Development Institute, 1983.

Japan Development Bank (Nihon Kaihatsu Ginkō). *Annual Reports*, 1978–91 eds.

———. ed. *Ashita e no Senryaku* (Strategies for Tomorrow). Tokyo: Nihon Kaihatsu Ginkō, 1976.

———. *Facts and Figures about the Japan Development Bank*. (Tokyo: Japan Development Bank, 1981, 1991.

———. *Forum on Policy Implementation Financing*. Tokyo: Japan Development Bank, 1983.

———. *Nihon Kaihatsu Ginkō Jyū Nen Shi* (Ten-year History of the Japan Development Bank). Tokyo: Nihon Kaihatsu Ginkō, 1962.

———. *Nihon Kaihatsu Ginkō Ni Jyū Go Nen Shi* (A Twenty-five-year History of the Japan Development Bank). Tokyo: Nihon Kaihatsu Ginkō, 1976.

Japan Electronic Computer Corporation (Nihon Denshi Keisanki Kabushiki Kaisha). *Konputa Noto* (Computer Notes). 1990 ed.

Japan Export-Import Bank (Nihon Yūshutsunyū Ginkō). *Ni Jyū Nen no Ayumi* (A Course of Twenty Years). Tokyo: Nihon Yūshutsunyū Ginkō, 1974.

Japan Information Processing Development Center. *Computer White Paper*. 1980 ed. Tokyo: JIPDC, 1980.

Japan Long-Term Credit Bank Industrial Research Association (Nihon Chōki Shinyō Ginkō Sangyō Kenkyū Kai). *Shuyō Sangyō Sengo Ni Jyū Go Nen Shi* (A Twenty-five-year Postwar History of Principal Industries). Tokyo: Sangyō to Keizai Kabushiki Kaisha, 1972.

Japan Shipbuilding Industry Association Thirtieth Anniversary History Publication Subcommittee (Nihon Zōsen Kōgyō Kai San Jyū Nen Shi Kōkan Shō Iinkai), ed. *Nihon Zōsen Kōgyō Kai San Jyū Nen Shi* (A Thirty-year History of the Japan Shipbuilding Industry Association). Tokyo: Nihon Zōsen Kōgyō Kai, 1980.

JETRO. *Nippon: Business Facts and Figures.* 1991 ed. Tokyo: JETRO, 1991.
"Jimintō Yūsei Zoku" (The LDP Telecommunications Tribe). *Kinyū Business,* 8 August 1986, 56–59.
Johnson, Chalmers. *Conspiracy at Matsukawa.* Berkeley: University of California Press, 1971.
———. *Japan's Public Policy Companies.* Washington, D.C.: American Enterprise Institute, 1978.
———. *MITI and the Japanese Miracle.* Stanford, Calif.: Stanford University Press, 1982.
———. "The Reemployment of Retired Government Bureaucrats in Japanese Big Business." *Asian Survey* 14, no. 11 (November 1974): 953–65.
Jones, Jesse H., with Edward Angly. *Fifty Billion Dollars: My Thirteen Years with the RFC.* New York: Macmillan, 1951.
Juhn, Daniel Sungil. "Entrepreneurship in an Underdeveloped Economy: The Case of Korea." D.B.A. diss., George Washington University, 1965.
Kakuma Takashi. *Ōkurashō Ginkō Kyoku* (The Banking Bureau of the Ministry of Finance). Tokyo: Taishindō, 1979.
Kani Hoken Jigyō Nana Jyū Shūnen Kinen Jigyō Shi Hensan Iinkai, ed. *Kani Seimei Hoken Yūbin Nenkin Jigyō Shi* (A History of Simple Life Insurance and Postal Pension Activities). Tokyo: Kani Hoken Yūbin Nenkin Kanyūsha Kyōkai, 1987.
Kankyō Eisei Kinyū Kōko. *Teiri no Seifu Shikin: Yuri na Karikata—Tsukaikata* (Low-Interest Government Loans: Profitable Ways of Borrowing and Using Them). Tokyo: Seiya Shoten, 1977.
"Kanpo Nenkin Dokuritsu Unyō" (Independent Management of Postal Life Insurance). *Kinyū Zaisei Jijō,* 3 November 1952.
Kanryō Kikō Kenkyū Kai. *Ōkurashō Zankoku Monogatari* (A Tale of Ministry of Finance Cruelty). Tokyo: Yell Books, 1976.
Kaplan, Eugene J. *Japan: The Government-Business Relationship.* Washington, D.C.: U.S. Department of Commerce, 1972.
Katzenstein, Peter J., ed. *Between Power and Plenty: Foreign Economic Policies of Advanced Industrial States.* Madison: University of Wisconsin Press, 1978.
———. *Industry and Politics in West Germany: Toward the Third Republic.* Ithaca, N.Y.: Cornell University Press, 1989.
———. *Policy and Politics in West Germany: The Growth of a Semisovereign State.* Philadelphia: Temple University Press, 1987.
———. *Small States in World Markets: Industrial Policy in Europe.* Ithaca, N.Y.: Cornell University Press, 1985.
Kawaguchi Hiroshi. "The Dual Structure of Finance in Postwar Japan." *Developing Economies,* June 1967, 301–28.
Kawahito, Kiyoshi. *The Japanese Steel Industry.* New York: Praeger Publishers, 1972.
Kawasaki Steel Corporation. *Aru Kigyō no Seichō* (One Firm's Growth). Tokyo: Kawasaki Seitetsu Kabushiki Kaisha, 1969.
———. *Kawasaki Seitetsu Ni Jyū Go Nen Shi* (A Twenty-five-year History of Kawasaki Steel). Tokyo: Kawasaki Seitetsu Kabushiki Kaisha, 1975.

Keizai Kōhō Center. *Japan: An International Comparison.* Annual 1985–92 eds.

Keohane, Robert. *After Hegemony.* Princeton, N.J.: Princeton University Press, 1984.

Keohane, Robert, and Joseph Nye. *Power and Independence.* Boston: Little, Brown, 1977.

Kindleberger, Charles P. *Economic Growth in France and Britain, 1851–1950.* Cambridge, Mass.: Harvard University Press, 1964.

Kinoshita Toshihiko. *Japan's Current Recycling Measures: Their Background, Performance, and Prospects.* Tokyo: Export-Import Bank of Japan, 1988.

Klein, Lawrence, and Kazushi Ohkawa, eds. *Economic Growth: The Japanese Experience since the Meiji Era.* Homewood, Ill.: Richard D. Irwin, 1968.

Kodama, Fumio. *Analyzing Japanese High Technologies: The Techno-Paradigm Shift.* London: Pinter Publishers, 1991.

Koizuka Fumihiro. *Kōzō Fukyō to Sono Jittai* (Structural Recession and Its Implications). Tokyo: Kyōiku Sha, 1978.

Kōkichi Asakura. "The Characteristics of Finance in the Meiji Period (The Period of Takeoff)." *Developing Economies,* December 1970, 274–300.

Komiya Ryūtarō. "Economic Planning in Japan." *Challenge,* May–June 1975, 9–20.

———. *Postwar Economic Growth in Japan.* Berkeley: University of California Press, 1966.

———. *The Japanese Economy: Trade, Industry, and Government.* Tokyo: University of Tokyo Press, 1990.

Komiya Ryūtarō, Masahiro Okuno, and Kōtarō Suzumura, eds. *The Industrial Policy of Japan.* Tokyo: Harcourt, Brace, Jovanovich, 1988.

Kondō Hiroshi. *Sumitomo Group no Subete* (Everything about the Sumitomo Group). Tokyo: Nihon Jitsugyō Shuppan Sha, 1976.

———. *Toyota Shōhō—Matsushita Shōhō* (Toyota's and Matsushita's Ways of Doing Business). Tokyo: Nihon Jitsugyō Shuppan Sha, 1977.

Kondō Kanichi, ed. *Sengo Sangyō Shi e no Shōgen* (Witnesses to Postwar Industrial History). 3 vols. Tokyo: Mainichi Shimbun Sha, 1978.

Konno Toyohiro. *Ginkō to Shōken* (Banking and Securities). Tokyo: Nikkei Shinsho, 1971.

Koo, Richard. "High-Quality Products but Low Profitability: Why Japanese Investors Are Increasingly Rejecting This Time-honored Formula." Mimeographed, February 1992.

Kōsai Yutaka. *The Era of High-Speed Growth.* Tokyo: University of Tokyo Press, 1986.

Krasner, Stephen D. *Defending the National Interest: Raw Materials Investments and U.S. Foreign Policy.* Princeton, N.J.: Princeton University Press, 1978.

———. *Structural Conflict: The Third World against Global Liberalism.* Berkeley: University of California Press, 1985.

Krauss, Ellis S., Thomas P. Rohlen, and Patricia G. Steinhoff, eds. *Conflict in Japan*. Honolulu: University of Hawaii Press, 1984.

Kure Bunji. *Kinyū Dokuhon* (A Financial Primer). Tokyo: Tōyō Keizai Shinpōsha, 1976.

———. *Kinyū Seisaku* (Financial Policy). Tokyo: Tōyō Keizai Shinpōsha, 1973.

Kusano Atsushi. *Shōwa Yon Jyū Nen Go Gatsu Ni Jyū Hachi Nichi* (May 28, 1965). Tokyo: Nihon Keizai Shimbun Sha, 1986.

Kusayanagi Daizo. "Kobayashi Ataru." *Bungei Shunjū*, January 1969.

———. "Sahashi Shigeru, Amakudaranu Kōkyū Kanryō" (Sahashi Shigeru, the High-Level Bureaucrat Who Didn't Descend from Heaven). *Bungei Shunjū*, May 1969, 162–74.

Kuznets, Simon, ed. *Income and Wealth of the United States: Trends and Structure*. Cambridge, Mass.: Bowes and Bowes, 1952.

Langdon, Frank C. "Big Business Lobbying in Japan: The Case of Central Bank Reform." *American Political Science Review*, September 1961.

LaPalombara, Joseph. *Democracy Italian Style*. New Haven, Conn.: Yale University Press, 1987.

Lasswell, Harold. *Politics: Who Gets What, When, How?* New York: Meridian Press, 1958.

Leonard, Herman B. *Checks Unbalanced: The Quiet Side of Public Spending*. New York: Basic Books, 1986.

Lincoln, Edward J. *Japan: Facing Economic Maturity*. Washington, D.C.: Brookings Institution, 1988.

———. *Japanese Industrial Policies: What Are They, Do They Matter and Are They Different from Those in the United States?* Washington, D.C.: Japan Economic Institute of America, 1984.

Lindblom, Charles E. *Politics and Markets: The World's Political-Economic Systems*. New York: Basic Books, 1977.

———. *A Strategy of Decision*. New York: Free Press, 1963.

Lockwood, W. E. *The State and Economic Enterprise in Japan*. Princeton, N.J.: Princeton University Press, 1965.

Lord, Guy. *The French Budgetary Process*. Berkeley: University of California Press, 1973.

Loriaux, Michael. "Comparative Political Economy as Comparative History," *Comparative Politics*, 21, no. 3, April, 1989, 357–79.

———. *France after Hegemony: International Change and Financial Reform*. Ithaca: Cornell University Press, 1991.

Lowi, Theodore. "Four Systems of Policy, Politics, and Choice." *Public Administration Review*, July–August 1972, 298–310.

McArthur, John H., and Bruce R. Scott. *Industrial Planning in France*. Boston: Harvard Graduate School of Business Administration, 1969.

Machiavelli, Niccolò. *The Prince and the Discourses*. New York: Modern Library, 1950.

McCraw, Thomas, ed. *America versus Japan*. Boston: Harvard Business School Press, 1986.

MacRae, Duncan, Jr. *Parliament, Parties, and Society in France, 1946–1958.* New York: St. Martin's Press, 1967.

Maeno Kazuhisa, "Yūseishō Kenkyū" (Research on the Ministry of Post and Telecommunications). *Gendai*, August 1985.

Mainichi Shimbun Sha. *Naze?* (Why?). Tokyo: Mainichi Shimbun Sha, 1978.

March, James, and Herbert Simon. *Organizations*. New York: John Wiley and Sons, 1958.

March, James G., and Johan P. Olsen. "The New Institutionalism: Organizational Factors in Political Life." *American Political Science Review*, September 1984, 734–49.

Maritime Industries Research Association (Kaiji Sangyō Kenkyū Kai). *Nihon Kaiun Sengo Josei Shi* (A History of Postwar Japanese Shipping Promotion). Tokyo: Unyū Shō, 1967.

Marshall, Byron K. *Capitalism and Nationalism in Prewar Japan: The Ideology of the Business Elite, 1868–1941.* Stanford, Calif.: Stanford University Press, 1967.

Masaki Hisashi. *Nihon no Kabushiki Kaisha Kinyū* (Japanese Corporate Finance). Kyoto: Minerva Shobō, 1973.

Matsuda Osamu, "Kōteki Kinyū no Mondaiten" (Problems Relating to Government Finance). *Senshū Daigaku Shakai Kagaku Nenpō*, no. 20 (30 March 1986).

Matsumoto Masao. *Seifu Kei Kinyū Kikan* (Government-affiliated Financial Institutions). Tokyo: Kyōiku Sha, 1978.

Matsumoto Seichō, ed. *Gigoku Hyaku Nen Shi* (A Hundred-year History of Scandals). Tokyo: Yomiuri Shimbun Sha, 1977.

Maxfield, Sylvia. *Governing Capital: International Finance and Mexican Politics.* Ithaca: Cornell University Press, 1990.

Mesato Yasunobu. "Sasebo Jūko o Tsubusenai Riyu" (The Reasons Sasebo Heavy Industries Cannot Be Crushed). *Bungei Shunjū*, August 1978.

Ministry of Finance (Ōkurashō). *Bessatsu Ōkura Yōran* (Addenda to the Financial Handbook). 1968–78 eds. Tokyo: Ōkura Zaimu Kyōkai, 1968, 1973, 1976, 1978.

———. *Ōkura Yōran* (Financial Handbook). Tokyo: Ōkura Zaimu Kyōkai, 1968, 1973, 1976, 1978.

———. *Ōkurashō Kokusai Kinyū Kyoku Nenpō* (International Finance Bureau Yearbook). 1982 and 1986 eds. Tokyo: Ōkurā Zaimu Kyōkai, 1982, 1986.

———. *Ōkurashō no Kikō* (The Structure of the Ministry of Finance). 1992 ed. Tokyo: Ōkura Zaimu Kyōkai, 1992.

———. *Shikin Unyōbu Shikin no Hanashi* (Talk about Loan and Investment Fund Money). Ōkura Insatsu Kyoku, 1978.

———. *Yūka Shōken Hōkoku Sho* (Report of Firms Issuing Registered Securities). Tokyo: Ōkurashō, 1951–78. Each firm listed on the national stock exchanges is required to file such a report annually. Reports for the following firms were consulted in the course of this research: Industrial Bank of Japan, Kawasaki Steel, Nippon Steel, Nippon Kōkan, Sumitomo Metals,

Nissan Motors, Toyota Motors, Tōyō Kōgyo Motors, Honda Motors, Fujitsu, Hitachi, Nippon Electric, Matsushita Electric, Nippon Yūsen, Japan Line, Mitsui-OSK Lines, Hokkaidō Tankō Kisen Collieries, Mitsubishi Corporation, Marubeni Corporation, Mitsui and Company, Tokyo Electric, Kansai Electric, Tōhoku Electric, Chūbu Electric. These reports provide detailed data on the specific banks from which various firms borrow.

—————. *Zaisei Kinyū Tōkei Geppō* (Financial Statistics Monthly: Loans and Investments Program Special Edition). Tokyo: Ōkurashō Insatsu Kyoku, 1977–92.

Ministry of Finance Budget Bureau Research Section. *Zaisei Tōkei* (Financial Statistics). 1983–92 eds. Tokyo: Ōkurashō Insatsu Kyoku.

Ministry of Finance Budget and Financial Bureaus (Ōkurashō Shukei Kyoku and Rizai Kyoku), eds. *Yosan oyobi Zaisei Tōyūshi Keikaku no Setsumei* (An Explanation of the Budget and Financial Investment and Loan Program). 1978–92 eds. Tokyo: Ōkura Insatsu Kyoku, 1978–92.

Ministry of Finance Financial Bureau. (Ōkurashō Rizai Kyoku). *Zusetsu: Zaisei Tōyūshi* (The Illustrated Fiscal Investment and Loan Program). 1982–92 eds. Tokyo: Tōyō Keizai Shinpōsha, 1982–92.

Ministry of Finance Financial History Office (Ōkurashō Zaisei Shi Shitsu), ed. *Shōwa Zaisei Shi* (The Financial History of Shōwa). Vols. 10–12. Tokyo: Tōyō Keizai Shinpo Sha, 1967–91.

Ministry of Health and Welfare (Kōseishō). *Kōsei Hakusho* (White Paper on Welfare), 1961 and 1987 eds. Tokyo: Ōkurashō Insatsu Kyoku, 1961, 1987.

Ministry of International Trade and Industry (Tsūshō Sangyō Shō). *Gaishi Dōnyū Nenken* (Yearbook of Foreign Capital Investment). Selected issues.

—————. *Nana Jyū Nendai no Denshi Kikai Sangyō* (The Electronics and Machinery Industries of the 1970s). Tokyo: Tsūshō Sangyō Chōsa Kai, 1971.

—————. *Sangyō Kōzō no Chōki Vision* (A Long-Range Vision of the Industrial Structure). Tokyo: Tsūsanshō, 1975–78.

—————. *Tekkogyō no Gōrika to Sono Seika* (Steel Industry Rationalization and Its Consequences). Tokyo: Kōgyō Tosho Shuppan Sha, 1963.

—————. *Tsūsanshō Ni Jyū Nen Shi* (A Twenty-Year History of MITI). Tokyo: Tsūshō Sangyō Shō, 1970.

—————. *Tsūshō Sangyō Gyōsei: Shihan Seiki no Ayumi* (The Administration of Commerce and Industry: The Course of a Quarter Century). Tokyo: Tsūshō Sangyō Shō, 1975.

—————, ed. *Tsūshō Sangyō Roppō* (Commerce and Industry Statute Book). Tokyo: Tsūshō Sangyō Chōsa Kai. Annual.

Ministry of International Trade and Industry Enterprise Bureau (Tsūsho Sangyō Shō Kigyō Kyoku). *Shuyō Sangyō no Setsubi Toshi Dōkō* (Capital Investment Trends in Basic Industries). 1960–73 eds. Tokyo: Ōkurashō Insatsu Kyoku, 1960–73.

Ministry of International Trade and Industry Industrial Policy Bureau (Tsūshō Sangyō Shō Sangyō Seisaku Kyoku), ed. *Atarashi Sangyō Kinyū* (New Corporate Finance). Tokyo: Tsūshō Sangyō Chōsa Kai, 1988.

Ministry of International Trade and Industry Industrial Policy Bureau. *Shuyō Sangyō no Setsubi Toshi Keikaku* (Capital Investment Plans of Major Industries). 1974–92 eds. Tokyo: Ōkurashō Insatsu Kyoku, 1974–92.

Ministry of Post and Telecommunications (Yūseishō). *Financial Deregulation in Japan.* Tokyo: Ministry of Post and Telecommunications Postal Savings Bureau, 1986.

―――. *Postal Banking Service in Japan.* 1984–88 eds. Tokyo: Ministry of Post and Telecommunications Postal Savings Bureau, 1984–88.

―――. *Yūseishō Hyaku Nen Shi* (Hundred-year History of the Ministry of Post and Telecommunications). Tokyo: Yoshikawa Kōbunkan, 1971.

Ministry of Post and Telecommunications Savings Bureau (Yūseishō Chokin Kyoku). "Tokubetsu Kōwa Shiryō." Special lecture data, 4 June 1987. Unpublished.

Mitsubishi Research Institute (Mitsubishi Sōgō Kenkyū Jo). *Kigyō Keiei no Bunseki* (Analysis of Corporate Management). Tokyo: Mitsubishi Sōgō Kenkyū Jo, 1976.

Mitsui Mining Corporation, Ltd. (Mitsui Kōzan Kabushiki Kaisha) *Miike Sōgi* (The Miike Dispute). Tokyo: Nihon Keieisha Dantai Renmei, 1963.

Miyake Seiki. "Ichimada Naoto Ron" (A Theory of Ichimada Naoto). *Bungei Shunjū,* September 1954.

Miyauchi Tsutomu and Chikao Asashi. *Sōgo Ginkō* (Mutual Savings Banks). Tokyo: Kyōiku Sha, 1978.

Miyazaki Yoshikazu. "Rapid Economic Growth in Postwar Japan." *Developing Economies* 5 (June 1967): 332–36.

―――. *Sengo Nihon no Keizai Kikō* (The Economic Structure of Postwar Japan). Tokyo: Shin Hyōron Sha, 1966.

Mizukami Tatsuzō. *Watakushi no Shōsha Shōwa Shi* (My History of the Trading Companies' Shōwa). Tokyo: Tōyō Keizai Shinpōsha, 1987.

Monroe, Wilbur F. *Japan: Financial Markets and the World Economy.* New York: Praeger Publishers, 1973.

Mori Takuya. *Nihon no Kōkyōsai* (Japan's Public Bonds). Tokyo: Zaikei Shōhō Sha, 1978.

Myōwa Tarō. *Tsūsanshō* (MITI). Tokyo: Kyōiku Sha Shinsho, 1974.

Nagatomi Yūichirō. *Antei Seichō Jidai no Kōshasai Shijō* (The Public and Private Bond Markets in a Stable Growth Period). Tokyo: Ōkura Zaimu Kyōkai, 1978.

Nakajima Masataka. *Nihon no Kokusai Kanri Seisaku.* Tokyo: Tōyō Keizai Shinpōsha, 1977.

Nakamura Takafusa. *Economic Growth in Prewar Japan.* New Haven, Conn.: Yale University Press, 1983.

―――. *Nihon no Keizai Tōsei* (Japan's Economic Controls). Tokyo: Nihon Keizai Shimbun Sha, 1974.

―――. *Shōwa Kyōkō to Keizai Seisaku* (The Shōwa Depression and Economic Policy). Tokyo: Nihon Keizai Shimbun Sha, 1978.

Nakamura Takafusa and Kumon Shumpei. "Nihon to Roshia no Keizai Hatten no Ruikei" (Types of Economic Development in Japan and Russia), *Keizai Hyōron*, no. 2 (1967).

Nakayama Hiroto. *Zōsen no Genkyō* (The Current Condition of Shipbuilding. Tokyo: Kyōiku Sha, 1978.

Nanto, Richard K. "The United States' Role in the Postwar Economic Recovery of Japan." Ph.D. diss., Department of Economics, Harvard University, December 1976.

Nester, William R. *Japanese Industrial Targeting: The Neomercantilist Path to Economic Superpower.* London: Macmillan, 1991.

Nihon no Jidōsha Buhin Kōgyō (Japan's Auto-Parts Industry). Tokyo: Nihon no Jidōsha Buhin Kōgyō Kai, 1971.

Nihon Keizai Shimbun Keizai Bu. *Documento: Ataka Sangyō* (Document: Ataka Industries). Tokyo: Nihon Keizai Shimbun Sha, 1977.

Nihon Keizai Shimbun Sha. *Documento: Sasebo Jūko* (Document: Sasebo Heavy Industries). Tokyo: Nihon Keizai Shimbun Sha, 1978.

―――. *Gendai no Shōhisha Shinyō Sangyō* (The Contemporary Consumer Credit Industry). Tokyo: Nihon Keizai Shimbun Sha, 1978.

―――. *Shin Kigyō Shūdan* (New Enterprise Groups). Tokyo: Nihon Keizai Shimbun Sha, 1977.

―――, ed. *Jimintō Seichōkai* (LDP Policy Affairs Research Council). Tokyo: Nihon Keizai Shimbun, 1983.

―――. *Kansai Keizai no Hyaku Nen* (A Hundred Years of the Kansai Economy). Tokyo: Nihon Keizai Shimbun Sha, 1977.

―――. *Kōshasai Hakkō Shijō* (Government and Corporate Bond-issuing Markets). Tokyo: Nihon Keizai Shimbun Sha, 1987.

Nihon Kōgyō Ginkō: Setsubi Shikin Ginkō no Ginkō Banare Jidai no Senryaku" (The Industrial Bank of Japan: A Capital Investment Bank's Strategy in an Era of Alienation from Banks). *Nikkei Business*, 11 April 1977.

Nikkei Business, ed. *Ginkō no Yūshū* (The Melancholy of the Banks). Tokyo: Nihon Keizai Shimbun Sha, 1978.

Nikkei Business Henshū Bu. *Nihon no Kigyō Kankyō* (The Japanese Corporate Environment). Tokyo: Nihon Keizai Shimbun Sha, 1974.

Nolte, Sharon H. *Liberalism in Modern Japan: Ishibashi Tanzan and His Teachers, 1905–1960.* Berkeley: University of California Press, 1987.

Nordlinger, Eric. *On the Autonomy of the Democratic State.* Cambridge, Mass.: Harvard University Press, 1981.

Nutter, G. Warren. *Central Economic Planning: The Visible Hand.* Washington, D.C.: American Enterprise Institute, 1976.

Odabashi Sadajū. *Nihon no Shōkō Seisaku* (Japan's Commercial and Industrial Policy). Tokyo: Kyōiku Shuppan Sha, 1971.

Ohkawa, Kazushi, and Henry Rosovsky. *Japanese Economic Growth: Trend Acceleration in the Twentieth Century.* Stanford, Calif.: Stanford University Press, 1973.

Ohkawa Kazushi, Shinohara Miyohei, and Larry Meissner, eds. *Patterns of Japanese Economic Development: A Quantitative Appraisal.* New Haven, Conn.: Yale University Press, 1979.

Ōhzono Tomokazu. *Kigyō Keiretsu to Gyōkai Chizu* (Industrial Groups and the Map of Industry) Tokyo: Nihon Jitsugyō Shuppan Sha, 1991.

Oizumi Tsuneo. "Buzumi Ryōdate no Jittai to Kinō" (The Reality and Function of Compensating Balances). *Ekonomisuto*, 14 January 1964, 40–43.

Okazaki Taizō. *Jūtaku Kinyū no Chishiki* (Knowledge about Housing Finance). Tokyo: Nihon Keizai Shimbun Sha, 1977.

Okimoto, Daniel I. *Between MITI and the Market*. Stanford, Calif.: Stanford University Press, 1989.

Okimoto, Daniel, Haruo Sugano, and Frederick Weinstein, eds. *Competitive Edge*. Stanford, Calif.: Stanford University Press, 1984.

Ōkura Mondo. *Ōkurasho Ginkō Kyoku* (The Ministry of Finance Banking Bureau). Tokyo: Paru Shuppan, 1985.

Olson, Mancur. *The Logic of Collective Action*. Cambridge, Mass.: Harvard University Press, 1965.

———. *The Rise and Decline of Nations*. New Haven, Conn.: Yale University Press, 1982.

Organization for Economic Cooperation and Development. *Banking and Monetary Policy*. Paris: OECD, 1985.

———. *Monetary Policy in Japan*. Paris: OECD, 1972.

———. *The Role of Monetary Policy in Demand Management: The Experiences of Six Major Countries*. Paris: OECD, 1975.

Oriental Economist. (Tōyō Keizai Shinpōsha). *Japan Company Handbook*. 1977–92 eds. Tokyo: Tōyō Keizai Shinpōsha, 1977–92.

———. *Kigyō Keiretsu Sōran* (Almanac of Enterprise Groupings). 1985–92 eds. Tokyo: Tōyō Keizai Shinpōsha, 1985–92.

Osborn, David, and Ted Gaebler. *Reinventing Government: How the Entrepreneurial Spirit Is Transforming the Public Sector*. Reading, Mass.: Addison-Wesley, 1992.

Patrick, Hugh. "Japan's Interest Rates and the 'Grey Financial Market.'" *Pacific Affairs*, Fall–Winter 1965–66, 326–44.

———. *Monetary Policy and Central Banking in Contemporary Japan*. Bombay: Bombay University Press, 1962.

———, ed. *Japan's High Technology Industries*. Seattle: University of Washington Press, 1986.

Patrick, Hugh, and Henry Rosovsky, eds. *Asia's New Giant*. Washington, D.C.: The Brookings Institution, 1976.

Pauly, Louis W. *Opening Financial Markets: Banking Politics on the Pacific Rim*. Ithaca: Cornell University Press, 1988.

———. *Regulatory Politics in Japan: The Case of Foreign Banking*. Ithaca, N.Y.: Cornell East Asia Papers, no. 45, 1987.

Pempel, T. J. "The Bureaucratization of Policymaking in Postwar Japan," *American Journal of Political Science*, 18, no. 4, (November 1974): 747–64.

———. "Japanese Foreign Economic Policy: The Domestic Bases for International Behavior." *International Organization*, Autumn 1977, 723–74.

———. "The Unbundling of Japan, Inc.: The Changing Dynamics of Japanese Policy Formation." *Journal of Japanese Studies* 13, no. 2 (Summer 1987): 271–306.

Pepper, Thomas, Merit E. Janow, and Jimmy W. Wheeler. *The Competition: Dealing with Japan*. New York: Praeger Publishers, 1985.

Pfeffer, Jeffrey, and Gerald R. Salancik. *The External Control of Organizations: A Resource Dependence Perspective*. New York: Harper and Row, 1978.

Porter, Michael E. *Capital Choices: Changing the Way America Invests in Industry*. Washington, D.C.: Council on Competitiveness, 1992.

———. *The Competitive Advantage of Nations*. New York: Free Press, 1990.

Pressnell, L. S., ed. *Money and Banking in Japan*. London: Macmillan, 1973.

Prestowitz, Clyde V., Jr. *Trading Places*. New York: Basic Books, 1988.

Prime Minister's Office Institute of Administrative Management. *Organization of the Government of Japan*. 1990 edition. Tokyo: Gyōsei Kanri Kenkyū Center, 1991.

Rapp, William V. "Japan: Its Industrial Policies and Corporate Behavior." *Columbia Journal of World Business*, Spring 1977.

Ratcliffe, Charles Tait. *Japanese Corporate Finance, 1977–1980*. London: Financial Times, 1987.

———. "Tax Policy and Investment Behavior in Postwar Japan." Ph.D. diss. Department of Economics, University of California, Berkeley, 1969.

———, ed. *Zaitech* (Financial Technology). Tokyo: Kinyū Zaisei Jijō Kenkyū Kai, 1986.

Reich, Simon. *The Fruits of Fascism: Postwar Prosperity in Historical Perspective*. Ithaca, N.Y.: Cornell University Press, 1990.

"Rinji Zōkan: Kinyū to Ginkō" (Special Enlarged Edition: Finance and Banking). *Tōyō Keizai*, 28 April 1977.

Roberts, John G. *Mitsui: Three Centuries of Japanese Business*. Tokyo: Weatherhill, 1974.

Rosenbluth, Frances McCall. *Financial Politics in Contemporary Japan*. Ithaca, N.Y. Cornell University Press, 1989.

Rosovsky, Henry. *Capital Formation in Japan*. Cambridge, Mass.: Harvard University Press, 1960.

Royama Shōichi. *Nihon no Kinyū Shisutemu* (The Japanese Financial System). Tokyo: Tōyō Keizai Shinpōsha, 1982.

Ryū Shōkichi. *Gendai Nihon no Zaisei Tōyūshi* (Fiscal Investment and Loans of Modern Japan). Tokyo: Tōyō Keizai Shinpōsha, 1988.

Saitō Hitoshi. *Nōgyō Kinyū no Kōzō* (The Structure of Agricultural Finance). Tokyo: Tokyo Daigaku Shuppan, 1971.

Sakakibara Eisuke, Robert Feldman, and Harada Yūzō, *The Japanese Financial System in Comparative Perspective*. Cambridge, Mass.: Harvard University Program on U.S.-Japan Relations, 1983.

Sakakibara Eisuke and Nagao Yoriyuki, eds. *Study on the Tokyo Capital Markets*. Tokyo: JCIF Policy Study Series, no. 1, 1985.

Sakakibara Eisuke and Noguchi Yukio. "Ōkurasho Nichigin Ōchō no Bunseki" (An Analysis of the Ministry of Finance and Bank of Japan Dynasty). *Bungei Shunjū*, August, 1977, 96–115.

Samuels, Richard J. *The Business of the Japanese State: Energy Markets in Comparative and Historical Perspective*. Ithaca, N.Y.: Cornell University Press, 1987.

Sanaka Nobu. *Nihon Kanryō Hakusho* (White Paper on Japanese Bureaucrats). Tokyo: Kōdansha, 1986.

Sarasas, Phra. *Money and Banking in Japan*. London: Heath Cranston, 1940.

Sasago Katsuya. *Seiji Shikin* (Political Finance). Tokyo: Kyōiku Sha, 1978.

———. *Shōsha Kinyū* (Trading Company Finance). Tokyo: Kyōiku Sha, 1979.

Satō Koi, Yamaguchi Shunichi, and Odaka Nobuo. *Mitsubishi Group no Subete* (Everything about the Mitsubishi Group). Tokyo: Nihon Jitsugyō Shuppan Sha, 1977.

Satō Tomoyasu. *Keibatsu: Nihon no New Establishment* (Marriage Cliques: The New Establishment of Japan). Tokyo: Tatekaze Shobō, 1981.

Saxonhouse, Gary. "Industrial Restructuring in Japan." *Journal of Japanese Studies* 5, no. 1 (Summer 1979): 289–95.

Schilling, W., P. Hammond, and G. Snyder. *Strategy, Politics, and Defense Budgets*. New York: Columbia University Press, 1962.

Schmitter, Philippe, and Gerhard Lehmbruch, eds. *Still the Century of Corporatism?* Beverly Hills, Calif.: Sage Publications, 1979.

Schumpeter, E. B., ed. *The Industrialization of Japan and Manchukuo, 1930–1940*. New York: Macmillan, 1940.

Semiconductor Industry Association. *The Effect of Government Targeting on World Semiconductor Competition*. Cupertino, Calif.: Semiconductor Industry Association, 1980.

Shiina Etsusaburō. "Nihon Sangyō no Dai Jikkenjō, Manshū" (Manchuria: The Great Proving Ground for Japanese Industry). *Bungei Shunjū*, February 1976, 126–34.

Shima, Y. "The Income-doubling Plan and Public Investment." *Kyoto University Economic Review*, April 1961, 14–52.

Shimokawa Kōichi. "The Structure of the Japanese Auto-Parts Industry and Its Contribution to Automotive Process Innovation." Paper presented at the International Policy Forum, Hakone, Japan, May 1982.

Shimura Kaichi. *Gendai Nihon no Kō Shasai Ron* (A Theory of Public and Private Securities Finance in Modern Japan). Tokyo: Tokyo Daigaku Shuppan, 1978.

Shioguchi Kiichi. *Kikigaki: Ikeda Hayato* (Reminiscences concerning Ikeda Hayato). Tokyo: Asahi Shimbun Sha, 1975.

Shiroyama Saburō. *Kanryōtachi no Natsu* (The Summer of the Bureaucrats). Tokyo: Shinchōsha, 1980.

———. *Shosetsu: Nihon Ginkō* (A Novel: The Bank of Japan). Tokyo: Kadokawa Shoten, 1971.

Sheard, Paul. "The Role of Firm Organization in the Adjustment of a Declining Industry in Japan: The Case of Aluminum." *Journal of the Japanese and International Economies* 5 (1991): 14–40.

Shonfield, Andrew. *Modern Capitalism*. London: Oxford University Press, 1965.

Simon, Herbert. *Models of Man.* New York, 1957.

Skowronek, Stephen. *Building a New American State: The Expansion of National Administrative Capacities, 1877–1920.* Cambridge, Eng.: Cambridge University Press, 1982.

Small and Medium Enterprise Agency (Chūshō Kigyō Chō), ed. *Chūshō Kigyō Hakusho* (Small Business White Paper). 1977–92 eds. Tokyo: Ōkurashō Insatsu Kyoku, 1977–92.

———. *Chūshō Kigyō ni taisuru Endaka Taisaku* (The Yen Revaluation Countermeasures Policy in Relation to Small Business). Tokyo: Chūshō Kigyō Chō, 1978.

Small Business Finance Corporation (Chūshō Kigyō Kinyū Kōko). *Chūshō Kigyō Kinyū Kōko Ni Jyū Nen Shi* (A Twenty-year History of the Smaller Business Finance Corporation). Tokyo: Chūshō Kigyō Kinyū Kōko, 1974.

Smith, Thomas C. *Political Change and Industrial Development in Japan: Government Enterprise, 1868–1880.* Stanford, Calif.: Stanford University Press, 1955.

Smith, W. L. "The Discount Rate as a Credit Control Weapon." *Journal of Political Economy,* April 1958, 171–77.

Smitka, Michael J. *Competitive Ties: Subcontracting in the Japanese Automotive Industry.* New York: Columbia University Press, 1991.

Stewart, John R. "Financing the New State of Manchoukuo." *Far Eastern Survey* 6, no. 5 (March 3, 1937): 49–53.

Stigler, George. "The Theory of Regulation." *Bell Journal of Economics and Management Science* 3 (1971): 3–21.

Stokeman, Fruns N., Rolf Zeigler, and John Scott. *Networks of Corporate Power: A Comparative Analysis of Ten Countries.* Cambridge, Mass.: Polity Press, 1985.

Suleiman, Ezra N. *Elites in French Society: The Politics of Survival.* Princeton, N.J.: Princeton University Press, 1978.

———. *Politics, Power, and Bureaucracy in France.* Princeton, N.J.: Princeton University Press, 1974.

———. *Private Power and Centralization in France: The Notaires and the State.* Princeton, N.J.: Princeton University Press, 1987.

Suleiman, Ezra, and John Waterbury, eds. *The Political Economy of Public Sector Reform and Privatization.* Boulder, Colo.: Westview Press, 1990.

Sumiya Mikio and Taira Kōji, eds. *An Outline of Japanese Economic History, 1603–1940: Major Works and Research Findings.* Tokyo: University of Tokyo Press, 1979.

Sun, Kungtu C. *The Economic Development of Manchuria in the First Half of the Twentieth Century.* Cambridge, Mass.: Harvard East Asian Monographs, 1969.

Supreme Commander Allied Powers, Natural Resource Section. *Basic Problems of the Coal Industry in Japan.* Report no. 3, November 1945.

Suzuki Yoshio. *Gendai Nihon Kinyū Ron* (Money and Banking in Contemporary Japan: The Theoretical Setting and Its Application). Tokyo: Tōyō Keizai Shinpōsha, 1974.

———. *Money and Banking in Contemporary Japan.* New Haven, Conn.: Yale University Press, 1980.

Suzuki Yoshio. *Money, Finance, and Macroeconomic Performance in Japan.* New Haven, Conn.: Yale University Press, 1986.

———. "Monetary Policy Yesterday and Today." *Shūkan Tōyō Keizai,* 29 September 1982.

———. *Seiji o Ugokasu Keieisha* (The Managers Who Move Politics). Tokyo: Nihon Keizai Shimbun Sha, 1965.

Sweeney, Paul. "When the Cost of Money Evens Out." *Global Finance,* August 1991, 34–37.

Tachibana Takashi. *Tanaka Kakuei Kenkyū: Zen Kiroku* (Research on Tanaka Kakuei: The Whole Record). 2 vols. Tokyo: Kōdansha, 1976.

Tahara Sōichirō. *Sengo Zaikai Sengoku Shi* (A History of Business World Warring States). Tokyo: Kōdansha, 1986.

Takada Kiyoshi, Sakaguchi Yoshihiro, and Kichikawa Shōji. *Kuromaku Kenkyu II* (Research on Political Brokers II). Tokyo: Shin Kokumin Sha, 1977.

Takahashi, Makoto. "The Development of Wartime Economic Controls." *Developing Economies* 5, no. 4 (December 1967): 656–61.

Takamoto Mitsuo. *Sengo Kinyū Zaisei Rimen Shi* (The Inside Story of Postwar Monetary and Financial Affairs). Tokyo: Kinyū Zaisei Jijō Kenkyū Kai, 1980.

Takamura Jūichi. *Mitsui Group no Subete* (Everything about the Mitsui Group). Tokyo: Nihon Jitsugyō Shuppan Sha, 1977.

Takayanagi Hiroshi, ed. *Kigyō Keiretsu Sōran* (Almanac of Corporate Industrial Groups). 1985–92 eds. Tokyo: Tōyō Keizai Shinpōsha, 1987–92.

Takehara Norio. *Sendo Nihon no Zaisei Tōyūshi* (Postwar Japan's Fiscal Investment and Loan Program). Tokyo: Bunseidō, 1988.

Takenaka, Heizō. *Contemporary Japanese Economy and Economic Policy.* Ann Arbor: University of Michigan Press, 1991.

———. *Kenkyū Kaihatsu to Setsubi Toshi* (Research, Development, and Capital Investment). Tokyo: Tōyō Keizai Shinpōsha, 1984.

Tarrow, Sidney. *Between Center and Periphery: Grassroots Politicians in Italy and France.* New Haven, Conn.: Yale University Press, 1977.

Tatewaki Kazuo. *Zai Nichi Gaikoku Ginkō* (Foreign Banks in Japan). Tokyo: Kyōiku Sha, 1978.

Teranishi Jūrō. *Nihon no Keizai Hatten to Kinyū* (Finance and the Economic Development of Japan). Tokyo: Iwanami Shoten, 1982.

Teranishi Jūrō, and Hugh Patrick. *The Early Establishment and Development of Banking in Japan: Phases and Policies, 1872–1913.* New Haven: Yale University Economic Growth Center Discussion Paper No. 294, August 1978.

Thurow, Lester. *The Zero-Sum Society.* New York: Basic Books, 1980.

———. *The Zero Sum Solution.* New York: Simon and Schuster, 1985.

Tilles, Seymour. "Strategies for Allocating Funds." *Harvard Business Review,* January-February 1966, 14–22.

Tobe Ryōichi, Teramoto Yoshiya, Kamata Shinichi, Suginō Yoshio, Murai Tomohide, and Nonaka Ikujirō. *Shippai no Honshitsu: Nihongun no Soshikironteki Kenkyū* (The Essence of Failure: Organizational Research on the Japanese Military). Tokyo: Diamondo Sha, 1984.

Toniolo, Gianni, ed. *Central Banks' Independence in Historical Perspective*. Berlin: Walter de Gruyter and Company, 1988.

Toyota Motor Corporation (Toyota Jidōsha). *Toyota Jidōsha San Jyū Nen Shi* (A Thirty-year History of Toyota Motors). Toyota Shi: Toyota Jidōsha, 1968.

Tsuru, Shigeto. *The Mainsprings of Japanese Growth: A Turning Point?* Paris: Atlantic Institute for International Affairs, 1977.

Tsuruta Toshimasa. "Yokin Meberi Soshō to Seifu no Sekinin" (The Savings Erosion Suit and the Government's Responsibility). *Ekonomisuto*, 4 March 1975.

Tsutsui, William M. *Banking Policy in Japan: American Efforts at Reform during the Occupation*. London: Routledge, 1988.

Tsutsui Yoshirō. *Kinyū Shijō to Ginkōgyō* (The Financial Market and the Banking Industry). Tokyo: Tōyō Keizai Shinpōsha, 1988.

Uchino Tatsurō. *Japan's Postwar Economy: An Insider's View of Its History*. Tokyo: Kōdansha International, 1978.

Ueki Saburō. *Kankoku no Kinyū Jijō*. (South Korea's Financial Situation). Tokyo: Asia Keizai Kenkyū Jo, 1968.

United States Secretary of the Treasury. *Final Report on the Reconstruction Finance Corporation*. Washington, D.C.: Government Printing Office, 1959.

Usami Makoto. "Kinyū Kai o Arau Atarashii Nami" (The New Wave Washing the Financial World). *Ekonomisuto*, 13 April 1963, 12–15.

van Wolferen, Karel. *The Enigma of Japanese Power*. New York: Alfred Knopf, 1989.

Vernon, Raymond. *The Oil Crisis*. New York: W. W. Norton, 1976.

———. *Storm over the Multinationals*. Cambridge, Mass.: Harvard University Press, 1977.

———, ed. *Big Business and the State*. Cambridge, Mass.: Harvard University Press, 1974, W. W. Norton, 1976.

Vogel, Ezra F. *Comeback*. New York: Simon and Schuster, 1985.

———. "Guided Free Enterprise in Japan." *Harvard Business Review*, May-June 1978, 161–70.

———, ed. *Modern Japanese Organization and Decision Making*. Berkeley: University of California Press, 1975.

Wade, Robert. *Governing the Market: Economic Theory and the Role of Government in East Asian Industrialization*. Princeton, N.J.: Princeton University Press, 1990.

Wako Shōken. *Tosho 1, 2 Bu Jōjō Kigyō no Shisan Saihyōka Kanren Shiryō* (Data Relating to the Revaluation of Assets by Firms in the First and Second Sections of the Tokyo Stock Exchange). Tokyo: Wako Shōken, 1977.

Weber, Max. *The Theory of Social and Economic Organization*, edited by Talcott Parsons. Glencoe, Ill.: Free Press, 1947.

Weidenbaum, Murray L., and Reno Harnish. *Government Credit Subsidies for Energy Development*. Washington, D.C.: American Enterprise Institute, 1976.

Weitzman, Martin. *The Share Economy*. Cambridge: Harvard University Press, 1984.

Welke, H. J. *Data Processing in Japan*. New York: North-Holland Publishing Company, 1982.

Wellons, Philip A. *Passing the Buck: Governments and Third World Debt*. Boston: Harvard Business School Press, 1987.

Wilensky, Harold. *Organizational Intelligence*. Berkeley: University of California Press, 1968.

Wilks, Stephen, and Maurice Wright, eds. *The Promotion and Regulation of Industry in Japan*. London: Macmillan, 1991.

Williamson, Oliver E. *Markets and Hierarchies: Analysis and Anti-Trust Implications*. New York: Free Press 1975.

Wilson, James Q. *Political Organizations*. New York: Basic Books, 1973.

Wilson, J.S.G. *French Banking Structure and Credit Policy*. Cambridge, Mass.: Harvard University Press, 1957.

Woo, Jung-En. *Race to the Swift: State and Finance in Korean Industrialization*. New York: Columbia University Press, 1991.

Wray, William D. *Mitsubishi and the NYK, 1870–1914: Business Strategy in the Japanese Shipping Industry*. Cambridge, Mass.: Harvard University Council on East Asian Studies, 1984.

Yada Toshifumi. *Sekitan Sangyō* (The Coal Industry). Tokyo: Kyōiku Sha, 1977.

Yamaguchi Hideyuji and Ishikawa Itaru, eds. *Zaisei Tōyūshi* (The Financial Investment and Loan Program). Tokyo: Ōkura Zaimu Kyōkai, 1973.

Yamaguchi Kimio, ed. *Nihon no Zaisei* (Japan's Public Finance), 1992 ed. Tokyo: Tōyō Keizai Shinpōsha, 1992.

Yamamoto Yūjirō. *Nihon Kōgyō Ginkō no Himitsu* (The Secrets of the Industrial Bank of Japan). Tokyo: Nisshin Hōdō, 1978.

Yamamura, Kozo. *Economic Policy in Postwar Japan*. Berkeley: University of California Press, 1967.

Yamamura, Kozo, and Yasuba Yasukichi, eds. *The Political Economy of Japan: The Domestic Transformation*. Stanford, Calif.: Stanford University Press, 1987.

Yamashita Takeshi. *Zaikai Shi Tenno* (The Four Emperors of the Financial World). Tokyo: Raru Shuppan, 1985.

Yasuhara Kazuo. *Ōkurashō* (The Ministry of Finance). Tokyo: Kyōiku Sha Shinsho, 1974.

Yasuoka Hiroshi. *Nihon no Zaibatsu* (Japan's Zaibatsu). Tokyo: Nihon Keizai Shimbun Sha, 1976.

Yeager, Leland B. *Proposals for Government Credit Allocation*. Washington, D.C.: American Enterprise Institute, 1977.

Yomiuri Shimbun Sha, ed. *Zaikai* (The Financial World). 2 vols. Tokyo: Yomiuri Shimbun Sha, 1972.

Yoshino, M. Y. *Japan's Multinational Enterprises*. Cambridge, Mass.: Harvard University Press, 1976.

Yoshino Toshihiko. *Nihon Ginkō* (The Bank of Japan). Tokyo: Iwanami Shinsho, 1963.

———. *Nihon Ginkō Sōsai Shi* (History of the Governors of the Bank of Japan). Tokyo: Nihon Keizai Shimbun Sha, 1973.

———. *Sengo Kinyū Shi no Omoide* (Reminiscences of Postwar Financial History). Tokyo: Nihon Keizai Shimbun Sha, 1963.

———. *Waga Kuni no Kinyū Seido to Kinyū Seisaku* (Our Country's Financial System and Financial Policy). Tokyo: Isseidō, 1954.

Yoshino Toshihiko and Katō Makoto. *Gendai no Kinyū* (Current Finance). Tokyo: Nihon Keizai Shimbun Sha, 1973.

Young, Michael K. "Judicial Review of Administrative Guidance: Governmentally Encouraged Consensual Dispute Resolution in Japan." *Columbia Law Journal* 84 (1984).

Yūbin Chokin Mondai Kenkyū Kai, ed. *Yūcho to Keiei* (Postal Savings and Management). Tokyo: Yūbin Chokin Shinkō Kai, 1984.

Yūbin Chokin Shikin ni kansuru Kenkyū. *Yūbin Chokin Shikin no Unyō no Arikata*. Tokyo: Yūbin Chokin Shikin ni kansuru Kenkyū Kai, 1985.

Zaikai Tenbō. "Tokushū: Nihon Ginkō Man no Karei naru Seisui" (Special Issue: The Rise and Fall of the Splendor of the Bank of Japan's Men). *Zaikai Tenbō*, June 1978.

———. "Tokushū: Ōkura Kanryō" (Special Issue: Ministry of Finance Officials), *Zaikai Tenbō*, September 1978.

Zaisei Chōsa Kai, ed. *Hojokin Binran* (Subsidies Handbook). 1978 and 1986 eds. Tokyo: Miyazaki Dō, 1978, 1986.

———. *Hojokin Sōran* (Subsidy Almanac), 1984–87 eds. Tokyo: Nihon Densan Kigyō Kabushiki Kaisha, 1984–87.

Zenkoku Ginkō Kyōkai. *Gaika Loan Nenkan* (Foreign Currency Loan Annual). 1970 ed. Tokyo: Zenkoku Ginkō Kyōkai, 1970.

———. *Ginkō Kyōkai Ni Jyū Nen Shi* (Twenty-year History of the Bankers' Association). Tokyo: Zenkoku Ginkō Kyōkai, 1965.

———, ed. *Ginkō Kyōkai San Jyū Nen Shi* (A Thirty-year History of the Bankers' Association). Tokyo: Zenkoku Ginkō Kyōkai, 1979.

Zysman, John. *Government, Markets, and Growth: Financial Systems and the Politics of Industrial Change*. Ithaca, N.Y.: Cornell University Press, 1983.

———. *Political Strategies for Industrial Order: State, Market, and Industry in France*. Berkeley: University of California Press, 1977.

Index

administrative cohesion: economic policy and, 46–49
administrative guidance, 88
agents de change, 239, 327n.79
"agricultural bill system," 80–81
agricultural policy: clientelism and government lending policies, 111; credit allocation policy and, 107–8, 228, 230, 325n.49; market forces and, 225
Agriculture, Forestry, and Fishery Finance Corporation, 231
Aichi Kiichi, 72–73
Aikawa Yoshisuke, 50
Aizawa Hideyuki, 94
Allied Occupation: banking industry during, 152–54, 264; breakup of trading companies in, 146; domestic politics and, 237–41; financial controls during, 41–44; industrial credit allocation and, 101–2
Allison, Graham, 47
All Japan Agricultural Cooperative Association (Zennō), 252
All Japan Bankers Federation. *See* Federation of Bankers' Associations of Japan
Amagasaki Steel, 114, 256; government neglect of, 131; venture capitalism and, 120
amakudari ("descent from heaven"), 69, 271, 320n.42
Anti-Monopoly Law, 154
Araki Eikichi, 301n.58
Araki Shinichi, 90–92
Arisawa Hiromi, 31, 58
"Army submarine case," 47
Asian Development Bank, 129
Ataka Trading Company, 150, 196
automobile industry: corporate-led strategic capitalism and, 110–11, 309n.14; emergence of, unrecognized by state, 4–8; government funding limited in, 107–8; IBJ credit allocations to, 169–70
Auto-Parts Capital Investment Committee, 318n.14
Auto-Parts Distribution Rationalization Committee, 18, 182, 318n.14

auto-parts industry: borrowing patterns, 175; credit controls and borrower response, 205–6; distribution policies, 181–82, 318n.16; government lending policies, 178–82, 255; loyalty strategy and, 176–83; MITI dominance of, 183; private sector organization, 178; rationalization plans, 181, 318n.15; wartime origins of, 177

balance of payments policies, 299n.32
bankers' associations: credit allocation policies and, 155–58; private sector role of, 151–58
Bankers' Kingdom: bankers' associations and, 153; banking and industrial profits, 139–42; borrowing patterns during, 233–34; credit allocation and, 263; exchange controls and, 216–18; funding relationships in, 136–42; IBJ role in, 160–61, 162; industrial credit policy and, 211–12; manufacturing bias of, 222–23; MOF regulatory powers and, 100; postwar emergence of, 41; regulatory structure of, 29; reliance on government financial institutions, 214–15; reliance on indirect financing, 213–14; Zenginkyō and, 157–58
Bank for International Settlements (BIS), 145
Bank Funds Utilization Order, 36
banking industry: domestic ties of, in Japan, 11–12; dominance as financial intermediaries, 43–44; foreign banks in Japan, 28–29, 260–61, 298n.20; government influence on lending behavior, 17; international operations, 264–67, 276–77, 331n.58; Kawasaki Steel and, 184–95, 319n.35; lending controls, 35–39; politics and, 230, 238–39; long-term financing policies and, 86–87; market-oriented central banking, 90–94; opposition to MITI controls, 64–66; Panic of 1927 and, 27–28; prominence of, in early history, 26–33; transnational politics and, 242–44, 327n.86;

chemical industry: IBJ credit allocations, 167–68

Chiba steel plant (Kawasaki Steel), 183–95, 320n.42; financing patterns for, 190–91; state structure and, 249

"circles of compensation": banking associations and, 156–57; biases in credit allocation due to, 130–33; electric power industry, 254–55; electronics industry credit allocation and, 116–27; industrial strategy and, 246–47; sectoral credit allocation and, 108; steel industry credit allocation and, 114; venture capitalism and, 120

Citibank, 331n.58

city banks: compensating balances and, 139

clientelism: Bankers' Kingdom and, 41; bias toward, 69–70; credit allocation policies and, 15–16, 261–68; electronics industry credit allocation, 119; future research on, 268; government lending patterns and, 107–8, 111; international comparisons and, 266–67; loan guidelines and, 83–84; MOF and, 97–98; political leverage and, 68; state credit controls and, 4–8, 207–10; venture capitalism and, 122–29

Clinton, Bill (president), 276

coal industry: Japanese investment in, 15; postwar crisis in, 30; rediscounting system in, 80; RFB loans to, 309n.21

commercial banking: BOJ opposition to, 191–92; cooperation with IBJ, 160; reliance on indirect financing, 213–14; role of, in Japanese economic strategy, 9, 294n.21

commercial paper, 222

Commodity Credit Corporation: U.S. exports to Japan and, 306n.29

Companies' Benefits, Dividends, and Accommodations Order, 36

compensating balances: bankers' associations and, 157–58; low-interest policies and, 138–39; politicization of, 235–37, 326n.68; regulation of, 93–94, 307n.41

competitiveness: banking-industrial networks and, 32–33; international changes in, 212

computers: electronics industry credit allocation and, 117–19; IBJ credit allocations in, 171–72; JECC computer leasing program, 147–48, 172. See also electronics industry

"concentration principle": foreign exchange laws and, 34–35

consumer activism: credit allocation and, 233–34

consumer electronics. See electronics

"control associations": establishment of, 152–53

Cooperative Loan Banks, 38

corporate behavior: consensus-building, constraints on state from, 39–41; liabilities and Japanese financial structure, 212–13; private sector funding and, 136–42; role of, in Japanese economic strategy, 11–13

"corporate-led strategic capitalism": credit allocation and, 7–8, 21–22; future research on, 268; government lending patterns and, 110–11, 273–74; industrial credit and, 261–68; international comparisons and, 267–68; Japanese economic strategy and, 6–7; long-term credit allocation and, 135; state credit controls and, 208–9; state structure and, 249–52

Crédit Agricole, 95

credit allocation: BOJ and, 77–94; borrower response and, 205–7; capitalism and, 261–68; cross-sectional government lending, 103–8; fragmentation and pluralism in, 247–53; government's role assessed, 12–13, 19–22, 25–26; industry-specific policies, 65–66; international systems and, 272–74; Manchukuo Model, 50; Panic of 1927 and, 27–28; political-bureaucratic interaction in, 12–13, 229–44; private sector borrowing and, 13–15, 129–33, 174–210; public action and private capital programs, 129–33; reform laws, 221–23; regulatory philosophy and, 72–76; rising liquidity in, 70–71; sectoral distribution, 104–8; *shokusan kōgyō* policies and, 26; state dominance of, 7–8, 13–15, 30–31, 206–7; success of assessed, 253–61; window guidance policy, 87–91, 307n.34

Crédit Foncier, 158

Krasner, Stephen, 9, 13
Krauss, Ellis, 9

laissez-faire economics: vs. state intervention, 5–6
Large Scale Loan Control Law (1974):
trading companies and, 150
Lasswell, Harold, 11
Law for the Facilitation of Research in
Fundamental Technologies (1985), 125
Liberal Democratic party (LDP): banking
industry and, 141, 157–58, 264–67;
compensating balances, 235–37; credit
allocation policy and, 252–53; developmental policies, 246; interest groups
and, 237–41; Sasebo Heavy Industries
and, 200–205, 321n.67; "small-scale
accounts" and, 234; trading companies
and, 148
life insurance companies: industrial financing and, 143–44
liquidity, in Japanese finance, 70–71;
Bankers' Kingdom and, 140–41; credit
controls and, 252; imbalance in financial institutions, 136–42; industrial
strategy and, 63; liberalization of financial policy and, 241
loan ceilings: of BOJ, 82–84; Japanese/
French parallels in, 303n.42
Lockheed scandal, 148, 313n.34
long-term credit allocation, 135; BOJ policies, 84–87; IBJ and, 160
Long-Term Credit Bank Act (1952), 159–
60
Long-Term Credit Bank of Japan, 158–59
Loriaux, Michael, 263
lottery associations (mujins), 26
Lowi, Theodore, 165
"low interest-rate policy," 138
loyalty strategy: auto-parts industry and,
176–83; private sector borrowing patterns and, 174–76; Sasebo Heavy Industries case and, 196
lumber industry: sectoral allocation of
government credit and, 107–8

MacArthur, Gen. Douglas, 240
machinery industry: IBJ credit allocations, 167–68; lack of reliance on government funding in, 107–8
Machinery Industry Promotion Corporation, 54, 180, 318n.12

machine tools industry: government
lending policies and, 255–56; private
sector credit allocation, 112, 114–19
Manchukuo Model, 50
Manchuria, 260; IBJ development programs in, 159; Japanese industrial
bases in, 50
Mansfield, Mike (ambassador), 210,
322n.77
Manufactured Imports Promotion Organization (MIPRO), 48
market forces and credit allocation: future research on, 270–74; government
financial institutions, 223–29; Japanese industrial strategy and, 14;
keiretsu role in, 144–45; trading companies and, 146–47
Matsukata Masayoshi, 27
Matsushita Electric, 171; financial surpluses, 213
mechatronics revolution, 260–61; credit
allocation policies and, 14–15; IBJ
credit allocations, 167–68; MITI's role
in, 5; origins of, 293n.7; state structure
and, 248
Medical Care Facilities Finance Corporation, 231
medical profession: credit allocations to,
231, 325n.52
military industries: government controls
over bank lending, 36
mining industry: clientelism and government lending policies, 111; credit allocation in, 107–8; JDB loans to, 169
Ministry of Commerce and Industry
(MCI), 49, 112; auto-parts industry and,
177–78; government financial institutions and, 38
Ministry of Construction: regulatory role
of, 74, 101
Ministry of Finance (MOF): alumni representation in Diet, 67–68, 76; Banking
Bureau, 48, 93, 98, 100, 150–51, 152,
198, 236, 314n.43; banking controls
and, 28–29, 35–37, 65, 129–30, 151–52,
154–58, 240–41, 303n.47; banking-industrial interrelationships and, 32–33;
Bond Committee and, 85; branching
restrictions, 250; Budget Bureau, 98;
centralization problems at, 96–98;
compensating balances, 236; conflicts
with underwriting syndicates, 219–20,

petrochemicals: government financing of, 131–32

Plan for Remodeling the Japanese Archipelago, 94

planning organizations: auto-parts industry and, 181, 318n.14

"policy ministries" vs. "regulatory ministries," 101–2

politics: auto-parts industry and, 182; compensating balances and, 235–37; consumer activism and, 233–34; credit allocation and, 229–44, 252–53; cross-national comparisons of, 69–70; distributive policies and, 232–33; IBJ and, 161; industrial credit policy and, 5–8, 211–12; machine-tool credit allocation programs and, 310n.29; postwar economic strategy and, 18–19; Sasebo Heavy Industries and, 199–202; securities industry influence on, 239–41; state credit controls and, 206–7, 207–10; trading companies' role in, 150–51; transnational trends in, 241–44; as welfare, 230–32

Porter, Michael, 21, 250, 267–68, 309n.14

postal-savings funds, 241; future trends, 275; government financial institutions, 223–29, 324n.37

Preferential Resource Allocation Policy (keisha seisan hōshiki), 111–12

pricing: credit allocation vs., 73, 305n.4

priority-production policy of credit allocation, 31, 56, 258; bankers' associations and, 154–55

private sector: auto-parts industry and, 178; bankers' associations and, 151–58; BOJ control over credit allocation, 77; capital spending patterns and, 132–33; cohesion in, 135; core keiretsu financial institutions, 142–45; credit allocation strategies and, 4–8, 16, 21–22, 129–33, 218–23; electronics industry credit allocation, 116–27; flow of government officials into, 15; future research on, 268–74; government financial institutions and, 17, 45–46, 223–24; IBJ and, 158–73; influence on bureaucracy, 63; Kawasaki Steel credit allocations and, 188–89; machine-tool credit allocation and, 114–19; migration of government officials to, 69;

MOF links with, 97–98; "para-public" functions of, 134; pluralism in, 248–53; political influence of, 12–13, 141–42; postwar dominance of, 41–44; priority production formula and, 31; public credit controls and, 129–33, 174–210; shokusan kōgyō policies and, 25–26; state credit controls and, 206–7; steel industry credit allocation, 112–14; transnational politics and, 241–44

Provisional Capital Investigation Committees, 40–41

quantitative allocation, 73, 305n.4

"real demand" rule, 221

Recession Industries Bill (1978), 66

"reciprocal consent" concept: Japanese political economy and, 11–12; state structures and, 251–53; venture capitalism and, 120–21

Reconstruction Finance Bank (RFB), 27, 258; credit allocation policies, 56–57, 59; long-term financing, 84–87; steel industry credit allocation and, 112–14; venture capitalism and, 121

Reconstruction Finance Corporation (U.S.), 74; steel industry credit allocation, 113

"redistributive policies," 165

"regulators": BOJ as, 77–94, 122; industrial credit allocation and, 74–76, 100–102; vs. "policy ministries," 101–2, 122, 165, 246; role of, in economic strategy, 68

research and development projects: foreign involvement in, 128; IBJ expertise in, 161, 163

research methodology on credit allocation: current goals in, 16–19; sources, 18–19; survey of existing theories, 8–13

Rosenbluth, Frances McCall, 11–12

Sahashi Shigeru, 50, 64–65, 130, 304n.48

Sakura Bank, 27. See also Mitsui Bank

Samuels, Richard, 11, 251

Sanwa Bank: industrial financing, 142–43; MOF alumni in, 96; political contributions of, 238; struggles with other banks, 160